D1565254

Ideology, Power, Text

Ideology, Power, Text

*Self-Representation and the Peasant
"Other" in Modern Chinese Literature*

Yi-tsi Mei Feuerwerker

STANFORD UNIVERSITY PRESS
STANFORD, CALIFORNIA 1998

Stanford University Press
Stanford, California
©1998 by the Board of Trustees of the
Leland Stanford Junior University
Printed in the United States of America
CIP data appear at the end of the book

Preface

THE IDEA FOR this book could perhaps be said to go back to many decades ago during those walks with my father, Mei Guangdi, in Zunyi, Guizhou, the location of Zhejiang University's last wartime campus during the War of Resistance against Japan. Zunyi was a small mountain town then, and when we ventured out in the cool of a summer evening it did not take us long to get out to the country, where my father often stopped to chat briefly with those winding up their labor in the fields. Noting little that seemed to be worthy of my attention, I would stand to the side and look at the sky, or idly trace designs in the dirt underneath my feet, impatient to get on our way and rather bored with the exchanges about this year's weather or next year's crops. My father was then chairman of the Foreign Languages Department at the University and had spent almost twenty years in the United States as a student and then university professor, but in showing his concern for how the peasant was doing, he was in many ways carrying out the obligations of a traditional Confucian scholar. I had also heard from him in quite another connection that we could claim Mei Yaochen (1002–1060), whose poem "Tianjia yu" ("The Peasants' Words") I discuss in chapter 1, as an ancestor.

I never had the opportunity after I reached adulthood to discuss these matters with my father, for he did not live long enough to return with the university to its original campus in Hangzhou after the war ended in 1945. But whether or not my "family background" had anything to do with my interest in the peasant in modern Chinese literature, the looming presence of the peasant image in that literature can hardly be ignored. Although I had begun with the idea of examining the metamorphosis of the peasant in fiction through several phases of twentieth-century literary history, my focus soon shifted to the writer/intellectual's self-representation in relation to the image of that peasant "other."

Instrumental in this change of focus was my participation at the conference "Contemporary Chinese Fiction and Its Literary Antecedents" held at Harvard's John King Fairbank Center for East Asian Research, May 11–13, 1990. My paper, "Text, Intertext, and the Representation of the Writing Self in Lu Xun, Yu Dafu, and Wang Meng," had little to do with the peasant image, but it reinforced my interest in issues concerning the writing self, language, and ideology. I am grateful to Ellen Widmer and David Der-wei Wang, the organizers of this conference—in many ways a landmark indicating that modern Chinese literature had come of age as an independent field of study—and to conference participants for their criticism and encouraging comments. I had the opportunity to follow up on some of the issues on January 12 the following year at a symposium organized by Theodore Huters on "Representation of the Self in Modern Chinese Literature" at the UCLA Center for Chinese Studies, in conjunction with the Southern California China Colloquium. As I continued research on my reconceived project, it was very beneficial to me to be able to present some preliminary findings at a University of Georgia Humanities Center Research Conference on "Re-imagining the Self: Agency, Representation, and Identity Politics," May 11–12, 1993. This "multicultural" and interdisciplinary conference, organized by Linda Brooks and Kam-ming Wong, was strategically designed to juxtapose Eastern and Western theories, and included scholars and critics from such diverse fields as philosophy, anthropology, gender studies, comparative literature, English, Romance Languages, and African-American Studies. These juxtapositions produced much stimulating discussion among conference participants. I am grateful to them, and particularly to Tu Wei-ming and Kam-ming Wong, for their thoughtful comments on my subject.

A research grant from the American Council of Learned Societies, funded by the Chiang Ching-kuo Foundation, and a fellowship from the Wang Institute of Graduate Studies, as well as an Arthur F. Thurnau professorship at the University of Michigan, enabled me to have time off from teaching and to carry out research in China and in various libraries in the United States. I am indebted to my sponsoring hosts, the Chinese Academy of Social Sciences in Beijing and the Shanghai Academy of Social Sciences, and particularly to the colleagues in their Modern Literature Research Groups for granting me access to their library and files and for their unstinting help in locating material. Many thanks to Ma Liangchun, Liu Fuchun, and Chen Yangu for their support. Among university libraries, it was a particular pleasure to work in that of Xiamen University, with its beautiful and almost distracting view of the water, and I am grateful indeed to Zhuang Zhongqing, Lai Ganjian, and Li Yijian of Xiamen University for their generous support and hospitality. The exchange of ideas with them and many other colleagues in China was very helpful to me in formulating ideas about my subject. The staff of the Shanghai Municipal Library, which became increasingly open as time went by, provided much valuable assistance.

I am grateful for the privilege of interviewing Li Zhun and Ma Feng, two well-known "peasant writers," who kindly shared their experiences and discussed their writings with me. As is evident in the notes to this book, I benefited greatly from the many opportunities I had of meeting and talking with Gao Xiaosheng and Bei Dao. Gao Xiaosheng's visit to the United States in 1987, which included a two-month stay at the University of Michigan, was sponsored by the Visiting Scholar Exchange Program of the former Committee on Scholarly Communication with the People's Republic of China. Bei Dao was the first visiting artist/writer of the University of Michigan's International Institute Distinguished Visiting Artist-in-residence Program. His year-long visit here in 1994 was also sponsored by the Department of Asian Languages and Cultures and the Center for Chinese Studies.

The list of friends and colleagues who have contributed toward the development of the ideas in this book is a long one; many of their names appear in the works cited in my bibliography. My thanks to Marilyn Young for the many provocative discussions we had when we taught a course together on modern Chinese literature at the University of Michigan's Residential College, to Leo Ou-fan Lee for incisive comments over the years on several of my papers related to the topic, and to Patrick Hanan for his support and guidance. Lydia H. Liu and Theodore Huters, both of whom read early drafts of the manuscript, provided thoughtful criticisms and comments that turned out to be invaluable to me as I carried out my revisions. Terre Fisher came through with timely and efficient help in preparing the final version of the bibliography. My thanks to John Ziemer for his encouragement of the project and to John Feneron and Martin Hanfft for their meticulous editing. I want to acknowledge the contribution of the University of Michigan's Center for Chinese Studies toward production costs. My husband, Albert Feuerwerker, discriminating critic and "computer guru," has been a source of constant support throughout. And finally I would like to thank my students who, over the years, have made the rereading of literary texts both necessary and rewarding.

Yi-tsi Mei Feuerwerker

University of Michigan

Contents

Accomplices
we are not guiltless;
long ago we became accomplices
of the history in the mirror,
waiting for the day
to be deposited in lava
and turn into a cold spring
to meet the darkness once again
                                        —Bei Dao

History, then, confronts the writer with a necessary option between
several moral attitudes connected with language; it forces him to
signify Literature in terms of possibilities outside his control.
                                        —Roland Barthes

Introduction: A Literature "Out of the Ruins"?

ONE OF THE most powerful yet enigmatic encounters between intellectual and peasant in modern Chinese literature occurs at the end of Zhao Zhenkai's 1978 story "Zai feixu shang" ("In the Ruins").[1] The story's events cover several hours in the life of Wang Qi, a middle-aged, Western-educated professor of history. It is at the time when the country is undergoing the self-destructive turmoil of the Cultural Revolution that had been launched in 1966, and this "Old-line British spy and reactionary authority" has been served a notice to appear without fail before the "organ of mass dictatorship of the Cultural Revolution" the next morning. His wife is dead, two months earlier his daughter formally denounced him and moved out, not long ago he witnessed the physical torture and death of an old friend. Rather than face what tomorrow will surely bring, Wang Qi has decided to hang himself. "In the Ruins" is an account of the walk he takes from the university grounds towards the site of his suicide.

It is the desolate season of autumn. The sun, having lost its warmth, is sinking behind the distant hills, and he finds himself at one point, without quite understanding how he got there, standing opposite the stone ruins of Yuanmingyuan, the Qing summer palace that was destroyed by invading Western troops in 1860. The ruins of this once glorious and opulent palace become for him a symbol of China's history, not just of the destruction of the past decades, but of the losses, the violence, and the suffering of the last centuries or millennia. History, time, life, all seem to have lost their purpose and meaning. He ties the rope he had carried in his pocket into a knot, and hangs it from the fork of a tree. Just as everything is set for him to end it all, he is startled by the sudden appearance of a little peasant girl (*xiangxia xiaoguniang*), who has come to cut grass to feed her rabbits. Seeing the noose, she innocently asks if it is for catching birds. Eager for her to leave so he can carry out his plan, he tells her to hurry back home for her father must be anxious, but she tells him that her father had been beaten to death the month before because he had stolen pumpkins from the brigade.

In an onrush of feeling Wang Qi clasps the child in his arms and finds himself shedding tears for the first time in many months. The startled little girl struggles to free herself and runs off into the woods in alarm. He remains seated for a long time until night falls. "All of a sudden he rose to his feet, and walked in the direction where the little girl had disappeared, without even turning his head." The story ends with the noose left dangling in the wind—and a question dangling in the reader's mind as to why he has apparently made the decision not to kill himself.

One can look for clues in the many flashback scenes from Wang's life as he walks, in his reflections about his wife and his daughter, his sense of time passing, but also of the ongoingness of history, in his belief that the young—his daughter, the young man who had written the threatening order—will perhaps some day regret what they have done, but the "explanation" for his renewed commitment to life (if indeed that is what it comes down to) is never explicitly given in the story, nor will a character analysis of the protagonist, should we attempt one, offer an adequate explanation.[2] Instead of trying to determine his personal motive, for my purposes I would like to explore some broader implications of the story's ending through considering the identity of the person he encounters and the class relationship between the two.

Up to that point the narrative has focused on Wang Qi's subjective state, reflected and externalized in the desolate landscape, and on the sense of passing time as he moves through the stages of his journey towards death. The momentary appearance of the orphan child, a reminder possibly of what his daughter would become when he is dead, calls him back to life. She is very young, naively matter of fact both in her comments about the crafty rabbits' preferences for a particular grass, and in her report of the cause of her father's death. Both signify her identity as a member of the peasant class, a subaltern "other." Whereas up till that moment Wang Qi had been despairing over himself and over China's history, this encounter with the peasant girl now arouses pity and compassion towards her; he realizes that her plight, although she hardly expresses a full awareness of it, might well be worse than his.[3]

The father's brutal death was due to his having stolen food, the struggle for which is the perennial focus of the peasants' harsh existence. At this moment such a reminder of their lot is itself heavily laden with irony, for after all the "reactionary" intellectual Wang Qi is being persecuted by a "mass dictatorship" that is presumably carrying out a revolution in the name of the peasant. Considered from the point of view of a class encounter, the final scene of "In the Ruins" resonates with themes that have long revolved around the crucial intellectual-peasant relationship in traditional and contemporary Chinese ideologies.

They are fellow sufferers, the little peasant girl and the middle-aged male intellectual, both entrapped by the catastrophes of history. When they meet, they may affect each other in fateful ways, but they do not, as the story strongly emphasizes, meet as equals. It is the intellectual who remains, as he apparently must, the center of consciousness, of himself, of his class, of his times, and of the whole of China's history. While this consciousness is the heavy burden that he bears, it also contains the possibilities of transcendence. Earlier, when contemplating the ruins of Chinese history and the ending of his own life, he had taken some solace in thinking about his books—they would survive him; although criticized today, they would be validated tomorrow. Through his ability to "speak his thoughts, write them down," he could hope for a "different kind of life," beyond death perhaps, a life that is denied to others. His representation is privileged, for he possesses the moral and intellectual capacity to reflect not only on his own situation but also on that of the little peasant girl, and to respond compassionately to it. Her subordinate status, her naiveté and her innocence, are further underlined by the fact that she is both a female and a child. Even though her presence and her plight may decisively impinge upon the intellectual's life—for in the end he walks "in the direction where she had disappeared," thus suggesting a possible further intertwining of their fates—she is represented as artlessly simple and unaware. If she does indeed possess a reflective consciousness of her own, she seems to lack the ability to articulate it.

While the contrast between the two characters has much to do with the wide gap in their ages and experience, it is also grounded in their "class nature" (*jiejixing*). They are both victims, both suffering from having recently lost someone near to them—the little girl's father fatally beaten for stealing food, Wang Qi's colleague tortured to death because of his Western academic background. Each of these violent ends is grounded in causes—hunger and poverty for one, intellectual status for the other—that are "class-specific."

The hierarchical intellectual/peasant class relationship is further mirrored on the level of narrative discourse. Most of the story is told by a third-person narrator who closely follows the protagonist Wang Qi step by step both in his external journey toward the palace ruins and in the movements of his internal state as he oscillates between observations, memories, and speculations. But this narrative stance changes once the peasant/child intrudes upon the scene. As the two characters interact, the narrator withdraws to a distance as it were, observing and recording their external actions and dialogue, and making no attempt to enter into the thoughts and feelings of either during the crucial confrontation. Whereas up till then the narrative had been intensely engaged in the subjective state of the protagonist, now both Wang Qi as well as the "other" he encounters become "objectified" as the text draws to its conclusion. It is as if the narration can focus on or identify closely only with the character self-contained within a developed consciousness to which there can be empathetic access. To the end the story remains the story of the intellectual; perhaps his story is the only one that can actually be told.

Such a shift in narrative position to the mere surface of the story's events, omitting any explication of the underlying reasons behind Wang Qi's critical decisions about life and death, or how much his decisions might actually have to do with the little peasant girl and her plight, invests the story's ending with an air of mystery or indeterminacy. But it is precisely this narrative reticence that opens up the text's final episode to multiple possibilities of meanings, meanings that lead us to many of the ambiguities and complexities of the long-standing bifurcation of Chinese society between intellectual and peasant.

Written in 1978, "In the Ruins," the story as well as its title, is first of all a comment on the Cultural Revolution (1966–1976), which had ended two years earlier with the death of Mao Zedong. Those "ten years of disaster," during which the orgy of mass self-destruction spurred on by ideological fanaticism seemed to be pushing to an extreme everything that had been going wrong with Communist Revolution, have occasioned much self-questioning among Chinese intellectuals, for they were the ones who had been its prime targets.

The story does not give any detailed information about Wang Qi's particular career nor state why he personally got into trouble, but there is no need to do so. In those days it was enough to be a high-level intellectual, a professor of history at the most prestigious university of the land, and to have furthermore once studied in Cambridge, England, for the "spotlight" to pursue him and finally fall upon his head. Their identity as high-level intellectuals was sufficient reason for his old Cambridge schoolmate to have the lead wire loaded with hand weights tightened around his neck (a foreshadowing of the noose that would soon be around Wang Qi's own), or for the head of his department—a Harvard Ph.D. in sociology—to be demoted to a yardman, fearful of implicating anyone who would stop to speak to him, or for Wang Qi's daughter to denounce her father—indeed for the repudiation of all normal human relationships. The post-mortem question asked by intellectuals when the Cultural Revolution came to an end then has been—why? Why were intellectuals, hundreds of thousands of them, targets of such brutal persecution?

The reasons are complex and deeply implicated in the history of China's turbulent move from the traditional past into the revolutionary present. In the view of several recent Chinese scholars, the Cultural Revolution had been but the extreme development of "contradictions between the intellectuals (*zhishifenzi*) and the common people (*minzhong*)," contradictions that had frequently been manifest in various forms in contemporary China.[4] The total denunciation of intellectuals was possible only because a radical leftist minority had been able to exploit the hidden prejudices that the masses had traditionally long harbored against them. Led by these extremists, the argument goes, the masses demanded absolute equality in everything, including equality in knowledge, what had most demarcated the intellectuals from themselves. For knowledge was also power, and since intellectuals were the ones in possession of that power, the people said, All right then, that power of yours will be destroyed, go toil in the fields, go forge iron, reform yourselves through labor. These contradictions had not newly emerged during the Cultural Revolution, but had been endemic in Chinese society. However, the traditional culture had always sought to evade them, to smooth them over, and in the interests of harmony, had idealized or managed to sublimate the uneasy and unequal relationship between the two.

Seen from such a perspective, the revolutionary upheavals of the past several decades can be primarily interpreted as the violent explosion of the forever oppositional yet inextricably interlocked intellectual-peasant relationship. Whether this indeed adequately "explains" everything that happened, these post-Mao critics are apparently subscribing to certain age-old assumptions about the traditional great divide in the Chinese cultural and political spectrum, a great divide that in their view has merely been recast by the Chinese revolution in terms of Marxist class struggle.

As a narrative representing a problematic encounter between writer/intellectual and peasant in the early post-Mao period, "In the Ruins" can be read as yet another exploration of a central theme in modern Chinese literature. When this literature came into being during the May Fourth period in the early decades of the twentieth century, it had conceived of itself as a "literary revolution," as a radical rupture from the traditional past, and high on its agenda was a commitment to make the peasant into a serious subject of literature. It began by "discovering" peasants as oppressed victims, as a subject to be used as a means for exposing that dark underside of Chinese society that the writers and intellectuals—the modern successors to the old scholar-official elite—had undertaken to reform. When the totalistic revolution envisioned by Mao Zedong took hold in the 1940's, it strove to reverse the age-old hierarchical structure by elevating peasants as vanguards of the revolution and instructing intellectuals to subordinate themselves, to go among the masses of peasants to study their language in order to create literature and art. To move the peasant to central stage, however perceived or constructed, has involved above all a correlative repositioning of the intellectual's role. Whatever the peasant might be "in reality", he or she has more often than not been a site or metaphor, a blank page on which various political visions and ideological agendas have been inscribed, articulated, and contested. Whoever the little peasant girl might be in herself, or even whatever the specifics of her individual suffering, is less important than the fact that she is there and the effect she has on shaping the story of the intellectual protagonist.

"In the Ruins" is an early example of the post-Mao challenge to the party-prescribed peasant image. Thirty years after "liberation", peasants are shown to be suffering still from hunger and rural violence, victims not of "feudal" landlords, but of party installed brigade leaders. Have peasants then been "rediscovered" merely as victims, in an apparent return to the May Fourth literature? One dramatic difference now some sixty years later is the downfall of the intellectual, who has become, under the Communist revolution, a fellow victim. During the Cultural Revolution thousands of intellectuals like Wang Qi were persecuted and driven to their deaths in the name of this peasant-centered revolution. If the peasant's lot continues to be characterized by hunger, poverty, and ignorance, that of the intellectual, the embodiment of historical consciousness, the agent of language and writing, whose assumed task is to represent the peasant, is a dark and uncertain hovering between survival and death.

The extreme manifestations of the Maoist revolutionary ideology and its disastrous consequences did not come to an end until Mao Zedong's death in 1976. In the period of relative "liberation" that has followed, modern Chinese literature has risen "out of the ruins" to enter a new phase of reappraisal and reflection, about the Maoist revolution itself, but also about the intellectual-peasant relationship. While the subject of the peasant has lost its clearly defined status as either oppressed victim or revolutionary hero, the writing/intellectual self has similarly become displaced. These new uncertainties have led most particularly to the "root-searching" (xungen) fiction of the mid-1980's, a fiction that attempts to go beyond immediate political history to question the fundamental nature of a culture that has for so long posited peasants and intellectuals at two opposite poles of the spectrum.

In this book I will attempt the reading of selected fiction in which a direct encounter between the intellectual and peasant "other" takes place. Peasants have been written about in many, many twentieth-century stories, and the correlative process of subject constitution and object formation has taken many different forms according to changing historical and ideological contexts. As self and "other," subject and object, the writer/intellectual and the peasant will occupy binary positions within a field of signification; each is posited, and takes on value and meaning in relation to the other. This is a dialectical process that will be explored in my selected texts.

My plan is to follow the confrontation between the writing self and the peasant other through four literary "generations."[6] Three chapters each center on one representative author. The fiction of Lu Xun (1881–1936) that initiated the literary preoccupation with the victimized peasant is also about the identity crisis of the intellectual. Zhao Shuli (1906–1970), upheld by the Communist Party as a model "peasant writer," tragically exemplifies in his career the inherent contradictions of such an assigned role. In the post-Mao era, Gao Xiaosheng (1928–) uses the ironic play of language to present a more ambiguous peasant while deflating intellectual pretentions. The chapter on the last of the four "generations" will examine several texts by Mo Yan (1956–), Han Shaogong (1952–), and Wang Anyi (1954–) as examples of "root-searching" fiction from the mid-1980's. While reaching back into the past, this fiction is paradoxically also experimental in technique: the encounter with the peasant will lead to questions about the self-construction of the intellectual and the nature of narrative representation itself.

My limited focus will be on texts in which some sort of representation or stand-in of the writer/intellectual self is present, as character, as witness, as center of consciousness, or as first-person or obtrusive narrator. Each story catches the writer in a self-reflective mode, the confrontation with the peasant "other" providing a theater for acting out varying dramas of identity, power, ideology, political engagement, and self-representation.

1

From Tradition to Modernity:
Intellectual and Peasant in Transition

THE BIFURCATION between the scholar-gentry class (*shi*) on the one hand, and the people (*min*) on the other, had always been one of the distinctive themes of the traditional Chinese agrarian-bureaucratic state. While inheriting that legacy, their twentieth-century counterparts, "intellectual" and "peasant," have also altered it in significant ways. In moving from past to present, the meaning of these two signifiers changed in themselves, and continually changed in relation to each other. The reconstitution of the people (*min*) into "peasants" (*nongmin*) was a corollary of the intellectuals' struggle for a new self-formation as they made the transition from the scholar-officials (*shi*) of the past, with their well-defined position within the state establishment, into *zhishifenzi*, the increasingly uncertain intellectuals of the modern period.

While "tradition" versus "modernity" is commonly used to refer to changes that began to take place as China responded to the significant impact of the West, how they should actually be defined within the Chinese context is far from clear. "Tradition" was, first of all, not something that was fixed and coherent. In discussing some of its central themes, I will highlight certain internal tensions and contradictions, especially regarding the situation of the intellectual. Nor does the transition to "modernity" simply mean the emergence of a marked break between past and present, the disintegration or radical displacement of what had been an

integrated, self-sufficient, and self-enclosed society.[1] One may further argue that the "tradition-modernity" paradigm itself is a product of Western parochialism or ethnocentrism that the Chinese too readily imported
or accepted as they found themselves faced with the unprecedented historical realities of the early twentieth century. If modernity means to
change in accordance with what the West defines as "universal," then
China could not but be entrapped forever in the effort of trying to
"catch up" in a losing game.

Yet that may be precisely the bind in which the Chinese placed themselves in their determined but problematic search for modernity. Whatever the definitions, one feature that seems above all to characterize the
modern generation has been the insistence on its own differences from
the past. All the while, however, it has continued to carry, as a conscious
or unconscious burden, themes and contradictions of tradition even as
that "tradition" has been constantly reinterpreted and reconstructed. The
debate between the traditional and the modern—neither of which is a
stable, essential category—would continue to be carried out on a shifting
ideological terrain caused by political upheaval.

All linguistic utterances, including literary and scholarly discourse, as
Pierre Bourdieu has argued, bear traces of the social structures they both
express and help to reproduce.[2] In the case of traditional China, the
functioning of such "symbolic power" or "symbolic domination" might
seem to have been glaringly obvious when we consider the political
authority the old imperial system invested in the intellectual elite, the
dominant producers of literary and scholarly discourse. But the ongoing
interplay between politics and literature in China was often a highly
complex and tortuous matter.

Due largely to the apparent coincidence yet constant tension between
the political and moral order, an important part of the self-image of
those who produced literature was their "sense of mission" (*shiminggan*).
This placed them and their literary enterprise in a peculiarly ambiguous
space vis-à-vis the authoritarian state structure. Among other things, the
sense of mission had also habitually obligated this intellectual elite to
take some account of the subordinate peasant class. It is against such a
tradition that we must examine the fluctuating relationship between the
two classes and its manifestation in modern Chinese literature.

The radically changed conditions for literary production brought
about by the collapse of traditional institutional structures in the twentieth century entailed reconceptualizations of writing as writers searched

for ways to discharge age-old moral and political responsibilities while engaged in the constant struggle to resituate themselves in an intensely problematic relation to power. Their attempts to forge a new literature has implicated them in concomitant exercises of textual self-inventions, most often against the process of constructing the peasant "other."

INTELLECTUALS AND THE STATE: COINCIDENCE AND
TENSION BETWEEN THE POLITICAL AND MORAL ORDER

When the philosopher Mencius stated in the fourth century B.C. that those who used their minds (*laoxin*) ruled and those who used their muscles (*laoli*) were ruled, he provided the classic formulation of the traditional binary relationship between scholar-official and peasant, while seemingly positioning the two groups into a perennial relation of domination and subordination. By *xin* Mencius was not simply referring to what is commonly rendered into English as "mind," for *xin* in Mencian philosophy was much more than a matter of the intellect; it was even more the seat of moral feelings. The power and authority of the ruling elite was therefore legitimated by their intrinsic worth, their highly developed heart-mind, their moral as well as intellectual superiority, which anyway were supposed to coincide.

But if the underdeveloped masses of people were thus "rightfully" relegated to the lower part of the power structure, they nevertheless had always to be taken into account, since the other side of the coin in the Mencian theory of government claimed that the mandate to rule was deserved only if the people's economic and moral welfare were properly attended to. Thus the people were always "there," both as objects of paternalistic concern and as a yardstick for evaluating governmental success. They were furthermore always present as a latent threat of insurrection, since the same ideology sanctioned the right of the ruled to rise in rebellion in the event that their rulers lost the Mandate of Heaven by failing to discharge their proper responsibilities toward those below.

When this Mencian political ideology was later institutionalized into the civil service examination, increasingly the route for recruiting the scholar-literati into the official ruling hierarchy, the rationale was that what most qualified candidates to administer the affairs of the empire was their mastery of the Confucian classics, their demonstrated indoctrination into the state ideology. By early Ming—that is from the fourteenth century on—Chinese society was dominated by a scholarly elite made up of officeholders in the imperial bureaucracy plus the many more who aspired to hold office, intellectuals who shared a remarkably uniform cultural outlook.

Political authority has always sought after the approbation of the learned, of the intellectuals. In behalf of its own legitimacy it needs to claim, as Edward Shils puts it, some sort of involvement with what is "essential," "ultimately right," the sacred, the ideal, involvement which overlaps with the normal preoccupations of intellectuals everywhere.[3] Conflicts will arise when intellectuals criticize the political establishment as wanting in these respects, or seem to infringe on its authority. What is remarkable in the Chinese situation was, first of all, a political ideology that tied the basis of legitimacy so explicitly to intellectuals as a group, and secondly, a political system that managed for centuries to give them a clearly defined and privileged place within its own structure, thereby incorporating or co-opting its potential critics into the system. While actual power always resided in the hands of the imperial state with intellectuals as its subservient subordinates, they could nevertheless, as carriers and interpreters of the Confucian ideology that legitimated that power, claim an allegiance to a "higher" authority from which they could exercise their right to judge those who held power over themselves. In its actual application, Mencius' principle that the "use of heart-minds" entitled those above to rule did not mean so much that the Confucian scholar possessed the political power to govern, but rather that he would be recruited to assist those who did, while at the same time being charged with the function of legitimating their authority.[4]

The outstanding characteristic, indeed one might say, the genius, of Confucianism, was the ethical continuum that linked individual person to state, subjective self-cultivation to social vocation and political service. "The Confucian intellectual" in Tu Wei-ming's words, "defines what politics is from the center of his moral being."[5] It was this dimension of moral aspiration and self-fulfillment, a feature shared by all religions, that so inspired personal commitment and that no doubt reinforced the performance of Confucianism as an ideology capable of holding together one of the longest continuing political systems in human history. Yet while many Confucian intellectuals did "take part in the governing process not as servants of the emperor but as messengers for their moral ideals,"[6] such a role carried within itself contradictions that were far from easy to reconcile.

The intellectuals' authority to speak or speak out was, after all, dependent on their status as officials. Their opinions and criticism could be expressed only within a clearly defined and circumscribed perimeter, and through a given set of specific terms; their remonstrations against the emperor, who might be incompetent, vicious, or moronic, were necessarily still couched in terms of personal submission to him.[7] To position himself vis-à-vis political authority, while functioning both as its servant and its critic, continually forced the scholar-official to carry out a precarious balancing act. Providing moral leadership, as government officials were supposed to do, did not mean that it was easy for those who were qualified in theory to maintain their own moral integrity in practice. Apart from the fact that "the integrity of Confucian teaching constantly had to be defended against the danger of debasement through its use as an official ideology or as mere professional qualification,"[8] were the dual Confucian values of self-fulfillment and official service ever wholly compatible? All in all, to be active in politics as a responsible literati-official could be as harshly challenging and demanding on the level of one's personal morality as embarking on the life of a religious devotee.[9] Chinese history may have been written as a mirror for good government, but its innumerable biographies of officials are no less the self-reflections of individuals who in the process of participating in that government have had to ponder excruciating moral choices.

There was always the alternative of withdrawing rather than serving in government, but then the Confucian "repudiated not only something outside himself—the corrupt and corrupting institutions of imperial authority, but also, and even more significantly, something within himself, some part of his identity and his duty."[10] To drop out of the system altogether entailed a loss to the self as well as becoming politically irrelevant. Throughout history Chinese intellectuals have not customarily thought of themselves as "independent, autonomous, endowed with a character of their own" that distinguished them in some "essential way" from all other social groupings, a charge Gramsci leveled against Western intellectuals connected with idealist philosophy.[11] The self-image and life work of Chinese intellectuals were always consciously enmeshed in the general complex of social and political relations.

In spite of their avowed break with tradition, China's twentieth-century intellectuals have not been able to free themselves from their contradictory legacy, but continue to carry within themselves, as survivals from the past, the "two deeply internalized roles" of "servant of the state and of moral critic of the ruler."[12] Throughout the past decades of political revolution, they have found themselves caught in a relationship with the state that is just as ambivalent and, if anything, even more fraught with wrenching tension and untold risk.[13]

WRITING AND THE AUTHORITY OF
LITERARY TRADITION

From the point of view of maintaining the state system through successful management of its intellectuals, the civil service examination must be considered one of the cleverest political institutions ever devised. Its integration of literature into the system played a decisive role in shaping the particular nature of the Chinese literary tradition. Based on the rationale that mastery of the moral teachings in the Confucian classics best qualified people for service in the upper echelons of government, literacy in the classical language became mandatory, and, as much as any factor, helped to perpetuate the division between the ruling and the ruled. The elite's intellectual and moral superiority was combined with a monopoly over writing and the textual tradition, which in a process of self-reinforcing circularity, embodied and perpetuated its particular ideology and values. Classical literature largely tended to be a carrier and purveyor of the dominant ideology, and therefore occupied a central and prestigious place in the political structure, a support and ornament of the imperial system it served.

The critical factor of literacy in dominance and subordination is highlighted in David Johnson's social-cultural analysis of late imperial China, which groups the population into nine categories within the "structure of dominance."[14] In between the very small legally privileged gentry class at the top, including those who had become officials and were at the very top of the top, and the largest group down below, including the urban but mostly rural poor, were seven other classes, ranked by their degrees of dependency. Those at the top were classically educated, in contrast to the dependent masses at the bottom, who were illiterate. Learning and access to the literary tradition were most conspicuously the means, but also the justification, for achieving elite status. In the orthodox view, as Johnson put it, "the learned deserved to rule" and the meritocracy, by Ming and Qing times, had become a "grammatocracy."

Literature in traditional China was thus deeply embedded in a broad network of public service, political power, class privilege, ideological imperatives, moral responsibilities, and an ongoing textual tradition.[15] This was the case even if not everyone who was educated passed the examinations into officialdom—in fact, by far the majority did not.[16] The number of men who were classically educated but who did not hold office because they had failed the examinations, or who, for one reason or another had dropped out of the system, continued to swell through the centuries,[17] since the territorial administrative structure did not grow proportionately as the empire's population increased.[18] But even if some may have felt freer to deviate from the orthodox line, classical literature was overall produced and consumed by an indoctrinated elite, and to be engaged in the act of writing was first of all to situate the self within the nexus of a complex and interrelated system.

For one who obtained political rank through mastery of the classical texts, the ability to manipulate them continued to be necessary throughout official life. Quotations from the Confucian canon were prevalent in reports, documents—the paperwork of one's bureaucratic career. They appeared in memorials to the throne, in imperial decrees, providing the textual authority for arguing positions, for determining policy, perhaps even to justify the choice of methods for flood control.[19] The scholar-official was ever aware of himself as a node in a vast and ongoing symbolic network, as he constantly evoked the texts of the past in his activities of administering and writing in the present. Even when turning to more personal genres such as the essay or poetry, he did not see himself as a professional or independent writer; his writing activities were regarded rather as a sideline, an avocation, the literary side of his public career as a scholar-official.

All writers in the classical language joined the same "in group," the exclusive aristocratic club whose members spanned the ages while seeming to possess a contemporaneous existence, as they reworked the formal conventions, the rhetorical formulas, the coded allusions, while adding through their textual production their own individual exemplification of an established genre. Classical Chinese writing was thus profusely and self-consciously intertextual, constantly incorporating and utilizing prior texts in the process of producing any new text. To write in the apparently timeless classical language was to be assured of immortality, to transcend one's personal death. Participation in the authoritative literary tradition united public role and personal transcendence; literature, in the words of Cao Pi (Emperor Wen of Wei,), was "a great force in the ordering of state, a glorious enterprise that never grows old."[20]

The written word itself was a privileged, visible sign of knowledge, power, and domination. In one of the first peasant/intellectual confrontations in modern Chinese fiction as portrayed in Lu Xun's "The New-Year Sacrifice," Xianglin's Wife accosts the I-narrator as someone who, in the customary phrase, "knows characters" (*Ni shi shizi de*). She assumes that he will therefore be in an authoritative position to answer her urgent question about her fate after death. In the eyes of the untutored, the written word could take on magical properties: "spring couplets" to bring about desired auspicious circumstances, or Daoist charms to cure illness, ward off evil. According to the *Yijing,* the *Book of Changes,* the beginning of writing, and thus of civilization, came about when the mythical Fu Xi, whom we must acknowledge as the world's first semiotician, observing the signs and patterns in heaven and earth and the markings of birds and beasts, modeled the hexagrams after them. The written word as sign was a link between the human and cosmic, the social and the natural order. Those who had mastered the exclusive art of writing held within their hands the ability to read the secrets of the universe, the power to rule over the rest, and indeed were in a position to affect reality. Such notions about the tremendous power of language would continue to have important consequences in modern history and in the turbulent relations between the writer/intellectual and the party-state.[21]

A TRADITION OF LITERARY MARTYRDOM

That writing was first of all a matter of participating in an inherited textual tradition was strongly articulated by Sima Qian (145–87? B.C.), subject of one of the earliest known autobiographies in China. In the prelude to her study of modern Chinese autobiography, Wendy Larson has discussed chapter seventy, the postface, to the *Shiji* (*Records of the Grand Historian*), as a "prototypical circumstantial autobiography" in which the author refers primarily to his social and material circumstances. Although in this text Sima Qian "deals with his life only in its official capacity and only in relation to external phenomena, social structures and institutions, and political ideology,"[22] he is, as Larson points out, "defining the self by its relationship to institutions and structures that signify status and power" (p. 11), and, one might add, status and power that, at time of writing, was actually lost to him. And it is against that critical loss that Sima Qian attempts to construct his writing self while relating that self to his conception of the textual tradition.

The motivation behind his autobiographical self-representation is to justify his choice of castration over death when punished for having offended the Han emperor. He had spoken up for general Li Ling, who had incurred the wrath of Emperor Wu in surrendering to the Xiongnu rather than fighting them to the death. The reason Sima Qian had chosen to live on, even in indignity, was so that he could carry on with the historical writing bequeathed to him by his father. He thus attempts to validate and justify not only his mission in life but also his very life itself, by linking up with an ongoing textual tradition, a linkage reinforced by filial obligations.

History, as Sima Qian, the founding father of Chinese historiography, wrote it was as much the assimilation of past texts into present texts as it was an investigation of what had happened in the past. Moreover, in "transmitting ancient matters and putting in order its hereditary traditions" he is claiming to be following the example of Confucius.[23] While explicitly denying a comparison of his own work to Confucius' *Spring and Autumn Annals*, he evokes it at length in his postface to emphasize that moral evaluation is inherent in what the historian writes. Although in disgrace, cruelly (and perhaps unjustly?) punished by his ruler at court, he will, however, in the time-honored tradition of the historian, assume the responsibility of sitting in moral judgment over political events. To write history is not only to be the center of consciousness in the narrative of history, it is also to be its abiding conscience.

Sima Qian's fate is paradigmatic of the double-edged relation of the Confucian intellectual to the structures of state power. In his letter to Ren An, a more emotional text of self-representation, he describes his personal tragedy in greater detail while constructing what may be termed a tradition of literary martyrdom. To claim to be witness to a higher moral truth while remaining subject to those holding absolute power, is the kind of situation particularly conducive to producing martyrs. And Chinese history, as Sima Qian goes down the list, has been full of them: King Wen expanded the *Zhouyi* while in prison, Confucius wrote the *Spring and Autumn Annals* when he was in straits, Qu Yuan composed "Encountering Sorrow" in banishment, Zuo Qiu lost his sight and so we have the *Conversations from the States*, Sunzi had his feet chopped off and thus *The Art of War* was put together, and so on.[24] Writing in the first century B.C., Sima Qian can already evoke a long list of august predecessors, great men who had produced important writings not only under conditions of physical suffering but also while in trouble with political authority. As Sima Qian implies, he himself (castration having denied him the production of progeny) is but the latest heir to that immortal tradition.

"Unable to put into action their principles (*dao*)," these writers "wrote of the past with their eyes on the future. . . . They retired (*tui*) to write books in which they expressed their pent-up feelings, hoping to realize themselves (*zixian*) in literature."[25] In this cause and effect sequence Sima Qian is suggesting that great writings are not just compensations for ultimate failure to attain public office (*zhong bu ke yong*) or alternatives to worldly success; they are born of, indeed are made possible by, such suffering or persecution.[26]

While it was Sima Qian who gave the most explicit expression to the "martyr syndrome" in his simultaneous construction of the writing self and the literary tradition, it is the figure of Qu Yuan, one of the names on Sima Qian's list and China's first named poet, that has been most frequently celebrated (or lamented) as the writer/martyr par excellence and that has been continually evoked down through the twentieth century.

Qu Yuan's dates as well as the historical circumstances of his existence are highly uncertain. The poetry attributed to him and supposedly produced when he was wandering in exile after his banishment from the court of King Huai of Chu (r. 328–299 B.C.), contains the self-portrait of a loyal, upright, high-minded official who has remained steadfast to his ideals, refusing to compromise even when suffering persecution. In his long narrative poem *Lisao* (*Encountering Sorrow*), the theme is expressed through a journey motif, during which the poet-subject moves toward a magical, supernatural realm while in quest of an ideal mate. But the journey ends in failure and despair, implying that he is an immortal exiled into an unworthy world. As Sima Qian put it in his biography of the poet some three centuries later, "It was the sense of wrong (*yuan*) that inspired Qu Yuan's composition of the *Lisao*."[27] In pointing out that historical examples are given in the poem "in order to criticize [or satirize] (*ci*) contemporary affairs (*shi shi*)," Sima Qian is, of course, referring to his own parallel practice of seeing the situation of the present self mirrored in the models of the past. The emotional affinity he felt with Qu Yuan is expressed in the "Historian's Comment" that follows the biography, in which he describes his tears both in reading the *Lisao* and when traveling to where the poet had drowned himself.[28] Large parts of Sima Qian's biography of Qu Yuan consist of extracts from other texts, and doubt has been expressed about the authenticity of the biography as well as the historical existence of Qu Yuan himself.[29] What is undeniable is how the retrospective reading of Qu Yuan as exemplified in the text has defined the Qu Yuan legacy.

In the *Lisao,* the poet at times adopts a female voice in lamenting the separation from his ruler or expressing his longing for recognition. The tradition of female impersonation was established early in the *Shijing* (*The Book of Songs*), most often in poems expressing the sorrow and longing of a neglected or abandoned woman. Sima Qian's "Letter to Ren An" similarly describes the aspiring scholar who searches for employment by a ruler as analogous to the woman who desires to be loved: "The scholar (*shi*) works for [or is employed by] (*yong*) the one who knows [his worth] (*zhi*), the woman makes herself beautiful for the one who loves her" (p. 357). Just as women were subordinate to and dependent on men, so were intellectuals in relation to their rulers, the apex of power in the patriarchal structure. In Sima Qian's case the analogy is all too painfully literal in view of his loss of masculinity, his political as well as physical "feminization" through castration.

The long Chinese tradition of the writer/intellectual as martyr syndrome is intertexually self-reinforcing through the common practice of allegorical reading, for earlier examples are not only seen as predecessors but also employed as metaphors of the present self. In twentieth-century literature, the figure of Qu Yuan remains an abiding presence;[30] most particularly he has appeared and reappeared in various guises as allegories of the tortuous relationship between Chinese intellectuals and the state,[31] of the struggle of moral integrity against official power. Textual self-representation has continued its dialogue with the tradition; even as intellectuals and writers reach for new autonomous definitions of the self, in many respects the new selves continue to be layered onto the old.[32]

In their assaults on the hold of tradition, or what they term the "feudalism" of China, contemporary critics like Liu Zaifu have decried intellectuals of the past for their willing co-optation into the imperial system, lamenting their tragic fates as "slaves" both to the emperor and to the scriptures of Confucianism. They are seen to have lacked "a self of subjective value."[33] According to Liu, May Fourth was the first "discovery of the human person" (*ren de faxian*) in Chinese history.[34] More specifically, Vera Schwarcz describes one important driving force during the

May Fourth "enlightenment" as the intellectuals' "urgent, almost incho-
ate desire for emancipation from the ethic of self-submission," the ethic
"of subservience to patriarchal authority be it that of family or of the
state."[35] And during those early decades of the twentieth century, as the
Qing dynasty came to an end, followed by the chaos of the warlord period and the Nationalist (Guomindang) Party's ineffectual attempts to
establish control, weak central government did make it possible for intellectuals to achieve a certain degree of autonomy. But then came
Communist Party rule, and as employees of state-sponsored cultural institutions, and again as "establishment intellectuals," they have seemed in
many ways to have been restored to or co-opted again into their integral
position in the state structure.[36] As contemporary critics look back on the
fate and situation of intellectuals vis-à-vis the Communist state, one agonizing question they are increasingly asking themselves is whether Chinese intellectuals ever managed to break out from that "slave"—or, to
continue with the traditional trope, "female"—position vis-à-vis political
authority.

But can the relations between the intellectual and the Communist
state be regarded merely as the continuation of what they had been under
the old imperial system? The successive campaigns for thought reform
that have punctuated the history of the People's Republic, the massive
persecution of intellectuals, leading to their condemnation as "old
stinking number nine" (*chou laojiu*) among counterrevolutionaries during the Cultural Revolution, all precluded the possibility of their exercising their traditional function as both servants *and* moral critics of the
state. One may well ask, as a result of such utmost downgrading, if the
old legitimated high moral ground in opposition to political authority,
or even that tragic but nevertheless respected status of martyrdom as
sanctioned by the literary tradition, has still been available to them.

Yet at least in the unvoiced consciousness of the public, the intellectual as martyr syndrome seems to live on in China today. There was
striking evidence of this when the students in Tiananmen Square undertook to fast during the student democracy movement in 1989. For it
was the demonstration of their willingness to accept martyrdom, to risk
their lives in remonstrating against the state, that turned out to be a major factor in galvanizing the public to rally to their cause. Whether consciously or not, the students became recognized heirs to a time-honored
tradition. On the other hand, the student movement had begun, paradoxically, as a direct harking back to the May Fourth period with its im-

ported ideologies of democracy, individual emancipation, and rejection of the traditional past. In spite of the plaster of paris statue of the "goddess of democracy" with its unmistakable allusion to America's Statue of Liberty, many traditional values and themes regarding the relation of intellectual and the state were being reenacted with multiple levels of irony during the tragic "June Fourth" drama of Tiananmen Square.

Whatever may or may not have actually been achieved by the May Fourth discovery of the "human person," it did indeed entail a radical questioning of the authority of the textual tradition. In the profusion of first-person fiction and autobiographies, it is the "I" as protagonist/ narrator that will be presented as a countersite of meaning and authenticity. Throughout the shifting politics of the twentieth century, literature and the writing self, for so long conceptualized in relation to the dominating political structure, have both had to be constantly questioned and reinvented. Our narrative texts of self-representation will each dramatize different stages of that ongoing and precarious quest.

THE PEASANT—SEEN, BUT HEARD?

The self-image of the scholar-literati elite, around which much of the literature in the classical tradition had revolved, included their "sense of mission" (*shiminggan*).[37] It is expressed in the famous motto by Fan Zhongyan (989–1052): "The *shi* must be the first to worry (*you*) about the troubles (*you*) of the world but the last to enjoy its pleasures." But beyond supposedly just being required to be more miserable than anybody else in the world, traditional intellectuals were specifically marked by their "worry or concern for the country and the people" (*you guo you min*). The responsibility of the practitioner of benevolent government was to nurture the moral nature of the *min,* those down below who were using their muscles, directly involved in the labor of producing food. It was important to ensure their economic livelihood first, otherwise they would not be able to carry out their family obligations, nor submit to his rule:

> Hence when determining what means of support the people should have, a clear-sighted ruler ensures that these are sufficient, on the one hand, for the care of the parents, and on the other, for the support of wife and children, so that the people always have sufficient food in good years and escape starvation in the bad; only then does he drive them towards goodness; in this way the people find it easy to follow him.[38]

The welfare of the "people" being the goal and criterion of good government, one of the duties of the scholar-officials, as transmitters and interpreters of the Confucian state ideology, was to see to it that the imperial authorities would continue to deserve to rule by discharging their responsibilities toward the people, the broad masses of peasants tilling the soil.[39] Therefore the peasants down below as oppressed and suffering human beings were not without a presence in the classical literary tradition.

In this respect, the traditional Chinese intellectual was "ahead" of his European counterpart, as this powerful and often quoted passage from La Bruyère (1645–1696), referred to by Fredric Jameson as "one of the first explicit descriptions of the peasantry in modern French literature," suggests:

> One sees certain ferocious animals, male and female, scattered over the countryside, black, livid, and burned by the sun, bound to the soil which they dig and turn over with unconquerable stubbornness; they have a sort of articulate voice, and when they stand up they exhibit a human face, and in fact they are men. They retire at night into dens, where they live on black bread, water, and roots; they spare other men the toil of sowing, tilling, and harvesting in order to live, and thus deserve not to be without the bread which they have sown.[40]

In China peasants had long been recognized to have been in fact men rather than animals, since they, like all humans, were distinguished from animals by Mencius because they possessed the same incipient moral tendencies that gave everyone the potential of becoming a sage king like Yao and Shun. And the main business of government was to nurture that potential.

While this was the political theory, it did not mean that Chinese peasants escaped victimization by political oppression and economic exploitation from above. Poets like Du Fu and Bo Juyi among many others, who wrote poems describing the hard lot of the peasants, did to some extent *see* what it was like for them. An occasional effort was made to *hear* the peasant as well, as would seem from the title of the following poem by the early Song poet Mei Yaochen (1002–1060):

> "The Peasants' Words" ("Tianjia yu")
> Who said the peasant's lot a happy one?
> Spring taxes still unpaid in autumn,
> The village officer bangs on our door

Pressing us day and night.
In summer the rivers overflowed,
Waters rose higher than the house,
Water has destroyed our beans,
Locusts eaten our millet.
Last month came the edict
Making people register again.
One in three men was drafted,
Cruelly forced to carry bow and case.
Now the prefect's even tougher,
Wielding whips, clubs, the draft officer
Seeks out young and old,
Leaving only those blind and lame.
Dare we complain in field or alley,
Fathers and sons each grieve and weep.
How can we till the southern fields,
When to buy arrows we sold our oxen.
The air of grief turns into long rains.
Jar and pan stand empty of gruel,
The lame and blind cannot plow
Death will be coming to us soon.
Hearing this I am ashamed
Receiving in vain my wages from the state.
Rather I should chant "The Homecoming,"
And cut firewood in a deep valley.[41]

The "peasants' words" are obviously not given in their own language, but have been "translated" into a classical five-character poem. Although Jonathan Chaves sees it as "essentially a believable lamentation by the farmers on their sad lot," he points out that the poem contains historical and poetic allusions with which they could not have been familiar. The poem is indeed in the "even and plain" (*pingdan*) style that Mei Yaochen was known for, and its accounting of the specific horrors of peasant life are given in a factual, straightforward tone. But it is hardly an authentic example of peasants speaking for themselves.

In the poem's long preface, Mei Yaochen describes the pressures exerted on the people by local officials vying to meet the imperial demand for conscripts: "High and low there were sorrow and complaints, the rains were extremely heavy. How could this assist the emperor's purpose of nurturing [his people]? So I have recorded the words of the peasants, arranged into a literary composition (*ci wei wen*), in readiness for the Poetry Collector." Here he is referring to an office, a sort of weathervane or public opinion pollster of ancient times, which supposedly collected songs and poems in order to let the emperor know how he was doing in discharging his responsibilities. Whether such an office ever existed historically, it certainly did not during the Song dynasty. But it had become a myth or a metaphoric convention of long standing,[42] and by referring to it the poem places itself within an orthodox tradition in which one justification of poetry was that it served the social purpose of informing those above about the conditions of those below.

The concluding lines of the poem shift from external observation to self-criticism, for the final importance of the peasants' words devolve upon their effect on the poet himself. Mei Yaochen was magistrate of Xiangcheng in Henan at the time he composed the poem, and he takes the hardships of the peasants as a sign that he is unworthy of his post. The way to deal with the problem is indicated in the allusion to Tao Qian's poem "Gui qu lai" ("The Homecoming") at the conclusion. When acknowledging that he was unfit for holding office, Tao Qian (365–427) resigned to return to his life as a farming recluse. For all his talk about cutting firewood in the deep valley, Mei Yaochen is not really envisioning a future shared with the peasant whose hard life he depicts. Rather his allusion to a poem written six centuries ago evokes a model that places himself within the alternative tradition of Daoist withdrawal from the political world. Although as a low-ranking official Mei Yaochen may have engaged in "certain interchanges in thoughts and feelings with the common people . . . his position towards them was after all that of a member of the ruling class."[43]

The title notwithstanding, the "peasants' words" on their immediate woes have in the process of being "recorded" (lu) been transformed by language, adapted to the conventions of classical poetry, and they end up primarily as a stimulus to the personal reflections of the poet, reflections which are in turn expressed in conventional ideologies or tropes drawn from the distant past. The term wo (I or we) occurs four times in the poem. In the first three, the wo is attributed to the peasant or peasants, and whether singular or plural, the wo speaks for the peasants en masse, as a spokesman of a large generalized group of oppressed and suffering people. But in the poem's final lines the referent of the wo shifts to the poet as an individual speaking from a particular subject position, possessing a reflective and inner life, engaged in the act of self-examination and contemplating personal choices. The two wos thus refer not only to two distinct social classes, but also to classes whose self-expression through language is of an entirely different order of subjectivity.

Although the poem expresses sympathy for the plight of the suffering peasants, ostensibly leading to the poet's sense of personal failure, the text reinscribes what Foucault would call the "power relations"[44] of the dominant culture. The way in which the peasants are interpellated and signified is from the speaker's position of superiority. They are presented as passive and observed objects to whom disasters befall; conscripted, pressured, and beaten, too intimidated even to avail themselves openly of the only responses possible, to complain and to grieve. Even in this attempt to present their "words" as if from their point of view, the peasants are consigned to their prescribed places, spoken by the text, with the poet, his inadequacies notwithstanding, occupying the position of the powerful speaking subject.

External depictions of the hard life of the peasants are indeed to be found among traditional writers sensitized by their Confucian sense of duty toward the people, but the enormous numbers of peasants basically existed as a marginalized mass, a looming but silent, inarticulate presence throughout the centuries. Those who labored on the land have traditionally been objectified as "others" against which the elite could define and express itself. The writing that may express compassion toward them, or even indignation on their behalf, will be produced within the relationship of domination, domination most conspicuously evident in the control over language and utterance. Not until the political and literary revolutions of the twentieth century have there been real efforts to reach peasants as people with a particularized voice of their own, who might perhaps be enabled to speak up by themselves, for themselves, or about themselves. Whatever the degree of their success—it is one of the issues this book will explore—such attempts took place at the same time that the entire literary tradition was under challenge, bringing about a concomitant identity crisis on the part of the writer/intellectual.

MODERN LITERATURE: CONSTRUCTING THE PEASANT/ SEARCHING FOR THE SELF

The minor theme of the peasant, however marginally acknowledged in the classical literary tradition, was to become a dominant one in the twentieth century, for "when China's new literature began, its pioneers already took the presentation of the fate of Chinese peasants as their historic mission."[45] From then on "peasant" would become a signifier whose meaning would be constantly constructed and reconstructed.

First of all a new term, *nongmin,* was apparently invented to refer to the farming *min.* This "new term" can actually be found in such early texts as the *Guliang* commentary on the *Chunqiu* (Spring and Autumn Annals), which covers the period 722–481 B.C. As a result of complicated translingual round-trip crossings, it found its way back as one of the many loan words "imported" from Japan into China during the nineteenth century and the early decades of the twentieth century.[46] It then took on a new meaning and soon replaced the traditional terms that had been more commonly used, such as *nong, nongfu, nongjia, tianjia, zhuangjia ren,* and so on. *Nongmin* became above all a "cultural and political invention," as Myron Cohen points out, a construction that was key to the "redefinition of traditional Chinese culture and of the vast majority, especially in the countryside, who still adhered to it."[47] For the intellectual elites of the May Fourth decades, to see the land-tilling rural population as "peasants" was to mark them as a reservoir of "backwardness," a major obstacle to the construction of a new society. This view was parallel to, and indeed was very much influenced by, the similar view that accounted for the Western choice of the term "peasant" over "farmer" in referring to the Chinese cultivators of "the good earth," suggesting that China was stagnant, "medieval," an underdeveloped land of peasants, held back by its peasants. Later, in the Maoist vision of revolution, these same culturally "backward" peasants would be yet again reconstructed as politically "progressive," the vanguard of the revolution and the motive force of Chinese history, now retold as having been propelled by a "tradition" of "peasant uprisings" (*nongmin qiyi*). In attempting to reverse the traditional hierarchy, the totalistic agenda of a sinified Marxism thus raised the peasant from neglected prime victim at the bottom of the old order to the exalted position of carrier of salvational hope, the hope of the utopian new order to come. The question of who the "peasant" might be "in reality" throughout such positionings and repositionings was neither answerable nor relevant.[48]

(To avoid awkwardness, I will be using the term peasant without quotation marks, with the understanding that the peasant as a signifier has always de facto been enclosed in quotes, a signifier whose shifts of meaning is being traced in this study.)

Whether peasants are subsistence producer-consumers or entrepreneurs producing for the market, they have been generally conceived not simply as an economic category, but also as a strata or group embedded in social relations.[49] In distinguishing the peasant from both the farmer and the primitive cultivator, the anthropologist Eric Wolf emphasizes the nature of the social order over the level of economic development. The farmer in the United States, for example, is an agricultural entrepreneur running his farm as a business enterprise. Primitive cultivators are those whose production is mainly geared to their own use or to discharge kinship obligations, and surpluses are exchanged directly among groups or their members. They control the means and their own labor in raising crops and livestock. Peasants, however, are those who have been relegated to a specific position as part of a complex social order. They are "rural cultivators whose surpluses are transferred to a dominant group of rulers that uses the surpluses both to underwrite its own standard of living and to distribute the remainder to groups in society that do not farm but must be fed for their specific goods and services in turn."[50] And the hallmark of civilization is this division of labor between rulers and food-producing cultivators.

Mencius had long ago pointed out the linkage between such a division of labor and China's bifurcated hierarchical state structure, while adding the all-important "Confucian twist" by explicitly identifying the intellectual—the users of heart/mind—with the ruling elite. With the end of the imperial state structure, the question for modern writers/intellectuals was how to position themselves in relation to the peasants, whose fate they were undertaking to present as they assumed their new "historic mission."

During the early decades of the twentieth century, the victimization of the peasant became a preoccupation of intellectuals, but unlike Mei Yao-chen, who saw it as due to a combination of rapacious officials and bad weather, modern writers seized upon the plight of the peasant as a means, a rationale, for indicting the entire system. But if the system was being discredited, from where then should the writer write? The situation was no longer clear-cut, as in the Song poet's case. Traditional alternatives of response, the established models from the past—to strive to fulfill one's duty as an official (even if shamefacedly) or to withdraw from public service as a recluse—were not available anymore. Modern writers could not make their individual choices within an established framework, which in any case they themselves were in the process of dismantling. In that process the peasant was becoming much more than an incidental subject that one might happen to observe, but was assuming an overwhelming presence that could neither be dismissed nor accommodated within the writer's or intellectual's own uncertain relationship with the world.

Even as the peasantry rose to assume central importance as a subject, engendering corresponding displacements in the writer's position, it remained geographically demarcated, accorded a clearly defined place by intellectuals in their discourses about the "countryside." A new genre or category of literature, "literature on the countryside" (*nongcun ticai wenxue*), whose ethos had little to do with the pastoral or idyllic "rural poetry" (*tianyuanshi*) of the past, came into being; it depicted the countryside above all as the site of peasant oppression and struggle. To write about the peasant in such a countryside was usually not to write about a unique individual who happened to be a peasant, but still to write about a specific class, a particularized space, a social entity, of which the individual, regardless of his personal qualities, was first of all a representative. In that respect the Mei Yaochen approach still holds.

The effort to redefine the intellectual vis-à-vis peasant relationship has gone through several phases as China has struggled to move away from its past. The peasant as such was not a dominant theme in what we might consider the transitional generation, the generation that recognized the bleakness of China's plight and engaged in an urgent search for solutions. This was the generation of the 1890's, the generation of Kang Youwei, Liang Qichao, and Yan Fu, whose lives had still largely been molded by tradition, and, while receptive to the new ideas from the West, they continued to believe that the tradition was encompassing and rich enough in resources that some rethinking of the old system would enable it to yield the solutions to current problems. Much energy was also expended in looking for parallel elements or comparable categories between traditional Chinese and Western thought—so difficult was it to accept the notion that the crisis China faced was an unprecedented one, and that what had seemingly worked so well in the past might be utterly inadequate for dealing with the crisis of the present.

It was not until the following generation, what we consider the generation of May Fourth, the students who participated in the movement and their somewhat older teachers or vanguard leaders, Chen Duxiu, Hu Shi, and Lu Xun, that the breakthrough occurred. This generation had also been educated in the classical curriculum, but with the abolition of the civil-service examination in 1905, when many were in their twenties, the traditional avenues of advancement were cut off. They had eagerly

absorbed the teachings of the previous generation, particularly its translations of works from the West, and many then went on to continue
their education in the outside world where those works had been produced. Turning their backs on home in more ways than one, after
reaching maturity in the alien environment of foreign countries like Japan and the United States they then returned to live and work in the in-
terstices of the large cities of Beijing and Shanghai that were undergoing
accelerating change.

Their search for alternatives from external sources with which to criticize tradition brought about a paradigmatic change, a "thorough radicalization." A notion that China could not join the modern world or
even survive in it without a "total demolition of the tradition"—"a
neoterist mentality" as Ying-shih Yü terms it—had been formed among
the Chinese intellectual elite, "a mentality obsessed with change, with
what is new."[51] In severing their links with the state system, the new generation of intellectuals were no longer its actual or aspiring government
servants. At the same time they lost their function as spokesmen and
transmitters of the values and ideologies that had given the system legitimacy and meaning. Uncertain of their place and identity, facing an
unknown future, they were the first truly alienated generation, the first
modern Chinese intelligentsia. In advocating totalistic change, the traditional intellectual had removed himself from the center to the periphery
and transformed himself into a marginalized modern-day *zhishifenzi*.[52]

This was the first generation to give up entirely on tradition, to commit itself to its rejection. Yet culturally and psychologically—as well as
biologically and genetically, for most were members of old gentry families in decline, a necessary condition for making it into the educated elite
to begin with—twentieth-century *zhishifenzi* were successors of the
scholar-literati of the past. They were openly iconoclastic yet inherited
many of the burdens of the traditional relationship, and it is in the writings of this generation that we see the beginnings of the obsession with
the idea of the peasant.

Scholars have noted certain parallels between the modern Chinese intellectuals' "discovery" of the peasant and the populist movements of
nineteenth-century Russia. In both situations, as Benjamin Schwartz put
it, the intellectual was part of the small group of elite "hovering above a
huge peasant mass—a group which very self-consciously distinguished itself from the mass, and tends to regard the 'people' as a sort of monolithic entity."[53] Like the Russian *Narodnik* movement of the 1870's, there

was a "going to the people" movement from about 1915 to the 1930's in
China, when intellectuals advocated the study and collection of folk
songs and folk literature, inspired similarly by a romantic view of the innocence and primitivism of rural life.[54] Folk literature was not only seen
as directly mirroring the different life and minds of country folk; it fitted
into the antitraditional, anti-Confucian agenda of Chinese intellectuals.
Going beyond such ideas as Rousseau's belief in the "goodness of simple
men," they endowed peasants with the "advantages of backwardness,"
perceiving them as outsiders of, or alternatives to, the political and cultural system in which they themselves had been so deeply enmeshed and
from which they now felt increasingly alienated.

Peasants emerged as new kinds of ideologized constructs in both
nineteenth-century Russia and twentieth-century China, as intellectuals
projected onto them their own visionary hopes for a brave new world. In
both cases the peasant masses were seen as an entity with an innate "revolutionary consciousness," or at any rate as a reservoir of revolutionary energy and creativity, for the purpose of serving assigned or imagined
functions in utopian political and modernizing agendas.

The specific political expressions of populism and their roles in Russian and Chinese socialist revolutions would turn out to take very different paths.[55] But there was one central dilemma shared by both, that is the
self-contradictory role of the intellectual toward the masses. Was the intellectual to learn from the masses or enlighten them and lead them? If
the masses were a repository of revolutionary consciousness and power,
how could those be turned into an effective revolutionary tool? Were the
intelligentsia to go among the people as pupils or as guides and stimuli
that could release that potential of the masses—or was the collective consciousness of the masses to become incarnate in a vanguard elite drawn
from the intelligentsia? Lenin would later resolve these contradictions by
placing a party that was assumed to embody the "proletarian consciousness" in the leadership and guiding role. The proletariat was in any case
not the peasantry, who could only play an ancillary role to the urban
proletariat in the bourgeois-democratic phase of the revolution. But in
China, due to different historical circumstances, notably the absence of
an urban proletariat, the peasantry was made into the centerpiece of the
revolution, with profound consequences for its relation with intellectuals. The dilemma of intellectual leadership and the masses' revolutionary
credentials was an issue that was never fully resolved. In fact, as compared with the conventional Marxist issues of proletariat versus bour-

geoisie, it was the problematic relationship between peasants and intellectuals that would continue to be a preoccupation of the Chinese revolutionary regime.[56]

While the populist movement among the Russian intelligentsia was mainly a passing episode before the revolution and died out soon after the 1880's, in the Chinese revolution it persisted, with various permutations, as a dominant theme. The difference can be ascribed to differences in the history of the two countries. The Chinese Communists may have imported the Western ideology of Marxism-Leninism for carrying out their revolution, but they also looked back into the Chinese past to find what evidence they could to support their political agenda, specifically in the tradition of peasant rebellion. Although peasants have been wretched and oppressed since time immemorial all over the globe, they do not frequently rise in revolt. In contrast to a country such as India, for example, where they have been relatively uncommon, widespread peasant revolutions have been endemic throughout China's history. Indeed one way to perceive the rise and fall of the dynastic cycles is as a recurring pattern of restoration of order and re-establishment of the intellectual-state relationship after its violent disruption by peasant rebellions.

Such was the case even when the new rulers started out themselves as peasant rebels—the old Chinese adage is that those who succeed become emperors, while those who fail go down in history as bandits—since it appeared that the only way to administer the empire was to follow established patterns. Founding rulers—one thinks of the stories surrounding those of the Han and the Ming—who might have started out as crude, ill-mannered peasants, arrived at court as uncouth outsiders. They initially outrageously flouted the rules of decorum, humiliating and terrorizing, if not outright murdering, scholar/officials, but then they soon learned that these were the people they had to depend on for managing the affairs of government. Essential to the institution of monarchy was their service as those in charge of rituals, forms, ceremonies, as manipulators of language and symbols, and the outward signs of imperial power, but even more important was their support, for they were the ones who could provide the ideological underpinnings to legitimate political authority.

The intellectuals, on the other hand, needed the state to maintain their privileged position, to carry out the clearly defined social roles on which they had always staked their sense of self. Sometimes the modus vivendi between emperor and intellectuals might take longer to achieve, at times not until the second or third generation of the imperial family, by which time the mutual dependence and working relationship would be reestablished, and both could work together in the task of governing the empire and maintaining the dynasty—that is, in holding off for as long as possible the next peasant rebellion.

The Chinese Communist Revolution deliberately set out to place itself within that partly retrieved, partly constructed tradition of peasant rebellion, a tradition with its own rich history and legends. This tradition had to be reconciled somehow with a Marxist ideology that was addressed to the urban working class of advanced industrialized nations. Beginning with Mao Zedong's Hunan Report of 1927, in which the peasant was put forth as the popular base of revolution, the peasant as embodiment of "proletarian consciousness" was both an adaptation of the Marxist ideological formula and a fresh interpretation of Chinese history which emphasized peasant movements as its motive force. At the same time, the Chinese Communist revolution, which would be far from content with seeing itself as merely being more of the same, in its grandiose attempts to reverse the traditional hierarchical structure would radically redefine the relationship between state, intellectual, and peasant.

CLASS-IFYING INTELLECTUALS FOR A "PEASANT REVOLUTION"

One of the complex dilemmas in adapting Marxism to the historical situation in China was where to place intellectuals in the party's class system as it carried out its program of overthrowing the existent structures of traditional society and building a new socialist society. "Class," and from it "class struggle," whatever the differences between Chinese and European society, were, after all, what a Marxist revolution was supposed to be all about,[57] and a central tenet in the Chinese revolution was that the traditional "feudal system" was one in which the labor of the producing peasant class was exploited by the oppressive ruling class. Intellectuals, just like "rich peasant," "capitalist," or "bad element," were assigned a ranked position in the system of "class status." As Tani Barlow puts it in her cogent genealogy of modern Chinese *zhishifenzi,* " 'Class status system' did not simply describe passively, but inscribed, produced, allocated and monitored power, social position, privilege and political wealth,"[58] and the assigned ranked position, one might add, could have for any particular individual fateful, indeed fatal, consequences.

But just as it had been tricky during land reform to distinguish between peasants who were rich, middle, or poor, or even to decide who should properly be labeled a landlord,[59] how to classify intellectuals, and more particularly, what their relative position was with regard to the peasant, remained, throughout the context of constant political change, a thorny issue.

These difficulties of defining the proper place of intellectuals in a revolution claimed to be centered on peasants as well as of overcoming the barriers between the two groups were articulated early on in a decision drafted by Mao Zedong for the party's Central Committee, December 1, 1939: "*Daliang xishou zhishifenzi*" ("Recruit large numbers of intellectuals").[60] Even though intellectuals here refer to those who have a middle school or higher level of education, hardly an exalted status it would seem, Mao noted the party cadres' discrimination against them and reluctance to let them join the party. Yet "without the participation of intellectuals victory in the revolution is impossible" (p. 301). For one thing they were needed to "organize the millions of peasants"; besides, "the proletariat cannot produce intellectuals of its own without the help of the existing intellectuals" (p. 303). The solution was to recruit them but "give them political education and guidance" so that they could "revolutionize their outlook, identify themselves with the masses, and merge with older Party members and cadres and the worker and peasant members of the Party." (p. 302). The inherent contradiction of both needing intellectuals for their unique qualifications but also determining to make them "become workers and peasants" like everyone else was to plague the party for years to come. This contradiction is certainly one more factor in the "cyclical policy towards intellectuals, which oscillated between periods of repression and briefer periods of relative relaxation," as described by Merle Goldman.[61]

In the 1920's and 1930's many Chinese intellectuals were early converts to Marxism, supporting its radical program to demolish the old society and build a new one. They identified their interests with that of the authority of the Communist state after its establishment, only to be stigmatized as heirs of the traditional scholar-official elite and persecuted as class enemies. Now in the post-Mao era, with its emphasis on modernization rather than class struggle, intellectuals have been recategorized;

no longer to be regarded as members of the ruling class, they have become elements of the laboring working classes. Indeed, there is to be no
political distinction between "the people" and intellectuals.[62] The renun-
ciation of the party's narrowly dogmatic Marxist "class-ification" has
permitted intellectuals to achieve a surface equality with peasants and
workers, removing them as automatically available targets of class struggle.

The ambiguity of classifying "intellectuals" as a group, and its shifting
relation to the emerging self-defined "peasant" revolution, has been a
running theme throughout the history of modern Chinese literature.
During May Fourth, even before the party was in a position as Mao Zedong had decreed to make over intellectuals in accordance with its own
construction of the peasant, their own representations of the "discovered" peasant had already initiated them into the process of rethinking
themselves. As relatively free subjects then, detached from a clearly defined position in the system, they sought to assume a role akin to what
Foucault, in describing the European left-wing intellectual, has called the
"universal intellectual,"[63] "who finds his fullest manifestation in the
writer (p. 70). As the voice of the "consciousness/conscience of us all,"
this writer/intellectual aspires to be a "clear individual figure of universality," a bearer in "its conscious, elaborated form" of a universality
which was embodied in the obscure collective, the proletariat [peasant, in
the Chinese case], unreflective and "barely conscious of itself as such"
(pp. 67, 68). While this may have been the self-conception that progressive Chinese writers were arriving at after the heated debates of the late
1920's and early 1930's, it remained uncertain just how they would articulate, clarify, elaborate, render conscious that which was embodied in
the peasant. In concluding that revolution was necessary and inevitable,
such an assumed role, so it seemed, was one way for intellectuals to as-
sure themselves of their continued relevance, or even more of their leadership function; it allowed them to do what they had always been best
at—putting things, reality, or whatever, into words. However, such a
role from the outset placed the writer/intellectual in a curious dilemma
which Foucault's statement does not address. If the proletariat, or the
peasantry as proletariat, was itself incapable of self-apprehension or articulation through language, how would access and understanding to its
consciousness by the nonproletariat be possible?

Perhaps what drove intellectuals into presuming they had the capability of speaking for or representing the peasant was not so much the old

awareness of privilege and superiority reemerging in a new guise, but rather a new sense of moral culpability when the peasant was taken into a new kind of serious account. Perhaps it was more a matter of felt obligation rather than capability. Just as "the enslavement of the peasants in Russia provoked such a feeling of guilt . . . that nothing disparaging could be said about" them,[64] while "all manner of extraordinary qualities" were ascribed to them, similarly in modern Chinese literature, a new "penitential consciousness" seems to have developed. While the "penitents" were those "well known by the author, belonging to his own social class . . . the principles of perfection in human nature were made incarnate in another sort of people not well known to the authors: such as workers, peasants or other laboring classes. This did not originate from their deep understanding or true feelings about the laboring classes; on the contrary, it was based on a lack of familiarity and sense of estrangement."[65] These observations suggest some of the moral, political, intellectual, and discursive complexities and contradictions that writers found themselves caught in as they attempted to represent—either to speak for or to portray—the emergent peasant in modern Chinese literature.

2

Language and Textuality: Toward an Analytical Methodology

WHEN THE WRITERS of the May Fourth era undertook to create a new literature while rejecting the literary tradition of the past, they began by conceiving of that rejection and their creation as primarily a matter of language. Their new literary movement was launched with proposals for language reform. From that time on, issues of language have continued to be the locus of contention and controversy throughout the historical shifts and ideological battles that have followed. Authors will be self-conscious in their choice of medium, since the particular language in which they speak will itself carry ideological implications; questions of language, speech, silence, therefore often become themes of their narratives.

Any overall generalizations about the changing conceptions of language and its historical role in modern China will inevitably be somewhat simplistic and one-sided. The purpose in underlining the issue of language in this chapter is mainly to provide both a context and a rationale for the kind of textual analysis to be carried out in this study. Since historically language seemed to be where "things were happening," I will be considering the way these "things" were inscribed on microlevels of narrative through the reading, or rather, the rereading of selected representative texts.

MAY FOURTH AND THE PRIMACY OF LANGUAGE

Language was a focus of concern as literature underwent the process of reconceptualization during the May Fourth period. To write was no longer primarily a matter of participating in an ongoing transcendent textual tradition as it had been in the past, but rather of turning away from tradition and responding directly to what was seen as social reality. From a diachronic perspective that had hitherto positioned the production of writing in relation to prior texts while looking forward to a hoped-for future immortality, writing began to reorient itself synchronically toward the world that was immediately present. Representation—the relation between language and the "reality" that supposedly preceded it or was external to it—then became a core issue around which others revolved.

That China's republican political revolution in 1911 was soon followed by a self-proclaimed "literary revolution" was due to the central and prestigious position that literature had occupied within the traditional cultural and political system. It was not just what classical literature *did*—its traditional function as embodiment and transmitter of state ideology or its symbolic power in the hands of the ruling elite's authority—that made it a necessary target of revolution, but also what classical literature *was*. The very nature of the medium itself in practice was viewed as complicit with an antiquated, self-enclosed system. In its reliance on quotation and cryptic allusion, in its deliberate intertextuality, the production of new texts always out of prior texts, it had, so it seemed, isolated itself from the contemporary "real world" in which it was situated.

When Hu Shi initiated the May Fourth literary revolution in 1917, six years after the overthrow of the Manchu dynasty that had brought an end to the old imperial system, with his article "Wenxue gailiang chuyi" ("Tentative Proposals for a Reform of Literature"), what he called for was a literature that would first of all be liberated from its bondage to the past. His eight proposals for "reform" mainly concentrated on the need to avoid imitating the ancients, to get away from the time-worn themes, clichés, allusions, parallelisms, outworn diction, etc.[1] The basic premise was that literature evolves and changes with time; therefore "today's China should produce today's literature" (p. 45). A language shed of classical allusions and formal conventions, plain, direct, and closer to everyday speech, such as that found in vernacular novels—the only writings that might be ranked with "first class world literature"—would be the proper medium for this new literature. A major theme in the writings of those advocating literary revolution would be that the classical literary tradition was dead and could have little meaning or relevance for the new national identity that China must assume in order to survive in the modern world. This revolution would not only bring into being a new literature, but also—for this was fundamental to the May Fourth agenda—a new China, a modern nation.

Language reform was irrevocably tied to political and social reform in twentieth-century China from the very beginning. To those advocating *baihua*, the language of the new writing was conceived of as a medium that would supposedly truly "reflect reality"; but it was furthermore an agent that would have the power to transform reality in accordance with predetermined goals. To faithfully mirror the present world but also to change it—"realism" and political agenda—the struggle to reconcile these two mutually contradictory notions is one that Chinese language and literature have been continually trapped in throughout this century.

Historical changes in political ideology have always necessitated new interpretations of reality, and, in the case of China, have therefore also continually and explicitly required new languages for writing. In accordance with the shifts in either self-appointed or assigned political tasks, writers of each phase of modern Chinese literature have found themselves at the edge of language experimentation, engaged in expanding the territory of language into certain areas while closing off others.

Although the May Fourth writers invested traditional vernacular literary forms with new significance, their dominating anxiety was to be free of the norms and influence of tradition. They made elaborate attempts to imitate Western literary models and to enlarge the possibilities of Chinese writing by embracing "Europeanization." Beginning in 1918, innovations derived from foreign languages, as Edward Gunn has usefully catalogued, "reached almost every category of linguistic analysis in terms of grammar, rhetorical invention, and sentence cohesion." These included techniques of syntactic suspension, lengthening sentences through new levels of embedding, the distribution of modifiers, and new forms of interjection and apposition.[2] Stylistic innovations, as Gunn indicates, have played an important role and indeed are a telling index to the changes that have been taking place in Chinese culture and society, but one thing that must be emphasized is that these innovations have been very much motivated and shaped by the need to position literature in specific ways according to changing views of that culture and society.

In order to discredit and overthrow the old cultural and political system, writers of the new literature undertook to expose its dark underside by turning their attention to those who had been its prime victims, peasants and women. To speak about and speak for these hitherto marginalized, silent, and invisible "others," writers felt they needed the new *baihua* language to enable them to break out of the self-immured classical literary structures of the past. But could this new language itself actually speak *to* those it was presumably speaking *about* and *for*? Was it accessible or even relevant to those who were its subjects or, it was to be hoped, perhaps its audience? This would evolve into a central issue during the debates in the early 1930's over the popularization—or, more accurately, the "massification" (*dazhong hua*)—of literature. To its critics, Europeanization had created but a new elite language, a "new classical language" (*xin wenyan*) in Qu Qiubai's words, just as inaccessible as the old classical language had been to the people that now this literature professed to be about and for.[3]

Even more directly and explicitly than during the early 1920's, the question of language was being linked to specific agendas for political action. Indeed, the need to close the gap between the new literature and the masses was part of the campaign for a proletarian literature (*puluo wenxue*) to serve the proletarian revolution to come, although how exactly this imported Marxist idea was going to work in the Chinese environment, or even who precisely the Chinese proletarian masses were, was not yet made clear. There was a call for new forms that were actually old (*jiu xingshi*), based on such traditional populist genres as oral storytelling, opera, or folk song as a way to turn away from Western literary models, to counteract "Europeanization," and accommodate or adapt a language closer to the people. Still largely a matter of contentious debate in the 1930's, so-called mass language would not have much of a concrete effect on literary production until the Communist Party assumed control over literature in the Border Regions.

LANGUAGE: A CHINESE COMMUNIST OBSESSION

Many points in Mao Zedong's milestone "Talks at the Yan'an Forum on Literature and Art" of 1942 had been anticipated by the earlier ideas of Qu Qiubai and others during the "massification debate," but, given Mao's newly consolidated position as leader of the party, they assumed a definitive authority, and the "Talks" remained the scripture—to be in-

terpreted with varying degrees of stringency—of the party's literary policies for the next forty years.[4]

On the question of language, the proper language for literature and
art, Mao Zedong was particularly explicit and prescriptive. His first
question: Literature and art for whom? and its answer, that they are for
"workers, peasants, and soldiers," seemingly established a basic premise
from which his exhortations that writers and artists "should conscien-
tiously learn the language of the masses" could naturally follow.[5] However, the ultimate objective, as given in his definition of "massification,"
was that "the thoughts and feelings of our writers and artists should be
fused with those of the masses of workers, soldiers, and peasants," those
that they would write for and write about. The fundamental assumption
was that language could somehow be taken as a true index of consciousness, an assumption that would turn out to have drastic consequences
leading to language manipulation for the purpose of carrying out
thought control and political persecution.

Whatever was specifically meant by the "language of the masses" or
indeed how the "masses" were to be perceived or ideologically constructed by the party, one important signal given in the "Talks" was the
radical reversal of status for the intellectual elite engaged in literary production vis-à-vis the others. Writers were, of course, no longer the members of the traditional scholar-gentry whose literary authority derived
from their responsibility to nurture and educate the people below. But
neither would they be permitted to maintain their self-image as the modern intelligentsia attempting to speak for and represent the oppressed
underclass in the process of forging a new literature to carry out a modernizing agenda. Now they were referred to as *wenyi gongzuozhe,* workers
in literature and art, but yet not workers just like everyone else. In fact
writers would be lesser or lower workers, for they were exhorted to go
among the masses, subordinate themselves as apprentices, and take lessons from them. Denied their hitherto assumed mastery of language,
their previous command of the tools of their literary production, writers
were being told to go and acquire a new language and start afresh. Their
ability to adopt the language of the workers, soldiers, and peasants, as
indicators of how well their "thoughts and feelings had been fused with
those of the masses" would henceforth be the criterion for measuring
whatever claims to validity and relevance their writings could still have.
Language would become the crucial touchstone of literary competence
and, even more, of political acceptability.

Language was assuming an extraordinary importance in Yan'an, the place where the Chinese Communist Party was establishing its revolutionary headquarters. Applying "discourse theory and a logocentric model" in their illuminating book *Revolutionary Discourse in Mao's Republic,* David Apter and Tony Saich describe Yan'an as above all a utopic community in which "themes, mythic stories, logical constructions, metaphors and metonymies, the mandated cosmos and the role of Mao as the purveyor of an inversionary discourse of his own" were all coming together in the form of symbolic capital.[6] They focus on Mao Zedong as the great storyteller who, through his speeches, talks, and other texts, created a master narrative about the Chinese revolution and forged a collective mythology out of participatory individual historical experiences. He was thus able to establish hegemony over a community that was discursively bonded. When we consider the astonishing evolution of the Chinese Communists in Yan'an from a band of stragglers who had barely survived the Long March into a political party that would take control of all of China within a short dozen years, Mao Zedong's narrative reconstruction of reality and its capacity to engage the broad participation of intellectuals and writers was singularly effective. However it was precisely the party's own skillful exploitation of language that made all the more necessary its unremitting vigilance concerning the uses that language could be put to by others. In looking back over the past half century, it is indeed striking to note how language increasingly became a fetish, an overriding obsession, of the Chinese Communist Party. Party ideologues and fundamentalists became adept practitioners of "close reading," zealously combing through texts, any texts, ferreting out clues to political views through meticulous "explications" of imagery and diction in order to determine the political standpoints of their authors. During the many campaigns that targeted intellectuals, countless "rightists," "renegades," and "counterrevolutionaries" were condemned on the basis of flimsy linguistic evidence, usually quoted out of context. Once anybody was named as a target, there was always some piece of text somewhere that could be unearthed and "explicated" to make a damning case against him.

The anxiety over the sheer power of language to subvert was conversely reflected in the Chinese Communist Party's own investment in discourse control and manipulation. Confucianism had always placed great emphasis on *zheng ming,* the correctness or rectification of names and terms, for correctness meant conformity to a particular moral standard as well as to truth or accuracy.[7] In this respect the Chinese Communists have followed the Confucian model in underlining the essential importance of language "getting things right," but have carried to extreme the belief that language can further be used to "make things right."

Everything depends on what language is used in referring to it, or perhaps on whether language is used to refer to it at all. "All propaganda work in China, of which literature is often considered a part, is directed towards spreading the belief," notes D. W. Fokkema, "that things do exist in reality if words only say so often enough."[8] Indeed the process of the Chinese revolution, at least in hindsight, suggests that if its leaders had, apart from the way they had presented it to themselves in words, truly understood what the reality was, they would never have been able to accomplish what they did. On the other hand, their faith in the power of language has also made the Chinese Communists victims of their own rhetoric. The disaster of the Great Leap Forward in 1958 and the devastating famine that followed could have at least been somewhat alleviated had the party not been carried away by its own slogans and stories about fantastic increases in agricultural production while refusing to recognize the mounting evidence that was exposing them to be little more than empty words. If the Communists had been but willing to see beyond the mystifying veil of their own language to a few hard facts, they could have backtracked on some of their unworkable policies or at least put in place relief measures to lessen some of the appalling death and suffering.

Among the documentation Michael Schoenhals has provided in his study *Doing Things with Words in Chinese Politics,* some of the most fascinating are the examples of party circulars (popularly known as *hongtou wenjian,* red-head documents, due to the red ink used to print across the top "Document of the CCP . . .") that deal with proscribing and prescribing terminology. These are directives giving precise directions about the appropriate formulation (*tifa*) for slogans, labels of political friends and enemies, forms of discourse, etc. A change in formulation could signify a major shift in the party line, as for example in the 1950's, when the formulation "Mao Zedong Thought" was first proscribed and then later revived. The question seems to have had to do with how to position the relation between "Mao Zedong Thought" and Marxist-Leninism, whether it could be seen as an alternative, or what. And in the 1984 campaign against "Spiritual Pollution," the directive to change the wording from eradication (*qingchu*) to a "long-term problem" to be "opposed (*fandui*) and resisted (*dizhi*)," had the effect of calling the campaign off.[9] Other forms examined by Schoenhals include mechanisms of "ghost-writing" for political authorities, direction of the press, and censorship in the fields of the humanities and social sciences. Language formulation with its goal of imposing uniformity in discourse is everywhere shown to be a "form of power managed and manipulated by the state" (p. 3). While formalized language is inevitably a part of politics everywhere—witness the rise and fall of the term "liberal," the use of Native American or Indian in the American context—the microcosmic, top-down, hands-on management by the Chinese Communist state apparatus seems unique in the extreme lengths to which it was carried.

The prevalence of "doing things with words" can be seen on many other levels as well. Each political campaign, each moment of revolutionary history, produced its own mass of slogans and documents to recite and study. Those whose thoughts were in the process of rectification or remolding were required to produce self-criticism (*jiancha*) after self-criticism, "to recall history and know the self" (*huiyi lishi renshi ziji*), revising in successive versions the situations and reflections of their lives, reaching hopefully for an acceptable rendering of themselves into language. There exist at least eight self-criticisms by the writer Zhao Shuli written during the Cultural Revolution, but only the one of winter 1966, because it was early and "less subject to external pressure," might "presumably be in accord with the truth of his own thoughts."[10] "If then," one might add, considering how a "life" could be subject to multiple revisions. It boggles the mind to consider the mountains of texts that were produced as people were directed to endlessly reconstitute their own identities in words.

(College students I talked to in 1981 said that regular self-reflections were still required, but instead of bothering to write an original piece each time to hand in, some of them were photocopying—presumably after some modifications, or by that time did it make any difference?—earlier versions, or even photocopying those of others. This saved time, even if it wasted paper!)

Since language was supposed to "get things right," it was always of the utmost importance how one was verbally labeled and classified. An individual was defined by the party through labels, names, tags, slogans, formulas, reports, documents as well as the self-criticisms one produced. Yet this same person could also be given a different name or label—which could well determine one's fate—at different points in one's career, depending on one's political standing in the party. Ironically, the most blatant manifestation of the power of language is that it need not be in itself consistent. On the surface the words could remain the same, even if their meaning and value were reversed—another demonstration of the arbitrary gap between word and referent. To be labeled a rightist had been of course to be a political anathema, while to be a leftist was progressive and good. But in post-Mao reappraisals of the Cultural Revolution it became retrogressive and bad to be "left," the same word taking on an opposite meaning when enclosed within quotation marks. Such a reversal points further to a paradox in the party's extension of the "getting things right" principle: when so much is at stake in naming and labeling, the "reality" or "identity," the referents of language—whatever they may be in themselves—seem to be of less concern than the names or labels used to refer to them. Whatever language was supposed to represent, historical fact or personal identity, could be further blurred by the instability of language itself.

Nevertheless, the faith in the ability of language to impose uniformity persisted. Its most extraordinary manifestation was probably during the Cultural Revolution, when all felt compelled to memorize, and thus internalize, "Quotations from Chairman Mao Zedong" as the script for every aspect of life and thought. During those final years of Mao's life, power and authority rested in a small collection of formalized texts, "the little red book."

The contemporary critic Li Tuo has argued that "Maoist language achieved a position of absolute dominion, or 'hegemony' . . . so that all other possible forms of discourse were excluded, driven out, or forgotten, to the point of extinction. As a result, not only was all writing done in one particular style of *baihuawen,* but all thinking and intellectual activity had to be carried out in one type of discourse and no other."[11] As Li Tuo has stressed in a number of articles, the importance of the new avant-garde fiction since the mid-1980's has been the "revolt of language" (*yuyan de fanpan*). Its deconstruction of the "Maoist style" (*Mao wenti*) has been bringing about the "second liberation of the Chinese language since the May Fourth movement."[12]

Whereas the "liberation" of language of sixty years earlier had taken place under the impetus of Western ideas of realism in literature, this "second liberation" in the post-Mao era has been taking place through the importation of poststructuralist notions of textuality and deconstruction. In the view of many Chinese critics, the specific meaning or content of the new avant-garde writing may be difficult or impossible to decipher. But no matter. What is much more significant for Chinese literary history is the sheer fact—and acknowledgment—of their opacity and indeterminacy. For it is just such notions, such new ways of looking at language, that are posing the greatest challenge to the claims of Maoist discourse as the transparent reflection of "reality" and the purveyor of clearly defined "truths."

LANGUAGE AND TEXTUALITY— (RE)READING THE TEXT

One may well ask, how much of the revolutionary turmoil of the past half century then has just been a matter of language? Now that the Great Chinese Revolution is over, some are questioning whether it ever happened, or questioning at any rate, whether what is *said* to have happened—socialist construction, the peasant revolution, the restructuring of the Chinese political order, etc.—actually ever happened. So has it all been language then, shadow-boxing with words against the background of modern China's turbulent history? Of course many events have taken place; after all, the world of China has undergone vast and irrevocable changes in the past century. Those changes have also been talked and written about in many ways, with varying distances between those innumerable texts and what "actually happened." There is a great deal of sorting out to do in confronting the enormity of events and happenings in twentieth-century China.

Yet it is remarkable to contemplate how much of the actual struggle to define and interpret historical events, to set political agendas, to exert power, and control the representation of "reality," has taken place through and within language. From the beginning of modern Chinese literature in the May Fourth period up to the present, writers, critics, literary reformers, political leaders, and party ideologues alike, from whichever end of the political spectrum and for the purpose of achieving whatever goals, have all in one way or another seen language or discourse not only as the weapon but also as the site of battle and contestation. It almost seems as if language is where everything is presumed to have happened.

Language was at the forefront of the writers' consciousness as they made the literary and political decisions to write the way they did. But whatever their expressed views, whatever they might have *said* they were doing—and this could be applied to all manifestos or self-proclaimed programs of literary or intellectual movements—the actual situation of language as used in practice, in the production of individual literary texts is a more problematic and ambiguous matter. While there is always a gap between what writers have set out consciously to do and what they have actually done, this gap becomes all the more important to explore when the literary enterprise is so evidently governed by explicit intentions. These intentions could be the announced reformist or iconoclastic agendas of the May Fourth generation, the accommodation to the prescribed ideology of Communist-directed literature, or the conscious questioning in the post-Mao era of preceding literary productions.

The May Fourth writers' break with the classical language tradition was never as clear-cut and absolute as they presented it as being. Their self-serving characterization of that tradition has long dominated all scholarly discourse but needs to be subject to re-examination. With all its claims about a "literary revolution" through the imitation of imported Western models, May Fourth writings continued to incorporate prior texts from the classical past and carry on an intertextual dialogue with that spurned tradition.

Under the influence of such nineteenth and early twentieth century literary historians as Hippolyte Taine and George Brandes, who had stressed literary history as the continuous process of evolutionary progress, May Fourth intellectuals made a sweeping condemnation of the Chinese literary tradition as stagnant and moribund. Moreover, their reinterpretation or rewriting of traditional Chinese literary history by setting up the two opposing categories of a dead *wenyan* which had to be replaced by a living *baihua* ignored the constant interactions between the two as well as changes in both due largely to that interaction. There were literary forms and texts that deployed language that was neither strictly classical nor vernacular but was somewhere in between or a hybrid of both.[13]

The May Fourth writers' reinvention of a to-be-rejected past was part of their construction of a self-image: A generation that was creating a radically new literature needed to reflect a newly evolving reality. But what are remarkable in many of their writings, once we stop looking at them through the lenses of their own version of Chinese literary history, are the tensions and ambivalences that arise precisely from their unresolved struggles against the past.

As for the Chinese Communist Party's program for literature, the main issue was that literature be subservient to the goals of the revolution. Therefore the party claimed the right to intervene in and control the literary process. But in spite of stringent thought control measures, the party's domination over the texts and their production of meaning could not be total. A literary text might conform to ideology by obscuring the actual conditions of peasant existence—for example, by smoothing over contradictions, and masquerading as solutions to intractable problems. At the same time it will also insist all the more that at every level—character, action, setting, symbolic imagery, language—it is an accurate transcript of a reality that is objectively "there," external to itself. But such a project, the attempt to create a coherent and internally consistent fictive world, is one that cannot ever be perfectly realized. No matter how much the dominating ideological code might seem to determine every aspect of textuality, an attentive reading will reveal gaps, fissures, absences, incoherencies, unanswered questions, and point to contradictions underlying the textual surface.

Post-Mao writers will be a much more diverse lot. Seeing themselves as products, indeed as victims, of recent history, they have been engaged through their fiction in retrospective questioning of the past as well as of its literary practices. "The revolt of language," to use Li Tuo's term, will be carried out through a wide range of narrative experiments, each posing different kinds of challenges to the determinate kinds of writing that had preceded them. Instead of a text that claims to be faithfully reflecting the world, as in party-controlled literature, some writers may deliberately create distance or discrepancy between the two by calling our attention to their own narrative process and the operations of language within their texts.

In all our examples of narrative fiction, whatever the expressed purposes of their authors, there will be discrepancies between intention and meaning. To some extent, all literature, or even all language, is, in J. Hillis Miller's words, "parabolic, 'thrown beside' their real meaning. They may tell one story but call forth something else."[14] The claim to unequivocal domination of one code or mode of signifying over others, making what the text tells seem inevitable, "natural," a self-present "truth," can often be called into question by a close reading, or rather, a close rereading. To extract from Roland Barthes' paradoxical argument on "How Many Readings?" in his introduction to *S/Z*, "Rereading . . . alone saves the text from repetition (those who fail to reread are obliged to read the same story everywhere), multiplies it in its variety and plurality."[15] In rereading we get beyond the "same story," the "already read" and become aware of the "text's difference," the "something else" the text might be calling forth.[16] It is rereading that enables us to uncover the discrepancies, inconsistencies, internal conflicts, the ways the text might be at odds with itself, and pose questions rather than provide answers.

This kind of interrogative, if not deconstructive, reading is particularly productive for modern Chinese literature, precisely because writers had announced agendas, or were subject to pervasive political control.

In any case, narrative texts—the focus in this study—are not stable and homogeneous entities; for one thing, they are not read as statements for information but experienced as process. Even when moving relentlessly toward narrative enclosure or a predetermined outcome, the textual journey is not a simple, direct linear one. "Something else," something diverse and heterogeneous, can and usually does happen as the reader travels from one end of the text to the other. On one level, this book can be seen as the result of one reader's journey through several narrative texts linked by a common theme that are representative of four different phases of modern Chinese literature.

For such a reading, details of language, facts of textuality will be all important. Rather than broadly discussing overall historical developments, I will be primarily focusing on a very limited number of texts and subject them to close analysis. This does not mean ignoring the extrinsic context. Whether indeed as Jacques Derrida's famous statement puts it, "There is nothing outside of the text," (*Il n'y a pas de hors-texte*),[17] what I hope to demonstrate is how historical, political, and cultural issues (however they exist "outside") are absorbed, articulated, and debated within the text itself. Each writer will be situated within a specific moment as I consider some of the critical issues going on at the time. My readings, or rather rereadings, will be moving back and forth between text or context, or, to put it another way, will be working on the assumption that there is no rigid boundary between text and context, intrinsic and extrinsic analysis.[18] Within the overall framework of historical change, each individual work, in its positioning of the writing self, in the narrative stance adopted, in the configuration of imagery and motif, will dramatize particular relations with and struggles against ideology. Not that the texts will be scrutinized in all these aspects; the choice, in each case, will be based on what seems to be strategic or problematic. All our writers invite a close reading, because along with their concern to express a particular vision of the world, all have at the same time been acutely conscious of themselves as experimenters in language. They have willy-nilly conferred a self-reflective "meta-dimension" to the "stories" they tell and to themselves as tellers.

Language has been at the center of action in the battles of the twentieth century, but the control of language, whether to push through an ideological agenda or establish political dominance, has proved to be an elusive matter. All texts are marked by "variety and plurality," as becomes evident in the rereading process. Perhaps it is this recalcitrant or indeterminate nature of language that enables human expression, however tyrannical the constraints, always to hold on to a certain measure of creative freedom.

REALISM, SELF, AND REPRESENTATION

All the fuss about language, beginning with May Fourth, has mainly been in the name of its relation to reality, the ability of language to represent the world. If literature has had to reform itself over and again, each time it has supposedly been for the purpose of making itself into a "truer," more authentic reflection of social reality. Each generation of writers has claimed "realism" to be its central literary doctrine, but the meaning of that term has undergone many transformations.

Realism, which was to become a watchword in modern Chinese literature, had been the dominant historical movement of the mid-nineteenth century in Europe. Its aim was "to give a truthful, objective and impartial representation of the real world, based on meticulous observation of contemporary life."[19] We moderns are no longer as confident about the possibility of ascertaining what might be "truthful, objective, impartial," nor are we certain of what and where might be "the real world." Furthermore, we see "representation" and "observation" as clouded by the process of representation and the functioning of the observer.

Such complexities must of necessity be ignored or dismissed by Chinese Marxist critics. When it comes to literature, they have been particularly adamant that it should be "realistic." Literature in the cause of the Communist revolution is required to reflect a world constructed or inscribed by a particularized hegemonic discourse; it must nevertheless paradoxically claim at the same time that it is directly reflecting reality, the "world as it is."[20] But the fact that Chinese Marxist critics have also felt it incumbent to precede that term realism with such modifiers as "critical," "socialist," "revolutionary," or even to resort to the oxymoronic phrase "revolutionary romanticism combined with revolutionary realism," suggests an unacknowledged uneasiness in making such a claim.

In the Chinese Marxist scheme of things, how to characterize a writer's "realism," will depend on the placement of his works in the historical timetable of revolution. For a writer like Lu Xun, with his undisputed position in the Communist canon, it is not only necessary to show that he was a writer of his time, producing fiction that was realistic as of 1918 to 1926, but also to argue that he was ahead of his time, somehow anticipating the socialist revolution to come. A recent study of methods and practice in modern Chinese literary criticism reviews some of the arguments over the proper formulation (*shuofa*) of Lu Xun's realism. Some have termed it "critical realism," while others insist that it had already manifested elements of "socialist realism," or was moving in the direction of "socialist realism"; still others would call it "revolutionary democratic realism."[21] The final irony of course is that all these tortuous arguments ignore the historical fact that the Marxist doctrine of realism was, to begin with, an inheritance from nineteenth-century Western "bourgeois" literary conventions.

In their ahistorical readings of Chinese literary history, Marxist critics have gone so far as to invent a tradition of "realistic literature," by ascribing a realist intention to those who in their view were reflecting the world of the past in a way acceptable by the Marxist standards of today. Much of premodern vernacular fiction, for example, could be made to qualify as "realistic." If it could be shown that it was in some way exposing the evils of the "feudal" system, then it could be considered an "objective portrayal of the way things actually were."

But the Western idea of mimesis, that literature should imitate or represent reality, was never an important part of traditional Chinese aesthetics. What was more characteristic of literary thinking were the "expressive theories" that focused on the relation between the writer and his work. The object of expression could be "variously identified with universal human emotions, or personal nature, or individual genius or sensibility, or moral character."[22] Even in literary genres like history, which may attempt to provide a record of events that took place in the past, or vernacular fiction, which often took pains to convey the impression—by giving names, dates, and addresses of characters, for example—that the story's events took place in the familiar, "real" world, the comments of the historian or the voice of the narrator as oral storyteller were constant reminders of the mediating presence of an implied author.

As Marston Anderson states in his important study of May Fourth fiction, realism was not primarily endorsed by Chinese thinkers for "its mimetic pretense," the "simple desire to capture the real world in language" as in the West. Instead it was "embraced because it seemed to meet Chinese needs in the urgent present undertaking of cultural transformation."[23] It was assumed that the turn of literature toward a "supposedly disinterested investigation of the external world," would "liberate the mind from the stranglehold of tradition" (p. 11). But like many other concepts that were eagerly adopted because of their potential to contribute to cultural transformation, and through that to national rejuvenation, realism was later reinterpreted or qualified when necessary to suit more specified political goals. While the term "realism" may continually appear throughout modern Chinese literary history, its meaning changes with the particular purpose it is supposed to serve.

From the very beginning the practice of May Fourth writers exposes an inherent paradox of the "mimetic pretense," a contradictory pull between objectivity and subjectivity. While realism is directed toward reflecting a supposedly objectified real world, it cannot do without the subjective author. Even the celebrated image of realist fiction as a mirror, as Anderson points out, predicates the framing and perspective of a viewer, the presence of an observing subject from its own specific space (pp. 10–11). Realist fiction thus paradoxically elevates the critical stance and authority of the individual writer, who, freed from the prejudices of received tradition, can now depict the external world on the basis of presumably direct, independent, and original observations.

As we shall observe, modern Chinese writers have found themselves caught in a contradiction of writing narratives that on the one hand presented themselves as "realistic," as direct and straightforward transcriptions of objective reality, while on the other hand as issuing from an intense subjective vision. The tension between the two can become all the more apparent and intense when, as is the case of many of our examples, the story or novel is told in the self-conscious mode of first-person narration, a new convention borrowed from Western models, that places an observer within the narrative itself. What the texts go on to dramatize then will be the uncertainties of knowledge and perception, bringing to the foreground a self engaged in a struggle to assimilate and transcribe the new external reality. The peasant, the perceived, objectified "other," construed as somehow representing the "real world," will change in accordance to how that world is seen and how the observer is positioned. In this way each encounter between writer/intellectual and peasant becomes a concrete enactment of a problematic representation process.

The specific conditions for such enactments will change as we move from one "generation" of writers to the next. As the first major writer to emerge from the May Fourth literary revolution, indeed the first major writer in modern Chinese literature, Lu Xun has often been credited with "discovering" the peasant. But what the discovery turns into is a crisis for the writer/intellectual, while posing profound questions about language and textual representation. His self-reflexive fiction will be the point of departure for our several textual journeys.

3

Lu Xun and the Crisis of the Writing Self

"LU XUN WAS the first in modern literature," as Yang Yi puts it, "to invite real and ordinary peasants, with their ragged clothing, sorrowful faces, and suffering souls, into the exalted halls of literature [*gaogui de wenxue diantang*]. With the blazing heart of a pioneer, he wrote the first volume of the bitter life history of peasants, who make up an overwhelming majority of the Chinese population."[1] The language here may itself be somewhat "exalted," but the observation that Lu Xun was the first to portray peasants is a commonplace among Chinese scholars. Typical also is the image of these new subjects as poor and tragic figures, with the condescending implication that their status has somehow been "raised" through literary attention and treatment. According to this persistent Chinese view, it is Lu Xun's pioneering writing about peasants that has more than anything else established "realism" (*xianshi zhuyi*) as the main stream of modern Chinese literature.

Lu Xun may indeed have been the first writer to figure peasants in his stories, but the "reality" of peasant life in its specificity is not the focus of his attention. Criticism that extracts a peasant figure like Runtu ("My Old Home"), or Xianglin's Wife ("The New-Year Sacrifice") out of the text for "character analysis," the most common practice among Chinese critics, has not led much further than to such vague attributes as "hard-working" (*qinlao*), "kind-hearted" (*shanliang*), "honest" (*pushi*), "well-behaved" (*anfen*). The peasants are all good, all alike, and, of course, all victims of the old system. An attentive reading will expose the inadequacy of such generalizations, but more particularly will also show that the main concern in these two stories is how the intellectual will attempt to posit and construct a self against the peasant as "other," an attempt that will in fact precipitate a moral and intellectual crisis. Whatever efforts may be made to promote Lu Xun as a realistic writer on the peasant, it is subjectivity and representation, the dilemmas for the self and writing when confronting the peasant, that will constitute the central drama in his stories.

I will begin by considering what was at stake for the individual writer during the May Fourth "literary revolution," then take a close look at the problematic textualized self and modes of representation in "A Madman's Diary" and "The True Story of Ah Q" as a preliminary for discussing the stories in which intellectual and peasant actually come face to face.

MAY FOURTH SUBJECTIVISM—THE STATE
OF THE INDIVIDUAL WRITER

The dichotomy between intellectual and peasant and their portrayal in May Fourth literature would seem at first glance to reflect its two major trends, romanticism and realism, with their respective orientations toward subjective self and external society. Imported from the West, each was represented on the Chinese scene by a major organization: the Association of Literary Studies, founded in January 1921, and the soon after founded Creation Society in July 1921. The association's slogan, "Art for life," indicated a social and humanitarian emphasis, an interest in the investigation of present social and economic "reality," which most often meant, as it did in mid-nineteenth century Europe, where the movement of realism began, a new attention to the experience and conditions of the oppressed lower classes. The early Creationists, on the other hand, were seen as preoccupied with the self, specialists in self-expression, in exploring the inner world of the individual psyche. But the two were not mutually exclusive, nor as diametrically opposed as their manifestos might lead one to believe.[2]

If, as Kirk Denton has rightly observed, "their battle may ultimately be seen as two different expressions of the same anxiety about the disintegration of cultural presuppositions of the self's unity with the outer

world," that "disintegration" was actually due in no small part to the
joint rebellion of both groups against the traditional social and cultural
system.[3] The assault on the old system could be carried out through an
exposure of its evils, its inhuman exploitation and oppression of those
down below. Or the system could be called into question on the basis of
one's direct experience and self-knowledge, by setting the individual self
up as an alternative source of meaning and authenticity. For both these
programs Western literature, however understood, provided not so much
models to copy, or a way "to replace the authority of their own tradition
with that of a new one," but, as Marston Anderson put it, a "lever" with
which Chinese intellectuals "could pry themselves free of their own tradition."[4]

While realism was never the objective reflection or direct transcription
of reality it might have aspired to be, the difference nevertheless made in
Chinese literature by the determination to take a good, hard look at
contemporary social phenomena cannot be minimized. Objective or not,
such an effort, for one thing, implied a conscious attempt to strip the
writer's mind of received knowledge and ready-made formulas from the
past. But even more important for our consideration here was the
"democratic" example European realism provided: ordinary people, including workers and peasants, in their everyday functions then "began to
appear on a stage formerly reserved exclusively for kings, nobles, diplomats and heroes."[5] In the case of China, that stage had also most particularly been the defined preserve of the scholar/gentry elite; in fact, it
was through their representations that the kings, nobles, diplomats, and
heroes appeared on the stage in the first place.

Now the stage had to make room for an enormous new group of
characters that had been largely left out of representations—a theatrical
concept, after all—in the past. But in introducing this cast of "ordinary
people," intellectuals had to search for newly self-defined roles as observ-
ers, writers, and impresarios, while simultaneously and awkwardly repositioning themselves on that very same stage.

No matter how rigorously attention was focused on the broad external
world, realist writers could not be as self-effacing as they might proclaim
to be. The May Fourth practice of realism inevitably involved a fundamental reconceptualization of the writer/intellectual. This reconceptualization overlapped in many ways, or was reinforced by, the other new image of the writing self, that inspired by European romanticism. In the
sense that all May Fourth writers wrote out of a sense of alienation from

established tradition and, "realist" or not, were engaged in a quest for a self from which to write, they all became part of, to borrow Leo Ou-fan Lee's phrase, "the romantic generation."[6]

In writings of the past, even when one's own ideals or values might be at stake, one could still maintain a clear sense of one's position and function in a larger, collective nexus. The aesthetics of lyrical poetry, expressed in such phrases as "poetry expresses intent" (*shi yan zhi*) or the "fusion of emotion and scene" (*qing jing jiao rong*), emphasized the active presence of an individual poet negotiating some sense of the self in relation to nature or the world.[7] Above all, to write was an act that situated the self within an ongoing literary tradition, since writing was consciously conceived of as textual transmission and constituted by intertextual activity.[8] As we have seen in the example of the historian Sima Qian when under pressure to commit suicide, writing was upheld as that which would enable him to justify his life and transcend his private mortal self. Through his commitment to literature as participation in tradition, his personal identity, even if set in opposition to political authority, would be valorized.

By contrast, the iconoclastic stance of May Fourth writers meant that they were driven to construct a new kind of selfhood through deliberately detaching themselves from the literary tradition. The new terminology for the writer as *zuojia*, as a creative writer, for example, reflected an apparent redefinition of the relationship with literature. To conceive of literature as creative activity was to emphasize the individual writing self as source or originator. If, as Yu Dafu, the "romantic writer" par excellence and one of the founders of the Creation Society, claimed, "the greatest success of the May Fourth movement, should be considered the discovery of the 'individual' (*geren*),"[9] then just who that individual was would become a question of capital importance. Yu Dafu's explorations of himself as an individual were carried out through his largely autobiographical works, in which his own personality and life experience were celebrated with a mixture of self-glorification and self-pity. His "determination to lay bare the naked truth"[10] was as much a search for the authentic true self as a deliberate flouting of the ideological ideals of selfhood upheld by the literary tradition. The extreme lengths to which he carried the disclosure of an inner life in his 1921 story "Chenlun" ("Sinking"), for example, its defiant exploration of sexuality, with shockingly candid accounts of sexual frustrations, compulsive masturbation, and ultimate suicide, certainly introduced a new kind of writing self into Chinese literature.

The story's departure from tradition is blatantly evident from the beginning, as the unnamed "he," a writer and student in Japan, "feeling pitifully lonesome (*guleng de kelian*)," begins his self-reflections with English phrases and extensive quotations from Wordsworth's "Solitary Reaper." He will continue to draw conspicuously from works of Western romantic literature as we follow him, not so much from one event to another, but from one emotional state to another. But he also writes poems in the classical Chinese style, and during his visit to a brothel toward the end of the story he chants one as a gesture of defiance against the bawdy songs in Japanese being sung in the next room. These might seem to be a reaffirmation of his link with the literary tradition, but, unlike the case of Sima Qian, that link is not enough, during the next to last moments of his life, to save him from himself. Thus self-annihilation remains the only way out.[11]

One thing the story shows in its relentless self-exposure is the great risks in resorting so utterly to the self and in confronting the private, dark side of the individual personality. How should one, how can one, ultimately make sense of such a self, such a "lonesome" (or "loathsome," one is tempted to add) self, moreover, as a writer? Does this story, an extreme case to be sure, raise the question for May Fourth writers of whether self-destruction is the other side of literary creativity?[12]

The question itself becomes thinkable because writing is no longer a matter of drawing upon tradition, but supposedly of creating out of one's own inner resources, whatever they might be. This solipsism, or need to fall back on the self, was re-enforced by the new uncertainties in the occupation of writer. Whereas in the past writing was an avocation, the "literary side" of the traditional scholar-literati, it now assumed the status of "an independent and honorable vocation,"[13] as the Association of Literary Studies proclaimed at its formation. But to be "independent" meant first of all that writers had lost the security that came with occupying a clearly defined place in the established system. The end of the civil service examination system in 1905 had cut off the traditional channels of advancement for intellectuals, and such new education as they received abroad or in Westernized schools might or might not equip them for public service. To be "independent" for many writers meant to produce for an as yet not clearly defined or emerging public, and to be en-

gaged in a struggle to make a precarious livelihood subject to the imper-
sonal and seemingly capricious "laws of the marketplace." They found
themselves more or less thrown on their own and trying to survive
somehow in the harsh urban environments of Shanghai or Peking that
were themselves being rapidly transformed by unpredictable external
forces.[14] All these factors contributed to the sense of loss and alienation,
intensifying the writer's preoccupation with the self, a self continually
proclaimed, but all the more at risk in the uncertain space they occupied
at the margins of society.

If May Fourth writers, the generation that began writing in the early
1920's, seemed largely obsessed with their personal hang-ups, it was also
because many were at an age when they were still emerging from adoles-
cence. Many of the earliest well-known writings of May Fourth were
produced by those in their early twenties; their literary experimentation
went hand in hand with youthful rebellions and identity crises. Lu Xun,
who published his first story in the vernacular at the mature age of
thirty-seven, was a major exception. His fictional self-representations
would be marked by a much greater degree of complexity and self-irony,
particularly in their relation to tradition, but he was no less driven by the
need to subject the self to examination.

THE PROBLEMATIC SELF IN THE TEXT

One of the outstanding features in Lu Xun's fiction is his frequent use of
a mediating subjective consciousness in the text. The position and the
function of the I-narrator as the "center of consciousness" will vary
sharply from story to story as the events unfold. He could be a paranoid
madman constructing himself through the writing of a diary, a self-
mocking narrator elaborately introducing the subject of his story, or an
elusive witness who is both revealing and evading his own moral culpability regarding the fate of a character. If the basic messages that all of his
stories come down to are somewhat similar, as Chinese Marxist critics
have claimed—the system is bad and due for a change—the processes of
self-representation and the self's implication in the system are very different. The range of Lu Xun's technical experimentation has often been
remarked upon;[15] where it may be most notable is in the range of narrative strategies employed in presenting the subjective narrator/intellectual
"I."

The process of narrative subjectivization began in late Qing fiction.[16]

One of the earliest examples of first-person narration is Wu Woyao's *Strange Events Seen in the Past Twenty Years (Ershi nian mudu zhi guai xianzhuang)*, but since the personal feelings and emotions of the narrator are almost absent, there is not a trace of "the typical Western search for self."[17] A more remarkable transitional work is the 1908 novel *The Travels of Lao Can (Lao Can youji)*. While it does not contain an I-narrator, there is a central protagonist who functions as a link for the various episodes of the novel and as a vehicle for communicating a personal view of the world. In Lao Can's prophetic dream described in the opening chapter, the ship of state is in peril of sinking, and the novel goes on to give a devastating account of an inept and corrupt system of officialdom. But the central figure is still very much a member of the old scholar-gentry class, just as the narrative itself, in spite of its attempts to limit the narrative point of view,[18] remains within the mode that evolved from the oral story telling tradition. The revolutionary breakthrough in both form and conception for textual self-representation would not take place until a decade later in Lu Xun's first short story, "A Madman's Diary."

Nine years after the story's publication, in a postface to a collection of essays entitled *Fen (The Grave)*, Lu Xun wrote in response to critics who had complimented him on speaking the truth in his works that theirs had been "excessive praise due to partiality." In fact, while not going out of his way to deceive people, neither had he given them his "innermost feelings as they are."[19] But he acknowledges that he himself had been an important subject in his works: "I have dissected (*jiepou*) others, but even more have I mercilessly dissected myself," although without "completely exposing blood and flesh" (p. 73). One of the most intriguing features of Lu Xun's fiction is how this dissection of the self actually takes place through the specific "I" constructed through the text (including the one for a nonfictional work such as the postface to *The Grave*).

All his fictional "I's" seem to share one common predicament that the self is caught in, a predicament that Lu Xun goes on in the same postface to describe in response to another kind of critical praise that had actually "sent a chill" through him. He had been mentioned in a Shanghai periodical as a writer who provided proof that those who want to write well in the vernacular should study classical writings (*guwen*). His response is that having read many old books and continuing to read them for his teaching, his writings inevitably reveal their influence. He will find himself writing the vernacular while "carrying the ancient ghost" of the classical language on his back. He thus sees himself as an example of "an in-between" (*zhongjian wu*), such as are always to be found in times of change or evolution. Now at the beginning of literary reform, it is inevitable and necessary that there will be some who are neither fish nor fowl (*bu san bu si*):

> Aroused, the in-between's job is to raise a new voice; and because he came from the old ramparts, he sees things more clearly, and in turning weapons around to strike, he can more easily render a fatal blow. But when light comes he should gradually fade away, at most having served as a piece of wood or stone in the bridge, but not a goal or model for the future. (p. 75)

The predicament is that of the transitional writer/intellectual, who will become obsolete once his function in the bridge between old and new has been fulfilled.[20] *The Grave* includes essays in both the classical and vernacular, so Lu Xun was justifying his inclusion of the former in spite of their "possible damaging effect on his readers." But having deplored, as it were, the unshakable influence of classical writings on his own, the last words of his essays are ironically given over to a quotation from a classical text. Taken from an elegy to King Wu of Wei (Cao Cao) written by Lu Ji (261–303), the quotation criticizes the king for giving injunctions to avoid an elaborate funeral while nevertheless outlining instructions about preserving his fur clothes, his seal, and the music of his courtesans. Is Lu Xun seeing an analogy here between himself and King Wu, who in death showed a reluctance to completely let go of the trappings of the past? Such an ending cannot but underline Lu Xun's continued use of the past, even when lamenting the negative consequences of its abiding power. At the same time, as he emphasizes, it is precisely this link with the past that enables him to strike back at it with greater telling effect. The point seems to be that the many-sided predicament of the in-between transitional person is grounded in the self-contradictory relations with the past. In the stories to be analyzed, the literary tradition continues to be very much "there," not just as targets of his "fatal blows" (although Lu Xun certainly struck plenty!), but also quoted, paraphrased, incorporated stylistically into the texture of his modernist texts. The ongoing dialogue with the literary past will be carried out on several levels and generate multiple tensions in his fiction.

Lu Xun's admission that he was "mercilessly dissecting" himself in his writings should not, nevertheless, encourage us to take his fictional representations as simply reflections of himself. In fact, what his stories strongly dramatize is the complex relationship or the fluctuating distance between the historical author and fictional self-representation that much of recent Western criticism has been emphasizing. Psychoanalytic theories on the preconscious or the unconscious, behavioral theories about role-playing according to social setting, have challenged all notions of a coherent, unified, clearly identifiable entity that once might have been confidently labeled an individual. These ideas about split selves have combined with post-Saussurian linguistic theories to emphasize a provisional, discursively constructed self, a self that comes into being in each instance of language.[21] If the human being is so split, unstable, and fragmented, is it even legitimate, in our reading of the narratives, to speak of one specific individual author, a certain identifiable "Lu Xun" "out there," who enters into a group of fictional texts in an array of different guises?[22] In any case, my purpose is not to determine how they stand in relation to the historical Lu Xun—an autonomous or personalized entity who might be considered as pretextual origin or source—but rather to examine the various selves that come into being through the textual processes of each individual narrative.

A PARADIGM OF THE WRITING SELF: A READING OF THE MADMAN AND HIS DIARY

As China's first major work of modern fiction, Lu Xun's 1918 short story "A Madman's Diary" ("Kuangren riji") has been subjected to innumerable interpretations.[23] What is truly remarkable is the range of crucial questions raised by this first story, making it in so many ways what Theodore Huters has called a "key meta-narrative in the subsequent development of modern Chinese fiction." While he points to its "authorial solipsism," its demonstration of the "impossibilities of representation,"[24] David Der-wei Wang sees it as posing "the problematic of the real" but generating "the conditions of writing and reading Chinese reality."[25] What I would like to focus on is the fragmentation of the self and the impasse created through the circularity of its self-text process.

On the most obvious level, Lu Xun was launching a full-scale assault on traditional Chinese society through the story, while rebelling against the entire classical textual tradition through the process of its discourse. But by presenting his story in the form of the diary entries of a designated madman, Lu Xun inserted into Chinese literature a newly problematic self that was in a state of crisis over its own identity. This self is further split into several conflicting "I's" within the text.

The madman's sanity is at stake as he struggles to sort out what the external world is, a world that he is trying to "read": "Everything requires careful consideration if one is to understand it," as he notes more than once. The diary is an attempt to record and express his emerging perception and understanding of the world and of his own relation to it. At the same time the madman is the "writer" of his own text, who comes into existence through the activity of writing. The problematic relationship between the text being written and the self writing that text will be a central issue explored by the story.

The madman's diary, which is written in colloquial language, is introduced by a preface in the classical language. This harks back to the convention in which works of traditional vernacular fiction were usually introduced by a preface written in classical Chinese, in contrast to the stories themselves. Presented as having been composed by someone other than the author of the book, it would provide an authoritative introduction to what followed, setting forth the purpose and circumstances of the stories' composition or compilation and making a case for its value and significance. At first glance the "I" in the story's preface would seem to be conforming to the tradition: He had received the diaries from a former schoolmate, the brother of the madman, and after reading it he recognized (knew, *zhi*) that the diarist was suffering from some form of "persecution complex." And although the language was "confused and incoherent, and contained many wild statements," he had copied out a part to serve "as a subject for medical research." But the convention of the preface is subverted here even as it is followed, for the immediate effect of this one is to alert the reader to look for an alternative reading, one other than the unlikely one of "medical subject" claimed in the preface.

The preface becomes an example of Bakhtin's "parodic stylization," in which the "intentions of the representing discourse are at odds with the intentions of the represented discourse."[26] By thus undermining the authority of the speaking "I" in the preface, the text signals that he is an "unreliable narrator" and that the reader must make the attempt to project an "implied author" whose view of the story will presumably be opposed to this narrator's.

The reader's complex processing of the story parallels what the madman must do himself. For the madman is first of all a reader who begins by questioning his reading of the classical texts, the traditional texts that have been defining his world for him. When the madman first puzzles over what possible offense he might have committed to account for the hostile gazes he encounters, the only thing he can come up with is that twenty years ago he had trod on the old account books of Mr. Ancient (*Gujiu xiansheng*)—the records of the past. He remembers that from ancient times human beings were often eaten, but he was "rather hazy about it." Looking it up in his history books, "scrawled all over each page are the words: 'Virtue and Morality.'" Unable to sleep, he reads intently half the night, until he begins to detect (*kanchu*) what is between the words (*zifeng*); they turn out to negate what the words themselves explicitly state: "Throughout the book were written the two words—'Eat People'" (p. 4). It is this deconstructive reading that enables him finally to arrive at the "truth" about the cannibalistic nature of Chinese society.

The texts produced by the madman himself are the thirteen disconnected, incoherent fragments in a nonclassical colloquial language that make up the diary. But his chronological recording of events, supposedly what a diary does, totally disorients him in time. In the series of undated "todays," incidents from myth, history, childhood, the last few days, dark times when day cannot be told from night, are jumbled together. People, events, dialogues, as well as historical texts, have no clear, stable meaning, but are subject to interpretation from opposite perspectives. Mr. He, the old man with glasses who visits him and feels his pulse, could be a medical doctor come to cure him *or* an executioner in disguise waiting for him to be fattened up for "eating"; the mother in the street may be scolding her son *or* indirectly threatening the madman, and so on. The reader is continually challenged either to choose between opposing possibilities or to search for alternative interpretations—to envision what is *probably* happening against what the madman represents *as* happening—in order to "make sense" of what is going on in the vernacular text. At the same time the reader, while questioning or rejecting the madman's view of things, must also go along and concur with his vision of the cannibalistic world for his story to have any significance, or indeed, to be worth reading at all.

On one level, the madman is "wrong," projecting his own "persecution complex" onto others, but on another level, he is "right," for he alone has truly perceived the cannibalism that characterizes Chinese society. Yet it is precisely this insight that makes understanding by others and communication with his spectator-audience impossible. His earnest message of reform, his exhortations to his brother, to the crowd to "change, to change from the bottom of your hearts, you must know that in the future there will be no place for people-eaters in the world," are merely seen as further evidence of his insanity; his isolation is intensified by his attempts to communicate what he has seen and knows.

Language itself, supposedly the medium of communication and understanding, contains figurative pitfalls and encoded cultural meanings that present another kind of indeterminacy. In his shifting between the literal and the metaphorical as he attempts to grasp the signifying operations of language, lies the insanity, or perhaps the "wisdom," of the madman. He discovers literal incidents of "people-eating" in the story told by the tenant of Wolf Cub Village, in the ancient story of Yiya's son, and in such bits of classical phrases as "eating exchanged children" (*yi zi er shi*), "eating the flesh and sleeping on the hide" (*shi rou qin pi*), to support his holistic reading of Chinese history. He recalls his brother telling him that one should be willing to "cut off a piece of one's flesh to feed one's parent," a reference to the phrase "cutting one's thigh to cure one's parent" (*ge gu liao qin*), in order to be considered a good person.

Through this most telling example of cannibalism in the name of virtue and morality, to be taken literally (or could it be metaphorically?), the madman's own complicity in cannibalism is literally "brought home"; for now he realizes that his own family approves of the practice, and that he may have participated in the eating of his little sister's flesh, perhaps served up by his brother—his mentor in classical texts and composition—when she died. The despair expressed at the end of the diary is over himself; the realization that he is personally implicated in the cannibalistic tradition: "Now I understand (*mingbai*), even though I did not know it at first; how can a man like myself with four thousand years of man-eating history (*lüli*) face real men?" (p. 11).

This realization engenders a further identity crisis. In the process of telling his own story, the madman had initially defined himself in opposition to the others, but as he becomes less certain about that difference, he is even more confused about who he is in himself. The individual's madness was first of all a defining characteristic, a condition of the moral authority that enabled him to expose the general cannibalism of "sane" society. It was the insight that set him apart, even if it brought on persecution, and that ensured him an independent identity. But as the diary moves to the self-discovery of the madman's own possible implication in society's evil practices, when he reaches the understanding (*mingbai*) that his own history is one of eating people for four thousand years, then he loses his individual sense of self.

How does the madman finally come out? The final entry of the diary, "Perhaps there are children who have not eaten people? Save the children . . . ," would seem to be a plea, to save the children from being eaten, but also from eating the food of their parents, from continuing the cannibalistic system.[27] But this wishful question, the poignant plea trailing off into ellipsis, is not where the story ends; the story actually ends where it began—in the classical language preface, in which the madman is described as having "recovered" and gone somewhere to await an official post—to continue perhaps his participation in the cannibalistic system? Has the madman finally, in William Lyell's words, rejoined "the ranks of the *truly* mad?"[28] Or has he, as the system would have it, been restored to sanity? Apart from the question of what constitutes madness and what sanity, there is the further question of which is the "real" madman, the one described "objectively" in the preface, or the one presented "subjectively" in the diary.

For this opening shot, as it were, of the modern Chinese literary revolution, Lu Xun has split the fictional "I" into several selves. The madman/narrator is not wholly identical with the madman/character within the diary, just as the speaking subject in any discourse cannot be collapsed into one with the subject of speech.[29] In her discussion of point of view in May Fourth fiction, Meng Yue sees an opposition between the narrator "I" and the character "I" in terms of their perception and feelings. The former mainly sees himself as a target of cannibalism, whereas the latter may have also practiced cannibalism himself, and thus is one of those "hated and feared" by the former.[30] There is also that split already mentioned between the subject "I" in the preface and the subject "I" in the diary; the two "I's" speak in two different languages, classical and vernacular, belong to two opposing ideologies, two distinctive literary traditions. Since the madman is the spoken subject of both discourses, each with its own encoded conception of reality and madness, the inability to agree on who he is points to the insurmountable barrier that separates the two. The madman as subject remains in a state of either/or dialogic tension, his identity ultimately unresolvable.

Even if one reads the diary without the framing preface and chooses to ignore the contradiction between the two, the diary itself, as a writing project for the purpose of constructing a self-identity, turns into failure. The literary tradition and its version of the subject may indeed have both been discredited and subverted through parody, but then neither can the experimental new language manage to bring into existence an alternative meaningful and coherent self. The mad diarist is the center of consciousness in his own narrative structure in which perception, meaning, and communication have become increasingly ambiguous and problematic. As the teller of his own story, the madman cannot be understood and cannot understand. In the end the circular and coincidental processes of text and self—mutually constructing and deconstructing—cause the madman/writer to disappear back into the established political system and its discredited literary tradition, against both of which he had initially struggled in order to affirm himself. When the madman discovers his own complicity in the system and rejoins it, the diary will have to come to an end. There is no longer a distinct individual self to write about, nor therefore, to write.

If, as Leo Ou-fan Lee has suggested, the madman may be "regarded as an artistic version of Lu Xun's inner voice" or an alter ego,[31] perhaps we can see the story as a self-reflexive mirroring of his own struggles at a time when literature itself was making the uncertain move from one literary tradition to the other. Like the madman, Lu Xun as writer was also an "in-between," caught in an impasse between dualistic discursive representations of the self. Paradoxically this vanguard short story of the new literature movement is filled with self-doubts about the validity, or even the possibility, of its own enterprise.

Doubts about the effectiveness of writing were voiced more explicitly four years later by Lu Xun in the 1922 preface to his first short story collection *Nahan* (*Call to Arms*). Responding to a request for literary contributions from *New Youth Magazine,* the journal which had first raised the banner of language reform, he describes a virtually indestructible iron house in which many people are soundly asleep and about to die of suffocation. What would be the good, he asks his visitor, of raising "a shout to wake up a few of the relatively light sleepers, making these unfortunate few suffer the agony of irrevocable death"?[32]

This famous iron house is most often interpreted as a metaphor for the stifling prison house of Chinese society, but in Leo Ou-fan Lee's provocative reading it signifies "a kind of interiority—the dark, shadowy abode of a disturbed inner psyche. The 'light sleepers' seem closer to Lu Xun's heart because they embody certain strains from his private experience and emotion."[33] They are the "loners who are unable to rouse the crowd." Light sleepers or mad diarists, all would seem then to be emblems of the self grappling with its own doubts about the literary project.

Lu Xun may never have succeeded totally in exorcising the inner demons of doubt and despair, but he did respond to *New Youth Magazine*'s request with "A Madman's Diary," thus not only joining their program of literary reform but also producing its first major work. Perhaps the way out of the impasse of writing is to write about that impasse, or, in any case, to write. Lu Xun's first attempt at the modern short story turned out to be a meta-narrative confronting the new dilemmas of the self and writing. It is also a powerful demonstration of how modern Chinese literature, in spite of external constraints or internal contradictions, in one way or another has always found itself writing against the impossibility of writing—and of why Lu Xun remains its greatest exemplar.

REPRESENTING AH Q AS PEASANT "OTHER"?

Peasants are present as evidence of the injustices in the madman's cannibalistic society—the tenant farmer (*dianhu*), for example, who asks the madman's elder brother to have his rent reduced and is refused. And among the crowd who gather around the madman, there are "people who have been pilloried by the magistrate, slapped in the face by the local gentry, had their wives taken away by bailiffs, or their parents driven to suicide by creditors" (p. 2). But the story, which takes place sometime in the last days of the Qing dynasty, primarily revolves around the intellectual, the "awakened" (and therefore "mad") member of the scholar-gentry class. Peasants are only marginally there, nor is class a focal issue.

In "The True Story of Ah Q" ("Ah Q zhengzhuan"),[34] written three years later, the principal protagonist is taken to be a peasant, although his "peasant identity" has often been a matter of contention. Chinese Marxist critics have struggled to resolve such questions as to whether Ah Q indeed is a peasant, or the more knotty problem, given the many negative features of this character, of what kind of peasant he is. What should be considered first, however, is the sort of personal identity Ah Q has, or rather, if he has any at all. Due to the presence of an intrusive, ironic narrator—first-person in the introduction and third-person in the "story proper"—the text of "The True Story of Ah Q," rather than creating the portrayal of an individual character, will continually undermine his personal identity and undo its own representation.

In "A Madman's Diary" the literary tradition is indirectly subverted through its "unreliable" classical language preface. "The True Story of Ah Q" openly takes tradition head on, as it were, through the use of a self-ironic I-narrator in the opening chapter that introduces the story. As Martin Weizong Huang's excellent analysis of the story argues, it is through the manipulation of the narrator's discourse that the dilemma of the modern Chinese intellectual, particularly his ambivalent relationship with the hapless peasant, is played out.[35] The introduction is not written in the classical language but incorporates many phrases and quotations from it in order to mock its literary modes and ideals. It begins with the I-narrator giving an account of his struggles to write about Ah Q, of his failed attempt to accommodate the "biography" that will follow within the classical literary tradition. Reiterating the unworthiness of his subject, he acknowledges that it will fit none of the existent traditional biographical genres, so in the end he has had to resort to borrowing the term *zhengzhuan* from the vernacular storytelling tradition for his title, thus inventing a new type of "biography," in order to portray what is, after all, a new kind of subject—a nonentity.

The narrator explains his difficulties in writing this long-contemplated biography, saying that he is not one of those who might achieve glory through writing (*liyan*),[36] as "it has always been that immortal pens should record the lives of immortal men." It becomes quite confusing as to whether "it is the man who is known to posterity through the writing, or the writing that is known to posterity through the man." In the process of the word play on the word *chuan* or *zhuan,* and its many traditional classifications, the narrator brings out its functions of "transmit," "impart," "portray," "represent," while recalling it as a generic term designating "history," "commentary," and "biography." The story that follows will set out to subvert the central Chinese tradition of biography, the tradition of portraying and transmitting (*chuan, zhuan*) noteworthy human subjects in language, by in every way performing the opposite.

The *zhuan* that the narrator specifically takes for his own use from the much less elevated tradition of vernacular fiction is that in the storyteller's stock phrase "Enough of this digression, and back to the true story (*zhengzhuan*) [or rather to the story proper]." It is the difficulty of conflating the operations of writing and the recognized conventions of writing that make it almost impossible for him to write about Ah Q. Through such self-deprecating comments, the narrator lets the reader know that in the story to follow one must be attentive to Ah Q, not so much as your normal "character" representing a "person," but as an unprecedented kind of subject emerging from a peculiar kind of discourse.

Patrick Hanan has discussed the story as an example of "presentational irony" in Lu Xun, in which the tone of the "more or less dramatized narrator standing outside the action" is in "violent contrast to the events described; the one is lofty, the other squalid, and the contrast makes the latter ridiculous."[37] I would like to emphasize that the tone of the narrator, precisely because it is so "lofty," makes *him* somewhat ridiculous as well. His exaggerated concerns about himself measuring up to the expectations of traditional literature ironically deflate both.

When it comes to introducing Ah Q himself, the narrator defines him first of all by means of a series of negations, a step-by-step stripping of the subject of history, native place, family, or personal name, of all the information that would matter most in a conventional biography and that would specifically locate him in the "real" world. Nothing can be ascertained about Ah Q's identity, the narrator says; the only sure thing left about him is the appellation "Ah," a vacuous, meaningless prefix like a "hey" that comes before all Chinese informal names. The implication is that this is a subject that could be anybody, or nobody, or perhaps everybody, and that is indeed what Ah Q simultaneously turns out to be in "his" story.

As to the second component, "Q," in itself a typographical oddity that sits uneasily in its surrounding Chinese text, it could be the first letter in a transliteration denoting any one of several common first names, but was chosen, according to Lu Xun's brother Zhou Zuoren, because its shape visually suggested a face with a queue (was a pun intended?).[38] On the one hand, this commonplace appurtenance can be seen in the story as playing a key role in defining people's identity, since it supposedly is an indication as to where they stand on the 1911 revolution that overthrew the last imperial dynasty, the Qing. On the other hand, the queue is a meaningless signifier, because it can so easily be worn hanging down or coiled on top of the head, depending upon which way at any given moment one thinks the revolutionary wind may be blowing.

Minus the pigtail, the letter Q becomes a cipher, a zero, which is what Ah Q is reduced to when forced to sign the final confession before his execution on the false charges of having taken part in a robbery. The only sign he is capable of making is a circle (how else can an unnamed, illiterate person represent himself?), a circle shaped also like a blank mirror. Not only do all Chinese share the "Ah" in Ah Q's name, they can all look into this character and see themselves. In a letter written in 1935, Lu Xun describes his own "method" in "Ah Q" by referring to a comment addressed to the audience in Gogol's "The Inspector General": "You're laughing at your own selves!" His own method was to make it difficult for readers to figure out who apart from themselves was being written about in the text, to "quickly shift it onto others and themselves become spectators;" they should "suspect that it seemed to be written about themselves, while also about everybody."[39]

Ah Q is a mirror because he lacks any individualized substance; he is concerned only with how he appears in relation to others. If his name signifies his paradoxical existence as both nobody and everybody, it is because he is engaged in a perpetual struggle to be a "somebody," a somebody with some kind of status that is forever beyond his reach. His constant but futile maneuvering for relative status, for a higher place, in comparison with whomsoever, will lead, on the contrary, to a diminishing of himself, a blurring of his personal identity. Ah Q had once boldly claimed that his surname was Zhao, when Master Zhao's son had just passed the county exam, only to be summoned and slapped by Master Zhao the next day for his presumptuousness: "How could we possibly have someone like you in the same clan?" As a consequence, Ah Q's surname was unknown (p. 69). His "résumé" similarly remains a blank, for his boast when quarreling with others, "We used to be much better off than you! Who do you think you are anyway?" is likewise a puffed up self-assertion that cancels out the possibility of specific information. The best known trait of Lu Xun's famous character, his "psychological or spiritual (jingshen) victories," is based on the same pattern of reality denial through verbal inflation.

These "victories" refer to Ah Q's habit of rationalizing his repeated defeats at the hands of others and of *talking* himself into thinking of them as something opposite—of telling himself after a beating, for example, "So it's just as though I've been beaten by my son. . . ." These processes of displacement by means of language not only show Ah Q as being out of touch with reality, they also continually empty him of any personal substance.

Ah Q's parochialism regarding anything apparently "foreign," his claims of "psychological or spiritual victory" when defeated by more powerful enemies, his opportunistic approach to the 1911 revolution, have been seen by many as typical of the Chinese response to the repeated defeats they have suffered at the hands of foreign imperialism. Ah Q thus becomes an image of China's desperate efforts in recent history to maintain its long-held "superiority complex" against the rest of the world in spite of all evidence to the contrary.

But whatever the particular historical moment of Ah Q, he has become famous and, indeed, one might say even "immortal" (another irony, if we recall the disclaimers in the self-mocking I-narrator's introduction) as a portrait of the Chinese national character. Lydia Liu has discussed the Western myth, as put forth mainly by missionaries, of the Chinese national character and its "translation" or importation to China as a source for Lu Xun's conception.[40] What may seem puzzling is why the Chinese were so ready en masse to accept such an unsavory character as a symbol of themselves. The lack of individual substance renders Ah Q into a blank mirror of nobody/everybody. But an even more important reason is the widespread acceptance of the May Fourth program of enlightenment and reform with the concomitant notion that only through national transformation could China hope to make it into the modern world. And for this transformation to take place the traditional Chinese lofty self-image would first need to be ruthlessly deflated—a project repeatedly enacted in the narrator's continual shifts between inflation and belittlement in Ah Q's representation.

Ah Q's particular language game can be learned and used by everyone, even against himself. When people beat him up physically, they beat him twice over through words: "Ah Q, this is not a son beating up his father, it's a man beating a beast. Let's hear you say it, 'A man beating a beast'" (p. 73). Ah Q, holding fast to the base of his queue and debasing himself even further would plead, "OK, beating up an insect. I'm an insect—now will you let go?" Jockeying for position and establishing one's relative status are very much matters of language, of adapting one's identity to words and terms to determine one's superiority or inferiority. The game works only because everybody in the village of Weizhuang has the same kind of obsession and goes by the same rules, from the scholar-gentry family Master Zhao down to the riffraff in the street.

Although Ah Q is one of the lowest of the low, a part-time laborer at the bottom rung of society, whose existence is recalled only when people need someone to do an odd job, his fortunes do have their ups and downs. They rise when he comes back from town with money and new goods to sell, when he implies he is in touch with the revolutionists, when he dubiously claims connections with the first family in the village. He even enjoys momentary respect and fame when he has the "honor" of being beaten by no less than Master Zhao himself. It is not just Ah Q who is a snob. Lu Xun is satirizing the mindless conformity, the excessive concern with surface appearances and hierarchical status—with "face"[41]—that prevails in Chinese society, of which Weizhuang is but a microcosm, with Ah Q as its quintessential representative character.

Who is above whom, even if ever so slightly, is an issue that comes up all the time. Ah Q may indeed be humbly submissive to Master Zhao and Master Qian, the heads of the two most powerful families in the village, but he will resort to any means to establish his superiority over the lowly Whiskers Wang. If he can't demonstrate his own greater prowess in lice-catching, then he will call names and pick a fight, even if, as usual, he is badly beaten yet again.

A bully like everyone else, Ah Q finally finds a target too weak to fight back: the little nun from the Convent of Quiet Cultivation. This time his "victory" is not a matter of private rationalization. He actually puts on a rather good public show, insulting the little nun, fondling and pinching her cheeks, while spurred on by the cheers of the onlookers in the tavern; when it comes to harassing a defenseless woman, everybody can share in the fun. This great "victory," however, leads to Ah Q's downfall, to a "tragedy of love" (the high-flown chapter titles are in ironic contrast to the ridiculous goings on). The extended treatment of this little drama, chapter four in the story, best exemplifies Lu Xun's particular mode of "characterizing" Ah Q. Thanks to that "smooth feel" lingering on his index finger and thumb after the encounter with the nun, Ah Q's thoughts repeatedly turn to "woman." The nun's curse, "May you die sonless!" arouses anxieties, the narrator tells us, that are in accord with the teaching of the sages about the unfilial sin of lacking descendants. But since Ah Q has always been most scrupulous in his views of "woman"—observing the "strict segregation of the sexes" and ready to denounce any woman of suspicious behavior—if he is now tempted, then it just shows how "women are a menace to mankind" (p. 80). In fact, the majority of Chinese men could become saints and sages, had they not been ruined by women. And Ah Q will indeed bring disaster down upon his own head when, aroused by the nun, he makes a pathetic pass at Amah Wu, the Zhaos' maidservant.

Juxtaposed against descriptions of Ah Q's own agitation are quotations from the Confucian classics and supporting "evidence" from historical examples. The material from the elite intellectual tradition is incorporated, not because it could have formed part of Ah Q's consciousness, but rather to hyperbolize the incident and turn it into a general satire on Chinese views of "woman." This episode is an illustration of how the textual process itself parallels Ah Q's own characteristic "approach" to life as he strives to aggrandize himself; in both character and narrative, the use of the language of inflation and exaggeration ends in the belittlement and effacement of the subject. What Ah Q might be in "himself" as a character, what he may "personally" have "experienced" as he suffered "the tragedy of love" is completely beside the point here.

The tragedy/comedy continues with further examples of Ah Q's lack of self-awareness during the aftermath of the "seduction." He fails to grasp that the whacks from the bamboo pole and the outraged crowd gathered in the courtyard could have some connection with what he has done. Leo Ou-fan Lee and Lin Yü-sheng have both commented on Ah Q's "lack of an interior self";[42] it is a lack that is due not so much to the story's mimetic representation of a hollow "person" who is Ah Q as to the narrative "treatment" he undergoes, the simultaneous process of fashioning and negating that absorbs the character utterly into the particular verbal texture of the narrative.[43]

But there is one final moment in the story, when Ah Q drops all his previous poses and pretenses, as he suddenly wakes up to the fact that he is being led to his own beheading. For the first time we see him forced to come face to face with his own powerless state, a state that cannot be glossed over anymore with grandiose language. At first he had been concerned about what kind of show to put on for those last moments of his life, looking for a suitable line to sing from a heroic opera, attempting a defiant half-sentence in bravado. But the crowd of spectators reminds him of the eyes of a hungry wolf who had stalked him in hopes of devouring him four years ago, and he sees the crowd's even more terrible eyes waiting to "devour something beyond his flesh and skin" (p. 108). In a flash he both sees into the true nature of the crowd and becomes aware of his own pathetic situation. "Help . . ." (or rather, the much more desperate Chinese "*jiuming*"), then the text reads, "But Ah Q did not say it." If not Ah Q, who then was speaking?[44] Has the narrator briefly dropped his detached, superior narrative stance to identify with his character, or perhaps to appropriate what may finally be a straight cry from the heart? At this moment before death have both suffered a simultaneous attack of aphasia, a loss of words? The uncertainty of speaker (perhaps no one actually spoke) underscores the symbiotic yet ambivalent relationship between narrator and character, the ironic distance between the two momentarily bridged, as Ah Q's "existence" and "his" story both approach their end.

The crowd following Ah Q to the execution ground in expectation of a spectacle is yet another re-enactment of the execution scene Lu Xun describes in his preface to his first short story collection, *Nahan*. According to the preface, the slide he was shown in his microbiology class in Japan, in which a Chinese spy surrounded by spectators was about to have his head cut off by the Japanese for having spied for the Russians,[45] was what turned him from medicine to literature. It struck him that rather than cure their bodies, the paramount need was to reform the Chinese spirit. The victim as a spectacle surrounded by an apathetic crowd becomes an almost obsessive image in Lu Xun; variations of it can be seen in story after story. But the crowd in Weizhuang is deprived of the fine show they had expected, since Ah Q was paraded through the streets without singing a single line from an opera, and was merely shot, not decapitated. In the end, "They had followed him for nothing" (p. 108).

Ah Q does possess certain important traits, as we have discussed above, but the process of ironic discursive deflation undermines our attempts to reconstruct or "put together" an individual "personlike" character. Among Chinese Marxist critics there has been "a great deal of confused controversies over what type (*dianxing*)" of character he precisely is.[46] One orthodox formula is that the image of Ah Q "sums up the class characteristics of poor peasants who had been deeply oppressed, and spontaneously demanded revolution" (p. 69), as if Ah Q's "fantasy of revenge" could be considered a bona fide revolution. First of all it seems that Ah Q should be classified as a peasant, not because he is engaged in farming—he is a lowly laborer who hires himself out for temporary odd jobs—but because he belongs to the oppressed lower classes (*diceng jieji*). But then this gives rise to tortuous arguments over whether his author endowed him with the proper class attributes.

Lu Xun is regarded as a "great writer who was very familiar with the society of the countryside, who understood the life of the peasants" (p. 65). But his seeing the "spiritual victory" of Ah Q as a kind of "abstract 'national character'" showed the limitation of his thinking at the time."[47] Not having yet "accepted Marxist-Leninist thought," Lu Xun "lacked a clear class viewpoint." And one line of defense argues that the peasant Ah Q's apathy and opportunism must somehow be attributed to his appropriation of the characteristics of the "feudal ruling class."[48] The many critics who try to "make sense" of him as a person on the level of verisimilitude are actually doing little more than projecting onto a blank space their own ill-fitting ideological stereotypes. But their basic problem is to discuss Ah Q as if he were a unified, determinate individual character with sufficient historic specificity to be isolated and abstracted from the ironic text into which he is assimilated. What Lu Xun accomplished was an antibiography of a nonperson that enabled him to savagely mock the elevated self-image and deconstruct the discourse of China's cultural and literary tradition.

This is not to say that there is not a problematized intellectual and peasant "other" relationship in the story. Events take place before and after the Republican Revolution of 1911 that brought down the Qing dynasty (hence the importance of placing one's queue), so Weizhuang has both old and new style intellectuals. Both types, county examination candidates and the queueless "Imitation Foreign Devil" who has studied in Japan, are targets of the story's bitter satire. But they are similar in their contempt for Ah Q; he gets more than one good thwacking by both sides.

The change in government does nothing to improve Ah Q's situation; in fact it brings about his unjust execution, and the great divide in status and privilege between the upper-class elite and those at the bottom rung of society remains. But there is a gap on the meta-narrative level as well, between the dramatized intellectual narrator and the illiterate peasant who is his subject. To consider their relative positions through the text's peculiar mode of representation raises all kinds of self-contradictions as one reads back and forth between the introduction and the "story proper." In order to represent his subject at all, the narrator claims he must break with the literary tradition. Yet as he works against the language and conventions of that tradition, he continually belittles and undermines his own subject throughout the process of representation. Even in "elevating" Ah Q into the realm of literature, the narrator maintains his own superior position as the one who manipulates the power of language and knowledge to reduce—as well as produce—his lowly subject.

"DISCOVERING" THE PEASANT AS "PEASANT"?

The relationship between the narrator and Ah Q is played out and problematized in the realm of discourse and representation, as Lu Xun attempts to claim a literary space for his unprecedented subject. Multiple levels of parody are carried out in the lofty tone of the introduction, the incorporation of traditional chapter headings, the use of verbal hyperbole and deflation, all of which are parallel to the grandiose yet pathetic efforts of the protagonist to make himself into more than what he is. In the process, literary tradition, intellectual pretentiousness, the national self-image, all become objects of satire and mockery. With the I-narrator standing outside the action, neither the particular character of Ah Q nor his class-specific condition is a matter of central concern. But in stories where the intellectual self and peasant "other" both exist on the same diegetic level and both inhabit the same fictional world, the situation will be very different. In those stories, class divisions will become a central issue. The indictment of culture and society becomes based more specifically on the plight of the peasant, and the intellectual will be directly challenged on issues of privilege, knowledge, and responsibility.

According to Lu Xun's own account, it was not a simple process for him to arrive at an awareness of the peasant as peasant. In 1933, seven years after his career as a fiction writer had ended, he wrote a preface to an English translation of a collection of his short stories. He used the occasion to give a succinct summary of his goals as a short story writer:

> In Chinese poetry there were at times references to the suffering of the lower classes of society (*xiaceng shehui*). But painting and fiction, on the contrary, generally spoke about them as being very happy, "Unknowing and unaware (*bushi buzhi*)/Following heaven's rules," placid as the flowers and birds. True, in the eyes of the intellectual class (*zhishi jieji*), the laboring masses of China were just like flowers and birds.[49]

Lu Xun goes on to describe his own growing up in a large family in the city, absorbing the teachings of the ancient books and his teachers, and entertaining a similar view of the masses. Contacts with peasants through his mother's family gradually made him realize that peasants were oppressed all their lives, full of suffering, and not like birds and flowers at all. "But I still had no way of making everyone know this."

Later the reading of foreign literature, especially that of Russia, Poland, and the Balkan countries, revealed to him that there were many others in the world who "shared the fate of our laboring masses, and there were some writers who were protesting and struggling against this," thus bringing to his mind even more vividly the situations he had seen of the countryside. "When I had an opportunity to write, I showed the degeneration of the upper classes and the misfortune of the lower classes in the form of several short stories. My original intention was merely to present this to the reader and raise certain issues; it was not for the sake of what the literary people of the time called art" (p. 632).

The brief preface apparently never appeared in any newspaper or periodical, and the translator and publisher of that anthology remain unidentified.[50] Nor is it clear which particular stories had been included. Nevertheless it is noteworthy for Lu Xun's explicit statement that an important motivation of his fiction was to let others share the *discovery* that he himself as an intellectual had made about the condition of the peasant. It may well be that it was only in retrospect that Lu Xun viewed his stories in such a light; after all, by 1933, with several years of fierce debates about revolutionary literature behind him, his "proletarian consciousness" had been raised to an extraordinary degree. But whether the "correctness" of its political standpoint truly reflects the writer as he was between 1918 and 1926, the great creative period of the stories, the preface does indeed underscore what is most distinctive in Lu Xun's approach when he made the peasant masses the matter of his fiction. The peasant does not appear so much as a subject in his or her own right, but rather as someone who is encountered by an intellectual. Several of his stories particularly dramatize the dual process of object formation and subject constitution, in which the perceived peasant "other" and the perceiving intellectual as subjective self are constructed and represented within the text in relation to each other.

While it is the harsh fact of the peasant's oppression and suffering that needs to be known, Lu Xun's point of departure in this preface, as well as in these stories, is what happens when the writer/intellectual becomes aware of that fact. Also characteristic in the preface is his description of the roles of traditional and Western textual traditions in educating one about the external world and in shaping that awareness. The quotation in the preface from the *Shijing* (*The Book of Odes*) provides an example of how the venerable classics mainly glossed over or covered up the peasant's true condition, whereas foreign literature provides not only a contrasting and seemingly more reliable view of the peasant, it concomitantly becomes the model for a new role for the writer. Foreign literatures suggest how the subject matter of Chinese literature could be expanded and become more consonant with one's own knowledge about life. Even more important, they point the way to the possibility of Chinese literature someday marching in step with world literature, by participating in a transnational historical movement toward revolutionary change. Such uses of the two textual traditions were essential to the May

Fourth agenda, which was to forge a new literature by rebelling against the classical past and learning from the West, with the presentation of the "fate of the laboring masses" seen as central to this agenda.

But it seems "unfair" of Lu Xun to target the *Shijing* here, since among the Confucian classics it contains the most descriptions of the activities and hardships of peasant life, including protests against harsh government.[51] There is some question as to whether the quoted "unknowing and unaware" refers actually to the peasants or rather to King Wen, the sage ruler, the eulogized subject of the poem, who without self-consciousness or self-awareness, naturally and automatically knew how to follow the ways of heaven.[52] Within the context of Lu Xun's preface, the quotation is used to underline a characteristic of the peasants—their lack of knowledge and self-awareness—which, whether it accounts for their "happiness" or not, most particularly sets them apart in the eyes of the intellectuals. This perception of the peasant has long persisted among modern Chinese writers when, under the influence both of foreign literature and the exigencies of history, they began to take a hard look at the peasants, and, appalled by the oppression and victimization they saw, engaged to represent them in the new literature. But the question was how were those who were themselves unknowing and unaware to be known? Only through an external observer? A knowing and aware intellectual?

THE PEASANT ENCOUNTERED—"MY OLD HOME" AND "THE NEW-YEAR SACRIFICE"

In Lu Xun's very first story on the peasantry, "Fengbo" ("A Passing Storm")[53] written in August 1920, intellectuals make but a detached, fleeting, appearance. The story begins with a panoramic view of a settlement by the river; in the light of the setting sun and against the waning chimney smoke, people are gathering for their evening meal. A pleasure boat carrying wine-drinking scholars passes by. Observing the scene from afar, they wax lyrical and exclaim: "Not a care in the world, a true example of the pleasures of peasant life! . . . The words of these literary lions, however, did not entirely tally with reality, but that was only because they had not heard what old Mrs. Ninepounder was saying" (p. 77). The narrative then moves into the conversations of the peasants themselves, which revolve around rumors about an emperor being back on the dragon throne again. They are filled with fear and consternation that those who have had their queues cut off will be punished. Set against the background of an attempt in 1917 by Zhang Xun to overthrow the republic and restore the Qing dynasty, this is a satirical story about the peasants' ignorance and backwardness, and their utter lack of understanding about the political realities of the post-1911 outside world. It closes with the telling image of the young daughter Sixpounder doing her chores with recently bound feet, "hobbling back and forth on the threshing ground" (p. 88). All these particulars of peasant life are unknown to those intellectuals whose contact with the peasant is limited to a distant view from a passing pleasure boat and ends with a reference to a literary cliché.

In two subsequent stories, "Guxiang" ("My Old Home") (1921) and "Zhufu" ("The New-Year Sacrifice") (1924), the intellectual's encounter with the peasant is face to face, direct and unsettling, an effect achieved by the strategy of a seemingly autobiographical I-narrator who is also a character within the story. This is Lu Xun's favored narrative device and appears in almost two-thirds of his stories. The narrative is cast in the form of the personal reminiscences and experiences of an intellectual that are often drawn from biographical facts of the historical Lu Xun, as his brother Zhou Zuoren has testified.[54] Lu Xun's statements toward the beginning of the 1922 preface of his first collection of stories, *Nahan,* also appears to bear this out. He wonders about the point of his "so-called remembrances," but suffers "from being unable to forget completely, and the part which I have not been able to forget is the source of *Nahan*."[55] The autobiographical base of many of the stories would seem to be underlined when they are located in S—, a reference to his home town of Shaoxing, or Lu Zhen, his mother's place of origin. However this does not mean that his fiction should be read as straightforward, confessional accounts of "what happened," nor that we should confuse the I-narrator with the author himself.[56] Indeed in many of the stories, and in marked contrast to other writers of the May Fourth generation, Lu Xun, as Leo Lee has observed, seemed to adopt "the device of the first-person narrator to *avoid* revealing himself."[57] On the other hand, it is precisely this device of the I-narrator that makes possible the unique combination in his fiction of such apparently contradictory qualities as introspection and detachment, lyricism and bitter self-irony.

Since "My Old Home" and "The New-Year Sacrifice" are both based on "so-called remembrances," the action will take place in several layers of time, in an intermingling of past and present. The past is evoked through a journey, a physical going back to a place one had left. That rural world, the countryside where the I-narrator once lived, is not just a "setting," but assumes a thematic significance. As a place showing the intrinsic connectedness of the temporal and the spatial, it becomes what Bakhtin has termed a chronotope (literally "time space"), "where the knots of narrative are tied and untied."[58] That place is where past and present meet and the only place where certain specific events can happen. The stories end with the actual or impending departure of the narrator, raising the question as to how or whether those events can actually be put behind.

"My Old Home" begins with a boat ride in desolate winter under an overcast sky to the "old home," or native place, which the I-narrator had left over twenty years before to go to the city to earn a livelihood, and, more important, to live the urban life of a modern cosmopolitan.[59] As he draws near he discovers that his old home is not in the least like the way he had remembered it; "it had been much better." This raises the question of whether his old home had always been like this, or whether it was "just a change in his own mood," but also of the reliability of old memories and their relation to transient feeling.

He will be departing soon in any case, and inevitably, since he will soon learn that he is geographically, temporally, and above all psychologically alienated, no longer "at home" there. He has returned only to say good-bye forever, to close up the clan's old house and move his family to the city where he is working. The major specific event that takes place during the narrator's brief sojourn is a fateful encounter with a peasant, or rather a re-encounter, for the peasant had always been there. It is just that the narrator had known him before only as Runtu, the high-spirited childhood friend he used to look up to. Now the suddenly revealed peasant identity of Runtu has a profoundly disquieting effect on him.

"My Old Home" is, for Lu Xun, remarkably free of ironic effects; it is one of the most deeply moving and personal of his stories. Not so much because the I-narrator is referred to twice as "Brother Xun," a direct use of Lu Xun's pen name, but because of its understated yet pervasive sense of personal loss and disillusionment, so tinged with nostalgia, giving the story an "autobiographical flavor." The narrator discovers that there is an impenetrable barrier between himself and his childhood friend when they meet again after almost thirty years, at the moment when Runtu returns his eager greeting by addressing him as "Master (*laoye*) . . . ."

Their old terms of address to each other as "brothers" will no longer do now. This barrier is the "lamentably thick wall" between their two classes, and its discovery seems to paralyze him, making him incapable of speech and communication with his old friend.

But the barrier is also brought about by the ineluctable passing of time, the unbridgeable gap between the carefree innocent past of childhood with its excitement of shared discoveries and the disillusioned present of the adult who has experienced the harsh "reality" of the world. The wonderful playmate who in the month or so they had spent together had enlarged his own limited horizon with such exotic wonders as colorful sea-shells, watermelon fields by the sea, hunting *zha* (whatever that was) under the moonlight, is now a shabby, wrinkled father of six, worn down by life, by "famines, taxes, soldiers, bandits, officials and landed gentry." Yes, his old home was "much better," for then he had not realized it to have been the place of stagnation and injustice, the locus of an oppressed, impoverished, backward, and inert peasantry. In this way the political message of "My Old Home," the protest against class differences and the lot of the peasant, is made to emerge from a deeply personalized life experience.

Yet at the same time it is precisely the presentation of the personal story that clouds the political message. Although the story covers a long period of time, its direct narration focuses on the momentary present—the brief visit home—while the past of almost thirty years ago is reconstructed as memories, or is it perhaps constructed out of the visual imagination? Much of the contrast between present and past is carried out through the use of visual imagery, between what is immediately seen and what is apparently remembered. Set in opposition against the cold wind, the graying sky, the drab and desolate countryside of the present, are the bright colorful images of flashbacks to childhood, where there was a golden moon in the dark blue sky, emerald green watermelons planted by the sandy seashore, and standing in the midst of it all, the high-spirited eleven- or twelve-year old boy Runtu, a silver ring around his neck, pitchfork in hand, thrusting mightily at a *zha*, which with a quick turn, escapes by running between his legs. This is the "marvellous scene" (*shenyi de tuhua*) that flashes in the narrator's mind when his mother brings up the name of Runtu. At that moment "I seemed to see my beautiful old home again" (p. 61).

Memories of the past are apparently conjured up to contrast with the dreary present. The "two worlds collide . . . most dramatically," in

Theodore Huters' words, when the adult Runtu makes his appearance in "real" time.[60] But one must ask, had the past ever really been that way? Had he actually ever seen, or had he merely heard about, that elusive *zha*? He admits he still doesn't know what a *zha* is. As the narrator had recalled the past, parts from Runtu's flow of talk, with its inexhaustible information of wondrous lore, had come to him as if verbatim, but now the once freely talkative Runtu is like a stone statue before him, a wooden puppet, suffering from his hard lot but unable to describe it (p. 64). He can only shake his head and speak generally about the lack of food, poor harvests, arbitrary money collectors. As a poor peasant, he has somehow become "dumb" in more than one sense of the word; he is no longer someone who can speak for himself nor does he seem to have much to say.

But to perceive his old friend as someone on the other side of the class barrier renders the narrator speechless as well. A few days earlier, he had been similarly tongue-tied when he was accused by Mrs. Yang, the "Beancurd Beauty" from across the street, of failing to recognize her. "A high-official with three concubines who sits in a sedan-chair with eight bearers whenever he goes out," as she describes him, he was now too "snooty" to remember an old neighbor who had carried him as a child. He feels unable to explain or defend himself, his verbal paralysis and helplessness stemming from the realization that he is being perceived (whether fairly or not) as privileged and powerful. While the specific reasons for silence for the narrator and Runtu may be different, once they become aware of their respective class status, communication seems to be no longer possible. What the narrator has discovered is not a particular individual peasant, but rather the difference it makes when a particular individual is perceived or redefined as a peasant, and the consequences for himself.

The constant juxtapositions between past and present lead to questions as the story closes about whether there is hope for the future. On the boat again as he departs with mother and nephew, the narrator returns once more in his thoughts to his old friend. His nephew expresses a wish to see Runtu's son again; might they not grow up, the narrator muses, without such barriers as there were between Runtu and himself? Could the younger generation not have a new life, a life that they themselves had never known?

But his hope for a such a future is fraught with uncertainty. He had secretly laughed at Runtu's burning of incense and candles as idol-worship, but was not his own hope for a new and better world no less an idol he had created himself? The difference is that what Runtu hoped for was "close at hand," while what he hoped for was "somewhere far off." This comparison is not without irony for someone who has expressed hopes for a better world, since it seems to suggest that the political goal of a more egalitarian society would be less realizable than the desires of a superstitious peasant.

The uncertainty about the future is intensified because of the narrator's ambiguous relationship with the problematic past. Was there indeed a time when his old home was "much better," when two boys from different classes could live and play in harmony and equal exchange, or is his nostalgia based on illusion and fantasy? In reality, Runtu was temporarily employed as the son of a poor seasonal hired hand and "Brother Xun" already a young master (*shaoye*). That imaginary past *before* class distinctions can neither be revived nor serve as a model for a better society to come, since it may never have existed. Can what is hoped for in the future really be projected from such a past?

Yet at the end it is the recurrence of the images of the "jade-green seashore" and the "round golden moon hung from a deep blue sky" that are implicated in his affirmation of the existence of hope, the road that is made "when many men pass one way" (p. 66). Traveling his own road now toward an indeterminate future, the narrator dozes off, while those images "spread themselves before my eyes" as if linking him again to his lost childhood, but the hard fact is that he is now leaving his old home forever, unlikely to return.

Three years later, in a different type of circular structure, issues of speech and silence, and their deep implication in power and subordination, are further explored in "The New-Year Sacrifice."[61] In different contexts, Marston Anderson has referred to this story as a "paradigmatic example" of confrontation between a member of the elite class with one of society's victims, and a "paradigmatic dramatization of [the] crisis of writing in Lu Xun's work."[62] Indeed the dilemmas of the writer when taking on the subordinate "other" as subject is confronted more directly and explicitly in this text than in any other by Lu Xun.

The story's central character, Xianglin's Wife, is a doubly subordinate "other," in that she is both peasant and woman. A victim of poverty and exploited for her labor by her gentry employers, she is also oppressed in the specific ways that only a woman can be oppressed: She is the property of her first husband's family, then sold in forced marriage to a second husband; she suffers the loss of her infant son to a wolf, and is in the end ostracized for her violation of the rules of chastity. A woman existing at the very bottom of society, she is the victim of multiple oppressions, as if the economic, social, religious, and moral systems had all conspired together to destroy her.

Written in 1924, the story is the first one in Lu Xun's second and final volume of short stories, *Wandering* (*Panghuang*). As the title indicates (Lyell translates it as *Wondering Where to Turn*),[63] and in comparison with the positively assertive one of the first volume, *Call to Arms* (*Nahan*), the mood here has become more somber and hesitant. In a preface to a self-selected collection of stories, Lu Xun had once referred to the stories in *Nahan* as "literature by command" (*zunming wenxue*), the "command of the revolutionary avant-garde" he was quite willing to comply with. But then *New Youth Magazine* disbanded, and he had become a "wandering warrior (*youyong*) out of battle formation." So although his technique had improved somewhat and there seemed be less restraint in his line of thinking, the fervor for struggle had cooled considerably. This was not good. Here were the eleven stories from this period, but he hoped he "would not be like this in the future."[64] Two lines from Qu Yuan then follow:

> Long had been my road and far the journey,
> I would go up and down in my searching.[65]

The volume adds six more lines in its epigraph. Here again, while writing to reject the literary tradition, Lu Xun has invoked the fourth-century B.C. poet for an image of his own condition, as a wanderer in political exile.

In "The New-Year Sacrifice" the moral and intellectual uncertainty on the part of the writing self is partly revealed and party concealed by the I-narrator. Unlike in "My Old Home," the reader is not invited to share in the narrator's subjective feelings but is placed rather at a distance from which to view him possibly as "unreliable," if not in regard to the facts, then certainly in his responses to them.

The story begins not with a journey home, but with the narrator already returned to his old hometown of Lu Zhen at the time of its annual New-Year sacrifice. He intends to leave on the following day, however, the ostensible reason being the discomfort caused by the volumes of neo-Confucian writings in the study of his Fourth Uncle's house, where he is staying. A new-style intellectual in his own eyes, he seems particularly anxious to distinguish himself from his uncle, a follower of neo-Confucianism, who twenty years later is still denouncing the 1898 reform "new party" of Kang Youwei. Indeed, no matter what, he must leave the next day. "Besides (*kuangqie*) the thought of my meeting the day before with Xianglin's Wife, made me feel I could not stay with peace of mind" (*shi wo buneng anzhu*) (p. 2). Thus almost as a casual afterthought, the other main character of the story is introduced, and it is the problem of his "peace of mind" regarding her that will be the main issue in the first and last sections of the story which are told by the I-narrator. These two sections provide a frame for the long central section which is told by the same narrator in third person. This splitting of narrative stance adds to the complexities and ironies in the story's representation of the intellectual-peasant relationship.

Two events dominate the first section: the encounter with Xianglin's Wife and her death either the same day or the next. Before anything more is told about her, the narrator's response to both events raises a question: What is the connection between the two? The possibility of cause and effect are suggested even more strongly, all the more so as he keeps striving to rationalize it away. In what way might that encounter have contributed toward her death?

She had approached him the day before, appealing to him precisely on the grounds that he is an intellectual: "You are someone who is a scholar [who can read, *shizide*] and has been out in the world; you've seen and know a lot" (p. 2). What she asks is whether there is a ghost or spirit after a person dies, and whether there is a Hell. What she really wants to know is what there might be in store for her—harsh punishment? something even worse?—after a lifetime of untold hardship and suffering. The narrator is initially sympathetic; he gropes for an answer that might help her. But whatever authority he might command as an intellectual is put in shambles by his utter failure in the end to cope with her probing questions. After some stammering, he can only respond by repeating, "I can't say for sure" (*shuo bu qing*), and beats a hasty retreat, trying to reassure himself all the while that by falling back on such a "most useful phrase" he has freed himself of all responsibility. He tells himself when he learns about her death the next day that it is just as well, for her as well as for others, that someone whom "people were sick of seeing around was no longer to be seen" (p. 6).

But his claims of feeling more relaxed and comfortable with himself notwithstanding, does he really feel he has freed himself of all responsibility? Without facing up to that issue, he proceeds, writer/intellectual that he is, to put together bits and pieces that he has seen or heard about her, so they will "combine into a whole." In other words, he resorts to what he is good at—he creates a narrative out of her life.

The switch to third-person narration in this narrative has the effect of distancing the narrator from any need to comment, respond, or involve himself in the tragic specifics of her story. In contrast to the disquieting introspections of the first section, the tone here is matter-of-fact and detached, allowing the events, as it were, to speak for themselves. Horrifying experiences, such as the kidnapping and the forced wedding, are further distanced by presenting them as reports by witnesses or through the hearsay of third parties.

The callous indifference toward what is happening to Xianglin's Wife is characteristic of all in the community. When her employers, Fourth Uncle and Aunt, learn about her situation, they are mainly concerned about "how this will make our family look," or "her bad influence on the morals of society." As in the episode of the harassed nun in the Ah Q story, Lu Xun is targeting the traditional idea that immorality in society is always the fault of the woman, even when, as in this case, remarriage and thus the loss of chastity, is cruelly forced upon her by others. Community indifference is all the more blatant when Xianglin's Wife repeatedly tells the story about the loss of her little son to a wolf. Her story arouses sympathy and interest at first, but soon begins to invite ridicule and parody, and she becomes crazed in her grief and in her isolation. It is the community, everyone, that has collectively driven her to madness, beggary, and death.

"The New-Year Sacrifice" is as much about the reaction of others to Xianglin's Wife's story as it is about Xianglin's Wife herself. We have here again another variation of Lu Xun's image of the spectator crowd that stands by watching with apathy as the victim is executed. But where is the narrator himself positioned in regard to the victim? Is he just another spectator, or can he claim some degree of superiority to the others because he, as a new-style intellectual, stands somewhat apart from the community and undertakes to tell her story?

Xianglin's Wife is a mere appendage to her husband (she has no name of her own), a piece of property to be sold by her mother-in-law, and she is reported on by the narrator mainly as an object observed from the outside; changes in her condition are noted by the changes in her physical appearance, her rosy cheeks, or sallow skin. Subjectivity denied, she is largely presented as dumb, inert, seemingly incapable of fully comprehending or articulating her own condition.

For writers producing literature to expose the injustices of society they want to reform, a peasant woman like Xianglin's Wife is a particularly available, "efficient," "ready-made" vehicle. Not only because her case can be used for mounting an attack on so many social evils all at once, but also because of her suffering. As in many other stories of the late 1920's and early 1930's, Rou Shi's "A Slave Mother" being a notable example, a woman's suffering often results from the loss of a child, since motherhood is what is most "essential" in defining woman as well as the area in which a woman is most vulnerable. A mother's sorrow is also what can be counted on to arouse the reader's pity. It is not so much the other horrors inflicted on Xianglin's Wife, nor even their cumulative effect, but rather the tragic incident about her child that pushes her over the brink into a pathetic psychotic state and that is the part of her story upon which she exclusively and obsessively dwells.

Woman as a passive, powerless victim, represented by a male narrator who places himself in a superior position because he is capable of understanding her suffering and its social context, and has the authority to speak about it, is a common theme in May Fourth fiction.[66] The victimized woman is usually presented as silent and helpless, (Rou Shi's "slave mother" submits silently and when she speaks cannot do more than stammer some half-formulated questions), denied her own mind and voice. Xianglin's Wife however is a somewhat more complicated case.

While the narrative emphasizes her subordinate and powerless condition to invite sympathy and indignation, she is not a totally passive victim. We can go beyond the narrator's text, as it were, to see how she does undertake actions on her own to fight strongly against her fate. To begin with she had run away from home to hire herself out as a servant; she does not go home willingly with her mother-in-law; and she puts up a fierce, though in the end vain, resistance to the second marriage. Furthermore, in her encounter with the narrator she is the one who speaks up first to challenge the narrator with her tough questions when they meet.[67] Nor is she completely silent. In her grief and despair she constantly speaks—in the telling of her own story. But the one "story" she tells is how her son was carried off by the wolf, and it becomes a monotonous litany of her dreadful pain and self-recrimination. "Rather effective" at first, it arouses much sympathy and tears, but soon everyone gets bored with it, and they turn around to use her own words to jeer at her. The repeated telling becomes a mark of her madness, a self-defeating effort that intensifies her isolation and hastens her destruction.

When Xianglin's Wife understands that no one will listen, she "keeps her lips tightly closed all day," finally, utterly silenced. What she had been repeating is, of course, truly "her own story," direct, authentic, coming straight from the depths of her deeply felt personal experience. But it seems that the victim cannot be expected to be capable of telling her own story. Her story can only be appropriated, enclosed, assimilated into the framework of the narrator's version of it, since his is the only one that can be expected to be taken seriously by the audience.

Speaking, communication, indeed the ability to express the self in language, the very activity which the story itself is performing, remain pre-eminently the prerogatives of the intellectual. When the story opened the I-narrator had presented himself as more "enlightened" than his reactionary Fourth Uncle, but in what way ultimately has his behavior toward Xianglin's Wife been better? In spite of his authority, based supposedly on his superior understanding and command of language, he had found himself at a loss when Xianglin's Wife appealed directly to him for help. After stammering some contradictory answers, he had beat a hasty retreat, rationalizing that "such a chance meeting could have no significance," and that the useful phrase "I can't say for sure " had nullified everything he had said before, so that even if something did happen, it would have nothing to do with himself (p. 4). Unlike Xianglin's Wife, who is "stuck" in her one speech, there is a contrast here with the intellectual who, with his ability to manipulate language, assumes that he can always evade or deny what he has said earlier, and therefore need take no responsibility for it.

The end of the story returns to where it began, with scenes of exploding fireworks celebrating the new year, as if nothing, including the tragic life and death of this one woman, had happened in between. Caught up in the atmosphere of the celebration by the community which has collectively accomplished the total erasure of Xianglin's Wife, the narrator comments that his personal doubts have been swept away. Considering his earlier behavior, his compulsion to reiterate that point raises precisely the opposite possibility. Meanwhile (in terms of text-time as opposed to story-time), he has, at any rate, told the story of Xianglin's Wife. But underlying the textual surface of rationalization and self-assurances, there are lingering doubts as to whether he has done all he could or should have done. As we readers become aware of the gaps created by the narrator's evasions, one question remains in our minds to haunt us: Face to face with the enormity of evil and pain in the world, is it good enough merely to take note of its victims and write (or just read) their stories?

Two years later Lu Xun would stop writing stories and devote his energy to writing prose essays instead, a genre in which he was to be much more prolific. Scholars have speculated as to why, especially in view of his artistic achievement in the short story form, Lu Xun would give it up and focus on a kind of writing considered to be, at least in the eyes of Western critics, less "creative." Since his fiction so often became a vehicle for personal soul-searching, for dramatizing the dilemmas and contradictions in the role and practices of the writing/intellectual self, perhaps he preferred a genre which lent itself more readily to intellectual argument and political debate. For these later prose essays would mark the stages of his difficult transition to the left. Whatever the reasons for his turn away from fiction, during his brief career from 1918 to 1925 as a practitioner of the form, Lu Xun paradoxically managed both to set modern Chinese fiction on its course, while simultaneously subjecting it to the most far-reaching self-interrogation.

THE MOVE TO THE LEFT

All the complex questions about subjectivity and language raised in Lu Xun's fiction have been largely disregarded, in spite of the evidence of the stories themselves, by Marxist critics determined to credit Lu Xun as the first writer to write about the peasant, and to ascribe his greatness to the true and realistic portrayals of the peasant in his fiction. But these ideologized efforts have often led to a simplification, if not distortion, of what Lu Xun is all about.

First of all there were the leftist critics who turned on Lu Xun as lacking in "revolutionary" credentials. A typical example is a 1928 piece by Qian Xingcun. The main point in his essay, "The Death of the Period of Ah Q" ("Siqu le de Ah Q shidai"),[68] is that due to revolutionary changes in the political situation of the past decade, the time for Lu Xun's writings had passed. Dissatisfied with the present, he only knew how to express his dejection, since he saw no way out, even with the "bright road" ahead of him. He could only "wander" as indicated in the title of his second short story collection. As for Chinese peasants, they were organizing and joining the revolution, "fully manifesting their revolutionary nature, no longer at all like Ah Q."

Communist revolutionaries were in the process of constructing a new peasant to suit their specific ideological purposes, a peasant capable of assuming the revolutionary character and vanguard role of the Marxist proletariat, but not to be found in Lu Xun's fiction; he was now therefore passé. This is an example of the sort of sweepingly dogmatic criticism that Lu Xun was subject to from 1928 to 1929 and it points to a key impediment—his representation of the peasant—in fitting or accommodating him as a writer within the framework of Chinese Marxist criticism.

During the acrimonious debates of the period, the nature of literature would also be specifically redefined to serve the revolution, and there was much discussion of the need for a proletarian (*puluo*) literature, a literature by and for the peasant and worker masses. Although Lu Xun was initially skeptical of the claims of his leftist critics, and openly scornful of their naive and extravagant notions about literature, toward 1930 his position evolved toward an acceptance of the class nature of literature and the role of literature in revolution. As Leo Ou-fan Lee concludes in his enlightening account of Lu Xun's changing perceptions about literature and revolution, he "was not a systematic or even a coherent thinker,"[69] and one would certainly be hard put to trace a clearly reasoned argument as he made the transition from 1927 and 1929 toward a leftist position.

But one question continued to haunt him: Who was capable of speaking for the common people, for the laboring lower classes, or the proletariat? This is hardly surprising since it was an urgent question already dramatized by the kind of I-narrators he depicted in his stories. In a 1927 talk on "Literature in a Time of Revolution," he expressed skepticism about those who were claiming to write people's literature: "Some people take the common people—workers, peasants—as subjects in their fiction and poetry and we call it literature of the people (*pingmin wenxue*)," but in fact it was no such thing, "for the people have not yet opened their mouths to speak (*kaikou*)."[70] He was still doubtful then about the usefulness of literature for revolution. Yet a short three years later he had adopted the concepts and the language of those leftist critics with whom he had been doing battle.

The reasons for this change, or "development" as the Chinese Marxists would say, in Lu Xun's thinking are complex—the impressive example of the Soviet Union and its literature was no doubt one. He made the effort to introduce some intellectual rigor into his polemical debates with his leftist critics by immersing himself in Marxist aesthetics. His translations (second-hand from the Japanese) of theoretical essays by Lunacharsky and Plekhanov, which were published in 1929 and 1930, may well have contributed to his ideological conversion. By the time he formally joined the ranks of revolutionary writers in becoming a member of the League of Left-wing Writers at its founding in 1930, he was referring to an expanding united front targeting the worker and peasant masses as in the conclusion of his inaugural speech.[71]

But above all what drove him and many others to the left was the pressure of political exigencies, most particularly the Nationalist government's increasingly harsh literary persecutions. When his disciple Rou Shi and four other young writers were executed in February 1931, Lu Xun expressed his sorrow and outrage two months later in a strong essay, "The Revolutionary Literature of the Chinese Proletariat and the Blood of the Pioneers" ("Zhongguo wuchanjieji geming wenxue he qianqu de xue").[72] The essay demonstrates how totally he had adopted the "jargon" of his former leftist opponents. It is also striking evidence of the powerful persistence, even in this very different context, of the Chinese tradition of literary martyrdom. Actually, twenty-three people were executed at the same time, but only the writers, in spite of their relatively negligible positions in the Communist Party, have been apotheosized as the "Five Martyrs."[73] Somehow it is the practice of literature that seems particularly to exalt people as martyrs; certainly Lu Xun is emphatic in making the link between their writing and the cause for which they had died:

> Our comrades' blood testifies that proletarian revolutionary literature is subjected to the same oppression, the same murderous terror as the revolutionary laboring masses, that it is engaged in the same battles and shares the same destiny, that it is the literature of the revolutionary laboring masses. (p. 268)

But sharing in the oppression, battles, and destiny of the revolutionary laboring masses does not necessarily mean writing a literature that is truly theirs. And in spite of Lu Xun's commitment to the Left-wing League's literary program, he continued to entertain doubts about the qualifications of intellectuals to speak for the people and write about the situation and characters of the proletariat, with which "they had never had any relations." He asks in a talk in 1931, "Can the present Left-wing

Writers write good proletarian literature?" He thinks it would be very difficult, since they are still all intellectuals (*zhishi jieji*), and "it would not be easy for them to write about the reality of revolution."[74]

While Lu Xun did not claim that he himself (or other contemporary intellectuals) actually wrote about the "reality of revolution," Chinese Marxist critical practice is to argue that he did, or rather, that he wrote about "reality" the way it was supposed to be written. Whatever controversies there were over Lu Xun's status as a revolutionary were settled when Mao Zedong chose to elevate him four years after his death in 1936, as the "chief commander of China's cultural revolution . . . not only a great man of letters but a great thinker and revolutionary."[75] The task then for Chinese criticism was set. From the 1940's on a steady stream of *sixiang yanjiu* (studies of thought) type books and articles appeared primarily to demonstrate the linear "development" of Lu Xun's thinking from Social Darwinian evolutionism to Marxism-Leninism–Mao Zedong thought.

The May Fourth movement itself was being redefined as a movement that had prepared for the Communist revolution, and with everything being made to fit into a predetermined course of history, albeit one retrospectively understood, the official canonization of Lu Xun's writings meant that they were in every sense nothing if not exemplary of his time. The standard interpretation was that before his conversion to Marxism after 1928, Lu Xun had been a "revolutionary intellectual of the petty bourgeoisie class,"[76] yet, of course, "moving towards the direction of socialism." As products from an early stage in their author's ideological progression, his stories had to be seen as both realistic—truly reflective of the way things were during their times, that is, from the eve of the 1911 revolution to the great national revolution—and yet unfalteringly meeting the prescriptions of an ideologized history.

Although Lu Xun as yet "could not analyze social relations from an explicit and conscious class point of view" (p. 57), his portrayal of peasants loomed large in these critical exaltations; it was most particularly seized upon as evidence that in his fiction he was already, before his destined arrival at the correct position, even then clearly on the right track. Study after study appeared on the "character" (*renwu*) or "image" (*xingxiang*) of the various peasants appearing in the fiction.[77] His achievement above all was supposedly the creation of a gallery of characters that were remarkable for their "typicality" (*dianxingxing*), the way they truly represented the historical reality of their times.

The critics' fixation on peasants has not rendered their task an easy one, since Lu Xun's own emphasis, as he more than once expressed himself, was to make everyone know the peasant as oppressed and suffering. The problem has been how to reconcile this kind of perception and motivating concern with a revolutionary ideology that was making the peasant out to be the heroic bearer of a proletarian consciousness with an inherent potential for revolution. Where is the revolutionary potential of the passive, inarticulate Runtu of "My Old Home" ("Guxiang"), for example, whose hopes for the future were solely invested in burning incense to the gods? Predominating views such as that "Lu Xun saw that peasants were an oppressed class . . . at the same time they were a class that wanted revolution. . . . Ah Q truly longed for revolution, in him all along [was] the potential for revolution,"[78] have been seriously challenged by Chinese critics in recent years only. In a 1986 article arguing that studies of Lu Xun have been biased in discussing the image of the laboring classes in his stories, Feng Guanglian provides some telling examples of the critical contortions of the past, that not only "exaggerated and heightened the positive and revolutionary aspects of the peasants" but also turned what had been "criticized and negated by the author into something positive."[79] Rather than seeing that "peasants are the important motive force of the Chinese revolution, containing within an enormous revolutionary power" (p. 60), what Lu Xun clearly saw was the "heavy material and psychological pressures on the laboring classes, and not the real possibility of their swift awakening or resistance" (p. 72). Exploitation and political oppression had in fact rendered his peasants "stupefied, apathetic, backward, stuck in old ways"(p. 58).

Such extreme fluctuations in accessing the ontology of Lu Xun's peasants, from backward, apathetic victims to potential revolutionary heroes, and then back again, would seem to depend mainly on the critic's ideological position regarding "historical reality," or rather on the degree to which he subscribes to the Chinese Communist interpretation of it. The fundamental premise shared by both critical positions is that literature is a transparent reflection of reality, that characters in a fictional work represent real people, so the argument revolves around what reality is, and what those people are like. Historical reality and peasant characters are in either case seen as external givens that pre-exist the text, which in turn is to be judged in accordance with its fidelity to, or degree of correspondence with, what is already "out there." But the mere fact that there could be opposing arguments over the nature of reality, or what the *same* "typical" people were actually like, would seem to indicate that the relation between literature and reality is not that simple and direct. And indeed it is Lu Xun's remarkable achievement as a writer that assumptions about this relation all become problematic as his stories unfold. This is a significant aspect or "lesson" that all these critics, whatever their ideological orientation, have chosen to ignore in their readings of his fiction. For beginning with his first story, "A Madman's Diary," the dilemmas of perception and representation are written into the very narrative processes themselves. Because of this, the intellectual I-narrator assumes a pivotal importance; when confronting the peasant, his uncertain and troubled response mirrors the struggle of the text in which both subject and object come into existence. If the peasant is an unknown and indeterminate "other," all the more then would the intellectual who is making the effort to know and be aware become the central "problem."

A PROPHETIC "SMALL INCIDENT"—
MOVING TOWARD YAN'AN

Lu Xun wrote several stories which feature intellectuals, and Chinese critics have usually slotted them into two main categories within a conventional historical framework. His intellectuals are either pathetic and contemptible remnants of the old "feudal" system, or disillusioned and retrograde intellectuals who have betrayed their early progressive and revolutionary ideals. They are primarily considered not so much as victims of society, but as targets of criticism: old intellectuals complicit in the discredited old tradition and evidence of its irrelevance; or "new" intellectuals, incapable in themselves of working toward a revolutionary future without, it is said, uniting with the peasants or placing themselves under the leadership of the Communist Party.

But again the categorization of intellectuals is not always quite as simple and clear-cut as such criticism makes it out to be, and there is often ambivalence as well on the matter of the traditional versus the new. Some of Lu Xun's stories are unequivocally sardonic in their treatment of the old intellectual, the hypocritical upholders of Confucian morality in "Soap" ("Feizao") (1924), for example. But in a story like "Kong Yiji" (1919),[80] the relation with the past is more complex. The story is not just about a down and out scholar from the "feudal ruling class" whose failures expose the bankruptcy of the old system, but also about the members of his community who have their "only fun" at his expense.

Through the use of the tavern boy waiter as a callous "unreliable" I-narrator, the reader's sympathy comes down on the opposite side, the side of the apparently targeted old scholar. What the reader sees in Kong Yiji is a traditional intellectual unwilling to totally relinquish his self-image while desperately trying to hold on to some last shred of dignity.

As the quintessential "in-between" (*zhongjian wu*) writer, Lu Xun develops this ambivalent dialogue with the past further in a later story that focuses on two new style intellectuals. "In the Tavern" ("Zai jiulou shang") (1924) has often been discussed as a portrait of backsliding intellectuals from the time of the 1911 revolution.[81] But Lin Weifu's moving of his little brother's empty grave—a symbolic gesture to the past even if it is no longer visibly there—"inconsequential" or "futile" (*wuliao*) as it may be, can be seen as a positive filial act to fulfill his mother's request. The once rebellious young intellectual who used to pull off the beard of the gods in the city temple, is now making a living as a tutor of the Confucian classics. Not a single thing of what he and his old friend, the I-narrator, had hoped and planned ten years ago, he tells him, has worked out. They liken themselves to flies flying in a circle only to come back and land in the same place. But could not such encircling be due both to an ambivalence toward the past as well as a loss of faith in the future?

In some other stories Lu Xun's satire targets intellectuals who are determined above all to be "modern"—i.e., "Westernized." The writer in "A Happy Family" ("Xingfu de jiating") (1924) tries in vain to shut out the sounds and affairs of his own everyday life in order to concentrate on writing a story that is modeled after Oscar Wilde's *An Ideal Husband,* a work he has never read. The "failure of modernity" is also allegorized in "Regret for the Past," ("Shangshi") (1925), in which the relationship between the two lovers is both set up and undercut by the narrator's own telling.[82] Those touted models of emancipation from Western literature, Ibsen, Shelley, etc., are used by the male narrator first to seduce the woman and then later to dismiss and ultimately destroy her. His reiteration of adopted foreign ideas about the "tyranny of the family, the break with tradition, the equality of men and women" (p. 107) are turned into a means for victimizing the woman in their "modern" relationship.

While intellectuals in Lu Xun's stories resist being simply classified as definitively backward or progressive on the basis of their position regarding tradition or its modern alternatives, the prevailing mode in his treatment is that of satire, ridicule, irony. In this he is far from alone.

From the late 1920's on, such fiction writers as Mao Dun, Ding Ling, Lao She, and Zhang Tianyi, among others, all added their contributions to the gallery of negatively portrayed intellectuals. Such unflattering self-representations of intellectuals may seem paradoxical for a generation which had initially invested extraordinary hopes in their own capacity to criticize and radically reform the world. While they had, of course, assaulted traditional intellectuals as integral parts of the old discredited political and cultural system, it seemed that, after the brief flurry of the excitement of rebellion, they soon gave up on themselves as credible leaders or guides to a brave new future. Their total rejection of the traditional past had led primarily to their own marginalization. But unlike the alienated artists of nineteenth-century European Romanticism, they could not develop an "ideology of the creative imagination" or a cult of the isolated but original individual genius in compensation.

This was largely because in spite of their iconoclasm, there was one legacy from the past the modern intellectuals could not shake off: the tradition of seeing the self in terms of a public role, and concomitantly, of evaluating the self as a moral exemplar. This sense of mission and accompanying culpability may help to explain why so many intellectuals, in later joining the Communist establishment, went along with the notion that it was they themselves that most stood in need of fundamental reform.

There is one early Lu Xun story that, brief as it is, exemplifies the intellectuals' unease about their own moral worthiness and seems almost prophetic in anticipating the changes in their status to come. For obvious reasons, Marxist critics have found "A Small Incident" ("Yijian xiaoshi"), written in 1920, an easy story to praise. It focuses on an intellectual's encounter with a member of the laboring lower classes, a rickshaw puller, probably a former peasant who has made his way into the city to make a living by selling his physical strength. The story is very brief, as its title suggests.[83] But this in itself is highly ironic. The incident, told by an I-narrator, is about how on one winter day in 1917, his hired rickshaw puller knocks down an old woman and then stops to help her up and take her to the police station, in spite of the narrator's commands to ignore her and go on. The "small incident" has in fact turned out to be so important that it keeps coming back to his mind even years later. Those texts that he had memorized as a child, the "sayings of the Master," or the "quotations from the Odes," he has forgotten completely, but this small incident remains ever before his eyes. It was a moral lesson for him, indeed a total reversal, one might say, of the Mencian principle that those who labor with their heart/minds—because of their moral superiority—are entitled to rule over those who labor with their muscles. For the narrator, the example of this rickshaw puller's behavior has supplanted the educational authority of the classics, making the intellectual reflect upon himself, spurring him on to reform (*zixin*).[84]

Lu Xun's slight narrative contains a particularly evocative image that foreshadows the coming shift in the relative position between the intellectual and the peasant/proletariat. Observing the rickshaw man helping the old woman toward the police station the narrator goes on:

> Suddenly I had a strange sensation that his dusty retreating figure had in that instant grown larger. Indeed the farther he walked the larger he loomed, until I had to look up to him. At the same time he seemed gradually to exert a pressure on me which threatened to overpower the small self hidden under my fur-lined gown. (p. 39)

An intellectual sitting high in a rickshaw and pulled at foot level by a straining human horse presents in itself a graphic image of the traditional hierarchical relationship between the two. But at this moment in the narrative, the intellectual finds himself looking *up* (*xu yangshi cai jian*) at the retreating figure, not just because of his "moral superiority" but also because of his looming, growing, overpowering presence.

This elevation of the peasant/proletariat and the corresponding downgrading of the intellectual will be the dominating theme in Chinese revolutionary ideology and literature as we turn to Yan'an and its most representative writer, Zhao Shuli.

BETWEEN THE DEATH of Lu Xun in 1936 and the emergence of Zhao Shuli on the literary scene with his first well-known story, "Blackie Gets Married" ("Xiao Erhei jiehun") in 1943, there is a chronological hiatus of some seven years. The gap in time is wider if we consider that Lu Xun discontinued his writing of fiction after 1925. From then on Lu Xun moved toward an acceptance of the lefist position, but he retained his reservations about the possibility of intellectuals writing authentic proletarian literature. He had stated in his 1931 overview of the Shanghai literary scene that what would most likely emerge in his time was resistance or exposé literature by those of the "petit-bourgeois class in revolt".[85] In adopting the term "petit-bourgeois" to refer to those including himself who were writing such literature, he was also subscribing to the ideology that he belonged to a class that was, as he himself said, on the way to extinction (*zheng zai miewang zhe de jieji*). In other words, there would be no room for intellectuals like him in the new revolutionary society. Lu Xun did not live to see the struggle against intellectuals nor the campaigns to remake them that were still down the revolutionary road. In fact none of the many writers who were zealously embracing the Communist cause during this time had any inkling of its tragic implications for themselves.

Zhao Shuli came into prominence as a new kind of writer, who was himself, it would be repeatedly claimed, from the peasant class and therefore eminently qualified to write as a peasant. How this manifested itself in practice will be examined in my next chapter. To move from Lu Xun to Zhao Shuli is to enter an entirely new phase in modern Chinese literature, to negotiate a vast geographical, cultural, and ideological distance. The center of literary production on the theme of the intellectual-peasant encounter will shift away from the cosmopolitan area around Shanghai to Yan'an and the Border Regions in the northwest interior. In Lu Xun the encounter with the peasants takes place during the intellectual's brief visits back to the countryside, as he temporarily leaves his work in the city and then quickly returns to it. Works of fiction by others about the peasant who followed him—Mao Dun's *Village Trilogy* investigating the bankruptcy of the silkworm industry or the disastrous rice harvest in southern Jiangsu, [86] Wu Zuxiang's dramatic narratives on the plight and upheavals of peasants in Anhui, Shen Congwen's lyrical yet ironic poetic visions about Western Hunan,[87] or Xiao Hong's powerful evocation of the elemental struggles of life and death in the Northeast, for example—have each journeyed further into the Chinese peasantry's territory. Nevertheless, none of these writers had been long stationed or actually employed in the countryside, as Zhao Shuli was, deep in the rural hinterlands of Shanxi and Shaanxi, isolated and far removed in cultural and economic development from the relatively accessible and affluent regions of the east.

In the 1940's literature was not only relocated to a very different kind of environment from that of Shanghai, it also required a psychological reorientation, a turning away from an urban audience and Western-inspired sources and techniques, toward the broad rural masses and their folk forms and popular traditions. The rural hinterland would also become the base from which the Chinese Communist Party would carry out its peasant-based revolution. "Peasant" and "reality" would all undergo redefinition. With politics strongly in command and literature under urgent pressure to serve the revolution in explicit ways, the crisis of self and writing that Lu Xun explored in his fiction could from that new perspective seem almost like a form of self-indulgent luxury. Literature produced in the Border Regions focused its attention on the peasant, making him assume even greater importance as "political and moral metaphor."[88] The "odyssey of modern Chinese intellectuals," continuing to unfold through their changing representations of the peasant, would take a radical turn upon reaching Yan'an.

4

Zhao Shuli: The "Making" of a Model Peasant Writer

IF ZHAO SHULI had not existed, he would have had to be invented, and perhaps to a great extent he was. Whereas the "great man of letters, great thinker and revolutionary" Lu Xun was a posthumous conceptualization by Mao Zedong, Zhao Shuli the model peasant writer was an ongoing joint creation of the living writer and party ideologues. In Lu Xun's case strenuous critical efforts had to be expended on fitting a finished, stable corpus of writings retrospectively into an assigned ideological niche. But Zhao Shuli's writings were contemporaneous with the formulation of the Communist Party's literary policies and, even as they were being produced, seemed to have been tailor-made to meet its specific requirements.

During the early 1940's in Yan'an, when Mao Zedong began calling for a specific kind of literature written for the masses, using the language of the masses, that would at the same time serve the revolutionary cause, coincidentally, as it were, Zhao Shuli and his fiction appeared just at the right place and the right time. His works were immediately available to be celebrated as a "victory in creative practice of Mao Zedong's ideas on literature and art" and to be upheld as models for the newly prescribed literature. By 1947, the constant exhortation was for all writers to "stride in the direction of Zhao Shuli," making him into a standard or ideal for creative writing.

Yet in spite of the hyperbolic acclaim with which it began, Zhao Shuli's literary career went on to have many ups and downs, and his creative output fell off considerably during the last twelve years of his life. Much vilified toward the end, he died tragically from the effects of cruel persecution during the Cultural Revolution; hardly the fate that would have been expected for someone who had once been praised as *the* writer who best embodied the party's notion of what a writer should be. In considering Zhao Shuli's literary career, the question one might well ask is, What happened? What could have caused the party to alter so drastically its evaluation of a writer it had once so enthusiastically endorsed?

The answer does not lie in any noticeable change or departure from his own earlier "direction" on the part of Zhao Shuli, for he remained steadfast both in his literary practice and in his self-conception as a writer. Nor do the fanatical excesses of the Cultural Revolution in themselves provide an adequate explanation for what ultimately happened to him. Yes, there were changing historical circumstances and increasingly stringent demands imposed on literature and art. And Zhao Shuli, of course, was by no means the only one who suffered when the Chinese Communist Party, in a frenzied orgy of self-destruction, turned on almost all of its writers and intellectuals. But others had not been elevated to the same model status as he once had. In retrospect, however, "what happened" to Zhao Shuli now seems in many ways to have been inevitable. For his spectacular rise and tragic fall were due above all to the inherent contradictions of the role he was given to play.

He has continued in the post-Mao era to be the subject of many studies, and the fact that they are by critics standing on opposing sides of the debate over the relationship between the party and literature is highly instructive. His case is drawn upon for support both by those who, praising him as an exemplar of the principles outlined in Mao's "Yan'an Talks," wish to reaffirm the correctness of the party's overall policy toward literature; but also by those who, lamenting his martyrdom, want to attack the later "leftist" bias of that policy, when the party, in their view, deviated from its correct path. However even more significant is the criticism that has gone further to use him as the pivotal figure for raising fundamental questions about party-directed literature even from its beginning, as in an important 1979 article by Liu Zaifu and others:

> The rise and fall of the Zhao Shuli school of writing, reflects in a typical way the distressful course of our country's revolutionary literature, particularly the

socialist art and literature of the thirty years since the establishment of the Republic. It is imperative that we consider the painful past, recall Comrade Zhao Shuli and the literary school of which he was a representative, assess their merits and defects, analyze their fate and fortunes, and draw valuable lessons from this process.[1]

What his career illuminates above all is the many dilemmas confronting those engaged in literary production during "the distressful course" of Chinese literature for thirty years, particularly since he had been set up to be its standard-bearer as a model "peasant writer."

The phenomenon of Zhao Shuli as "peasant writer" represents a complex interweaving of personal biography, ideological criticism, and literary production. Before proceeding to the reading of some representative texts, we need to consider what it *meant* to be a peasant writer and the issue of peasant versus intellectual in Yan'an's cultural policy. To discuss the work of Zhao Shuli, more than of any other writer in this book, it will be necessary to bring in various aspects of his biography as well as comments by his contemporary critics. Salient facts of his life were continually processed into legend, as he was presented and interpreted by those engaged in defining the party's literary policies.

THE WRITER AS PEASANT

Zhao Shuli was "discovered" as the first bona fide "peasant writer" (*nongmin zuojia*), the title conferred upon him by those in charge of party policy. Given the special status of the peasant in the Maoist revolutionary ideology, its application as the defining label of an author was intended both to serve as evidence of his impeccable credentials and to highlight his special achievement. But the term is loaded with several meanings, together suggesting the multiple burdens placed on the writer. First of all, *nongmin zuojia* was a summary description of Zhao Shuli's subject matter, pointing to the fact that his fiction was always *about* peasant characters and life in the countryside. It also underscored the notion that his fiction was the first to be produced *for* a rural audience as well, and therefore appealed to their interests and represented their point of view. But even more important—and this gets to a basic tenet in Chinese Marxist criticism—it signified his identity as *being* a peasant writer, a writer who, as it was endlessly stressed, came from a peasant family and had lived and worked as a peasant. This explained what he wrote about and whom he wrote for. And the label encompassed his appearance; it was important that Zhao Shuli should *look* like a peasant as well.

This is how Chen Huangmei, who as vice director of the Writer's Union (*Wenlian*) of the Shanxi-Hebei-Shandong-Henan Border Region was one of Zhao Shuli's important early promoters, recalls his first meeting with the writer in 1946:

> He looked just like a common Shanxi peasant: a small cotton-padded black jacket buttoning down front, a pair of cotton trousers such as one often sees in the countryside, and a brown felt hat. His face was rather pale and sallow; there was not a trace of the intellectual in his appearance; he did not even resemble an ordinary village cadre.[2]

On his part, Zhao Shuli lived up to his expected role by initially showing some uneasiness during that meeting, because, as he confessed to Chen Huangmei later, he thought he was going to meet with some "big intellectual" (*da zhishifenzi*). The contrast between "peasant" and "intellectual" underlined by both participants in referring to the meeting is characteristic; it would be a persistent refrain in eulogistic articles about Zhao Shuli. An important question raised then is, Why such an insistence on the opposition between peasant and intellectual?—which normally includes those who produce literature—and the corollary question, what does it mean anyway to *write* as a peasant, as opposed to writing as an intellectual? The ominous implications of this opposition would emerge more clearly in subsequent attempts to characterize the so-called peasant literature that Zhao Shuli presumably wrote.

Since he was a peasant writing about peasants and for peasants, his work could claim to be "realistic" and authentic, because he was supposedly writing from first-hand experience and "knew" what he was writing about. As a peasant he also had the right class background to guarantee that he would be writing from the correct political standpoint. Not only was the relation between text and historical "reality" considered to be direct and transparent, but the author was also always emphasized as the source and origin of the work. Therefore one was totally responsible for everything in it. You were what you wrote, or rather, you wrote what you were (an argument that was continually utilized for persecuting writers).

These were some of the themes repeated ad nauseam by Zhao Shuli's early champions. Yet as time went on, such impeccable credentials turned out to be inadequate to shield his work from negative criticism, or to protect him from his persecutors during the Cultural Revolution. Evaluation of Zhao Shuli often revolved around the question of how peasant characters were portrayed in his works. He had been hailed for his great innovating achievement, as the first writer to "write about peasants who were truly like peasants."[3] When he later got into trouble it was because some of his peasants were found not to have been portrayed as they ought to have been, but had, on the contrary, been "slandered" (*wumie*).[4] Such drastic reassessments were dictated by a changing political environment. As his writing career continued, Zhao Shuli had to struggle to come up in his fiction with ever more heroic peasant characters to meet ever more exacting standards. At the same time, as he represented himself in comments and discussions about his own work, he was under constant pressure to live up to his own identity or persona as a peasant writer.

Ironically, tragically, one way to view what happened to Zhao Shuli after 1958 was that he committed the major offense of continuing to take his persona as spokesman for the peasants all too seriously. His assigned/assumed persona led him to believe that he indeed had an obligation to speak out on behalf of the peasants. And he did so when he began to perceive that the party was failing in its responsibility toward them. It was primarily his attempts to speak and write about his concerns over conditions in the countryside that brought down upon his head the terrible persecution that in the end cost him his life.

Although Zhao Shuli was a loyal and conscientious adherent of the party line in literature, and many of his individual works were produced by assignment while following required formulas, they are actually more complex, more problematic, than the simplistic, highly ideologized readings his critics have given them. Certain interpretations were imposed upon his fiction for political reasons, at times almost in spite of the fiction itself. It is not so much what Zhao Shuli himself wrote as *how* he was *read* by ideologues that gives him an exemplary significance. From the start, Zhao Shuli was participating in the construction of a mold for "revolutionary literature," a mold that was being defined even as his own writings were interpreted as fitting into it. Literary production and critical context became a mutually reinforcing two-way process.

The fit between Zhao Shuli's narrative fiction and its reading by the critics is by no means perfect. Dominating as the revolutionary ideology might be, it cannot quite succeed in coercing or subsuming every aspect of the texts' meaning, and a close reading will uncover discrepancies and contradictions.

Zhao Shuli was defined the way he was because at a particular historical moment political circumstances had required that there be a peasant writer like Zhao Shuli. He emerged in 1943 with his first major work to provide the necessary exemplification of the new literary policy that was being formulated in Yan'an.

PEASANT VERSUS INTELLECTUAL IN
YAN'AN CULTURAL POLICY

Mao Zedong's "Talks at the Yan'an Forum on Literature and Art" were a watershed in the history of modern Chinese literature. Much of what Mao said in May 1942 about writing for the broad peasant masses had been anticipated by earlier developments, but his remarks on literature, if not original, were explicit, definitive, and set the parameters and the major themes for all writing about literature and art for the next three decades.

One of the controversial issues during the leftist debates in Shanghai during the late 1920's and early 1930's on creating a new revolutionary literature had concerned the role of intellectuals in such a task. In his influential 1928 piece "Cong wenxue geming dao geming wenxue" ("From a Literary Revolution to a Revolutionary Literature"), the linguistic inversion neatly summing up developments since May Fourth, Cheng Fangwu had already stated the central problem that would be developed later:

> If we want to shoulder the responsibility of revolutionary *yin-tie-li-geng-zhui-ya* [intelligentsia], we must yet again negate ourselves (the negation of negation), we must strive to acquire class consciousness, we must make our medium (*meizhi*) close to the language used by the peasant and worker masses (*nonggong dazhong*); we must take the peasant and worker masses as our target.[5]

Cheng Fangwu's own language, littered as it was with the new jargon of political neologisms and transliterated foreign borrowings, could hardly be considered "close to the language used by the peasant and worker masses," but his emphasis on the reform or transformation of the intelligentsia, and its linkage with the problem of language, was one that anticipated a critical component of Yan'an policies.

Qu Qiubai, leader of the Shanghai League of Left-wing Writers, had also called for narrowing the distance between the intellectuals and the "laboring masses." The May Fourth "literary revolution," in his view, had merely created a "Europeanized gentry" and a new Europeanized classical language, totally cut off from the common people. What had to be done in writing was to make use of the "modern vernacular spoken by living Chinese," but reflecting the antirural bias of both the urban intellectual and of Western Marxism, Qu Qiubai made the point that he was referring specifically to the modern language spoken by the proletariat:

> This newly arisen class cannot be compared to the "country folk" peasantry (*"xiangxiaren" de nongmin*). The language of "country folk" is primitive and obscure. Whereas the language of the newly arisen class, in the big cities that draw from many regions and in the modernized factories, has actually already evolved a Chinese common vernacular (*putonghua*). . . . It is not the same as the new classical language of the intellectuals. . . . In sum, every work written should "be understood when read aloud."[6]

Two years later, in 1934, Qu left the urban environment to work as commissar of education in the Jiangxi Soviet, where he no doubt found himself facing "country folk" and the necessity to look into their language, but his execution by the Guomindang the following year did not allow him time to put in writing much about his experience.

Many of Qu Qiubai's ideas on the popularization of literature and art would be echoed in Yan'an a few years later, but by then the peasantry had replaced the new proletariat and assumed the role as the central force of the revolution. Speaking to and writing for the "laboring masses" would then take on a different and much more specific meaning, since the notion of what was a "peasant" would be utterly redefined by the Communist Party in Yan'an. Marx had seen little revolutionary potential in peasants; the socialist revolution was expected to succeed only in industrially advanced capitalist countries anyway. Mao Zedong's great contribution to revolutionary ideology and the main feature of his "sinification" of Marxism-Leninism is widely considered to be his reconceptualization of the Chinese revolution as a peasant-based revolution. Of course once the Chinese Communist Party had been driven to the countryside by Guomindang terror and its successive encircling campaigns, it had little choice but to work with what was there. And what was there for the ragged survivors of the Long March to work with when in 1935 they arrived in the Border Regions of the Northwest—where they would set up their revolutionary base—was not an urban proletariat, but the poverty-stricken peasantry of a remote and peripheral area of China.

There are those who have argued that what gave legitimacy to the Communist Revolution was its ability to link up with a spontaneous peasant revolution.[7] Peasants may be driven by harsh conditions to rebel, but these rebellions normally take the form of agitations that do not aim to establish an alternative political system to replace what is traditional or familiar. What more plausibly describes the Chinese case was that a small group of visionary revolutionaries inspired by a foreign ideology, found themselves able to exploit peasant discontent and mobilize the peasantry as a means of achieving political power.

That this minority group was able to accomplish such a feat had much to do with the state of crisis in the Chinese countryside. Peasants do not survive much above the subsistence level even in the best of times and conditions will vary from region to region, but between 1920 and 1949, there were wide areas suffering from famine, mass migrations, massive rural unemployment, widespread debt and dispossession of land, the degradation of women, and the selling of children.[8] Without the depth and magnitude of rural poverty, exploitation, and suffering, especially in the north and northwestern areas where the Communist Party would have its base, there would most likely have been no socialist revolution in China. The invasion by Japan also played a crucial, and in the view of some scholars decisive, role in rallying the rural populace behind the Communist Party.[9] And without question Japan's invasion made its own monstrously brutal contributions toward rural misery. Unlike previous peasant rebellions, which were usually based on a yearning for the past, displaying a form of nostalgia for what might have been good or at least better than the present, the Marxist-inspired rebellion held out a radically new vision that aimed at a fundamental reversal of the traditional order.

When Mao Zedong in March 1949, on the eve of taking power over all of China, summarized the party's revolutionary work from 1927 on, he put it in terms of "surrounding the city by the countryside."[10] Once the focus of the party's work shifted from the countryside to the city as it then achieved victory and was in position to carry out its goal of rebuilding China, that countryside with its peasant manpower and woman power—for the mobilization of vast resources of female labor through collectivization efforts was another great achievement of the party—could be exploited in order to squeeze a surplus for use in rapid industrialization. The miserable conditions of the countryside had provided the party with a vast reservoir of discontent to mobilize for revolutionary change, but sincerely moved and indignant over the plight of the peasantry as the Communist revolutionaries were, "the liberation of the peasantry was not, and never had been, the fundamental aim of the Chinese revolution."[11]

But even if revolution by, of, or for the peasant was not what in fact the Chinese Communist Revolution was all about, the party did develop a peasant-based revolutionary ideology. In Yan'an, as the party was spelling out its vision of the revolution and forging the strategies that would eventually turn out to be so successful, "the possibility of rendering the 'peasant other' into a redeeming national class became the object."[12] Its elevation of the peasantry into the leading force of the revolution was primarily a matter of defining and constructing a peasantry, whatever it may have been in itself, in accordance with revolutionary needs. This is not to say that the party under the leadership of Mao Zedong was deliberately practicing deception. Way back in his 1927 "Report on an Investigation of the Peasant Movement in Hunan" Mao had articulated in stirring words his notion that only the impoverished peasantry, those on the bottom rung of society, were capable of turning things upside down and of carrying out revolution, a revolution in which "several hundred million peasants will rise like a mighty storm, like a hurricane, a force so swift and violent that no power, however great, will be able to hold it back." "To march at their head and lead them" was the only choice, in his view, the revolutionary movement should make.[13]

Whether or not Mao's report may have been, in the words of Roy Hofheinz, "an utter fantasy,"[14] it nevertheless evoked a grand vision, a powerful projection containing elements of recognizable reality that could be made into the effective foundation of radical revolutionary practice. Whatever the relation to historical reality, as Mao Zedong assumed the role of the great storyteller in Yan'an, his master narrative of revolution would continue to feature insurrectionary peasants as its heroic protagonists.

The achievements of the early years of the peasant movement in China were hardly impressive. No large-scale organization of peasants, no strong mass base was established from 1928 to 1935. But the party was learning useful techniques, in many of which the Red Army played an important role, for coordinating military, political, and cultural work to set up a network of peasant associations and rural governments. Always efforts were made to inquire into local conditions, to deepen contact with the villagers, to encourage and listen to their stories of bitterness. The party's penetration into the countryside was historically unprecedented in its scale and depth. But as it turned out, it was not so much to arrive at an "objective" understanding of the peasant as to shape an image of the peasant tailored to accommodate a specific revolutionary vision.

These were some of the revolutionary concepts and techniques that came together in the Yan'an period, when the party had a decade to refine and give them definite form, and also to supervise their translation into artistic and literary expression.

The purpose of Mao Zedong's "Talks at the Yan'an Forum" in May 1942, as he clearly stated in the introduction, was "to ensure that literature and art become a component part of the whole revolutionary machinery, so they can act as a powerful weapon in uniting and educating the people" in the struggle against the enemy.[15] The idea of appropriating literature and art into the all encompassing process of revolution and their use as a weapon for struggle stems from Lenin, whom Mao quotes and refers to in the "Talks," but it also had behind it the experience of the Jiangxi Soviets from 1931–1934 in which certain agitational forms, written, oral, or pictorial, had been adapted from Soviet models; the propaganda network of the Red Army on the Long March and after; and the many local mobilization efforts in the war of resistance against Japan. Although Chinese critics have continued to quote the "Talks" as if they represented a discussion of the theoretical issues of art and literature— audience, effect, criteria, language, form, etc.—Mao's statements were oriented toward the pragmatic and largely concerned with functional revolutionary strategy.

Once Mao Zedong raised the question of literature and art "for whom?" in the Yan'an "Talks," it would seem that the rest of his ideas followed naturally. The shift was, as Bonnie McDougall describes it, from an "elitist, author-centered culture (i.e., designed by authors) into a mass, audience-centered culture (one designed by or for the audience)".[16] But it is important to keep in mind that while the author was indeed being "de-centered," the audience was not what was actually "there," but an audience projected and conceptualized by the party. (This suggests an intriguing contrast or comparison with the money-driven American media's justification of immorality and violence by claiming merely to be "giving the public what it wants." In other words, we're not responsible;

it's the audience—as we perceive it.) The audience that Mao invokes in the "Talks" were the "great masses of workers, peasants, and soldiers"; and since what workers there were constituted but a tiny number, and since soldiers in any case were workers and peasants "who had taken up arms," what this mass audience comes down to is that same peasantry as defined and constructed to serve the party's program for revolution.

As for the immediate audience for the "Talks" themselves, they were not the broad masses, but the writers and artists along with newly recruited party members, the main targets of the Rectification Campaign of 1942–1944. These writers and artists, "the literary intelligentsia" in Ellen Judd's term, were composed of people "with some formal education implying at least moderate literacy and exposure to indigenous or foreign elite culture."[17] The central question was how to remold or transform those whose educational and social status set them apart from the broad peasant masses, so that they would be able to perform effectively the all-important grass-roots-level work of the revolution.

The policies of the party toward art and literature as set forth in the "Talks" had far-reaching consequences for the role that the literary intelligentsia—most particularly in its position vis-à-vis the peasant—henceforth was to play in the revolutionary society now coming into being. To ask writers and artists to submerge themselves among the masses was first of all a means for bridging the distance between the two classes.

While the boundaries between the traditional gentry ruling elite and the ruled peasant masses had always been sharply drawn—access to education and control of literacy being a critical demarcation line—they did in many respects share in a common culture, occupying two ends of a cultural-social continuum. This continuum had been ruptured by the May Fourth intellectuals' rebellion against the traditional system and adoption of foreign values and ideas even as they made deliberate efforts to write about the lower classes. The distance between the intellectual and peasant classes was further widened by the breakdown of traditional social institutions and the shift to the modern urban centers as the focus for intellectual activity and the cultured life. Since the late 1930's, intellectuals and writers, driven in part by the Japanese invasion, had been leaving the coastal cities of the east and arriving in increasing numbers at the Border Regions to join the revolution. The gap between the two classes would need to be narrowed for this cosmopolitan-trained and -educated corps to work effectively in the countryside. A goal of the Rectification Campaign of 1942–1944, the context within which the "Talks at the Yan'an Forum on Literature and Art" were given by Mao Zedong, was a preparation for sending intellectuals to the countryside, to set aside for a while their professional activities and lifestyle (still relatively privileged even under the harsh conditions in the Border Regions), and live and work among the laboring masses.

But party policy further required intellectuals to subordinate themselves to the masses. They were urged to "become one with the thoughts and emotions of the great masses of workers, peasants, and soldiers" (p. 521), to serve them, learn their language. It was not just a matter of breaking down the old Mencian distinction "between those who labor with their heart/minds, and those who labor with their muscles," when not to dirty one's hands through manual labor had been a mark of the higher and privileged status of the intellectual elite. What was gone were the claims to intellectual and moral superiority that had legitimated that status. In fact, now intellectuals would need to examine themselves continually to see whether they were living up to their obligation to serve those who had once been considered their inferiors. This reversal of the traditional hierarchical relationship placed the intellectual in the position of being subject to the control and direction of the broad masses, or rather of the party that had appropriated the masses and was carrying out revolution on their behalf. Party domination over literature and art—always in the name of the peasant masses—became the central feature of literary history for the next thirty years.

At first glance, the Communist Party's prescription for the writers of literature, that they learn from and write for the people, the masses, would seem to be providing a solution to the intellectual's dilemma when confronting the peasant. When the writers of May Fourth, with their notions of literature as a tool for dissecting social reality, turned their attention to the oppressed peasant as subject matter for their stories, they were often overwhelmed, as shown in story after story, by the injustices and suffering they discovered. The sense of anguish and moral culpability, such as we have seen in Lu Xun's fiction, was a major factor in their leftward turn. It made them receptive both toward the Communist Party's program for radical reform and toward its new conception of the downtrodden peasant. From such a perspective, their acceptance of the downgrading of their own status as intellectuals and willingness to subject themselves to thought reform and learn to write a new literature become more understandable.[18]

The exhortation to learn to speak the language of the masses, to write for them as the primary audience, provided a major impetus for utilizing "national or popular forms" which were widely used in various agitprop work—street plays, wall newspapers—in the bases there. Some of the newly arrived urban intellectuals, Ding Ling being the most prominent among them, had organized propaganda troupes like her Northwest Front Service Corps, to take the patriotic message of resisting Japan to remote villages in Shaanxi and Shanxi.[19] Many of these troupes studied and adapted popular traditional forms, such as drum songs (*dagu*), clapper talk (*kuaiban*), comic cross-talk (*xiangsheng*), two-man comedy acts (*shuanghuang*), and the song-and-dance *yangge*.[20]

Yan'an's interest in national popular forms marked an important shift away from the May Fourth use of Western models, and parallels the move from city to countryside of intellectual revolutionary work and literary production. Many questions could be raised as to what precisely were the national forms that were appropriated and how much of their original character was preserved as they were removed from their original ritual contexts. The entire project was based on rather naive notions about art, notions that one could simply put "new content" into old forms, or pour new wine into old bottles (a common analogy used) without in fact destroying them. But it did have a distinct effect on the new literature and art that was being produced, and its indeterminate nature made this literature and art even more amenable to party control.

As a model peasant writer, Zhao Shuli had to, first of all, focus on featuring in his fiction the new idealized and ideologized peasant the party's revolutionary work was bringing into being. But he was also in much demand to write and talk about his literary approach. Reiterating the party's dogmas on the inevitable class-based nature of literary genre and language, he would present himself as a promoter of the folk or popular tradition in Chinese literature—i.e., the "folk tradition of folk songs, drum songs, oral story telling, regional operas, etc." He distinguished this literary tradition of the proletarian class first from the tradition produced by "the ancient scholar-gentry class (*shidafu jieji*), such as ancient poetry, classical language, traditional painting, the ancient *qin*"; and also from a second tradition produced since May Fourth by "cultural circles" (*wenhuajie*), including new poetry, new fiction, "talking drama," oil painting, the piano, etc.[21] The first clearly belonged to the "feudal" past; the problem was with the second, in that literature from May Fourth was still considered to be main stream, not just by the "authoritive types who uphold the tradition of the 1930's, but all those with student backgrounds," because of its higher literary and cultural level. More "progressive" to be sure, than the classical language tradition, it was nevertheless a product of the capitalist or bourgeois class. The emphasis on purported class origins thus sets the folk or popular tradition in opposition to the "bourgeois" intellectuals' tradition, and reinforces further the implied anti-intellectualism of the party's literary policy.

While it may seem on the one hand that by subscribing to such a policy the writing self could be transcended in serving collective goals, on the other hand, what comes through more strongly, as in the telling example of Zhao Shuli, is the complicity of Yan'an nurtured writers in the downleveling of culture and literature, and the simultaneous devaluating of themselves. This is a contradiction that will be dramatized in much of his fiction.

Zhao Shuli wrote his stories to fit into the discursive community, to participate in the theories, the stories, the stock language, that were being generated in Yan'an. In these stories the themes of Yan'an cultural policy, the adoption of mass language and popular national forms, the predilection for processing history into myth, are extended into the realm of literary creativity and given concrete form. Yan'an was not just a background that was reflected in Zhao Shuli's work; it was the environment that created it but it also created his "life" as well.

THE "MAKING" OF A PEASANT WRITER

In any account of Zhao Shuli's career, it is difficult to separate fact from legend, substance from image, for it was the mixture of these together that made him into the consummately representative peasant writer that he was. Discussions of his fiction tend to make much of the fact that he was born into a poor peasant family, and that due to "his blood and flesh ties with the peasant masses," "within the peasant characters in his fiction beats the heart of the peasant, flows the blood of the peasant."[22]

What is most typical of this kind of criticism is the emphasis on character creation as the foremost criterion of artistic achievement and the drawing on the writer's life to back up that achievement. Yet considering the great importance placed on the writer himself—specifically on class background, political consciousness, personal character—as the source of the literary work, it may seem curious that, until the post-Mao era, full-length biographies of literary writers, with the exception of Lu Xun, hardly existed as a genre in revolutionary China. It might be risky to get too deeply into a writer, since anyone could, with a change in the political winds, suddenly fall from grace and become the target of a campaign, leaving the biographer in the lurch. In Zhao Shuli's case there was the additional burden of maintaining the legend of an anointed model peasant writer; it would not do should any inconvenient facts of his biography turn up to blemish it. Thus any information about Zhao Shuli's life was of necessity highly selective and consisted of variations on a few reiterated themes, all to affirm and reaffirm his status as a peasant writer.

It is only since around 1981 or so that book length biographies of Zhao Shuli have appeared.[23] Basically these are "life and work" hagiographies that do not fundamentally challenge the basic premises of the legend. Still they contain enough new detailed information to call into question the simplistic correlations made between biographical fact and literary practice during his lifetime and suggest that more than a few qualifications could be made of the "peasant writer" label.

Zhao Shuli was born in 1906. The sixteen-room, storied brick and tile Zhao family compound in Yuchi village of Shanxi's Qinshui county was built by an ancestor during the Qianlong era. A student of the Imperial College, and later probably even a military official (*wujuren*), he was in any case an "intellectual of the feudal class."[24] Although the family had declined considerably by Zhao Shuli's time, its material circumstances and cultural level (*wenhua shuiping*) were considerably above those of the average peasant.

Zhao's grandfather had worked in a dry goods store in Zhoukou town in Henan and later returned to the village to operate a school. To the twenty-odd students, including his only grandson, he taught the *Four Books* and other classics. Zhao Shuli continued his classical education under a local scholar (*xiucai*) who instilled in him a love of classical poetry.

Zhao's father farmed the land, but supplemented his income by practicing medicine; he was a skilled fortune teller and geomancer as well. From his grandfather and father the young Zhao Shuli studied the "Classic of the Three Sage Sect" and learned by heart the formulas of the manuals of divination. He thus had opportunities as he was growing up for classical as well as other kinds of less orthodox forms of traditional learning. After he had been attending school off and on, his father borrowed fifteen yuan to send him at age nineteen to the Number Four Provincial Normal School in Changzhi, where he entered the equivalent of the first year of junior high. There a whole new world was opened to him. He discovered the new literature of May Fourth, the works of Lu Xun, Guo Moruo, Yu Dafu, and such foreign authors as Ibsen and Turgenev. He was also introduced to writings about Communism. Two years later, in 1927, he became a member of the Communist Party. Forced to flee the white terror of Yan Xishan, he took on a vagrant life as teacher, itinerant mountebank, seller of calligraphy and paintings, etc.

For a time he was imprisoned in the Self-renewal Institute, a sort of Guomindang thought reform place, and his short stories in the "Europeanized vernacular," required for the "Self-renewal Monthly" may have been his first "published" works. In 1930, shortly after his release, he published a long classical poem in a Beijing newspaper, where his writing career may be more properly considered to have begun.

Then followed seven years of wandering again, and eking out a living as substitute teacher, teaching assistant, clerk, bookseller, diviner, storyteller, etc., but the activities of Zhao Shuli during this impoverished and unsettled period of his life are not fully known. In many respects Zhao Shuli's background and training—a gentry family in decline, albeit declining farther than most, early education in the classics, followed by introduction to foreign literature, teaching, clerking, and other "intellectual jobs"—conforms to the pattern of many other modern Chinese writers. What is distinctive is his participation during his childhood and youth in village musical groups, mastering the wooden clappers for the local opera by eight and the drum by fifteen, parts which required him to memorize numerous libretti and much dialogue,[25] and his exposure to, and mastery of, storytelling and other traditional folk forms. These would be frequently drawn on in the writing he was to do in the future.

Zhao Shuli's background and travels did provide him with an intimate knowledge of life in rural Shanxi. And he never experienced in his formative years the urban cultures of Shanghai or Beijing. But he was, as his biographer Huang Xiuji writes in 1981, "after all, not a peasant, not a folk artist, but an intellectual who had been influenced by the May Fourth new culture movement."[26] Another recent biographer, Dong Dazhong, makes a similar point in commenting on two essays Zhao Shuli published in 1936 and considering their range of knowledge and literary style: "Reading these essays, you would not think of him as a peasant writer, in fact he was an intellectual writer who then changed into a peasant [or "became peasant-like" (*nongminhua le de zuojia*)]."[27] Quite understandably these were sides of Zhao Shuli that had been much played down, in fact, totally ignored, as the writer-as-peasant legend was being constructed.

One crucial preparation for Zhao Shuli's later role was the propaganda posts he held in southern Shanxi. He had rejoined the Communist Party in 1937, whereupon his life of precarious vagabondage came to an end. The party was establishing its base in Shanxi with the 129th Division of the Eighth Route Army, by working through the "Alliance of Sacrifice and National Salvation," a united front organization under Yan Xishan, the Shanxi warlord and Guomindang commander-in-chief of the Second War Area. Zhao's assignment in the party for the next several years was to put out newspapers, mostly in lithographed or mimeographed form, in the small towns among the Taihang Mountain area, functioning often as editor, typesetter, illustrator, proofreader, as well as writer. For these "one man shows" (*dujue xi*), as he was to call them, he wrote and published, under a variety of pseudonyms, essays, short stories, poems, plays, clapper talks, jokes, folk songs, which are now for the most part lost. Such a prodigious and wide-ranging output was for the overall purpose of arousing the populace to support the anti-Japanese war effort.

In sharp contrast to the older May Fourth generation, who came mostly from eastern and southern provincial towns and then migrated to the coastal metropolises to begin writing careers with professional aspirations, and similar to his contemporary northern writers, such as Ma Feng, Li Zhun, Du Pengcheng, Zhao's literary activities began in the interior as propagandist for the party. As he commented in 1955:

> In the early stages of the Anti-Japanese War I did propaganda work in the countryside, then later became a professional writer in what can only be called a "transfer" (*zhuanye*). Writers who start out in this kind of work will often attempt to coordinate [their writing] with current political propaganda tasks and aim for quick results.[28]

This explicitly acknowledged blurring of the distinction between literature and propaganda would indeed have a profound effect on the way this younger generation conceived of the nature of their writing activities and must be kept in mind in any analysis of their works. Unlike the May Fourth writers, these writers who began their careers in the 1940's, were committed to party work from the start—indeed, as they emphasized, they had been nurtured into being writers by the party in the first place.[29]

During the War of Resistance against Japan, patriotism was a major motivation for writing, but there were also many times when it was called upon to respond directly to a more specific situation. When an uprising of a religious sect instigated by the Japanese to oppose the Eighth Route Army took place in November 1941, Zhao Shuli was asked by the party leadership to write a play against superstition; he complied.[30] The incident also prompted the Taihang area Party Committee and the Political Department of the 129th Division to organize a forum in January 1942 to discuss the question of intensifying cultural education work among the masses. When Zhao Shuli addressed the forum he is reported to have exhibited a collection of popular reading material that he had gathered from people's homes: divination texts, love and adventure stories, pictures of deities, religious scripts, examples of "the 'North China' culture that prevails over all else among the people,"[31] in order to make a dramatic plea for a popular literature that could reach the masses by using forms that had appeal for them. He had always been aware of the "competition" in his work, and made the point that the "struggle for position against the forces of feudal culture" involved strategies of form and language. The solution that Zhao Shuli proposed: "learn from these forms" while giving them "correct content," rested on the questionable assumption that "form" was easily separable from "content"; but it was an assumption that would guide both party policy and his own writing in the future.

Sometime in the spring of 1943 he was transferred to the Party School of the Central Committee's Northern Bureau and assigned the task of collecting material from the lives of the people to use for purposes of education and propaganda. He was told he could write in any form he chose so long as it could be understood by the masses. By the time Mao Zedong's "Talks at the Yan'an Forum on Art and Literature" had reached the Taihang area in the summer of 1943, laying down the principle that in order to write for the masses, writers must go among them and learn from them, Zhao Shuli was ready with the major work that was to make him famous.

WHY BLACKIE HAS TO GET MARRIED

"Xiao Erhei jiehun" ("Blackie Gets Married")[32] is a story about two young lovers who overcome the opposition of their "backward" parents and the intimidation of the village bullies in order to marry. After initial rejection the book was finally published when Peng Dehuai, vice commander in chief of the Eighth Route Army, wrote a promoting inscription ("It is rare to have a popular (*tongsu*) story like this written out of investigation among the masses") and gave it to Li Dazhang, the head of the Northern Bureau's Propaganda Ministry, to hand over to the Xinhua publishers. The book was an instant success, reportedly selling an unprecedented thirty to forty thousand copies within the Taihang area alone. It could be argued by the party that the masses had finally been given what they wanted.

According to Zhao Shuli the material for his stories was mostly "picked up" stuff that he had "run into (*pengle tou*), and could not dodge even if [he] had wished to."[33] Beginning with Peng Dehuai's inscription, the close relationship between Zhao Shuli's fiction and the life and experiences of the masses will be a recurrent theme in any discussion of his work, but the precise nature of that relationship, over which enormous amounts of ink have been spilled, is actually a problematic matter. Zhao Shuli's treatment of the material he had "picked up" from life in this particular story points to the predicament Chinese criticism finds itself in when simultaneously insisting on a literature that must be based on life (*cong shenghuo chufa*) and yet meet a priori ideological requirements.

During a major Japanese offensive in 1943, Zhao Shuli's cultural unit was evacuated to a village where the Liao county government was then stationed. A relative of his landlord came to bring a lawsuit against a group of local cadres who had beaten his nephew Yue Dongzhi to death and then hung the corpse in the cow shed, clumsily arranging it to look like a suicide. The young man's father had already bought him a child-bride, but he had fallen in love with Zhi Yingxiang, a young girl from the same village. There were obstacles to their relationship on her side as well. Her mother, a member of the Three Sage Sect (*Sansheng dao jiao-hui*) had a year ago arranged for Yingxiang to marry a forty-year old merchant, but then when she ran into opposition by her two sons as well as the daughter, she hanged herself. Yue Dongzhi had another rival in the person of the married village head, the son of a rich peasant, who was pursuing the same girl. Several village cadres organized a "struggle meeting" to accuse Yue Dongzhi, who was captain of the people's militia, of dissolution, and pressure him to break off with the girl. Yue was beaten and killed. Zhao Shuli investigated the case and used it as the base of his story.[34]

The events of this multiple tragedy are worth recapitulating in order to show the drastic transformations they undergo in Zhao Shuli's story. Most striking of the changes, and most characteristic of the new fiction ushered in by "Blackie Gets Married," is the happy outcome. Instead of suicide and lynching, the story ends with the mother seeing the error of her ways and the two young lovers being married with the blessing of the district head (*quzhang*). While the degree of fidelity to "reality" by no means determines the quality of a work, it has, for ideological reasons, been a cardinal principle in Chinese Marxist criticism. How was this up-beat ending, which would have profound consequences for the story's other structural elements, such as mode of characterization, plot motivation, and narrative closure, to be reconciled with Peng Dehuai's recommendation that it was "written out of an investigation among the masses"? But Mao Zedong had stressed that in serving the goals of the revolution, literature and art should portray the "bright side," not the dark side, of reality. The victory over feudalism could not have been won without showing Blackie happily married.

Zhao Shuli's version plays down the villainous role of the village cadres—that is, the peasant hoodlums who had now become local representatives of the party and were in a position to terrorize the village. In his 1949 account of Zhao Shuli's handling of the material, Dong Junlun writes:

> Zhao Shuli considered the conclusion of the original story overly tragic. Since he was writing something in opposition to feudalism, he thought he should give the positive characters a way out. . . . But that was during the early period of the revolution, there were not yet many examples of victories by the people; the sprouting of brightness, was still only from the top down to below . . . so Zhao Shuli could not think of another solution except to go to a higher level, thus a happy ending was brought about by the district head and the village head.[35]

The awkward mixed metaphor of sprouting brightness aside, the passage reveals a problem Zhao Shuli had to confront from the very beginning: how to come up with that obligatory positive ending when the peasants and lower-level village cadres (some of whom were themselves responsible for the crime) were not actually capable of bringing it about themselves.

But it is not only in the happy ending that the story departs from the original tragedy; in fact the opening sentences prepare us immediately for something that is quite the opposite:

In Liujia Valley there were two immortals (*shenxian*) known to everyone around: one was Second Zhuge of the front hamlet, the other was Third Fairy of the rear hamlet. Second Zhuge was originally called Liu Xiude; he had been a small merchant and never made a move without consulting *yinyang*, the Eight Diagrams, or looking at the zodiac and the stars. Third Fairy was the wife of rear hamlet's Yu Fu; on the first and fifteenth of each month she draped a red cloth over her head and strutted about masquerading as a heavenly spirit.

Second Zhuge shunned as taboo the phrase "not propitious for planting"; Third Fairy, the phrase "the rice is mushy." Herein lie two little stories.[36]

We hereby enter a fictional world dominated by two comic figures, both foolish and ridiculous, both magnificently exaggerated personifications of village superstitions. They are the "villains" introduced by Zhao Shuli into the story, who will attempt in vain to obstruct the path of true love. Second Zhuge is the father of the boy Blackie (Xiao Erhei), and Third Fairy is the mother of the girl, Xiaoqin. These two parents will of course be defeated in their schemes to stop the marriage, a signal we pick up from the moment they appear on the scene; we sense that any threat posed by these two need not be taken seriously.

The story continues to be narrated in this style, with an omniscient third-person narrator adopting the lively, chatty tone of an oral storyteller familiar with the community he is describing: "The young men again started calling on Third Fairy. Rather than say that they went to consult her oracle, one should say that they went to gaze on the heavenly image" (*yao shuoshi . . . hai buru shuoshi . . .*) (p. 2). What most undermines the substantiality of the two comic characters is the playful language in which they are represented from the beginning, language that calls attention to itself rather than to its supposed referents. There is artful symmetry in the names, Second and Third, front and rear hamlets, in the parallel sentence structures used to depict parallel behavior. Each is animated by habitual, jerky gestures: Second Zhuge won't "lift his feet or move his hands" (*taijiao dongshou*) without consulting articles of divination; Third Fairy "sways and struts about" (*yaoyao baibai*) draped in a red cloth. The rapid and abrupt rhythm of the description of weird facts make them seem like marionette-like figures, characterized and "fixed" by their nicknames. Two little stories then follow to explain why the two phrases they shun like a taboo are attached to them; these will become identifying labels repeatedly used by the village community to remind all of their pathetic absurdity. One thing lacking in "Blackie Gets Married" is an explanation of what motivates their change of heart in the end, when they withdraw their opposition to the marriage. Since the story never explores their behavior to begin with, it need not go into the reasons when that behavior happens to change. In the concluding lines of the story the village children give the two immortals new nicknames, Third Fairy is now called "Heaven-ordained Marriage," and Second Zhuge "Unmatched Horoscope"; it is a way to continue to ridicule them in their defeat. That the story closes with this replacement of linguistic tags rather than any further discussion of the fate or character transformation of the two figures reinforces the impression that Zhao Shuli's characters are not so much modeled after people, in spite of the fact that he once claimed that Second Zhuge was a miniature (*suoying*) of his father,[37] as creations of verbal artifice.

According to semiotic theories, characters are textual constructs anyway and should not be equated with "real people," so we need not insist that Zhao Shuli's characters be coherent or plausible or even "person-like." The problem of "characters as people" arises because both Zhao Shuli himself and his critics have insisted on discussing his characters (*renwu*) as if they were real people drawn from real-life situations, and have focused on character as the main, if not sole, carrier of the story's meaning. This is a characteristic of all didactic literature in general. Character is regarded as the site where the moral and political issues of the story are supposed to be fought out and resolved; it has been used over and over again by Chinese Marxist critics as the measure of ideological correctness. This demand about "character" placed a burden on Zhao Shuli which he consciously assumed, but which was in effect contradicted by his actual narrative practice.

Since the story is supposedly reflecting ongoing historical reality, Zhao Shuli's characters fall into several distinct categories to conform to the party's strategy for revolution in the countryside. As Huang Xiuji points out, "Blackie Gets Married" already contains the major character series (*xingxiang xilie*) that were to appear in Zhao Shuli'ss fiction thereafter. These Huang categorizes as the Second Zhuge series: old peasants, poor, passive, superstitious, "feudalist" in their thinking; the Third Fairy series: the "backward" women in the countryside, "the most vividly characterized" of his creations; and the young peasant series: Xiao Erhei and Xiaoqin, positive characters who represent the new society. These three types represent the major character series that will appear in all of Zhao Shuli's fiction.[38]

Although portrayals of young peasants are more numerous than those of any other characters in Zhao Shuli's fiction, few can compare, in the view of Huang and other critics, with the vivid portrayal of his old peasants. The young Xiao Erhei and Xiao Qin are seldom on stage or given more than a sentence or two here and there in the course of the narrative. Instead it is the backward, feudalistic, superstitious peasants of the older generation in Zhao Shuli's fiction that have created stronger and lasting impressions. This is not so much due to their being truer to life, or because, as critics have often taken pains to note, these old peasants were the kind he was most familiar with, as to his particular mode of characterization: the witty phrase, the deflating rhetoric, the use of surface verbal play instead of in-depth representation of motivation or behavior, and most memorable of all, the colorful, outrageous nicknames that he confers on them. In addition to Second Zhuge, Third Fairy, other examples include Aching Shank (*Xiaotui teng*), Unfillable Stomach (*Chi bu bao*) (from "Duanlian duanlian"), Ever in the Right (*Chang you li*), No Can Do (*Neng bu gou*), Muddlehead (*Hututu*), Can't be Offended (*Rebuqi*) (from *Sanliwan*)[39] that in fact almost make them into cartoon figures. These peasants of the old and passing prerevolutionary world should in theory be rich with possibilities for tragedy and conflict, since they are caught in the momentous transitions from old into new, but they are robbed of any subjective substance and turned into comic objects of satire.

Unlike landlords who are negative and irredeemable, these old "feudalistic" peasants will undergo transformation (*zhuanbian*) in the course of the story, transformations of personalities that illustrate the "world-shaking changes taking place in the Chinese countryside,"[40] even if these transformations, as we have seen, are often just a matter of verbal manipulation. What makes it possible for the two lovers to achieve their desire and marry in the end is not any change in the behavior of their obstructive parents, but the freedom of choice provisions in the new Marriage Law as expounded by the head of the district government. The happy outcome is imposed from the top down, official authority coinciding nicely with the desire of the two lovers and the parents' change of heart. Old peasants can thus remain salvable; they certainly must not be presented as posing any serious threats to the revolutionary victory to come. Zhao Shuli felt less free to indulge in verbal histrionics with the younger generation; Xiao Erhei and Xiao Qin are just like many other heroic idealized peasants: indistinguishable one from the other and utterly forgettable.

In "Blackie Gets Married" a tragedy taken from life is turned into a comedy in which the individual characters do not in themselves warrant serious attention. But in his pursuit of satirical and comic effects, Zhao Shuli falls back on blatant sexism in the portrayal of "Third Fairy" type characters. In addition to being "feudalistic" and backward like their male counterparts, these backward females are often presented as somewhat warped personalities, suggesting a weird mixture of sexual enticement, shamanism, and superstition. Whereas thirty years ago the young men used to flock to Third Fairy and flirt with her as the prettiest girl in her village, now she must lure them with her colorful religious rituals. In the end she is supposed to be funny when she is exposed to be an old, balding coquette with embroidered shoes and decorated trouser cuffs, with a wrinkled face covered with powder, which makes her look at age forty-five like a "frosted donkey turd" (p. 3). Third Fairy does not really "reform" and change her attitude toward her daughter; she is merely made to look ludicrous in her downfall. Nothing is an easier butt for ridicule than an old woman who has lost the charms that the village men were once only too ready to succumb to. She is portrayed as little more than a comic villai*ness,* but how did she become that way? The fact that Third Fairy had been married off at age fifteen to a man with whom she had nothing in common and later resorted to shamanism in desperation, that she herself should be considered a sad victim of the "feudalism" that is the story's target, is hardly acknowledged, much less examined.

THE WRITER'S ROLE—TELLING A "TRUE STORY"

The following year Zhao Shuli wrote a story about a woman's liberation, her "turning over" or "standing up" (*fanshen*). As an editor of the Xinhua book store, he had attended a 1944 conference of model workers of the Taihang area; "Meng Xiangying fanshen" ("Meng Xiangying Stands Up"),[41] one of the two pieces he wrote on the model workers he met there, was completed a few months later. After talking to people who knew Meng Xiangying, the material he collected was not so much on her heroic efforts in mobilizing the village women to unbind their feet, attend literacy classes, and gather wild plants to stave off famine, but, as he stated in the story's preface, rather on how she had "been liberated from under the oppression of the forces of old society (*jiu shili*)," and because "I thought that how a person changed from not ever being a hero into a hero was also what everyone would like to know, I wrote this little book."[42] Most of the story focuses on the horrors of Meng Xianying's life as a young bride: Beaten by her husband, oppressed by her mother-in-law, she makes two failed suicide attempts before she becomes a village cadre as leader of the Women's National Salvation Association with the support of the party. She then moves on to her leadership position and is chosen as a labor heroine to attend the conference.

In biographical and critical studies on Zhao Shuli, the generic designation of this piece varies from reportage, feature, story, to biographical story, a reflection of the uncertain assessments of its degree of fictionality. Significantly, the story is subtitled "a true story" (*xianshi gushi*) and indeed the achievements of Meng Xiangying were reported on numerous times in the party newspaper, *Jiefang ribao* (*Liberation Daily*), but these were not aspects of the subject's life that Zhao Shuli covered. That the story was not entirely based on specific facts from her personal life but deduced from generalized situations is evident in a comment Zhao Shuli made many years later. In making the point that one "should not be in a rush to write, should not write on what one is not familiar with," he stated that the events he wrote about in "Meng Xiangying" were not his own life, but "were prevalent in the society of those days, and I had been used to seeing them."[43]

"Meng Xiangying Stands Up" may be seen as an example of the kind of genre that was an important "happening" during the Yan'an period, when poems, plays, and stories based on "true stories about real people" (*zhenren zhenshi*) were produced and performed before audiences, sometimes with the "real people" themselves participating on the stage. They presented heroic models for all to emulate. As Meng Xiangying comments on her experience within the story, one needs to "lead by doing the work oneself, and first set a good example (*mofan*)." (Confucianism had, of course, always placed much importance on models, but instead of the mythical sage kings Yao and Shun, the model is now an illiterate, impoverished, and oppressed peasant woman.)[44] The vision of the Chinese revolution had been premised on the ability and power of the masses to raise their consciousness, realize their latent resources, and transcend themselves through the revolutionary process. The "true story" of Meng Xiangying, who "changed from not ever being a hero into being a hero," is an example of how literature was being recruited to give form to this vision. Whether the events were entirely true mattered less than whether it conformed to the formula and served proper political ends. By professing to represent uplifting events taken from real life, from history actually in the making, and showcasing those whose powerful potential was being uncovered through participation in the process, literature could claim to be "realistic" and also serve the cause of revolution.

But the light-hearted tone of the narrative, given the tragic circumstances of Meng Xiangying's life as a cruelly victimized wife, creates a curiously discordant effect. When her husband, Meini, "hacked a bloody wound on Meng Xiangying's forehead, from which the blood kept gushing out even after they had been pulled apart,

> those who broke up the fight seemed to think that Meini had done wrong. Almost everyone said, "If you want to hit her, hit elsewhere, how come on the head?" They were only saying that he had hit her in the wrong place, nobody asked why he had hit her. According to the "old rules," there was no need to ask why a man had hit his wife.
>
> After the fight everyone dispersed; there wasn't any business left for them. The only person not to take it all so casually was Meng Xiangying herself.[45]

She makes her first suicide attempt. Another failed one follows. Regardless of what is happening, the narrator seems to take it all rather "casually" himself due to his determinedly upbeat manner, even when it seems incommensurate with the awful events narrated. Perhaps it is that facetious tone that enhanced the much touted "entertainment value" of Zhao Shuli's fiction. The audience knows that there is no need to be overly concerned, since the "bright side" will always win out and lead to a predetermined happy outcome.

Again, as in "Blackie Gets Married," most of the blame is placed on an old woman, on the upholder of "the old rules," Meng Xiangying's mother-in-law. She has a sharp tongue and heaps verbal abuse on her daughter-in-law. But nothing more is made of the physical violence Meng Xiangying endures from her husband nor is he described in any way. Certainly he was a major cause of her suffering, yet he occupies a strangely passive, faceless space in the narrative. Is it necessary to shield him from criticism perhaps because he is a male peasant of the younger generation, who are usually portrayed as "progressive" in Zhao Shuli's fiction?

In showing the hardships endured by Meng Xiangying under the old system, the story focuses its evils on one person—another woman—and moreover, an older woman, an easy target for satirical criticism. She is bad, but also portrayed as somewhat ridiculous. Such sexism is particularly hard to reconcile with the central message of the story which ostensibly is about how an oppressed peasant woman succeeds in "standing up" through the empowering efforts of the party.

In spite of all the rhetoric about equality between men and women, the party never mounted an effective challenge to masculine hegemony in rural China. Among the many reasons for its failure to deal with the multiple issues involved in women's oppression, one is no doubt the fact that the men who dominated the revolution never questioned their own sexist assumptions. These assumptions form part of the unconscious of Zhao Shuli's text.[46]

Questions can also be raised as to just what the celebrated liberation of woman means in the story's treatment of speech and language. Much is made of the fact that Meng Xiangying can talk; this is why the villagers recommended her to the party worker as possible leader of the Women's National Salvation Association in the first place. She also talks back to her mother-in-law, giving rise to some lively exchanges between them. Her later empowerment is due to her acquisition of party language through her participation in the revolutionary process. When a meeting against an enemy agent is organized, she hesitates at first about attending, then goes at the urging of the party worker, while wondering if she could avoid having to say anything: "Couldn't I just not talk?" (p. 76). But once she gets there and sees the crowd and the collective scramble to speak, she "soon leads the Xiyaokou villagers in shouting slogans" and "after the struggle meeting she became bolder." The woman speaks up, she has a strong voice, but is it mainly a voice through which the party communicates its revolutionary message? Will that be the only way in which she can speak from now on?

Throughout most of the story, the narrator assumes the stance of a chatty oral storyteller in giving out occasional background information: "But you mustn't think that just because they've been intermarrying for generations that every couple is happy, actually a lot of them are in an awful fix" (p. 67). But at the end, he interposes himself as the writer of the text to explain his conception of his task—primarily by playing down his own role. Since Meng Xiangying's remarkable achievements have all been reported in the press, he comments, "there is no need for me to go on about them" (p. 80). The story concludes with an imaginary dialogue between the narrator/writer as "I" and some readers asking questions about what's happening now and whether the characters of the mother-in-law and husband, written about rather "disrespectfully," would be given a chance to change. His closing response is that of a writer with a continuing commitment to record events as they unfold: "Meng Xiangying is only twenty-three years old this year. From now on a chapter will be added at each year's Labor Heroes' Conference. We'll see who has changed for the better and who for the worse, why should you worry that the writing might not be continued next year?" (p. 81).

In writing this "true story" about a revolutionary heroine, the writer defines himself as a mere transcriber, as one who places the act of writing in the service of real and ongoing facts. His only function is simply to follow them and write them down as they are and as they will be.[47]

There is little trace here of the self-reflexive questioning about writing, representation, and the positioning of the subjective self that was so prominent in Lu Xun's stories about oppressed peasants. In writing this "true story" to show how the party can empower even a poor woman peasant to transcend herself and contribute gloriously toward its collective goals, the writer need only become a self-effacing observer and transcribing medium. The operations of the writer, in serving the party's revolutionary goals, are now, it would seem, crystal clear. It would be the representation of the new peasant—in this case the new peasant woman, the doubly oppressed victim turned revolutionary model—who was, above all, "real," "out there," already in existence, a ready-made object merely requiring direct transference into literature.

Such a reduced, minimal conception of the writer, in which writing is treated as an activity of near self-erasure, since all the writer had to do was simply record the "true stories" of "real peasants," turned out, of course, to be impracticable (as well as contrary to the nature of writing.) For one thing, even if party ideologues could downgrade the mediating operations of the writer, or in effect deny the literary act itself, they would, as time went on, find it very difficult to be consistent about who the "real peasant" was. By the late 1950's, it would become increasingly impossible for Zhao Shuli to sustain even such a minimized writer's role.

A few months before "Meng Xiangying Stands Up" was written, Zhao Shuli had begun to examine the concept and role of the writer from several different angles in a longer work. In "Li Youcai banhua" ("The Rhymes of Li Youcai")[48] the relationship between oral folk tradition and the writer's textual production, and the multiple levels of self-representation this generates, are explored together against the party's function in the authorization of language and the literary process.

Li Youcai is a local folk artist, a "clapper talker" (*banren*), whose rhymed stanzas are inserted into the prose narrative. A supplemental source of information, his twelve verses also provide important commentary on the story's characters and events as they unfold. He is introduced by an I-narrator in the first section, "The Origin of the Book's Name:"

> From the time of the anti-Japanese war, many changes took place in Yanjiashan, and Li Youcai made up some new clapper talk (*kuaiban*) about them. This got him into trouble. I want to talk about these changes and have copied down some parts of his clapper talks during those changes for your diversion. As a result this book was written. (p. 20)

After speaking here as the author, the narrator drops the first-person narrational stance, and throughout the rest of the book assumes the voice of an omniscient third-person narrator to share the narration of the story with Li Youcai. The clapper talker functions alternately on both an extradiegetic (as narrating agent) and diegetic (as narrated object) level in that he also is described externally as he participates in the story's action.[49]

As one who has a clear-eyed view from above, as it were, of what is going on, Li Youcai plays an important role in the unfolding of the plot. The main action in the story revolves around the struggle to establish grass-roots level political power through the election of a village head in coordination with the movement for the reduction of rent and interest announced in January 1942. Although located within a Communist-controlled base area, the village is still in the hands of the entrenched "feudal" power of the local landlord, Yan Hengyuan, who has managed to manipulate the election process and through kinsmen or flunkies continue his stranglehold on the village offices. It is Li Youcai who through his clapper talk uncovers the villains and exposes their schemes.

An image of Li Youcai at work in this supra-narrative role is embedded in the story when one day he "happened to be on a hilltop, guarding someone's wheat" (p. 34). Looking down from that high vantage point, he observes the landlord Yan Hengyuan and his flunkies measuring the land and using false markers to conceal their actual holdings. The event is made into the subject of his new verses. Apart from this chance observation, the story does not otherwise explain how it is that Li Youcai comes to his superior understanding of a political situation so adroitly managed by the local power structure that even the authorities are fooled at first into conferring on the corrupt Yanjiashan the title of "model village."

With all his perspicacity, Li Youcai is nevertheless in his other role as narrated character just another poor peasant, another victim of the local landlord, who appropriates his land and expels him from the village when the verses exposing the land-measuring fraud spread in the community. Li's wisdom and talent are "officially" recognized when, his land restored and justice done, Comrade Yang, the chairman of the County Peasant Association who has come to investigate the village, gives him the assignment of composing a verse to sum up the events and commemorate the villagers' victory over the villains Yan Hengyuan and others. The "natural," intuitive wisdom of the peasant as embodied in this one character is thus shown to coincide with the party's final analysis of the situation and lends support to its policy.

As C. T. Hsia has noted, Li Youcai is largely a self-portrait of the author,[50] but the relationship with the author is carried out on several levels within the text and through a complex interaction between them. Li Youcai is, to begin with, a representative of one aspect of Zhao Shuli's creative activity, in that, as several critics have pointed out, Zhao himself similarly produced works in the clapper talk genre.[51] Even more important, as a fictionalized persona of the author within the text, Li Youcai functions as a mirror, an idealized self-image of the peasant writer, a literary species who can have it both ways: one who has the capacity to present the events of the story from a superior, authoritative stance of vision, knowledge, and literary skills, yet somehow manages to maintain his identity as "one of the peasant masses."

Through its incorporation of clapper talk within the narrative, "The

Rhymes of Li Youcai" is above all a response to Mao Zedong's call for
the use of national or folk forms, a practical example of the writer
speaking to and for the masses in their own language. The active presence of the peasant's voice would seem to be particularly appropriate in
this story, given its theme of peasants having their consciousness raised
by arriving at an awareness of their own participation in the revolution
and acting to overthrow the entrenched local power structure. But abstracted from its normal cultural context and endowed with a new political function, not much of the traditional popular clapper talk genre,
apart from some superficial formal trappings, survives the transplant into
Zhao Shuli's story. The writer's task, which was to transvalue popular
folk entertainment "meant shifting conventional associations of such
rhymes with the risqué and ribald release of sexual tension, and sometimes political ones as well, to new associations with political activism
and ultimately political panegyric, to express the will of the Communist
leadership on behalf of the peasantry."[52]

The first examples of Li Youcai's clapper talk in the story are two sat-
ires in verse, one on Yan Hengyuan who manipulates his re-election as
the village mayor year after year, and the other on his constantly blinking
and conniving elementary school teacher son. (As the only intellectual in
the story he is negatively portrayed.) The last examples are composed at
the request of the chairman of the County Peasant Association for the
purposes of recruiting for the peasant association and of celebrating in a
mass meeting the victory over the oppressors in the village. The folk en-
tertainer thus shifts from subject matter of the kind that could well have
been accommodated within the traditional popular genre to what is
unabashedly party-assigned agitational propaganda. Far from existing as
they are, national forms in the story are in effect being detached from
their folk origins, revised and adapted to new use.

Like Li Youcai, the narrator of the prose sections presents himself as a
type of folk artist as well. He assumes the persona of an oral storyteller as
he explains local terms and customs to the reader: "Songs like these are
called *geliuzui* around Yanjiashan; *kuaiban* in official speech (*guanhua*) "
(p. 18). He thus sets himself up as the mediator between the village
community and the broader readership "out there," between the two
languages of folk idiom and "official speech"—that is, standard Chinese.
The alternation between verse and prose throughout the story is likewise
inherited from the genre of oral storytelling, but the storyteller's traditional prerogative as commentator on unfolding events is given over to

the clapper talker, while the author/narrator remains in charge of plot action.

Along with this division of labor, the author/narrator incorporates local idioms and strives for a folksy down-to-earth style himself, seeking to make his own language and vision converge with that of the folk artist's, which is of course, actually created by him. The juxtaposition of two genres of different language and compositional forms—one more literary, intellectual, and modern, in spite of its adoption of the oral storyteller's voice, the other folk and traditional—within this joint narrative enterprise enables them to interact and create a relationship of mutual endorsement in the text.

Li Youcai's disconnected clapper verses are valorized by their placement in a modern narrative structure that links them and provides them with a framework of significant context. Within that structure the people will appear to have their say; their wisdom, their true perceptions of the world, are given a vocal presence. On the other hand, even though the "I" as narrator/author somewhat self-deprecatingly states at the beginning that the verses are merely offered up for "diversion" (*jiemen*), those verses evince the subordination of his literary craft to the masses and thereby validate his own credentials as a revolutionary writer.

Nevertheless both the story's narrator and the clapper talker are ultimately dependent for their legitimacy as "literary and art workers" (*wenyi gongzuozhe*) on the blessing of the party, represented in the story by Comrade Yang, chairman of the County Peasant Association. He is an example of a key figure who typically appears near the end of almost all of Zhao Shuli's stories. As the idealized party cadre sent down from "higher up," he can do no wrong and he can be counted on to set everything right in the end. In the process he himself will play a simulated two-way role of power and authority vis-à-vis the villagers.

When the chairman of the County Peasant Association first arrives at the mayor's office, it is in the guise, as it were, of a common peasant. Wearing a white shirt, dark blue trousers, and old, heavy shoes, a white towel wrapped around his head, he is taken for a mere messenger and rudely ignored. Zhao Shuli works in some nice comedy here as the mayor is required to carry out an abrupt about-face in his behavior when Comrade Yang's letter of introduction is produced, revealing that he is in fact a high level cadre. Rudeness immediately turns into fawning obsequiousness. But then when Comrade Yang demonstrates his willingness to join the poor peasants in their labor in the threshing field—he had worked ten years as a farmhand before—and eat the very same food they eat, they are convinced that he is "indeed one of us" (*zhenshi zijiren*) (p. 47). He is the exemplary upper-level cadre who can appear to be truly at one with the peasant masses.

But once Comrade Yang uncovers the true conditions of the village and identifies the villains, he will start throwing his weight around. It is his power and authority as a superior after all that enable him to summarily dismiss the chairman of the Village Peasant Association and bring in various district leaders to an organized mass struggle meeting. The meeting ends with Yan Hengyuan and his gang forced to refund extorted money, return foreclosed land, and effects a complete changeover in village administration.

Although Comrade Yang will claim that victory came about through the efforts of the people working together, he is in fact a deus ex machina who comes down from above and through authoritative intervention solves all problems and brings the events to a triumphant conclusion. For a work ostensibly about the rising revolutionary consciousness and power of the masses, most particularly of the lowest stratum of poor peasants, this reliance on a solution from top down may seem ironic and paradoxical. Yet it is a general pattern in Zhao Shuli's fiction, a pattern that is also reflected in the stratification and interaction of the several levels of discourse within the text.

For all the attempts to incorporate folk tradition, to promote the language, forms, and voices of the common people, the last word is given to the official voice and language of the party. This is the ultimate contradiction in the professed message of adopting the speech and enhancing the power of the common people. To carry out revolution in the Chinese countryside, the party was in fact not drawing upon the language as spoken by them, but imposing a new abstract language translated from the West or borrowed from Japan. In "The Rhymes of Li Youcai" these would include, as Edward Gunn has pointed out, such phrases as "importance" (*zhongyaoxing*), "significance" (*yiyi*), "organize" (*zuzhi*), "status, identity" (*shenfen*), and others.[53] Although such language is mocked by Li Youcai when evoked in meetings by the party worker Zhang (a "bad" cadre who is out of touch with the people), it is the same kind of Euro-Japanese bureaucratic language that is used in the "good" cadre Comrade Yang's letter of introduction. To stand up for themselves, take charge, speak up in struggle meetings, overthrow the traditional power structure headed by the local landlord despot, peasants will need to subordinate themselves to the party authority, and do all that, not through their own language, but through the new empowering partyspeak.

While "The Rhymes of Li Youcai" is both thematically and formally constructed around the speech of peasant oral storytelling, that speech loses its autonomy once it is framed within the context of the author's narrative. And whatever possibilities there might be of internal dialogism between the languages of the people within the text are finally suppressed in order to unify all under a single ideological system represented by a dominant discourse.

When Little Yuan is scolded by his uncle Old Chen for acting like a big shot after he is elected head of the local militia, the (unnamed) visiting chief of the district militia issues him this stern reprimand:

> "I'm giving you one month to correct all these faults and I'm telling all the village officials to keep their eyes on you. If you haven't changed within one month, don't expect any polite treatment!" When Old Chen heard this, he slapped his knee in approval. "Good old comrades! You've said it all! Everything that I wanted to say to him!" (p. 58).

What the plot action contrives to bring about is the peasant's recognition that the official final word turns out exactly to express his own intentions. And when Li Youcai composes a final verse that is authorized by Comrade Yang as the grand conclusion of the struggle (*douzheng*) depicted in the story, these two kinds of discourse, that of the people's artist and that of the party, through the mediation of the authorial discourse, converge to bring the narrative to closure. The voice of the party authorizes the wrapping up of the traditional oral storyteller when Comrade Yang comments: "That rhyme about sums up the whole business!" His presence is mandatory, both to effect the positive outcome of the story's action, but also to endorse the literary efforts of those who represent it, including by extension the implied author behind the scenes.

In 1950 Zhao Shuli adopted the storyteller form (*pingshu*) in the short story "Dengji" ("Registration"). Although the storyteller/narrator "I" there makes a strong overt presence at the beginning of the story, engaging in direct dialogue with his audience, the "friends who are listening to this story," he withdraws toward the end, and the last section, "Who should do self-criticism?" (*gaishui jiantao*), ends with the district party secretary giving a summarizing speech apportioning praise and blame and extolling the virtues of the marriage law.[54] Zhao Shuli also wrote an unfinished novel *Lingquandong* (*Lingquan Cave*)[55] in *pingshu* style, the first part of which was published in 1958. Besides these works in the storyteller genre, Zhao Shuli used other traditional folk forms such as drum songs (*guci*), and clapper talks (*kuaiban*), but "The Rhymes of Li Youcai" is the only work in which the "author" and folk artist interaction is written into the course of the narrative.[56]

IDEOLOGY, REALISM, AND THE PEASANT CHARACTER

The three stories I have analyzed above were all produced between 1943 and 1944, when Zhao Shuli was starting out on his career as a peasant writer under the enthusiastic sponsorship of the party. Both writer and party were engaged in a cooperative effort to define, shape, and indeed create the mold to bring such a writer into being. Yet from the very beginning, as we have seen, there are observable fissures and discrepancies in the goals and process of that project. Each story demonstrates in different ways the tensions between supposedly reflected "reality" and predetermined ideology, between popular tradition and textual authority, while pointing up the uncertain role of the writer caught between the proclaimed empowerment of the people on the one hand and authoritative party control on the other.

The dilemmas of a "peasant writer" are enacted within these stories through various stand-ins as folk artist, as oral storyteller, or as self-effacing transcriber. But even on the level of revolutionary content, there is a question as to whether the stories manage to communicate an unambiguous message of liberation of the oppressed, particularly of women. Zhao Shuli's early fiction is especially instructive when subjected to rereading, because even as he was working out the formulas for this newly programmed literature, its inner contradictions were already being revealed in various levels of the text.

Many of the difficulties that Zhao Shuli went on to experience in his subsequent career can be traced to the attempts of ideology to repress or gloss over these unresolved contradictions, and these difficulties are demonstrated most concretely in the controversies over his treatment of the peasant.

When Zhao Shuli began, it was his images of the new peasants that were quickly seized upon by his early promoters, who saw them as a new phenomenon in literature and a particular cause for celebration. The comments in 1947 of Chen Huangmei, vice director of the Writer's Union of the Shanxi-Hebei-Shandong-Henan Border Region, while more effusive than most, are nevertheless characteristic:

> When his pen turns to peasants and the young generation, it flows with am-
> ple sympathy and warm love, the tip of his pen begins to vibrate, how lovable
> does he make those new peasants who have grown to maturity in the midst of
> bitter struggle! He eulogizes these characters, eulogizes their youth, their en-
> thusiasm, their bravery and resourcefulness, their hatred of the landlord.[57]

The goal of critical practice was to read Zhao Shuli's characters primarily
for the purpose of finding images of the new peasant that would confirm
the ideology of a peasant-based revolution.

It was to reinforce the claim that these portraits of the new peasant
were accurate, "true" reflections of reality, that much emphasis was
placed on the writer's first-hand knowledge of the peasantry. As Chen
Huangmei goes on to say, everything in Zhao Shuli's works seemed so
natural and free of artifice: "We believe the reason is that he has a clear
class standpoint; he lives with the characters in his works, struggles together with them, his thoughts and feelings are totally merged with those
of the people, with those of the peasants he portrays." His proper class
background was all important: "Of course, Comrade Zhao Shuli came
from a family of poor peasants, grew up in the countryside, was familiar
with the life of the masses. . . . Like a peasant he lived together with
peasants, he has a very concrete understanding of the people. This is
something we should emulate also" (p. 199).

Zhou Yang, who between 1942 and 1966 increasingly took on the role
of chief interpreter of Mao's ideas on literature, had made the same point
the year before: "These are nothing more than ordinary (*putong*) peasants. . . . Struggle has educated them, nurtured the activists (*jiji fenzi*)
among them. What Comrade Zhao Shuli's work reflects is the wisdom,
the strength, the revolutionary optimism of the peasants."[58] Again situating the writer "with" his characters: "He has not stood outside the
struggle, but has stood inside it . . . stood on the side of the peasants, he
is one of them (*tamen zhongjian de yige*)" (p. 186). In this way, Zhou
Yang argues "it is possible truly to integrate the standpoint of the masses
and the method of realism (p. 187)."

But in spite of such euphoric beginnings, it was precisely this yardstick of the "realism" of his peasant portrayal by which both fiction and
writer were to be measured that would later turn out to jeopardize Zhao
Shuli's standing as a "peasant writer."

As the political climate changed, increasingly stringent demands were being made on literature. The precarious balancing act required to portray "true" peasants was becoming more difficult to sustain, as can be seen in the title of an article that appeared in *Wenyibao* in 1959, attacking a story written by Zhao Shuli the year before: "A Story that Distorts Reality: Reflections after Reading 'Duanlian duanlian.'" Pointing to the lazy women, "classless, backward, selfish to the point of committing thievery" in the story, the critic asks, "Does this indeed correspond to the reality of the countryside (*fuhe nongcun xianshi*)? Could this be a true portrait (*zhenshi xiezhao*) of peasant women?"[59] Whereas criticism some ten years earlier had nothing but praise for the "truth" of Zhao Shuli's peasant portrayals, he was now attacked for "distorting and vilifying" the peasant, for failing to truly reflect reality as it was.

What had changed, what was different from before, was not so much the writer, nor his subject, but the demands to construct an ever more positive and heroic peasant. The "reality of the countryside" was in the process of being redefined to meet new requirements of party policy. Driven by the need to overcome the sluggish performance in the agricultural sector, but also frustrated with the problems of excessive centralization and a bloated bureaucracy, Mao Zedong was pushing for rapid transformation through the mass campaign approach, in order to unleash and mobilize peasant know-how and energy in a bottom-up process. Greater and greater stake was placed on the quality of the common peasant that would make everything possible. Peasants were what the revolution was counting on to work with; they constituted the material, the energy, the resources that party leadership could tap and mobilize to carry the revolutionary experiment to a victorious conclusion. The obstruction of a few backward peasants that might be left could easily be neutralized. As the momentum of mass movement fed upon itself, spiraling into an unfounded optimism and wildly inflated estimates of increased production, it seemed that even the propagandists themselves came to accept their wishful thinking for the future as present fact. Peasants were collectively transformed into superheroes, remaking history, accomplishing the impossible; a "reality" that would shape their representation in literature.

The antirightist drive had begun in June 1957; the Great Leap Forward's basic principles were formulated in August 1958. All these intensified the pressure on literature to support and illustrate the new policies (*tujie zhengce*). No one would deny that "realism" remained the basic premise of literature, but it was a realism that in fact was already being somewhat qualified when in the 1940's it began to be preceded by the modifier "revolutionary." In March of 1958, Mao Zedong imposed further modifications in decreeing that "proletarian literature and art should adopt the creative method of combining revolutionary realism and revolutionary romanticism."[60] To combine realism and romanticism was to blur the line between the projection into a utopian future to come and the description of the actual conditions of the historical present. All discourse, official and literary, came to be locked into the mode of celebration; indeed the language of celebration, or rather of self-congratulation, was the only one sanctioned.

Zhao Shuli's *Sanliwan* (*Sanliwan Village*) of 1955, based on material about the experiment in agricultural cooperatives in 1951 and 1952, was advertised as a work that "truly reflects the new face of the countryside" (*zhenshi de fanying le nongcun de xin mianmao*).[61] Yet it was also "endowed with a long-range perspective and elements of 'idealism.'"[62] Embedded in the novel is an episode that mirrors its own imaging of the future within the present.

The novel's action focuses on the "ideological struggle" (*sixiang douzheng*) that takes place in a remote, drought-plagued mountain village when the peasants are being mobilized to expand the agricultural cooperative and dig an irrigation canal. They must overcome the opposition of backward "feudal" old peasants as well as those middle peasants with "capitalist tendencies" seeking to enrich themselves. To this process of struggle a local painter, Lao Liang, makes a significant contribution with a realistic panoramic water color of the village. The peasants are dazzled: "It really looks like the place." "From a distance it looks as if one could walk right into it!" Then Wang Yusheng, a character with little schooling but a talent for technical innovation—in C. T. Hsia's words, a "sort of youthful Edison,"[63] or, perhaps one could say, an embodiment of peasant wisdom and ingenuity—asks Lao Liang whether he could paint something that does not exist—"Sanliwan after the canal is built".[64] The painter obliges. Within a matter of days, he produces not only "an elevated Sanliwan," "tomorrow's Sanliwan," showing an early autumn scene with the finished canal with tributaries, seven water wheels, abundant water flowing through a land of bountiful harvest, but also a third painting, "Sanliwan in the Era of Socialism," including thick forests, a north—south highway, automobiles, electric wire poles, new houses, complete with harvesters, hoeing machines, purported to be "very much like today's state farms" (p. 128).

In this emblematic episode, Lao Liang becomes a stand-in for the writer himself, as one who creates a work for peasants who "had never seen Sanliwan in a painting before"—a work by and about peasants— and now praised "for having made it much more beautiful than the original" (p. 128). His painting enacts the role that all literature and art were expected to play in a revolution conceptualized as continuous: to provide a vision of the future and thus raise the consciousness and generate the will to make possible the collective's movement from the present onto the next stage of development. In the representations of this continuing process, the emphasis cannot be on a reality as it is, but on a reality coming into being. The "three paintings" of present, tomorrow, and socialist future are superimposed in a form of telescopic perception, and the idealized future incorporated, portrayed, as if it were already in the present.[65] Whereas in his earlier fiction, when Zhao Shaoli was portraying peasants making the transition from the old society and was mainly required to be "realistic," in this time of "socialist construction of the countryside," he was expected to move beyond present reality into a visionary future.

The same blurring of "realism" and "romanticism" can be observed in the useful ambiguity surrounding the term *dianxing* as applied to fictional characters. Engels' definition of realism in his letter to Margaret Harkness, as "the truthful reproduction of typical characters under typical circumstances,"[66] was quoted by many critics who took *dianxing* in its meaning of "model," or "standard," rather than "characteristic" or "representative." Since all these meanings can apply in the Chinese term, its ambiguity made it particularly suitable for a literary approach demanding that peasant characters be both "reflections of reality" and inspirational role models in revolutionary struggle.

Sanliwan was initially greeted as the first novel to present "socialist new peasants," but later, as with other works of Zhao Shuli, it was criticized for being far more successful in its portrayal of characters from the "old" generation (*lao zi bei*), than of those from the "new" or "little" generation (*xiao zi bei*). Zhao Shuli himself fretted over this nagging defect in his fiction, acknowledging that he "wrote more about the old than about the new" because he had more contact with and a better understanding of old—as opposed to new—people and old events. "It was easier to make the old more lifelike (*shengdonghua*), whereas unavoidably the new might be written somewhat according to a general concept, formularized (*gainianhua*)."[67] Perhaps the writer was admitting more than he thought here by setting up a comparison between what was more "lifelike" and what conformed to "concept" or "formula." He is reported to have told his fellow writer Kang Zhuo in 1952 when chided for his failure with new characters, "But I've never seen one" (*mei jian guo*). In the following year he was taken by Kang Zhuo to Hebei to visit villages and meet "new characters,"[68] and he continued to seek out such opportunities for the purpose of transcribing them into his fiction, but the fact that he never managed to overcome this "shortcoming" points up the conflict between basing literature on experiences derived from "life" and meeting the requirements of party policies. This was the crux of the problem in representing the new peasant character.

COMPLIANCE AND PROTEST—THE FATE OF ZHAO SHULI

As Zhao Shuli continued his writing career the strains in the constant struggle to reconcile a realist aesthetics with the party line become more pronounced. It had seemed at first that a combination of the two was workable because his fiction was oriented toward the immediate and the pragmatic. In 1949 he had written that his themes came from his work among the masses, the problems he encountered "that had to be solved but were not that easily solved,"[69] so he wrote about them in what he would later call "problem stories" (*wenti xiaoshuo*). Then six years later in a somewhat self-critical piece, he emphasized that from the beginning he had tried to coordinate his writings with political tasks of the moment;[70] perhaps problems arose, he said, when in rushing to write, he might not have been adequately prepared. The dual commitment to work among the masses and to adhere to party policies created dilemmas that drove him to vacillate between compliance and protest, and, as it turned out, created a gulf between his published fiction and some of his "unpublishable" writings.[71]

His struggle to reconcile what he knew about the countryside and what was required of him as a writer is implied in a talk, "Dangqian chuangzuo zhong de jige wenti" ("Some Current Problems About Writing"). He refers (characteristically) to a leader's (*lingdao tongzhi*) comments that it is only when one is separated from the people that literature for the purpose of "carrying out assigned tasks" (*gan renwu*) becomes a problem. For the "tasks" put forth by the higher authorities are all problems that had already long existed among the people.

If you live among the masses and contribute your own efforts, all you have to do is to write about the fresh things (*xinxian shiwu*) that you personally experience, then your work will coincide with the commands of the authorities. You won't feel they are sudden, nor will you feel you are carrying out an assigned task.[72]

But by 1959, when this talk was given, the Great Leap Forward had been launched, and the underlying assumption that the leadership was infallible, always truly in accord with the people, so that the writer need only go among the people to get things right, was being more and more questioned by what Zhao Shuli was "personally experiencing" in the countryside.

When the People's Republic was established, the peasant writer, like so many other writers and intellectuals, had moved to the capital city of Beijing and was ensconced in the establishment as a bureaucrat, editor, and professional writer in the pay of the state. Within a short time, he became editor of *Wenyibao,* was on the editorial board of the Popular Literature series, was elected chairman of the Association for the Study of Mass Literature and Art, and was appointed head of the Folk Art Reform Section in the Ministry of Culture, to mention a few of his posts. In the 1950's, there began pro and con debates over his individual works, criticism of his editorship of the journal for popular literature, *Shuoshuo changchang* (*Telling, Singing*), and of his positions during the Wu Xun and anti–Hu Feng campaigns. These criticisms Zhao Shuli more or less weathered while he continued to produce stories and novels to portray what was going on in the contemporary countryside to reflect the successive phases of "revolutionary struggle." He would return to the countryside for months at a time to maintain contacts and collect material for the stories that would continue to "document" the phases of rural socialist construction. But during those times he was also observing the actual conditions of the countryside. And in letters and talks he spoke of his concerns over lowered production, shortages of food and fodder, excessive control by bad cadres, and decline of morale—in spite of the collectivization efforts about which he had written so glowingly in his fiction.

He submitted letters and memos to the authorities, to the Changzhi prefectural party committee, among others. One long essay of some 230,000 words, that came to be known as his "Ten Thousand Word Document" (*wanyan shu*), "My Views on How the Commune Should Lead Agricultural Production," was addressed all the way up to the

party's Central Committee. In it he listed the problems with party policies as administered in the countryside. He submitted it in September
1959 to the party periodical *Hongqi* (*Red Flag*), but it was never accepted
for publication and only excerpts survive.[73] (That this document should
be categorized as a *wanyan shu* links it in a rather striking way to the tradition of literary martyrdom. Apart from the matter of length, the term
referred to long memorials to the throne, especially from officials who
were earnestly remonstrating or presenting proposals for reform that
could, and often did, have serious consequences for their careers or even
their lives.)

The unpublished *wanyan shu* became known when it was used by the
party group of the Writers' Union as damning evidence of Zhao Shuli's
"rightist tendencies" in a campaign of criticism against him that ran from
November to the following February. But in August 1962, during a period when the party was making some attempts to correct "leftist errors,"
the Writers' Union convened a meeting of sixteen writers at Dalian for a
discussion of short stories on countryside themes. The talk then was
about the need to "go deeper into realism" and accommodate "middle
characters" in fiction.[74] During this Dalian meeting the earlier verdict on
Zhao Shuli was reversed; now his "writing about the duration and hardship of struggle" was lauded as a victory for realism.[75] But the rehabilitation turned out to be all too brief. Two years later the attack on "middle
characters" began; he returned to work in Shanxi, determined to write
about "heroes."[76] But the Cultural Revolution soon followed, and Zhao
Shuli became a main target of struggle. His submitted document on
commune leadership as well as other unpublished pieces were brought
out as the grounds for branding Zhao Shuli one of the "reactionary
gang" (*heibang*) and a "capitalist roader."[77]

These are just some of the highlights in Zhao Shuli's later career to
indicate its up-and-down pattern as he sought to sustain the difficult
synchronization among party policy, work with the masses, and literary
practice. He confessed in one of his self-criticisms (at least eight survive),
written during the early stages of the Cultural Revolution, that it was
during the organization of communes that his "own thinking began to
fall out of step with work in the countryside . . . was unable to keep up
with the political mainstream . . . so he had failed to reflect in his writings the unimaginably (*buke xiangxiang*) great accomplishments of the
state."[78] He is confessing to his failures here, but admitting, perhaps
ironically, that he indeed had had problems with the credibility of the

party's grandiose claims. He is quoted as having once said in a talk some years earlier, "I do not have the courage to add more idealization in my works, I would rather believe my own eyes,"[79] an explanation, it would seem, for the falling off of his fiction writing during his last years.

Self-confessions always make for painful reading, but as the persecution of Zhao Shuli intensified, he was no doubt pressured to go further in his later confessions (which are unpublished) in abject, self-demeaning admissions of failure. And how is one to gauge their reliability as indexes to what the writer really thought? During a struggle session in 1967, Zhao Shuli is reported to have expressed some doubts as to whether, in spite of his great efforts to make his fiction easy to understand (*tongsu yidong*), it had really been read by that many who were truly peasants (*zhenzheng de nongmin*). After some investigation, he had discovered that those who liked to read his fiction were mainly middle school students and teachers of middle and elementary school. He should therefore turn to writing plays instead. The discovery had "greatly disappointed" him.[80] Whether Zhao Shuli ever actually came to this conclusion himself, it is more likely than not that his fiction never really succeeded in reaching the broad peasant masses as his party promoters had continually claimed.[81]

The Cultural Revolution of course put an end to his writing activities, but even during the five or six years before that, Zhao Shuli's creative output had been showing signs of decline. Only one of the eight stories from that period was written entirely on his own initiative, the others having been assigned by Party cadres or produced at the request of periodical editors.[82] Two stories on model peasants, "The Unglovable Hands" ("Tao bu zhu de shou") and "The Down-to- Earth Worker Pan Yongfu" ("Shiganjia Pan Yongfu"),[83] are more in the nature of character sketches. On the one hand his idealized treatment of the protagonists in the two stories can be seen as conforming to the higher standards for model heroic figures, but on the other, their selfless and pragmatic conduct has been interpreted by some as counterexamples, "going against the prevailing wind" (*dingfeng*) of empty "boasting and exaggeration." As is so often the case, in his efforts to walk the fine line between "truth to life" and ideological conformity, even in these rather simplistic pieces, Zhao Shuli produced fiction that critics, depending on their point of view, have been able to read as expressions of either compliance or protest.

During the Cultural Revolution campaign against him, a few of the stories written after 1958 had been singled out as "poisonous weeds," but from the time the campaign began in August 1966, his attackers focused primarily on letters, talks, the "Ten Thousand Word Document," and other memos he had submitted to party authorities.[84] The accusations against him as "reactionary," "anti-party," "the deadly enemy of poor and middle peasants," etc., appeared to target him not so much for his published fiction, but for having expressed his concerns in various forms over the effects of misguided party policies in the countryside.

Had this "peasant writer" misunderstood his role as representative and spokesman for the peasant in taking it so seriously? Zhao Shuli repeatedly risked speaking out in protest because he apparently believed he indeed had an obligation to speak for the actual conditions of the peasantry—and that he would be heeded. This may be an indication of the idealism—and naïveté?—with which he submitted himself to participate in the construction of his role as a writer. He willingly accepted his assigned place, without realizing that its limits would become ever more restrictive, that his own perceived commitment to the people he spoke for would turn out to be a transgression. In the end he was fated to suffer under a brutal campaign when the single-minded ideological fanaticism of the Cultural Revolution closed in on him.

Zhao Shuli's fate may have been sealed in March 1965 when he was sent (whether at his own request or in exile) to Jincheng, Shanxi, as deputy secretary of the county party committee, in charge of the work in the culture office. Fourteen months later the attacks against him began. The campaign in Shanxi against Zhao Shuli was pursued with particular ruthlessness, eighty-eight articles attacking him having appeared in the local provincial paper alone between July 1970 and July 1971,[85] including one that attacked him as a "deadly enemy of poor middle and lower peasants."[86] He was shunted back and forth between Changzhi and Taiyuan for struggle meetings, beatings, labor reform, and periods of "cow shed" imprisonment. During one of the struggle sessions in 1967 his ribs were broken, making every breath painful for him for the last three years of his life. The terrible physical sufferings of Zhao Shuli ended only with his death in September 1970.

THERE IS A tragic dimension to the life of every writer that appears in the pages of this book; each one in a different way has been a victim of political persecution. The case of Zhao Shuli is particularly problematic. Shortly before he died, during his daughter's last visit to him, when he was being held in the Military Control Unit of the Higher People's Court of Shanxi Province, he gave her a poem of Mao Zedong's that he had just painstakingly copied to give to the party. The poem is in traditional *ci* form, written by Mao in 1961 as a counterresponse to a poem, "On the Plum Tree" ("Yong mei"), by the Song poet Lu Yu (1125–1210). At this moment, Zhao Shuli the peasant writer would seem to be making an oblique connection between himself and the classical literary tradition, but it places him in an even more ambiguous relation to political power. While the plum tree that blooms in the snow in Mao Zedong's poem may be read as a harbinger of spring, traditionally it is also a symbol for protesting one's personal integrity, particularly in the midst of political adversity.[87] Does Zhao Shuli, albeit using words of Chairman Mao, intend it as an image of himself? How should one interpret this final gesture on his part, or consider him overall as a martyred writer?

In many ways he can be accused of complicity in his own calamitous fate, in that he not only accepted party control over his own writing, but actively promoted and enthusiastically supported that control through his own creative efforts. It is ironic to note that his fashioning of idealized peasant images is parallel to the party's effort to process him into a model peasant writer, and how both become unsustainable in the end. The folk artist Li Youcai, whose clapper talk verses are featured and celebrated in Zhao Shuli's story, is apparently apotheosized but also diminished. Liberated from the landlord who could evict him at will, he then comes under total party control, able to speak only at its sufferance, and only according to its prescriptions.[88] This may be considered yet one more way in which Zhao Shuli's fictional character mirrors the condition of its author.

Within the narrow restrictions that Zhao Shuli chose to operate in, he was able to explore in his fiction through various forms of textual self-representations some of the contradictions of the peasant/writer role. The divergent interpretations possible of his stories show that he was not just a literary hack blindly submitting to the authorities and merely reproducing formulas. His stories need not be read for their portrayal of peasant characters or information about the historical transformation of the countryside, for what might be called their "realistic" content. Rather their interest lies in the experimental adaptation of folk forms, the lively play of language and surface textual complexity.

With all his efforts to conform to the escalating demands of party policy, Zhao Shuli sought to preserve some space in which he could carry out his commitment to the peasant as well as cultivate his literary craftsmanship. In his fiction, but even more outside of it, he incurred the risks of speaking up for those he was supposed to represent. If one may be permitted a value judgment, Zhao Shuli comes off much better than the party that created him, and that later, while itself caught in a self-destructive mode, also destroyed him. What the radical reversals in the career of this once model peasant writer dramatize are the extreme consequences of the party's peasant-centered revolutionary ideology for literature.

5

Reassessing the Past in the "New Era": Gao Xiaosheng

WHEN GAO XIAOSHENG'S stories began to appear to wide acclaim in 1978 and 1979, almost a decade after Zhao Shuli's death, he was immediately heralded as a new "peasant writer," an example of the "new realism" characteristic of literature in the post-Mao era. His portraits of peasants had broken through the ideological mold into which they had been cast for the past three decades, and were, so it seemed, much truer to life and "reality."

Unlike Zhao Shuli, he was considered qualified to assume the mantle of new spokesman for the peasant by credentials that did not originate from his class background, but rather from the fact that just as he was beginning his literary career, he had been sent down to the countryside as a rightist in 1958 for labor reform. After twenty years of living and laboring among the peasants, he was supposedly someone who could come back and "tell it like it was."

The fiction that has been produced by Gao Xiaosheng indeed mostly takes place in the countryside, but to say that what we are getting is finally the "real" peasant is to oversimplify what this writer is about. His early narratives about the countryside undergoing socialist reconstruction cover much of the same period as those of Zhao Shuli, but his peasants are not featured as heroic protagonists of class struggle. As Gao Xiaosheng himself has put it, peasants had not been the "main character" in the literature of the revolution, but rather had been used as "a foil, a piece of material evidence. The main characters have been the basic-level cadres, who may have been peasants to begin with, but are now carrying out policy in the countryside. The peasants are there to prove that the policy is correct."[1] In fact, one might almost say that the fiction of this writer, in portraying Chen Huansheng's ongoing hunger or the repeated failures of Li Shunda to build a house, would seem to provide "material evidence" of the opposite. Instead of illustrating the correctness of the party's policy, the conditions of the peasant become a means to challenge it, indeed to contest the master narrative of the Chinese revolution.

Because there is always an implication that more is going on than is evident on the surface, a Gao Xiaosheng story about any individual character will lend itself to being read as a distillation of larger issues. While his peasants are often shown as victimized by misguided party policies, a question often raised by his fiction is to what extent the general nature of the victim (for in spite of the range and complexity of his peasant characters, the tendency to consider them as a somewhat monolithic mass persists) may have contributed to his own condition.

These issues are not discussed explicitly in the texts, but are mostly suggested through the adroit use of irony and the ambiguous stance adopted by the narrator toward his subject. Gao Xiaosheng takes great pains to situate his characters in the specific context of Party policies toward the peasant, just like all the socialist realists who are presumed to be faithfully recording events taking place in the Chinese Communist version of the historical world. But the way he incorporates into his own narrative texts the slogans, formulas, and propaganda stock phrases of each political moment in effect shows how this party language, as literally understood and applied by his peasants, will turn out to work against itself.

In Gao Xiaosheng's fiction, intellectuals who have had, as a result of campaigns against them, to submit to the life and labor of the countryside, most often under the "supervision of the masses," are placed in a rather ambiguous position vis-à-vis the peasantry, neither one of distinct superiority nor of subordination. Similarly caught in the political confusion of the times, they are fellow victims themselves. What their portraits reveal, as compared with those of the peasant, is a greater self-awareness, particularly of their own fumbling inadequacies. Gao Xiaosheng's fiction has raised the representation of the peasant and his relation to the writing self to another level of moral and political complexity. This complexity comes through in the situational and verbal irony of his stories. One finds little drama there; instead what matters are details of events and the nuances of language in depicting them. Because so much takes place on the micro-level of language, extensive quotations will be necessary to convey a sense of the characteristic effects of his distinctive narratives.

ANOTHER ZHAO SHULI OR ANOTHER LU XUN?

One initial critical reaction when Gao Xiaosheng's stories appeared on the scene was to see him as the successor, or even the "reincarnation," so to speak, of Zhao Shuli. As one 1982 article enthusiastically put it, "those peasant masses who had deeply cherished the memory of the people's writer Zhao Shuli were rushing about spreading the news that 'Old Zhao has returned, Old Zhao has come back to life.'"[2] Leaving aside whether this comment is based on factual observation or whether the peasant mass-es indeed ever constituted the core readership of either writer, to place Gao Xiaosheng's fiction within the hallowed tradition of "peasant writer" established by Zhao Shuli is first of all a mark of positive endorsement.

In their comparisons, critics would go on to point out the differences between the two, or more particularly, the ways in which Gao Xiaosheng, while carrying on from Zhao Shuli, is seen as having sur-passed his predecessor: "The mission that Zhao Shuli had not been able to complete has fallen on the shoulders of a new generation of writers. Gao Xiaosheng, in portraying the tortuous and tumultuous past thirty years of the historical fate of contemporary peasants, has continued in greater depth the explorations of Zhao Shuli."[3] In making the point about the "historical limitations" of the fiction of Zhao Shuli, who after all had to labor under severe constraints at a time when literature was "in the service of politics" (wei zhengzhi fuwu), these critics were also cele-brating the relative openness of the post-Mao era that was making fiction such as that of Gao Xiaosheng possible.

What is implied, if not explicitly stated, is that the peasant need no longer be conceived only as an ideological construct of the party tailored to its revolutionary strategy. The "peasant," either as portrayed in fiction, or as an assumed component of the writer's identity, could, due to the current "deepening of realism," be expected to be a different kind of character. In other words, literature was now said to be "realistic," not because it conformed to the party's version of history, but rather because it questioned it. Making much of Gao Xiaosheng's twenty years of exile in the countryside during which he lived and toiled like a peasant, these critics have centered their arguments around the authenticity and "realism" of his representations.

On the other hand, Gao Xiaosheng has also been increasingly compared with Lu Xun, not so much—with the exception of Ah Q[4]—for his peasant characters, but for the ironic effects of his language and his subtle techniques of satire.[5]

In Mao Zedong's 1942 "Talks at the Yan'an Forum on Literature and Art," intellectuals had been exhorted to learn from Lu Xun's example of serving the proletariat and the masses, but at the same time warned against writing satire in the Lu Xun manner, since there is no need to be "obscure or devious" in the Border Regions where "revolutionary writers and artists are given complete democratic freedom".[6] If critics have emphasized the linkage between Lu Xun and Gao Xiaosheng, now writing some sixty years later, it has been to hail the welcome revival of the satirical tradition. This revival is perceived as another indicator of the relatively liberalized situation in the post-Mao era. When literature was under the domination of Maoist control, the mode of satire, which relies always on indirection, implication, if not "obscurity or deviousness," had been seen as incompatible with the requirement that literature be a direct, "realistic" reflection of life and carry a clear and explicit political message. But "now after the great [historical] turning point" as one critic put it, "how the new era of modernization longs for literary history to give us a new Lu Xun!"[7]

The claim that Gao Xiaosheng has "inherited the tradition from Lu Xun to Zhao Shuli, and thereby achieved the image of the third generation of peasants in modern literature" emerged soon after his fiction appeared.[8] Frequent comparisons have been made with the portrayal of peasants in the two earlier writers, each supposedly having represented a different generation. But quite apart from the question of whether Chinese peasants in fact can be so neatly slotted into clear historical categories, what does it really mean to compare Gao Xiaosheng to two such utterly dissimilar writers as Lu Xun and Zhao Shuli?

In his self-conscious exploitation of the resources of language to achieve satirical effects, Gao Xiaosheng may be said to be reminiscent of Lu Xun. And like Zhao Shuli he meticulously follows the events of recent political history in situating his stories, while often adopting the chatty tone of an oral storyteller. However, whatever he may have "inherited" from either is combined into something quite new, in which the "two sides," so to speak, of Gao Xiaosheng—verbal play and historical specificity—will be found to exist in creative tension.

Many of his stories foreground the opacity and materiality of language, directing the reader's attention away from a close, direct relation with historical reality. Others thematize the problematics of that relation through events within the fictional text. By means of his own special use of language, Gao Xiaosheng deflates the construction through language of history. He has turned out to be a prolific writer since his return from exile in the countryside, experimenting with a wide range of themes and methods that challenge the earlier—and less complicated—paradigms of the peasant, whether as the oppressed victim of the May Fourth generation or as the revolutionary vanguard of Maoist ideology as molded in Yan'an.

REAPPRAISAL OF LITERATURE ON THE COUNTRYSIDE AND THE "NEW REALISM"

It is not only Chinese critics, but their Western counterparts as well, who have viewed Chinese literature in the post-Mao era as a "return of 'critical realism.'" Michael Duke describes it as a return to the tradition of realist fiction with a "critical edge and humanistic thrust" that developed during the May Fourth period, a tradition that was suspended when literature became "the handmaiden of the Party."[9] Understandably, many Chinese critics are not yet ready to discuss the issues of realism versus party domination in such stark oppositional terms. Instead they have engaged in tortuous debates over how to formulate and reassess the relation between party-dominated literature and the historical reality of the period during which it was produced.

The problem of reconciling the dual requirements that literature be "realistic" and that literature "serve politics" has always been particularly acute in fiction on the countryside, since the "cooperative transformation of agriculture" had been one of the dominant themes under party-directed literature. That problem is enormously compounded now since it is precisely in that area where the most drastic revisions of party policies in the post-Mao era have been made. When historical reality had been defined and conceptualized in terms of party policies toward the countryside, Maoist literature, to be deemed realistic, had to reflect the struggle—since that was what was going on—between the two lines of collectivization versus individual entrepreneurship.

However, with the adoption of the "contract responsibility system," the dismantling of communes, the encouragement to individuals to get rich, and with the official ending of such slogans as "Take class struggle as the key link" and "Continue revolution under the dictatorship of the proletariat" (December 1978)—with the undoing, in short, of the cooperative transformation of agriculture—"agricultural reality" was radically changed. How then should the "realistic" literature of the past that had described "agricultural reality" exclusively in terms of the two line struggle be evaluated in the present?

During the first few years of the post-Mao era, what was termed the "reevaluation of fiction on the countryside" (*nongcun ticai de zai pingjia*) was indeed a thorny issue in literary criticism.[10] It was the focus of a typical discussion at a conference on contemporary Chinese literature held in 1981.[11] Now that the agricultural policies of the previous three decades had been superseded, the debate was over whether "agricultural policies of the present should be used to negate literary works of the past." How should the once highly praised short story by Li Zhun entitled "Buneng zou na tiao lu" ("You Must Not Take that Road"),[12] for example, be evaluated, now that the "capitalist" road of individual enterprise which one was not supposed to take has turned out on the contrary to be the road that one now must take? Had such works then, as some are now willing to point out, merely been occasional pieces written in response to political policies, policies, furthermore, that the party now rejects or admits to have undertaken in error? How did the writer understand the "reality" of the countryside which he was supposedly portraying in his works? Should the writer be discredited today for having followed the party line of yesterday, for not having known better than the party what was, or what should have been, going on in the countryside? Should the literature of the past thirty years be condemned wholesale as not actually having been "realistic"?

Central to the many debates over the degree of "realism" or the proper criterion for judging literature on the "cooperative transformation of agriculture" has been the treatment of character. The action or process of struggle in the standard "collectivization novel" was invariably carried out through a standardized repertoire of fictional characters—the progressive poor peasant supporting the movement toward the collective, the reactionary rich peasant bent on pursuing private profit, the initially wavering "middle characters" who eventually see the light. In works that were produced to illustrate or coordinate with specific policies, this repertoire of characters would be presented according to formula or generalized preconceptions (*gongshihua, gainianhua*), and not, despite all their claims to the contrary, it is acknowledged now, drawn from "real life."[13] When writers without exception placed the peasant characters they portrayed against the historical background of agricultural cooperation, that movement became "the entire contents of the life or fate of the peasants; characters were always differentiated and represented through the contradictions and struggles of that movement."[14]

Thus Gao Xiaosheng's representation of the peasant "broke through the formula" (*tupo gongshi*); his characters are not conceived first of all as embodiments or carriers of ideology, but are complex mixtures of good and bad. For the most part they are actually not able to make much sense of party policies in the countryside, policies of which they are supposed to be the chief beneficiaries or that are carried out in their name.

Critics may claim that peasant characters are now finally "realistic" because they are no longer being shaped by a monolithic political code, but there remains the problem of how to define this "new realism." To make the case that Gao Xiaosheng's characters are based on the close observation and intimate knowledge of "real life"—ironically the same argument made for Zhao Shuli's very different peasant characters a generation ago—both the writer himself and his critics have drawn heavily upon what may be construed as the "evidence" of his biography.

THE INTELLECTUAL-PEASANT BOND

Certainly during the first few years of his rehabilitation, as he re-emerged on the literary scene with his first stories centering on peasants and peasant life, Gao Xiaosheng continually emphasized his own identity as a peasant, as one who had shared in the peasants' lot and in their fate through the story of his own life.

He had begun his writing career soon after graduating from the Sunan School of Journalism in 1949, writing plays, essays, and stories for propaganda work of the Southern Jiangsu Writers' Association in Wuxi. He also published several short stories.[15] In 1957, caught up in the spirit of the "Hundred Flowers," he and several other Jiangsu writers published an article, "Yijian he xiwang" ("Opinions and Hopes"), calling for reforms in the party leadership in literature and for the freedom to organize literary groups. They were proposing to form a group, "Tanqiuzhe" (Explorers) and publish a journal.[16] Unfortunately for Gao Xiaosheng, he was the one who drafted its manifesto. The group never formally came into existence, its journal never appeared, but this "aborted fetus that had not even taken shape in the womb" as one of the founders described it, was considered criminal evidence enough for him and his several colleagues to be labeled an antiparty clique during the antirightist campaign. When the manifesto was later published, it was only as a target for criticism.[17]

The antirightist movement abruptly put an end to Gao Xiaosheng's fledgling literary career. In 1958 he was expelled from the provincial writers' union and exiled to the southern Jiangsu countryside to undergo labor reform. His wife, a schoolteacher who had followed him into exile, died within about a year, a tragic experience that formed the basis of his novel *Qingtian zaishang (Blue Heavens Above)*. In 1972 he married the widow of a peasant out of a sense of hopelessness; if he could not produce writings, he should at any rate, he said to himself, have a son.[18] When he was rehabilitated in 1978 after twenty years in the countryside, he presented himself as having become a peasant:

> I formed a bona fide peasant household. Like all the other peasant households, we constituted one cell in the commune, the brigade, the production team. The members in my family like everyone else took part in labor of the production team. ... Like everyone else we were allotted our grain, our plants, and other things. Our furnishings were those of peasant households, we had the tools necessary for our labor, there we kept our fowls and animals, we had the various jars and pots for storing things, and we had our private plot to work.[19]

Sharing the life and labor of the peasants, he was subject as they were to the same dominant control of party policies:

> Whether the harvest of the team was good or bad, rich or poor, whether the measures taken were correct or wrong, whether the consequences of a policy were good or bad, whether the cadres' style of doing things was upright or evil, a big wind or heavy rain, all these affected me in the same way as they did the peasants. My fate was just like theirs, our pulses beat together as one. p. 24)

These common experiences became the sources of his fiction, and what he portrayed in his stories was nothing more than what had also happened to himself:

> That is why I can feel relatively free when I write. For example, I did not just observe the difficulties Li Shunda had in building a house, I went through the

same battering experiences myself. I did not just see the "funnel-householder's" empty rice pot, I went hungry also as I desperately labored to fight for a life with warmth and food; like them I straightened my back to get through those times of hardship. We have lived and died together, shared in all hardships, we have exchanged our hearts and our minds. (p. 24)

Although Gao Xiaosheng has thus gone beyond any writer in claiming an identity with the peasants—"I did not need to make out what they were thinking; I knew that my thoughts would not be different from theirs"—the moment he writes about that close relationship, he must at the same time inevitably reveal his distance from them.

The story "Jixindai ("The Bond of Hearts"),[20] written in December 1978, whose apparent theme is the close relationship between intellectual and peasant, has been seized upon by critics as a telling motto for summarizing Gao Xiaosheng's works.[21] That the writer himself used this story as preface to an anthology of fourteen stories on the countryside written from 1979 to 1981, the first phase of his postrehabilitation career,[22] suggests his concurrence with such a view.

The story does not narrate a sequence of events but is rather a prolonged reflection by the central character while he waits for the bus that will take him away from the countryside. The "period of turmoil" over, Li Jiafu is now returning to his original work unit. He had arrived at this unknown village a full ten years ago, "an intellectual of rather dubious background," and with "all hope destroyed," had been extremely anxious about how he, a "reactionary scholarly authority" (*fandong xueshu quanwei*) and "capitalist roader," would be treated.

But due to the urgent need for modern know-how among the villagers, he discovered that he was able to do a great many things for them. "He had not imagined that with merely the most common skills" he would be able to "tear down the thick wall between himself, who was there to undergo 'reform through labor,' and the local people." He knew how to give injections and spare them the trip of several miles to the commune hospital; he improved the shape of the stove chamber to increase the combustibility of coal; he figured out the most efficient posture for mowing wheat. He had also proposed that the commune establish a stone quarry, recalling happily how he had participated in its planning and how he had instructed the new workers, "men who had barely put down their hoes," in the use of dynamite. That small factory he developed now brought in over two million a year. People soon became solicitous toward him, for he was perceived as a "good and useful person"; they quietly but determinedly, and in spite of their political misgivings, invited him to their homes for meals. Li Jiafu quickly understood that

> this was their special way of expressing their feelings for him, of expressing their protest against those who were his persecutors. Such a form of protest showed that the people were also oppressed, and that he, without any doubt, was now considered by them to be one of their own. He was moved to shed hot tears; the people were really too good. He condemned himself for his faults of the past, for the inadequacies of his own work. (p. 9)

Grateful for their trust and their honesty, from then on he held back nothing from them; he was like a kite with the end of the string placed in their hands, determining where he would be positioned.

The meditation on the relationship between the intellectual and the peasant is carried out through several metaphors, the binding string between them that would never break, that "could at any time transmit the pulse beat of both sides" (p. 4) merely being one of the most elaborate. However, their separation is ultimately inevitable, as expressed in one developed metaphor that also concludes the story.

With the quarry, stone had become more and more a common building material in the village, and "one brown stone, level enough to serve as a stool," had somehow been moved to the bus stop. It was now worn smooth by countless waiting passengers, for persistent experience could have an enormous effect, just as Li Jiafu himself "was no longer the person he once was." Seated on the stone, he thinks that lonely and isolated as it had been, it had nevertheless each day provided rest to travelers, had everyday "sensed the heart beat and breathing of those seated on it, and, witnessing joys and sorrows, unions and partings, it understood everything that had passed. It had sufficient reason to be satisfied with its closeness to the people" (p. 6). Yet at the end, this symbol of himself that again represents his relation to the people is left behind. The bus finally arrives and he gets on. As the door closes behind him and the bus moves away, "he suddenly felt something was missing. Looking out back at the bus stop, he couldn't help a smile, he had intended to carry the stone away with him" (p. 10).

In spite of Li Jiafu's decade-long immersion in the life of the countryside, when things are back to normal and he is restored to his former status, he must leave that life behind. True, he had shared the lives and the hardships of the people, he had contributed to them his knowledge and expertise, but the kite, to continue with the earlier metaphor, is not as completely earthbound as they are; unlike them, he has the capacity to soar high in another sphere.

Although not narrated in first-person like Lu Xun's "My Old Home," this story also has a deeply felt autobiographical meaning. What "Brother Xun" discovers when revisiting his "old home" is the unbridgeable distance between himself and his once childhood friend, whereas Li Jiafu in exile is able to forge a close relationship with those whose hard life he has been forced to share over ten years. But both stories end in departure; both intellectuals will in the end leave the countryside behind.

Gao Xiaosheng has referred to "The Bond of Hearts" as describing his relation with peasants; "otherwise, I would not write."[23] Its tone is more somber, notably free of Gao Xiaosheng's characteristic irony. Much more typical in his stories about peasants is the mixture or continuous alternation between empathy and irony in the narrator's stance toward his subject.

LI SHUNDA AND BUILDING THE MANSION
OF SOCIALISM

The double-edged narrator's stance is particularly evident in "Li Shunda zaowu" ("Li Shunda Builds a House"),[24] written four months later and regarded by some as Gao Xiaosheng's masterpiece.[25] The story was written after "The 'Funnel-Householder'" ("'Loudouhu'zhu'"), so nicknamed because his stomach is never filled, in which the problem addressed is the basic one of food. (It will be discussed below as the first one in the Chen Huansheng series.) "Li Shunda Builds a House" followed to address the problem of shelter. It was only afterward that Gao Xiaosheng realized that the "disasters" during those thirty years had not only prevented Li Shunda the individual peasant from building his house—"even more serious, it had obstructed the building of the mansion of socialism," and that the story took on the "meaning of reexamining a period of history."[26]

This re-examining of history is first of all a retelling of historical events from the perspective of the peasant's fate under Communist rule. But beyond this exposure of the reality of peasant life, the story, through its use of parody and irony, interrogates the role of language throughout that history. It contests the party's claims that it has always represented the peasants and their interest by introducing extensive quotations from the party's own language into the narrative and applying it to Li Shunda's frustrated struggle.

Li Shunda and his family of four had received one-sixth of an acre of good land in 1951 during land reform. Before "liberation," his two parents and younger brother, for lack of shelter, had frozen to death one cold stormy day in 1942. Now inspired by the promising vision of socialism, he decides to build himself a house. With the devoted help of his wife and sister, and after scrimping and saving for years, he finally has but one more year to go in getting the remaining necessary materials. But with the Great Leap Forward of 1958, when everyone is required to donate everything to the new collective society coming into being, he is forced to give them all up. He starts from scratch again, careful to save cash rather than materials this time, only to have it taken away from him during the Cultural Revolution by a blackmailing, "little red book"–toting rebel type (zaofan pai) carrying a gun. Li Shunda suffers incarceration, physical punishment, but is finally released. When that ordeal is over, the problem is the scarcity of materials and the need to "go through the back door." By 1977 he seems to be on his way to acquiring what will be needed, but when the story ends, his house, after over twenty-five years of struggle, remains unbuilt.

Since Gao Xiaosheng has himself acknowledged that the story can be read as an allegorical account of how the Chinese Communist Party, with all its promises of a better life, has failed to build what it calls the "mansion of socialism," the inescapable question is, What are the causes of this failure? The story strongly suggests that it is the party's own misguided policies and disastrous campaigns that have time and again subverted its own progress toward that goal.

As "an embryonic myth of Sisyphus, Chinese style,"[27] a tale of unending striving and failing, "Li Shunda Builds a House" adds an "existentialist" dimension to the seemingly insurmountable odds of lifting China's peasantry from its dire poverty. In discussing the story, Gao Xiaosheng quotes a peasant saying on the impossibility of Li Shunda's enterprise: "To build a house is to lay the foundation and establish the family; it is also to lose your fortune and ruin the family."[28] Li Shunda could not even have entertained the ambition of building a house until after Communist liberation. But the system that holds out hope for those who had never had any, also constantly sabotages the realization of that hope. The self-destructive effects of its utopian vision is demonstrated in an emblematic episode when those who take charge after defeating the "capitalist roaders" decide to "reorder the land" by mobilizing thousands of laborers to turn a river "bent crooked like the back of an old man" into a "ramrod straight model river." What it primarily achieves after such a massive effort is the dislocation of many peasant homes.

As the story emphasizes, Li Shunda is a "follower" (*gengen pai*), one who sincerely follows the Communist Party all the way, and literally accepts, believes, and obeys everything it says. This "literalism" on the part of the character creates many opportunities for a kind of verbal play that accounts for the story's most telling ironic effects. By presenting events as understood "literally" from the character's point of view, the story suggests that it is not just the gullible peasant, but the party itself that is undone by its own political rhetoric. That party language, as interwoven into the narrative text, is unquestionably accepted by Li Shunda; the effect will be to deflate it and expose its inherent absurdity.

Language is a central motif in the story and plays a major role in shaping its "action" and plot development. Li Shunda pins his faith on the symmetrical rhymed slogan that summarizes the promise of the good life to come in a socialist society. He has heard that "socialism meant 'upstairs and downstairs, electric lights and electric phone'" (*loushang louxia diandeng dianhua*). Personally he'd rather just have the downstairs without the upstairs, but then "he didn't know whether a one-story house was considered socialism or not." Electric lights were fine, but what use would he have for a telephone? If the child broke it, repairs would cost money, "wouldn't that ruin the family?"[29]

Literalism may be a matter of naive misunderstanding on the part of this honest peasant, but it is used for their own ends by those "making revolution" as well. During the Cultural Revolution Li Shunda is arrested and tortured because, among other things, he had made "reactionary statements." For example, he had said "a two-story house is not as practical as a one-story house, he couldn't afford to fix a broken phone; these were poisonous attacks on socialism" (p. 21). Language perverted and quoted out of context has been much used throughout the Chinese revolution as an expedient means to target those perceived as its enemies. The irony here, of course, is that the "follower" Li Shunda is merely doing what the party authorities themselves do, taking language literally as the "real thing." It is language that holds out promises of the future, and language again that is used as a pretext for persecution. Is the socialist vision, even to its believers, nothing but a matter of fussing over empty words? The house, after all, whether one story or two, does not exist, is not even in the process of being built.

The physical effects of Li Shunda's confinement and torture leave him feeling so unlike himself that he begins to have nightmares about turning "revisionist" (*bianxiu*); he has seen the consequences in others. Again because he takes the political metaphor "bearing a black pot" (*bei heiguo*)—that is, to be blacklisted—literally, he becomes terrified that he may find himself turned into a black pot unawares some night while asleep. But since he "maintained a high degree of vigilance" (another borrowing of current political vocabulary) he "until now has not been transformed" (p. 22). Absurd as Li Shunda's fears may be, they are merely a reflection of the utterly irrational and arbitrary way in which the Cultural Revolution selected and condemned its victims.

In the process of building his house, Li Shunda himself becomes a master of language manipulation to gloss over hard facts. When the daily income of himself and his family is not sufficient to cover expenses as they struggle to save for their house, they decide to go hungry, each person eating half a bowl less of gruel at each meal, and "what was saved would be considered surplus." When they have to skip meals because they are "unemployed," and are down to two meals instead of three, "they counted what was saved from the meals not eaten as income." A spoonful of rice broth would be used for cooking snails instead of wine, since "wine was made from rice in the first place" (p. 14). The process becomes a parody of the way the party has handled or rationalized information and statistics to reflect wishful projections rather than hard realities in its construction of a socialist society.

In the elaborate language play in the text, the overt narrator assumes an active role that operates in multiple ways. He comes on the scene with a voice much like that of a traditional storyteller, displaying his familiarity with the community he is describing, quoting peasant sayings, engaging the reader with a conversational tone:

> The older generation of peasants always used to say, "Eat thin gruel for three years, then you can buy an ox." It sounds easy, but it's really not. Think about it: if you have to skimp on rice for three years, wouldn't you have to cut back on everything else? What's more, it's all mostly empty talk! If you can't afford to eat in the first place, what's there to save? (p. 11)

In the traditional storyteller manner, Li Shunda's family is introduced as an individual example of this general situation. But as the story unfolds the narrator will often shift his stance in relation to the central character. A strong sense of empathy is expressed in describing Li Shunda's loss of parents and younger brother in a snowstorm: "In the end they all simply froze to death in the snow. Heaven lacks eyes, earth has no conscience. The plight of the poor is unthinkable, unrecountable. . . . Those who have no house, Alas!" (p. 12). At other times the narrator will adopt a satiric language to distance himself from the central character. His critical comments challenge the reader to come up with a different—presumably more sympathetic—response: "This Li Shunda, like a lot of peasants, was clever enough only in little ways. So just when he thought he was sure he would not fall into the same old trap, he tripped on the road again. To tell the truth, the arm gets tired supporting and helping such people move forward" (p. 19).

More typical of the story's mixture of irony and sympathy are the passages in which the narrator's voice and the thought processes of Li Shunda apparently blend into one and together read like "us" reciting party propaganda: "One morning Li Shunda woke up and suddenly heard that the world of Great Harmony (*datong*) had been achieved, and there would be no more distinctions between 'yours' and 'mine.'" It is the time of the Great Leap Forward and Li Shunda will be forced to donate the material he has saved after years of hard work and self-denial to the collective:

> In the eight years since Liberation, the masses had managed to have some things on hand. For example, didn't Li Shunda now have the materials for a three-room house? So why not put what everyone had together to speed up our construction? Our construction being for the benefit of all, every one should pitch in. There is no need for individual plans; in the future everyone's lives would be equally wonderful. What's the big deal in that pathetically small amount of private property? Contributing it all to the great enterprise is the only glorious thing. No need for misgivings, everything will become public property, everyone will be the same, no one will be cheated. (pp. 16–17)

While the passage seems to begin with the narrator speaking, his voice is subsumed in the merging of Li Shunda's thought processes with party language, an example of how Li has internalized whatever the party says, for "his thinking was now completely liberated" (p. 17). And "everyone" (*dajia*), "our" (*women*) become the signifiers in which character, narrator, and party blend together.

When the Great Leap Forward turns out to be a collective disaster and Li Shunda finds that he has lost everything, the problem is to make him accept his sacrifice willingly and be satisfied with the lowest possible compensation: "The only thing the cadres could do was to put everything into ideological work (*sixiang gongzuo*), and raise the political consciousness of people like Li Shunda" (p. 18). In fact this is the first time anyone has put so much painstaking effort into his ideological education. The district party secretary, Liu Qing, comes to see him and through a convoluted argument attempts to makes the best case for the party, focusing on its eagerness to compensate the people for their losses (although in fact it does no more than let Li Shunda move into a pigsty). "Who other than the Communist Party would ever do something like that? It was certainly unprecedented in history. Only the Communist Party has been so concerned for the peasant" (p. 18). Li Shunda is moved to shed tears of gratitude. "While the losses incurred by Li Shunda were not at all small, his political awareness had definitely been raised."

Political consciousness raising would seem to be a matter of sheer language, of putting the proper "spin" on whatever disasters party policies may bring about. The more mistakes the party makes, the more important the work of ideological education, or in this case, the more intense the manipulation of language to gloss over or reinterpret existent reality. The narrator first uses a mode of free indirect discourse here but then shifts to directly reproducing the utterances of the party secretary. This suppression of the narrator's voice to allow the voice of the party to talk on and on in its own words at such a moment is an example of a type of "double-voiced discourse" in which speaking in "someone else's discourse . . . introduces into that discourse a semantic intention directly opposed to the original one."[30] Narrative commentary becomes superfluous when party discourse is allowed to go on and practically turn into a parody of itself.

Political slogans are adapted only to give them an ironic twist. Li Shunda compares his own resolve to "the Foolish Old Man Removing the Mountain" (*Yugong yishan*). His application of Mao Zedong's reinterpretation of a Chinese myth as metaphor for the inevitable victory of the revolution both trivializes it,[31] and reveals "the utter discrepancy between ideological fantasy and the raw reality of peasant life."[32]

Through the operations of language on the levels of both story and discourse, on the *what* and the *way* of the text, "Li Shunda Builds a House" provides a capsule account of thirty years of revolutionary history, while exemplifying the determinant role of language in that history. But if peasant and party, victim and perpetrator, are both bound by party language, the peasant in the end is able to break away and rise above the party, if only in rather uncertain and tentative ways.

Li Shunda learns from his suffering and at one point finds a different form of language to express his view of the world. Furthermore, he turns out to be capable of a kind of moral introspection that allows this "follower of the party" to maintain a degree of independence and integrity. Although the story centers around him, Li Shunda is given few opportunities to speak in his own voice. The most extended occasion is after the Cultural Revolution, when drawing on oral traditions of the past, memories of stories from childhood, opera lyrics, and folk songs,[33] he composes a ditty about the "strange, strange, truly strange" phenomena he has seen:

> Grandpa sleeps in the cradle . . .
> Rats bite the cat's belly . . .
> The dog sends the weasel to guard the chickens . . .
> Swan flesh falls into the toad's mouth . . .
>
> (pp. 22–23)

Whereas in Zhao Shuli's " Rhymes of Li Youcai" folk forms are introduced only to be harmonized with the party's totalistic view of events, Li Shunda's "Song of the Strange," made up of individual, discordant instances of absurdity, in which common sense and traditional sayings are inverted, is a falling back on his "peasant's" or "folk" way of voicing protest. Given the odd gaps between language and the actual happenings in the story, Li Shunda's "Song" is also a metastatement embedded within the text about the inability of language to describe or explain the "strange, strange, truly strange" ways of the world.

In 1977, with the help of District Party Secretary Liu Qing, Li Shunda again begins to acquire the materials for his house, but "through the back door." He has to bribe the man at the brick factory and the concrete factory with "horizontal beams"—cigarettes—before he can be given the goods. Ashamed of having "corrupted others . . . he had no peace of mind, and sometimes would wake up in the middle of the night thinking about this and he would scold himself saying, 'Ai, I must change myself for the better!'"

Thus the story concludes with a subjective introspection that sets Li

Shunda apart from all the "corrupted" others. In spite of his passive and gullible nature, this peasant does hold on to a sense of right and wrong, even if only using it to judge himself. Throughout hardships and victimization, whether by party policies or economic corruption, he manages to retain a core of decency and integrity to the end. The peasant, unknowing as he may have been, remains a yardstick by which to evaluate a society that has gone wrong and that has wronged him.

THE PEASANT IN A CHANGING WORLD— THE CHEN HUANSHENG SERIES

The "character" of the peasant, distinguishing as well as moral attributes, are examined from different points of view in the series of stories that follow his transition into the post-Maoist world. These center around the peasant Chen Huansheng. The first four, written between 1978 and 1982, are probably the stories for which Gao Xiaosheng is most widely known. They include "'Loudouhu' zhu" ("The 'Funnel-Householder'"), 1978; "Chen Huansheng shangcheng" ("Chen Huansheng Goes to Town"), 1980; "Chen Huansheng zhuanye" ("Chen Huansheng Transferred"), 1981; and "Chen Huansheng baochan" ("Chen Huansheng under Production Contract"), 1982. Then Gao Xiaosheng announced the conclusion of the series, stating that he "would no longer give Chen Huansheng any more trouble, but would let him take a rest."[34] Eight years later, however, he "went back on his word" (zi shi qi yan) to resume the Chen Huansheng series, and added three more stories, including a final one in which the character is packed off to America for a new set of adventures.[35]

It seems rather unlikely that the last three stories will capture the same kind of critical attention. The great impact of the early stories of 1978 to 1982 was due to their being perceived as a clear departure from the optimistic formulas of Maoist literature and a rejection of the heroic revolutionary image of the peasant. Instead of positive, upbeat endings in which stories portrayed only the "bright side," as one critic put it, "what is outstanding in this author is his grasp of the tragic factors in social life," not only such external factors as the party's "leftist errors" but also "the weaknesses of the people themselves, which is also an important factor in the making of [their] tragedy."[36] The mutual complicity between party and peasant, in essence a discrediting of both, has been a common theme in the criticism of these stories.

The first story, "The 'Funnel-Householder,'"[37]—a nickname given to those peasant households who like "funnels" that could never be filled were always hungry, always in debt from borrowing grain—was, in the author's words, a piece of "literary reportage," for it had been almost all based on the situation, personality, and experiences of one person, someone who had lived for a long time near himself.[38]

Chen Huansheng is an honest, hardworking peasant who continually subsists on the margin of starvation but never gives up on his trust in the promises of the party. He is puzzled though over its agricultural policies that in effect decree that any surplus that could feed him and his family or help him get out of debt must be donated to the state, to avoid "black marketeering." Once he asks his cousin, an elementary schoolteacher, to write a letter on his behalf to the newspaper, but the cousin refuses, since as he puts it ironically, there is no way that the central fact of Chen Huansheng's life—his perpetual hunger—could "possibly exist in a socialist society" (p. 107). Throughout the history of misguided agricultural policies Chen Huansheng does not give up, but continues to teeter between hope and despair, repeating to himself year after year: "We'll go hungry another year and see."

Things improve for Chen Huansheng in 1978 with the implementation of the *sanding* policy (three fixed distribution quotas for production, purchasing, and marketing). When the new grain is allotted, all agree that he should be the first one to receive his share. His eyes fill with tears as his mound of grain gets higher and higher; wiping them away, embarrassed, he smiles faintly at the crowd gathered around. "But seeing that many eyes were wet, he could no longer control himself and let his tears flow freely in a cataract" (p. 113). Not a few critics have confessed to shedding their own tears upon reading this last sentence in the story: "Chen Huansheng is weeping, Gao Xiaosheng is weeping, and we are also weeping."[39] The ending of the story is a moment of catharsis, when, after thirty years of a peasant-centered revolution, literature can finally, openly acknowledge the actual sufferings of the peasant.

Gao Xiaosheng has referred to his own deep emotions in writing the story,[40] a story that only someone like himself, who had lived among peasants for decades, would be capable of writing. It was in a sense a "ready-made story." For literature to portray openly the fact of hunger in the countryside (although there were some who continued to deny that it could exist) was for many the beginning of a "new realism" and resolve:[41] "We must never let our peasants go hungry again!"

Chen Huansheng is a victim twice over. His hunger is the consequence of bad party policies, but also of the party's persistent continuation of them due do its refusal for so long to face up to the reality of their consequences. In his muddled way Chen Huansheng knows that something is wrong with the policies: "Deep in his heart there was a vague question, but it was stuck in his chest and he couldn't articulate it" (p. 101–2). "He could only sink into silence, his expression becoming more and more apathetic." "His mind, rather simple to begin with, could concentrate only on one simple thing—food" (p. 106).

The struggle to penetrate into and express the truth during a time of official lying and concealment is an important theme within the story. Chen Huansheng's groping but ultimately failed attempts to do so is a major facet of his character. As in much of Gao Xiaosheng's fiction, ironic effects are built on the uncertain degree to which his protagonists are capable of understanding their own situation. One question repeatedly raised by his fiction is whether the party's successful imposition of its own view of reality was possible in part because of the susceptibility of the general populace.

If peasants have been dupes of party rhetoric it is also because they are good, honest, industrious; they trust authority and are able to endure incredible hardship while always hoping for the best, or the better. The stories take pains to celebrate these very positive qualities while showing them to be inseparable from and intertwined with such negative qualities as passivity, acquiescence in their own oppression, and a "slave mentality" (nuxing). This double-edged nature is represented as a critical factor in their victimization. To emphasize what has been termed this "other"—i.e., negative—side of the character of the peasants not only goes utterly against the exalted image of the revolutionary hero in previous party-dominated literature but also departs from the image of the simple, downtrodden victim of the May Fourth period.

"The 'Funnel-Householder'" and other Chen Huansheng stories that followed unleashed a spate of critical analyses of the "real" and complex peasant character: Chen Huansheng was seen to represent its manifestations in history, its rootedness in tradition, its two-way relation to the party, its responsibility not only for the general backwardness of Chinese society but also for its complicity in the tragedies of recent history, in what had gone wrong with the "peasant-based" revolution.

After "The 'Funnel-Householder,'" Gao Xiaosheng called the Chen Huansheng character "back to life," as he put it, in "Chen Huansheng

Goes to Town," making it a sequel in order to call attention to that first story. He already had a good grasp of that character and it was "more convenient than creating a new one."[42] If extra-textual consistency in character is a primary concern, however, it may well be debatable whether the Chen Huansheng in both stories is indeed the same "person." Historical circumstances have changed, but more important, the shift in mood from pathos to comedy primarily effected by the increasingly overt and ironic presence of the narrator places the two "Chen Huanshengs" in quite different fictional worlds.

"The 'Funnel-Householder'" takes the peasant up to the threshold of the post-Mao era. Hereafter the question will be how well Chen Huansheng, given his traditional peasant character, will be able to meet the challenges of the ever-changing state of affairs brought about by Deng Xiaoping's economic reforms. He is no longer a long-suffering victim of wrongheaded rural policies. Now he functions more like a character in the role of a country-bumpkin confronted with a new, complex, and more sophisticated urbanizing world. His innocence, naïveté, bewilderment, and tenacious clinging to old values involve him in a series of bungling activities that at the same time provide a critique of that very same world.

In "Chen Huansheng Goes to Town" he takes advantage of the more open policies toward sideline production and free market trade and goes to town with his homemade *yousheng* (a kind of fried dough twist) to sell at the railroad station. He falls ill there and is discovered by the county party secretary, Wu Chu, whom he had met earlier that fall when Wu visited their production brigade. Secretary Wu takes Chen Huansheng to a clinic for medicine, then instructs his driver to deliver Chen Huansheng to a guest house to rest for the night while he resumes his own journey by train.

The comedy begins when Chen Huansheng awakes to find himself in the unfamiliar and to him incredibly luxurious surroundings of the guest house room and is shocked later when he is billed for five *yuan,* more than his pay for seven days of labor. Besides, he had been there only half the night! He goes back to the room to get what he can out of it, even if it means just messing it up. Then on his way back to the village, he consoles himself for his financial loss by thinking that finally he has something to talk about: He has had an adventure unlike that of anyone else, a ride in the county party secretary's car and a stay at a high-level guest house. His five yuan then is a cheap exchange for such "spiritual satisfaction."[43]

Critics have detected echoes here of the "spiritual victories" of Lu Xun's perpetual loser Ah Q, who is placed in a similarly snobbish community obsessed by status rankings. But despite all his failures, Chen Huansheng is never subject to the same kinds of humiliation as Ah Q. He is granted a subjective consciousness, adding an ethical dimension to his behavior that makes judgment of him a much more ambiguous matter. Most particularly, the narrator's relation to the central character, Chen Huansheng, an admixture of gentle satire and empathy, manifests itself in a style that is very much Gao Xiaosheng's own. This unique combination is achieved primarily through the use of an overt narrator who seems to move inside and outside of Chen Huansheng throughout the narration.

As the story begins, the narrator adopts the tone of an oral storyteller commenting on events from the outside: "Carefree and at ease, Chen Huansheng, the 'Funnel-Householder,' is going to town today."[44] The weather has turned warm and breezy after a cold spell, and with a full stomach, a new set of clothes, swinging a neat and full holdall bag, he saunters along enjoying the scenery of spring. The narrator calls our attention to his own overt presence through the dialogue format in several following paragraphs:

> Why is he going to town? He is going to do some trading . . . a little sideline occupation. . . .
>
> What's he going to sell there? *Yousheng.* Made with his own flour, his own oil, and by his own hands. . . .
>
> What'll he do with the money he makes? . . . (pp. 15–16)

Life has improved greatly for this former "funnel-householder" and he believes it will be getting even better: "Shouldn't he be satisfied? He is thoroughly satisfied." But he has always had trouble expressing himself or finding anything to talk about. "To speak of talking, is to touch upon a shortcoming of Chen Huansheng" (p. 16). He would like to talk, but there did not seem to be much of anything to say:

> For instance, about farming. All he could say was "to plant wheat, you use the hoe to break up the soil," "rice is transplanted in bundles of six." . . . No one would want to listen to that. As for this business of selling fried twists, he didn't think it up. Lots of people had been doing it for some time now. How to do ingredients? How to work them? How to package them? How much to charge? How much profit? Where to go at what time for the most customers, for the best business? He had learned all that from others. For him to brag

about it to people, now wouldn't that be a joke? . . . It would be better just to keep his mouth shut. (p. 17)

The ironic tone is retained but instead of "going over the head" of the central character to address an audience with an external, "objective" description of the situation, the narrator has switched to a position of "internal focalization,"[45] entering into Chen Huansheng's thought process and speaking from his self-deprecating point of view.

The special relationship with party secretary Wu is not in itself without ironic implications. When Chen Huansheng first reflects on the kind concern of the good Secretary Wu, who he believed may have saved his life, his "heart feels warm, hot tears flow," for here is someone who "although an official has not forgotten the common people." That is what the character thinks. What the story conveys though is the wide gap between the two, the discrepancy in wealth, life-style, privilege, status (without the secretary's "connection" Chen Huansheng would not even have been able to stay in such a guest house), and indeed the carelessness or nonchalant unawareness on the part of Secretary Wu about these matters when he left his peasant acquaintance in the lurch. A dualistic perspective on the character and his adventures is thus provided on several levels.

As economic reform proceeds apace, other opportunities are opened up for enterprises in the countryside. "The world, ha, ha, is like a kaleidoscope, transforming endlessly and truly fascinating,"[46] as begins the story "Chen Huansheng Transferred," for although everyone assumed that the "Funnel-Householder" would be working as a peasant all his life, and he himself had never considered anything else, "he has suddenly been targeted by the brigade leader, who wants to transfer him to the brigade factory." Chen Huansheng's potential for contributing to rural industrialization has nothing to do with his own abilities, but everything to do with his being perceived as having a special relationship with Secretary Wu. That relationship becomes a critical issue in this story and the next, "Chen Huansheng Under Production Contract."

The brigade factory wants Chen Huansheng to be its purchasing agent, now that Wu Chu has been promoted to secretary of the District Party Committee in charge of industrial matters. Since one can only hope to get materials through special connections, Chen Huansheng, with his presumed access to them, is pressured to undertake the job. He travels to the city and finds Secretary Wu. But the secretary has to rush off to a meeting, and Chen Huansheng must stay around for a couple of weeks at Wu's home. Idle, and unable to bear the sight of a piece of wasted land in the courtyard, he cultivates it into vegetable plots. When Secretary Wu returns (having in the meantime forgotten to look into the matter) he is embarrassed, and moved by Chen Huansheng's sincerity and patient waiting, he sends him to the proper places with the requisite statements of introduction, helping him succeed in his mission. Considering it extravagant to spend the 60 yuan to rent a truck, Chen Huansheng laboriously spends two days hauling the material to be shipped to the train station. When he returns to the village, he is "praised to the skies," but he cannot figure out why he is not compensated for that strenuous physical labor, yet given a 600 yuan bonus for having secured the material for the factory, a matter which did not involve any work on his part. He feels uneasy to be accepting such an enormous sum of money, nor can he understand the workings of a system that turned down one request for two tons of material but granted another for five. "All these question swirled around in his brain, trapping him in a bewildering maze. No one explained anything to him, and he was too embarrassed to ask, afraid that they would say he was stupid" (p. 60). The system of connections, bribery, underhand favors, and bureaucratic irrationalities appears unjust and does not make sense to the "stupid" peasant. But could it not be because the system is unjust and does not make sense to begin with?

His success in obtaining the material creates a "Chen Huansheng rage" in the commune, and there is much pressure on him to continue as purchasing agent and exploit his "connection" with Secretary Wu further. He wavers between that and going back to his occupation as a peasant under the new contract production responsibility system. This is the "action" in "Chen Huansheng Under Production Contract."[47] Initially the new system causes him a great deal of anxiety, for one thing, he remembers previous campaigns: "'Would it be considered the capitalist road?' he asks uncertainly" (p. 73). Besides, how was he going to go about farming on his own? "For twenty-eight years now, he had followed the behind of the team leader, when the leader pointed east, he went east, when he pointed west, he went west." He had been on his own before he was twenty but now he was all confused about the varieties of rice or wheat, planting methods, chemical fertilizers, pesticides. After almost three decades of submitting to the guidance of party leaders, peasants now lack know-how and initiative.

Giving in to the flattery and cajoling of the local party secretary and the team leader (both of whom had cursed him as a "funnel-householder" in the past), Chen Huansheng finds himself one day on his way again with a present for Secretary Wu. But a conversation with his schoolteacher cousin puts into words his own reservations about "going through the back door." The cousin, Chen Zhengqing, asks whether he will tell Secretary Wu about the 600 yuan bonus he got last time and accuses him of compromising Secretary Wu in order to enrich himself. Chen Huansheng weeps with shame and decides not to go. He'll be diligent and work hard; along with everyone else he will learn to farm and operate under the new responsibility system.

For some critics this fourth story in the series is a literary failure. By focusing on Chen Huansheng's psychological dilemma the story lacks action or comic peripeteia, in comparison with the others. But one reason for the dissatisfaction is that Chen Huansheng, "who had manifested an incipient modern consciousness for industrialization, has retrogressed back to farming under the contract system. This violates the developmental logic of the character's soul."[48] For the assumption is that "Chen Huansheng's psychological progress is a microcosm of the peasant soul during the new era," his transformation is that of the peasant who "bears the heavy historical burden of the small producer into a peasant of socialist modernization."[49] Another critic describes the phases of Chen Huansheng's development as "funnel-householder—parasite [of Secretary Wu]—right to independence.[50] These critics may be said to represent the "optimistic view" that conforms to the new political line—the inevitable successful economic transformation under socialism—but there are many others who take the "pessimistic view."

In their view what the fourth story shows is really the true state of things. The peasant "has been for so long stuck in the straits of collectivized small production, whose economy and means of livelihood have been so controlled leaving no room for planning (*yi chou mozhan*). Without true independence, truly becoming the master, the forbearance and slave character of the peasant will never disappear . . . The image of Chen Huansheng is a self-portrait of the small producer in a position of weakness, without any right to independence."[51] In other words, Chen Huansheng basically does not progress or transform throughout the series, and the fourth story is mainly the clinching revelation of that fact.

What both "optimists" and "pessimists" share in common is the notion that Chen Huansheng is more than just an individual character, but a highly representative portrait of the Chinese peasant. Their disagreement is over how the peasant in general should be characterized and what the relationship of the peasant might be in the development of Chinese history.

The last three stories in the Chen Huansheng series, which was resumed after an eight-year hiatus, would seem to support the "pessimistic view" that Chen Huansheng is "stuck" in his ways. The incongruity of his experiences, as the author sends him on a trip to the United States in the last story, underlines his fundamental conservatism, but it takes two stories to get him on his journey.

In story five, "Zhanshu" ("Tactics"),[52] Chen Huansheng continues to be twitted by friends and neighbors for his decision to quit the factory and contract to farm. But what causes him the greatest anxiety is the pressure from the factory director and the party secretary. "He had never liked to use his mind much; from childhood he had grown up following what was arranged by others"; his parents had been in charge then and his older siblings ordered him around. When it was explained to him that *guojia* meant that the country was everybody's family and that Chairman Mao and the Communist Party were the heads of the family, were "our own father and mother," he "gave his buttocks a slap in joy," because it made everything clear to him. In the same way the production team leader, the brigade leader, the commune leader would be his father, grandfather, and great grandfather. But for team members, "father" would be the team leader, the one directly in charge of you; in the factory, "father" would be the factory director (p. 91). The relationship with Wu Chu introduces complications, since there are obligations toward him as a member of the "older generation" as well. What this direct representation of the thought process of Chen Huansheng, a parody of the Communist Party's perversion of the Confucian "state as extension of family" idea, manifests is the peasant's naive faith in political rhetoric and his unquestioning subservience to those who represent the party.

Nevertheless Chen Huansheng puts everything into farming. His few attempts at such sideline occupations as raising rabbits or chickens fail, so he is earning money the hard way, but he does begin to prosper. And in the sixth story, "Zhongtian dahu" ("The Rich Farming Householder),[53] he manages to build a house, even if unhappy that he must give gifts and go through the back door to get his materials. "So it turns out that it was impossible for anyone to live by doing right" (p. 126). He is helped in his house-building by the former team leader, who now works as the purchasing agent at the factory, as he gives Chen his own land but then borrows the new house for illegal gambling parties.

Chen Huansheng continues to work his land, refusing offers to go into other kinds of profitable business. "His response to all change was not to change and to remain firmly rooted to the land underneath his feet." The narrator then extends his commentary to the Chinese peasant as a whole:

> For this is Chen Huansheng thought. It has been forged and tempered in the long river of history, could he become rich? . . . He is easily satisfied. To this day he is still the backbone of society—he fills our stomachs, but he cannot consider whether society has shortchanged him; because he has long been used to shortchanging himself.
>
> Chen Huansheng decided to continue on this way. If there would be change, it would have to wait till the children grew up.
>
> Who knows what it will be like in the future! (p. 129)

The story ends with the family's adoption of a baby left at their doorstep. Given the name "son of heaven" (*tianzi*), he is both an allusion to tradition and a symbol of the uncertain new order to come.

The final story, "Chuguo" ("Going Abroad"),[54] finds Chen Huansheng getting older and letting his son increasingly take on the responsibilities of farming. Secretary Wu has also retired, and

> could no longer help Chen Huansheng create any miracles; even the writer of fiction would probably be unable to come up with any fantastic ideas!
>
> But things are hard to predict. From the time Chen Huansheng "went to town," his fate was already being arranged by the old lord in the sky, and he was to spring up anew and become an even more dazzling shining star." (pp. 135–36)

The "writer of fiction" turns out not to be "Gao Xiaosheng," a "nonexistent person," but Teacher Xin Zhuping, who had been assigned to their village for labor reform during the Cultural Revolution. Now restored to his old position, Xin Zhuping has received an invitation to visit and lecture in the United States. His American hosts, who have read his stories, are inviting him to bring along one of its central characters, Chen Huansheng.[55] In the strange new world of America, the earth-bound but always well intentioned Chinese peasant gets himself into some embarrassing situations, passing out from fright when approached by a group of Californian seminude sunbathers of mixed sexes, or digging up a lawn to plant it with vegetables when house-sitting for an American professor. But on the whole, the opportunities for comedy, especially when compared with the earlier Chen Huansheng stories, are not fully exploited. Chen Huansheng is impressed by the degree of automation in American farms and marvels at the wasteful practices of this affluent society, but he returns home, as the story hastens to its end, without observing much and basically unchanged. The only things from America that he takes away with him, seeds of certain vegetables not available at home, he— symbolically—loses at the airport.

Even back home the world around the peasant had been changing too rapidly for him to adapt to its seemingly irrational and immoral ways. Given his fixed, tradition-bound character, confirmed even more by his American adventures, a central question raised by the Chen Huansheng series would seem to be, Will this Chinese peasant ever be ready to move with his society into the future?

INTELLECTUALS AND THEIR ROLE

During the first years after his rehabilitation, while exploring the nature as well as considering the fate of such characters as Li Shunda and Chen Huansheng in his stories, Gao Xiaosheng also wrote and lectured extensively, stressing that what he was doing was "writing for the peasant." It was the peasants' example of fortitude in the face of adversity that had sustained him and enabled him to survive his twenty years of exile in the countryside, and he "became one of them."[56] He writes in order to serve them, because "peasants lack culture, some are illiterate; they would like to express themselves, but are unable to."[57] One of the important motifs in the Cheng Huansheng stories, as we have seen, is the character's inability to articulate his thoughts, or indeed to "use his mind" much and come up with something to say. The writer/intellectual therefore first of all assumes a self-appointed role as a spokesman for the peasant, speaking in his place.

The assumption of such a role may be reminiscent in certain ways of the May Fourth writers when they initially took up peasants as a serious subject in literature. Stories were written on the backward practices and superstitious beliefs of the peasantry, but the writers' educational function in transforming its character was not their explicit goal. The peasants' oppressed condition was used primarily to substantiate a strong case against society in a reformist or revolutionary agenda. It was the social and political system that had to be changed. Gao Xiaosheng, however, presents a different conception of his writing in relation to the peasantry. Literary works on peasants should enlighten them, "stimulate them toward self-knowledge . . . to know their own strengths and weaknesses, their own history and present condition" so that they will not only possess the consciousness of being masters of the nation, but also possess the capability of being masters of the nation."[58] To raise the question about their "capability" to perform their dominant revolutionary role not only challenges the party's ideologized representation and construction of the peasant masses, it is also a reversal of the Maoist dictum that intellectuals should subordinate themselves to learn from them.

Whether capable of being a revolutionary vanguard or not, in Gao's view, peasants have nevertheless, precisely because of their traditional and backward ways, been enormously influential in the Communist revolution. Without peasant "backwardness," the negative and destructive aspects of that revolution would not have been possible. Peasants "worshipped the Communist Party like an idol,"[59] and if their weaknesses are not overcome, "China could still produce emperors."[60] Li Shunda's "slave mentality, his accepting submission to adversity" may have been contributing factors to the years of disaster.[61] In other words, the collaboration between party and peasant has indeed been crucial, not so much in advancing the cause of the Communist revolution, but rather in accounting for its most devastating consequences.

One of the most striking images in Gao Xiaosheng's peasant stories occurs at the end of "Da haoren Jiang Kunda" ("The Very Virtuous Fellow Jiang Kunda"), when the barefoot peasant carries the boot wearing Director Liu of the Satellite Brigade Factory of the Great Leap Commune on his back to spare the less than sure-footed cadre from slipping and falling in the mud.[62] The moment provides a telling symbol of the peasant-party relationship.[63] As they slog on, Director Liu asks at one point, "Aren't you tired, carrying me on your back?" "No, no, I'm not tired," Jiang Kunda responds, "I'm used to it." Without the peasant's age-old "slavish character," could the party cadre have come to occupy his privileged, superior position?

The emphasis on the intellectuals' responsibility to educate and enlighten the peasant may be regarded as a going back beyond May Fourth to link up with the traditional Confucian idea of those above nurturing those down below, even if the content of the education would be dissimilar. However when one examines intellectuals as portrayed *within*

Gao Xiaosheng's fiction, they would hardly seem to be up to such a task.

Chinese critics have been almost uniformly enthusiastic in their praise for Gao Xiaosheng's peasant characters, but are mixed in their views of the intellectuals in his fiction. The problem, according to some, is that the two are actually difficult to distinguish from each other. As Wu Liang put it, "Gao Xiaosheng's fiction is almost without exception about peasants; when occasionally he writes about intellectuals or cadres, they become like peasants (*nongmin hua*)."[64] The writer himself has acknowledged that the "thinking and habits" of peasants "have an enormous influence on all classes in society"; since they number eight hundred million, "we are all heavily surrounded by peasants." Therefore "peasants in a literary work should also be a mirror of all classes in which we can see ourselves reflected."[65] Gao Xiaosheng's intellectuals cannot lay claim to any intellectual or moral superiority over peasants; indeed, both are similar in the attitude of resignation and passivity toward whatever befalls them. What differentiates intellectuals, if anything, is their high degree of self-consciousness; they feel particularly anxious, insecure, ill at ease—characteristics that lend themselves to become targets of the writer's irony and satire.

Things always seem to happen to these intellectuals; they are perpetual victims of circumstances they cannot control. A vivid example can be found in "Diejiao yinyuan" ("Falling into a Marriage")[66] in which everything in the subsequent life of the research scientist Wei Jiangang is determined by the happenstance that one day when walking out to buy soap, his future wife fell out of a two-story window, crushing him to the pavement. This accident "brings them together," but her dubious class background, from having once been the concubine of a capitalist, makes him into a target of political criticism. He flounders between commitment to his wife and submission to pressure from his unit while his chances at a career are wasted away by suspicion and harassment. What the story dramatizes is the fortuitous nature of one's political fate and the helplessness of the intellectual in trying to cope with his vulnerability.

This sense of insecurity is shared by many other intellectuals in Gao Xiaosheng's fiction. The writer Hu Yanping in "Hutu" ("Muddled"),[67] even after his rehabilitation twenty-some years after the antirightist campaign, continues to be beset by worries about its possible revival. In the unit to which he has returned, he feels hounded by rumors, petty slanders, insinuations about his past due to his political history and his peasant wife, as well as criticism of his politically problematic writings; all conspire to make him live in a state of constant "fear and trepidation" (*chenghuang chengkong*). He would seem to be entitled to enjoy a sense of success when his novella *Yuanshangcao* (*"Grass on the Plain"*) is about to be made into a film. The director, a former acquaintance, has arrived with a crew to discuss the film with the writer and investigate the locale where the novella takes place, the village to which Hu Yanping had been exiled as a "rightist" in 1957. But the district minister of propaganda and the district party secretary in charge of culture, both treat the filming team with less than cordiality when it first arrives. Hu Yanping cannot but attribute this to his own insignificance and political vulnerability. But suddenly there is a complete about-face in the attitude of the local cadres. There are some scenes of high comedy as Hu Yanping reacts with bewilderment and embarrassment while he and the filming team are treated to dinner, provided with escorts, as his hosts inexplicably trip over one another to entertain them. Later he learns the reason for the dramatic change in treatment: The cadres had received information that his work had been praised by "an important responsible person in the provincial Party Committee." Suddenly then "it all makes sense." Objects of rueful self-irony, these hapless intellectuals, like Gao Xiaosheng's peasants, also serve as a means for exposing the snobbery and irrationality of the system and its representatives against which they feel so utterly powerless.

Such are the persisting effects of having been targets of persecution during political campaigns. The 1991 novel *Qingtian zaishang* (*The Blue Heavens Above*)[68] draws heavily ("sixty percent," in his own words) on Gao Xiaosheng's personal experience to portray an intellectual in exile. It begins in the spring of 1957, when Chen Wenqing, a newly condemned "rightist," is being "sent down" from Nanjing to his home village for labor reform. His lover, Zhou Zhuping, or Zhuzhu as he calls her, a former schoolteacher hospitalized with a severe case of tuberculosis, insists on following him into his life of hardship. They arrive in the countryside as it becomes increasingly embroiled in the turmoil of the Great Leap Forward. Suffering from tuberculosis himself, Chen Wenqing begins his life of labor reform under the "supervision of the masses." Meals become a problem for Zhou Zhuping when all supplies and utensils are confiscated for the collective (a metal pot is returned to her later in return for her services for the welcoming ceremony of the provincial party secretary, but that work brings about the worsening of her illness), and she, because she is not a registered resident member of the commune, is not allowed to eat in the communal dining hall like everyone else. Relatives and friends do what they can to bring her food, but scarcity due to disrupted production as the Great Leap process accelerates soon begins to affect all. They run out of rice and live on rations of what is euphemistically called "health flour," a mixture of husks and bran. Zhuzhu's condition deteriorates rapidly and she dies in the winter of 1959.

As in Gao Xiaosheng's earlier fiction, the senseless injustice of the political goings on is exposed through naive questions from honest peasants. Chen Wenqing's clansman are puzzled as to why he could have gotten into trouble merely because of what he seems to have said or written, as the documents indicate. To be punished by the Communist Party this way, he must have done something really evil. After all there were cadres "who were corrupt, had beaten people to death, fooled around with the wives of others, raped young virgins, and they had never been considered enemies, or kicked aside. Whatever evil Wenqing had done was obviously much more serious than these" (p. 106).

The commune's minister of public security, Wang Guoguo, a former peasant who single-mindedly follows and transmits orders from above, and now put in charge of supervising the production brigade's Great Leap Forward, is, however, quite clear about the matter. As he says to Zhuzhu, "The antirightist campaign is anti you intellectuals. Intellectuals look down on the Communist Party, just because they think they've been to school for a few years. . . . They don't follow the resolutions of the party committee; they're critical and say we are wrong" (p. 206). Against this context of avowed anti-intellectualism, the fate of the one magnificent building in the village may be seen as symptomatic of the status of intellectuals. Built long ago by a clan relative who had passed the highest imperial exam (*jinshi*) and become an official (p. 98), it has functioned ambiguously both as a symbol of evil, "feudal" power, and an exhortation to people to follow the path of learning. Now the great hall is packed with row upon row of stinking pig sties, and it is later dismantled for its lumber (pp. 203, 253). An early ancestor had once cautioned his descendants against learning (*nianshu*), since learning gets people into trouble (p. 99), a prophecy that would seem to have come true with Chen Wenqing, the only person in the village who had gone to college.

It is a time of red-hot revolutionary fervor. Commune members are terribly busy shouldering the heavy burdens of history. "'Long live the people!' 'Only the people are the creators of history,' What stirring words! These two phrases alone made those politically awakened work willingly to the death."

> Their leaders were considerate of them, realizing that they had to put all their time into physical labor; no time now to use their brains. For them this would really be difficult, so excessive demands must not be made on them; all they needed to do was obey orders and listen to commands. Therefore leadership had to be strengthened. (p. 143)

For this reason various levels of cadres are sent to each district, each brigade; these were the cadres that took total responsibility (to spare people from using their brains). This was Wang Guoguo's role. "Because if some one was not fully responsible for [or in charge of, *bao*] a production brigade, how could its thousand-odd members become the masters to create history?"

In a speech to commune members explaining what the Great Leap Forward is all about, Wang Guoguo, with a glance toward Zhuzhu, since "intellectuals all like to pay excessive attention to wording (*yaowen jiaozi*)," launches into his own wordy explication of the movement that reads like a parody of party language:

> To leap, is to jump, to leap forward, is to jump forward, we're not leaping in the ordinary way, but like Monkey turning a somersault of ten thousand miles. . . . You must not be afraid to fall. You're holding on to your bottles and jars, afraid to jump, afraid that they will break. So to dare to jump you must first hand over your bottles and jars, to the production team, to the brigade, to the commune, in a word, to the Communist Party. (p. 198)

Everyone realizes that tremendous changes will be taking place, "so immense, immeasurable, that no one could find the accurate language (*yanci*) to describe them, therefore it was all right to use any language to describe them" (p. 200). Since language need not correspond to any reality, all the people, Chen Wenqing among them, are completely carried away by it.

The Great Leap Forward becomes a test of whether one is "left" or "right." As a "rightist intellectual" trying to reform himself, Chen Wenqing measures his progress in terms of how well his own mind can go along with "this brand new reality" (p. 117). He watches the slogan set up along the bend of the Grand Canal, exhorting them to "Strive for the upper reaches [of the river *li zheng shangyou*], strive for a thousand catties per *mu* yield," escalate its target every few days from one to two to three to five to eight to ten and finally to twenty thousand catties per *mu*. But since his "intellectual's brain was good at thinking," he is persuaded to believe in the possibility of such miracles. "Without the Great Leap Forward, he wouldn't have seen that; with the Great Leap Forward, his consciousness was raised ... which shows that thought reform in his case was quite effective" (p. 120).

If "intellectuals good at thinking" are so lacking in critical intelligence as to accept without question the grandiose schemes and outrageous claims that marked the Great Leap Forward, then "thought reform" has been effective indeed. But is this what Chen Wenqing, the one highly educated person in the village, "really" thought? Whether the text is attempting to give us a *plausible* representation of the penitential intellectual's process of conversion to the party line, even of one who, under social and psychological pressures had no choice but to conform, may well be beside the point. Events are described in an apparently matter-of-fact tone from the perspective of the main character here, but the narrative is not so much informing us about what was happening within the internal world of the individual Chen Wenqing as targeting its satire against both the madness of the period and the intellectuals in general who somehow (mindlessly?) went along. Even in this semi-autobiographical piece with all the tragic events to follow, it is the mode of satire and irony (or self-irony) that dominates the text.

As the situation worsens toward the end of the novel, Zhuzhu goes to visit uncle Yaoming. By now every family has contributed its tools and furnishings to the commune, and she walks into an utterly empty room: "A guest could only sit on the floor. Zhuzhu felt however that the room had become more airy and spacious. Chairman Mao's portrait was still enshrined on the wall facing the front door, just as dignified, kindly, poised and magnanimous as ever, not at all bothered by what things were or were not here" (p. 234). The scene of the deified Mao magnanimously presiding over the space devastated by his policies may be read as a metaphor for the consequences of the Great Leap Forward. It is ambiguous whether it is the narrator or the character who is speaking and making this observation, but again the point is more satire than a description of whatever "actual" emotional reaction the character Zhuzhu may have had.

In many other passages the two intellectuals in the novel are similarly represented as products of thought reform and used as a means by the implied author to achieve his satiric ends; of necessity they are more or less deprived of such qualities as a critical consciousness or an independent self-awareness. They are not shown to question, much less resist or challenge, even in their own minds, the senseless things happening around them. No doubt one point of the novel is that intellectuals were dupes of party policies just like everyone else. The problem is that such passages tend to undermine the persuasive force of the other "story" being told about Wenqing and Zhuzhu in the novel—the story of their love and loss.

That other story with its tragic ethos would seem to demand that the individual thoughts, feelings, and motivations of the two people involved be "taken seriously." Zhuzhu's beauty and goodness, at times bordering on idealization,[69] the couple's intimacy, their devotion to each other, scenes of tenderness, the terrible pain of parting in death are indeed there, but these moments coexist rather uneasily with those in which they are present more as vehicles of the implied author's ironic strategies than as characters "in their own right." At different moments they seem to straddle different narrative levels.[70] Certainly novels are not required to produce "consistent people," but such contradictory attributes work against the reader's efforts to integrate these two into the "more or less unified construct" that can be perceived as "character," and in this example, undercut the pathos of their story.

WRITING AT WHAT COST? LIU YU AND HIS BOOK

The fate of the intellectual in "Liu Yu xieshu" ("Liu Yu Writes a Book"),[71] is also a tragic one, but its pathos is subdued and accommodated within the story's consistently self-ironic mode. Written in 1981, a few years after Gao Xiaosheng had returned from the countryside and begun to resume his writing career, the story centers around a writer whose experience of exile and rehabilitation closely parallels his own. It is a searching exploration of the moral responsibility of the writer, particularly in relation to the peasant.

After a twenty-year hiatus when he was doing labor reform, the former "rightist" Liu Yu determinedly takes up his writing again. But he finds himself in a frantic race against time when hospital tests reveal that he has cancer and but a brief time to live. Already in ill health, and now totally obsessed with his desperate, painful struggle to finish his book before he dies, Liu Yu neglects his peasant wife, Li Suying, leaving her to toil alone in the fields under the broiling sun and to shoulder all the tasks of sustaining the family. The information of his impending death he has kept from her. While he devotes his time and energy to his writing, she assumes all the work of the household until she suddenly dies from heat stroke and exhaustion. Expecting to follow her soon, Liu Yu labors on to finish the book, only to be told that the hospital had made a diagnostic error and that he does not have cancer after all. The story ends with his collapse on the floor as he is abruptly given this shocking information.

As Liu Yu contritely reflects, it was his fiction writing that had brought about his wife's death, *bei ta xie xiaoshuo xie si le.* (Gao Xiaosheng has acknowledged that in his own life the person who died was actually his stepmother, who for this reason was a person very much on his conscience. He wrote the story the way he did because he was so totally absorbed in his writing that even if it had been his wife, he would have done the same thing.)[72] The mea culpa message of the story—the writer/intellectual as parasite, as exploiter, whose literary production comes at the expense of the laboring peasant—turns it into a parable of the relationship between the two. At first glance the surprise ending à la O. Henry may seem to suggest that but for that bit of ill luck at the hospital, the wife's life could have been saved and the husband spared a lifelong burden of guilt. Yet given the harsh environment in which the events take place, the poverty and hardships of the peasant, the brutality of the system, the precariousness of the writer's fate, there is a relentless inevitability in what happens. If the writer too readily accepts the hospital's verdict, it is because a terminal illness merely reinforces his existent uncertainties about how much time is left to him to write anyway—he has already lost over twenty years, and policies toward intellectuals are always subject to arbitrary change.

The story details the relentless pressures on the wife Li Suying, the strenuous toil, the struggle to come up with the 200 yuan needed for the grain ration for the family of six with herself as the only laborer. She has to work their private plot at dawn and night before and after laboring all day on the land of the production team (she was not one of those "smart" people who dawdled along in the team's work, in order to save their energy for working later on their own land), and the heat and drought require her to carry water endlessly to keep the crops of soy beans, sweet potatoes, and vegetables going. On the other hand, there is the despair of the writers who have had to endure decades of persecution in campaign after campaign and been denied all opportunities to write;

they must wrest whatever possibilities there may be for creative production within the narrowest of margins. Fellow victims of thirty years of
disastrous party policies, neither intellectual nor peasant has a monopoly
on pain and suffering.

In spite of their common harsh fate and the fact that intellectual and
peasant are yoked in the intimate relationship of marriage—the love of
husband and wife for each other is often referred to in the story—a wide
gulf exists between the two. The clearly marked spatial boundaries of
work—he writes inside at the table, she works outside in the fields, a reversal of the age-old "men outside, women inside" (*nan zai wai, nü zai
nei*) division—recalls Mencius' sharp demarcation between those who
labor with their mind and those who labor with their muscles. There is a
stark contrast in narrative stance. Toward Li Suying it takes a sympathetic outside view, in spite of, or perhaps, paradoxically because of, the
greater gap between narrator and character. Toward Liu Yu it is ironic
and critical, a stance possible precisely because it goes so much more
deeply into his inner world. The struggle and turmoil of the writer, his
reflections on his coming death, his efforts to position himself in writing
as he recalls literary examples of the past, are indications of a rich and
complex subjective life that is apparently denied to her. Lu Xun's "The
New-Year Sacrifice" is much on Liu Yu's mind.[73] Almost six decades
apart, the two stories have in common the theme that the relationship
with the peasant woman "other" brings on a moral crisis for the writ-
ing/intellectual self.

Those moments when the narrator focuses on Li Suying's thoughts as
she watches in awe the single-minded efforts of her husband to write and
write and write mainly underline her lack of comprehension of what it is
all for, or what it is all about. She first thinks he is doing work for the
school from which he is on sick leave. When he reveals that he is writing
a book, her first alarmed query is "Wasn't it writing a book that got you
into trouble before?" (p. 128). What is also incomprehensible to her is the
persistence of his struggle. To withstand the extreme heat Liu Yu sits
with his feet in a pail of well water (like an icebox), and to ward off the
mosquito hordes he hangs a hot methane lamp over his head (like a
stove)—they burn to death as they hit the chimney—thus he persists
"midnight after midnight assailed by heat and cold." The image conjured
up here, which is not without its comic aspects, reminds his wife of
Buddha in the temple, for "she had never seen any one else sit still for so
long" (p. 134). In her eyes there seems to be a circle of light—a halo per-

haps?—over his head. She vaguely senses that her husband "must be engaged in an extraordinary enterprise, otherwise he wouldn't be so determined"; to her "the Liu Yu of this moment seemed truly as great as Buddha, presumably cultivating himself toward enlightenment" (p. 135).

The hyperbolic image produced by Li Suying's naive, uncomprehending perception emphasizes the distance between intellectual and
peasant, but it is not without parallel in the representation of Liu Yu's
own thoughts on his situation. As he meditates on the writer's fate and
his own imminent death, irony is created in language that similarly in-
flates and deflates his ego.

Quotations from the venerated classics, including Sima Qian's letter
to Ren An,[74] in which he had weighed the consequences of death and the
pressure for suicide against his mission to complete his history, while
placing himself in the immortal tradition of literary martyrs, add to the
self-irony of Liu Yu's reflections: "Yes indeed, Liu Yu was about to die. A
man dies only once, whether it be weighty as Mount Tai or light as a
goose feather [as Sima Qian said]. If Liu Yu dies, whether it should be
considered Mount Tai or goose feather, only heaven knows" (p. 129).
When he had to give up his writing, he had made himself think there
was "no happiness greater than the death of the mind" (a play on "There
is no grief greater than the death of the mind" from the *Zhuangzi*),[75] re-
signing himself to his condition, but now he found he was facing the
death of the self (which the original text emphasized to be of lesser importance). Other texts quoted and given an ironic twist include lines of
ci by Li Yu (937–978), tragic poet-ruler of Southern Tang; and by Yue
Fei, Song general executed for his patriotism. The invocation of these literary martyrs seems on the one hand to link Liu Yu to the hallowed tradition of the past, but the recasting, inversion, or parody of textual quotations on the other hand simultaneously punctures what grandiose literary pretensions he might have had in seeing himself as a participant in
such a tradition.

He is driven also by the notion that the time has come for him to fulfill his writer's role as prescribed in a revolutionary society. During his
youth, "Liu Yu had firmly believed that the meaning of life lay in serving
the people." But when he was labeled a "rightist" and there seemed to be
no reason to value his own life, he had resisted the temptation to die,
letting things take their natural course. Now "the wheels of history were
moving forward again (p. 130) . . . the meaning of life was returning and
was even more significant than during his youth." Now "he truly under-

stood the people, understood their lives—joys, hardships, strivings, hopes. Understanding the multiple nature of life, he was truly qualified to be a writer" (p. 131).

The final irony here, of course, is that while so earnestly rededicating himself to "serving the people" through writing, he seems in the process to be actually oblivious to their "hardships, strivings, hopes," most particularly in his selfishly causing the death of one of them right within his household. Moreover, apart from the fact that he is writing a work of fiction, we are never told anything about the work itself; an absence, a blank cipher in the text represents what is being produced at such a great cost. And it is around such a negative space that life and death, and questions of the writer's moral responsibility, revolve.

For writers who have suffered unjust persecution and finally have been allowed to resume writing after two decades of enforced silence, a posture of self-pity or self-importance would be thoroughly understandable. Through its deflating irony, this story ultimately avoids both. It asks whether the intellectual, his own loss and fortitude notwithstanding, may not be writing at the cost of those supporting him with their labor, and whether the prerogative the writer is reclaiming may all along never have been available to the peasant "other." As Liu Yu laments his wife's death, he speculates that she could well have had a subjective life that had never attained expression. She was gone "without leaving even a word. Both were human beings; before Liu Yu died he had so much to say that he had to write a book. But didn't Li Suying have something she wanted to say?" (p. 137).

"Liu Yu Writes a Book" is indeed a tragic story and can move one to tears,[76] but under Gao Xiaosheng's ironic self-mocking treatment the writer/protagonist is not allowed to attain the status of a tragic figure. When the doctor nonchalantly informs him that the fluoroscopy and x-ray were after all negative, and assures him that everything is all right, "Liu Yu's breath stopped, his eyes blank, his head dizzy, and plop! he fainted on the floor" (p. 138). End of text. At the final climactic moment of revelation, the writer is denied a dignified exit.

THE TRANSITION FROM REALISM

Gao Xiaosheng has been a prolific writer since his rehabilitation. With a kind of grim determination (shades of Liu Yu here?) to make up for lost time, he restarted his literary career by publishing one volume of eight or nine short stories per year for six years. He has not maintained that pace of short story production, having branched out into such longer forms as novellas and novels, but he has succeeded in any case in portraying a wide range of peasant characters. His fiction has been rightly celebrated as a breakthrough from the political formulas of revolutionary literature, when writing about peasants was a matter of tailoring them to fit into the a priori formulas of class struggle in the countryside. This has had far-reaching implications for a revolution that has featured peasants in its ideology and certainly has been a major stimulus in the move to "reappraise the literature of the countryside" of the previous thirty years. He has also gone beyond the tendency of much of May Fourth fiction to see peasants simply as so many downtrodden, inaccessible, and inarticulate victims, adding much depth and complexity in his representations.

Nevertheless, one notes a family resemblance among his peasants: They share such characteristics as diligence, honesty, an extraordinary ability to endure; they are also naive, trusting, tradition bound, and submissive to authority. These are the qualities that have stood in the way of their adapting to change and made them susceptible to political domination and manipulation. In many ways they can be seen as accomplices in their own oppression. But victimized as peasants have been, they have at the same time managed to preserve a core of goodness, maintain a standard of integrity against which their oppressors can be judged. One is broadly generalizing here, of course, and there are many sharply etched individuals among his peasant portraits, but the fact that one can risk generalizations at all raises certain questions.

In spite of the refreshing close look at peasants and the intimate knowledge of their lives evident in Gao Xiaosheng's fiction, is there still not a tendency, on both the writer's and reader's part, to "objectify" peasants as a separate category of people, to see them as possessing a distinctive ontology, as a collective mass about whom generalizations can be made? Whether as the oppressed victims for exposing the evils of Chinese society, the vanguard for carrying out political revolution or the backward factor impeding China's progress toward modernity, peasants have continued to be seen as "others," against which agendas about reform, revolution, and modernization are projected. Gao Xiaosheng's peasants, their diversity notwithstanding, still fall within that tradition.

In looking at peasants as a way to understand what is going on or what is wrong in Chinese society, Gao Xiaosheng can be seen as retrospectively bypassing the intervening period when they were elevated as the centerpiece of Communist revolutionary ideology, "going beyond" the fiction of Zhao Shuli, and returning to the earlier May Fourth agenda of realism and reform. It is what many Chinese critics have hailed him for in upholding his works as a manifestation of what has been optimistically termed the "new era" in modern literature. Literature, based as during May Fourth on the close observation of "reality," will, in representing peasants, again generalize from individual characters to the broad masses and position them against the specifics of ongoing history, in which they are perceived as bearers of a political or social message for reform or protest.

But while Gao Xiaosheng may in some respects be considered an heir to the May Fourth writers, his experiments in narrative strategies and his ironic use of language also undermine their realism/reform agenda. For one thing, the encounter between writer/intellectual and peasant becomes a much more problematic matter. Chinese critics have noted that in a Gao Xiaosheng story, the fact that one cannot distinguish which is character and which is author when the character's inner processes are described is a source of confusion, indicating an inability to command a stable view from above. Due to his having resided too long in the countryside he has found it difficult in their opinion to distance himself sufficiently from the peasant.[77] This would be in marked contrast to the superior position maintained by the May Fourth writer/intellectual even while taking on the peasant "other" as subject. However, as we have seen, it is precisely the fluctuating distance, the particular mixture of empathy and irony, that enables Gao Xiaosheng's fiction to carry out his exploration of a more intimate yet more ambiguous relationship between the two.

As a writer Gao Xiaosheng has shown himself to be highly self-conscious and meticulous in his use of language, yet also paradoxically quite aware of the impossibility of completely controlling its meaning.[78] Such a notion of language poses a challenge to the realist project, which usually assumes a direct correspondence between language and what it supposedly represents. By adroitly incorporating party rhetoric into his own narrative processes, he has questioned not only the history of the revolution as given but also the relationship between language and reality. His fiction exposes the ways in which words gloss over reality and are employed as substitutes for concrete action and achievements. Whatever the situation, political slogans, labels, and words have made it seem otherwise. Through irony and satire his fiction shows how in the arena of politics, words are deeds; symbolic representation, the reality. In the end, Gao Xiaosheng's use of language manages to have it both ways. On the one hand his fiction questions the use of language in a revolution shown to be constructed out of words. On the other hand it demonstrates the exquisite power of language, when it can be put to such deconstructive use.

Through his particular method of reassessing the past, Gao Xiaosheng marks a transition from the central tradition of "realism," however variously interpreted, in modern Chinese literature. By uncovering the contradictions in the agenda of realism, he anticipates the experimental fiction to come. Many writers from the younger generation who have become prominent since the mid-1980's have very different literary concerns; when they write about peasants, neither "realism" nor reform politics is high on their agenda. Some examples of their fiction will be the subject of the following chapter.

6

The Post-Modern "Search for Roots" in
Han Shaogong, Mo Yan, and Wang Anyi

FOCUSING ON TEXTS in which the peasant is their subject, I have been considering the fiction of Lu Xun, Zhao Shuli, and Gao Xiaosheng as participating in a continuing tradition, with each writer representing a distinctive change as the political context has shifted. But when we come to the writers to be discussed in this chapter, such a tradition can no longer be taken for granted. While the fictional narratives produced by Han Shaogong, Mo Yan, and Wang Anyi as they appeared on the literary scene during the mid-1980's may continue to feature peasants, they do not resort to political classification or historical conditions for their conception of character; indeed, reform and revolutionary agendas have almost become irrelevant. The countryside may still be the locale of fictional events, but no longer primarily as the site of a time-specific, class-based struggle. Nor can the stories of this "fourth-generation" of writers, unlike those of their predecessors, be accommodated within the category known as "fiction on countryside themes" (*nongcun ticai xiaoshuo*), with all the political implications or attendant conventions expected of that genre. What has taken place is a movement beyond the confines of explicit ideology and the concomitant deconstruction of peasants as a politicized literary category; peasants will emerge from the texts of these writers as a new kind of discursive subject.

This radical turn in modern Chinese literary history, which has become increasingly manifest since the decade after Mao Zedong's death, requires a different critical approach. Each of the preceding chapters on the representation of the writer/intellectual self and the peasant "other" has focused on one individual writer. And if it was possible to consider these writers individually as representative of a particular phase in literary history, it was mainly because the fiction of each could be characterized by certain overall distinctive patterns, patterns that could be discerned through the reading of selected exemplary texts and related to a specific historical context. Such a possibility is, of course, particularly evident in Lu Xun and Zhao Shuli, whose careers can be seen as a whole. Gao Xiaosheng continues to be actively productive, but his large output of stories on the peasant so far exhibits common features about which certain generalizations can be made.

The only generalization one could reasonably make concerning the three writers of the new generation, however, would be about their striking diversity, diversity not only from one author to another, but even among the individual works each individual author has produced. Not only are the authors still relatively young, having all been born between 1953 and 1956, their commitment to continual thematic and formal experimentation means that their fiction has yet to coalesce or crystallize like that of those earlier writers into clear-cut overall patterns. Such diversity reflects, and is made possible in the first place by, the fluctuating and increasingly variegated context against which they are writing. Instead of focusing on the production so far of any single writer, the discussion in this chapter will revolve around one particular "moment of convergence"—1985–86—in their widely divergent literary careers, when each of the three published fiction regarded as outstanding examples of "search for roots" (xungen) literature, a movement that dominated the mid-1980's literary scene.

Peasants became prominent subjects in specific ways then because for many intellectuals the site of China's "roots" was located within its enduring, earthbound peasantry. In reaching for this new "cultural agenda," writers shifted from writing about peasants as a politically determined class, positioned either as oppressed victim or proletarian vanguard, to writing about them as somehow embodying or emblematic of what in their view were enduring characteristics of Chinese culture. This displacement has signified a new representation/construction of the peasant, a breaking away from the bonds of previous political agendas into a much expanded territory of narrative time and space.[1]

It was the fiction the three writers produced at this point in their careers that contributed importantly to what has been termed the "repeatedly occurring miracles" that took place around the year 1985.[2] Indeed some scholars have seen the moment as signifying a "century-type transition" (*shiji xing zhuanbian*),[3] from nineteenth-century "realism" to twentieth century "modernism" or "postmodernism."[4] Among other works, what marked this "breakthrough," signaling nothing less than a "second literary revolution," was the appearance of Han Shaogong's "Guiqu lai" ("Homecoming"), "Ba Ba Ba" ("Pa Pa Pa"), Wang Anyi's *Xiaobaozhuang* (*Bao Village*) in 1985, followed the next year by Mo Yan's *Honggaoliang* (*Red Sorghum*), the major texts to be analyzed in this chapter.

While the "search for roots" label has certainly not been limited to these three writers, they are particularly included here because several major themes we have observed so far in the stories of Lu Xun, Zhao Shuli, and Gao Xiaosheng happen to re-emerge in their fiction, but only to be developed in significantly new ways. To reconceptualize the peasant as in some way emblematic of the "roots" of Chinese culture will, first of all, involve a repositioning of power and moral responsibility on the part of the intellectual self in relation to a redefined "other." Their fiction reacts against the Communist Party's dominion over literary production not only by presenting peasants who depart from its ideologized categorizations, but also by calling into question the direct relation with empirical reality or historical "truth" upon which that dominated literary production was supposedly premised. Each writer utilizes a wide range of textual strategies, such as the disruptive treatment of time and chronology, the uncertainty of identity and memory, or the questioning of narrative authority, among others, to indicate their departure from the realist tradition. Even more remarkable in all three writers is the self-conscious way in which literary representation and the functioning of language in the duality between intellectual and peasant are explored and problematized, most often through the processes of narrative itself.

At this point it is of course impossible to determine whether it will turn out in hindsight that the mid-1980's were indeed such a dramatic turning point in modern Chinese literary history, or whether these particular authors will actually stand out as the most representative of their period. Nevertheless, when taken together, even as they re-examine the age-old theme of the intellectual/peasant encounter, they do suggest many of the important new directions contemporary literature was taking at the time as it began its accelerated move away from tradition.

It may seem paradoxical at first to note that examples of what is considered "new wave fiction" should be so closely associated with a movement that apparently focuses its attention on China's cultural past. And there are Chinese critics who would refuse to accede modernist or postmodernist credentials to "root-searching" fiction because in their view the return to the past is a culturally conservative agenda.[5] But as we shall see, the attitude toward tradition among these writers is not only marked by ambivalence and contradictions; there is discrepancy between their theoretical pronouncements and fictional praxis as well. However we wish to understand the relationship between the quest for a primordial tradition and the experimentation with Western modernism, both are impelled by the same desire—to break away from the concepts and techniques of literature that had prevailed in recent decades.

The increased exposure to works of foreign literature possible in the relative liberalization of the post-Mao period has not only introduced writers to new ways of writing, it has also made them aspire to create a Chinese literature that could "move toward the world" (*zouxiang shijie*)—i.e., measure up to "world standards" while at the same time not losing its "Chinese" character. In the view of several critics, the example of Gabriel Garcia Marquez's *One Hundred Years of Solitude* and his winning of the Nobel prize for literature in 1982 turned out to be an inspirational model.[6] Columbia was, after all, a developing country like China, and now with a writer whose subject matter was primarily his own culture and history, it had managed to make a spectacular entry onto the world literary scene. Could not China, it was asked, with its long (and asssumed to be more glorious) literary tradition, hope too for something similar? Furthermore, Garcia Marquez's "magic realism" seemed to suggest an effective way out from modern Chinese literature's hidebound commitment to the "realistic" mode of writing. A new conception of and methodology for fiction was therefore arrived at, according to Chen Xiaoming, through combining "ideas and techniques of modernism (or postmodernism) with China's native culture."[7]

It was in such an environment that the slogan of *xungen* was first raised in an 1985 essay, "Wenxue de 'gen'" ("The 'Roots' of Literature"), by Han Shaogong. Its appearance was quickly followed with essays by Zheng Wanlong, Li Hangyu, and others on the same topic.[8] Although for the past few years such writers as Jia Pingwa, in his Shangzhou series, or Li Hangyu in his Gechuan River series, had already been producing notable fiction that drew upon the material and local color of specific regions, regions that were often perceived as living in a past that was on the verge of fading away, it is with these essays that "search for roots" became a fully self-conscious movement and suddenly the most visible and lively scene in town.

The authors of all the above essays had been brought together the year before, in December 1984, in a meeting sponsored by the periodical *Shanghai wenxue* (*Shanghai Literature*) in Hangzhou.[9] Significantly, a main topic of much of the discussion was how to look for ways to break out of existing artistic norms in fiction. It seemed to many that while Western models might point the way toward new literary forms and techniques, the subject matter, under the notion of *xungen,* could remain Chinese.

The turn to the West for literary ideas and forms in the post-Mao era recalls the May Fourth writers' struggles some sixty years earlier to forge a new literature for China. But whereas that earlier generation mostly stressed its own clear-cut rejection of, or severance from, the traditional past, the new writers of the 1980's deliberately take it on, or rather take on what they consider to be the perennial or age-old in Chinese culture as their primary target of textual exploration. They turn their attention to the past with its traditions and myths, not in order either to reject or rehabilitate them downright, but rather to emphasize their staying power while subjecting them to a radical interrogation.

The devastations of recent history and their own coming of age during the traumatic years of the Cultural Revolution did much to propel them into such an interrogative mode. Those crude excesses of the Cultural Revolution when the whole country seemed to be caught up in a self-destructive orgy of ideological fanaticism, did not, in the view of many intellectuals, erupt out of nowhere, nor could they have; more than just a bad moment in the Communist Party's history, those excesses have been increasingly viewed as an extreme manifestation that finally and fully exposed some inherent problems in the party's agenda.

Furthermore, although the party itself had always proclaimed its goal of liberating China from its "feudal" past, perhaps it had been much less than successful in achieving that. Many have attributed what had gone so horribly wrong in the Communist Revolution to "feudal remnants," claiming that it was the persistence of the past in collusion with Maoism that was responsible for the disasters of the present. In that case, the question to be asked should not only be what might have gone wrong in the party's program and performance, including its failure to break with the past, but what might have been basically wrong with China from the start. What could be the fundamental nature of a culture, the "historical, cultural foundation" that had made the horror of the Cultural Revolution possible?[10]

On the other hand, the "search for roots" movement has not been simply driven by a radical iconoclasm, a protest that the Communist revolution had not gone far enough. With many writers the search for the past has also actually become, to borrow David Der-wei Wang's phrase, an exercise in "imaginary nostalgia,"[11] a remembrance or perhaps re-creation of what had been before. As an aftermath of the Cultural Revolution, this search can in any case be turned into an implied critique of the Communist present and its suppression of the past. In such a critique, traditional culture and its ancient myths are evoked to emphasize a sense of loss, a decline from or impoverishment of what had been before. Han Shaogong's recall of the "many-splendored" culture of ancient Chu in his manifesto, Mo Yan's lament at the decline of the race in the *Red Sorghum* family saga, Wang Anyi's depiction of Bao Village as a place where Confucian virtue (*renyi*) governs human behavior and relationships, can all be seen as expressions of an "imaginary nostalgia." In these writers the past is used both as a vehicle for questioning the present and as a source of renewed creative energy. Even as writers seek to "move toward the outside world," their reaffirmation of the hold of the past, either in denouncing or longing for it, makes their attitude toward China's past into a much more complex and ambivalent matter than the explicit iconoclasm of the May Fourth generation.

With the initiation of the "search for roots" movement in 1985, Chinese writers were caught up in the grips of a "culture fever" (*wenhua re*), engaging in feverish debates over the fundamental nature of Chinese culture and producing widely varying perceptions or assessments. Whether positive or negative in their conclusions, the debates have usually reached beyond contemporary revolutionary ideologies, even beyond the long-standing moral and political systems of state Confucianism, into early folk myths or the cultural preconscious. The old culture under appraisal is not necessarily that from a remote historical period, for the main point is how its manifestations persist into the present. Rather than an attribute defined by chronological time, cultural roots are considered to be that which is enduring and primal, representing ahistorical features that go deep into the bedrock, perhaps the preliterate roots, of Chinese civilization. In this "root-searching" process the peasantry becomes reconceptualized as the incarnation of that primal bedrock culture, particularized anew as an "other" against which modern writers carry out the quest for their own cultural past. Within such a context, the intellectual/peasant encounter in each of our three writers will take on many different meanings.

INTERROGATING SELF, LANGUAGE, AND TEXT

Han Shaogong, Mo Yan, and Wang Anyi belong to the generation who spent important periods of their growing up as "educated youth" (*zhi-qing*) among the peasant masses in the countryside. That traumatic experience of massive dislocation underlies their fiction of 1985–86, a fiction that often revolves around a crisis to the self brought on by crisscrossing the spatial, temporal, and cultural boundaries of country and city, past and present.

It is one of the great ironies of history that the post-Mao deconstruction of peasants as a special category of party ideology has in many ways been a direct result of a campaign in which they had theoretically been elevated to the absolute pinnacle as a class. The "up to the mountains and down to the villages" (*shangshan xiaxiang*) campaign was an outstanding feature of the Cultural Revolution. Between 1968 and 1975, Mao Zedong took the injunction outlined some twenty-six years earlier in his own "Talks at the Yan'an Forum on Literature and Art" that writers and artists "go among the masses," "serve the masses . . . become their student," to fantastic extremes, sending some twelve million young urban intellectuals to resettle in the countryside or border areas for periods ranging from one or two to ten or more years, or even a lifetime. Only after Mao's death was this extensive program dismantled and condemned along with the Cultural Revolution as yet another disaster of the "ten years of tumult" (*shinian dongluan*).

Like many other "mistakes" (*cuowu*)—as the party is wont to label even some of its most disastrous policies—in the history of the Chinese Communist Party, this campaign could be seen as yet another example of Mao Zedong "going too far" in carrying out the demands of his own revolutionary rhetoric. The campaign did indeed mingle intellectuals and peasants together on a historically unprecedented scale, but in the end the grand experiment may be said to have backfired, for what the young intellectuals actually learned from the masses as a result of their rural so-journ was not quite what the party chairman had envisioned. On the contrary, exposure to the poverty and the backward conditions of peas-ant existence in the countryside revealed to them the inadequacy, if not the sheer fallacy, of the ideological construct of the generic peasant as "revolutionary vanguard," as masters of the nation.

Even more unsettling for those who went to "resettle" among the peasants to work with and learn from them, was the effect of that experi-ence on their notions of themselves. Large numbers of them had origi-nally responded to Mao Zedong's call in fits of genuine revolutionary fervor and idealism. They had seen themselves as participating in another "Long March," their move to the countryside as an opportunity to break free from all oppressive authority (including parents, school, even the party's bureaucratic apparatus), but above all to carry on with the task of the great revolution and of building a new society. But instead of realiz-ing the utopian vision of the brave new world to which they had so ar-dently committed themselves, they found their years in rural exile lead-ing to dead ends in their lives, and to a state of profound disillusion-ment—and not just with those who had initially swept them up in the great revolutionary experiment.

The death of Mao Zedong in 1976 was soon followed by a wave of new literature born out of this disheartening experience. For the first few years many of these young writers wrote about their sense of personal loss and the deprivation of normal human relationships. They themselves as victims, exploited and betrayed by what they had invested their hopes and ideals in, were one of the central themes of "scar literature" or "literature of the wounded" (*shanghen wenxue*).

Like Xiaohua, the protagonist in Lu Xinhua's story "Shanghen" ("The Wound," or "The Wounded"), from which this whole genre of literature derives its name, they turned to scrutinize themselves and saw themselves as suffering.

It is 1978, the eve of the spring festival, and the story opens with Xiaohua (Dawning China?) on the train returning to visit the mother she had heartlessly rejected nine years ago when her mother was denounced as a "renegade" party member. Fervently believing in the correctness of the party's position then, she had left home to join the "up to the mountains and down to the villages" movement before graduating from high school. But now the "Gang of Four" has fallen, her mother has been rehabilitated and is gravely ill. As Xiaohua journeys back in the dark train, one of the first things we see her do is to furtively take out a small square mirror from her bag and look in it: "She had never before examined with such care her own young and beautiful face. But as she looked and looked, she suddenly realized that her eyes had begun to fill with tears."[12] To take a mirror out and look at oneself may be a small and commonplace gesture, but at this historical moment it was a significant indication that literature was moving away from the only themes that had been allowed during the Cultural Revolution: optimistic celebrations of the collective experience and its victories. These had precluded any introspective examination of the individual's condition, much less any acknowledgment that she might be in pain.

Xiaohua continues on her homeward journey to Shanghai. But of course by the end she arrives too late; of course she finds that her mother has just died that very morning. The outcome is inevitable, for this story is *meant* to be a tearjerker, an openly sentimental story staking a claim for the legitimacy of personal feelings which had for so long been suppressed. But the tragic ending of the journey home also emphasizes that for this generation of wounded youth there could be no recovery of what has been lost, no going back to pick up again where they had been before. The wounds suffered in her child's heart, as the dying mother wrote on the last page of her diary, are "deeper than those that have scarred my body"; these wounds are something the newly self-aware will have to live with for the rest of their lives.

There are more than a few lingering traces of the Maoist formula in this Lu Xinhua story, including the customary reference, for example, to the "poor and middle peasants" who had, during Xiaohua's long sojourn in the countryside, shown "much sincere concern for her. They took her in; they encouraged her." And they had collectively written to the Youth League to ask that she be approved for membership. But the fact remains that the story ends with Xiaohua holding on to the arm of her boyfriend, with bold steps heading toward "the bright lights of Nanjing Road." Her future, it is suggested, will henceforth not lie in the countryside to which she had once been so willing to dedicate herself, but here in the modernizing city of Shanghai.

In "scar literature" the self is a wounded subject, a means for revealing what the revolution had wrought on its children. It was fashionable in 1977–78 "to flaunt 'scars' left on one's body or mind by the Cultural Revolution,"[13] but by the 1980's, introspection in literature moves from

narrow self-pity to a broader search for the self. By this time the "educated youth" have already made their journey back to the urban environment from which they came and settled back where they might pre-
sume to feel more at home. They discover, however, that their problems
lie not only with what they find (including finding out what they may
have lost) upon their return, but whether they can really leave the past
behind and just turn their backs on those in the countryside with whom
their lives had once been so intertwined. In stories by Han Shaogong and
Mo Yan, crises of identity and moral responsibility will be precipitated
when the protagonists revisit their old rural communities and are forced
to confront not only that past but also themselves.

While these stories on re-encounters bypass the party's political categorization of peasants as basically irrelevant to the events, they pose a
further, even more direct, challenge to party doctrine in their apparent
foregrounding of the self. In 1985, at the same time the self-conscious
"search for roots" movement emerged, Liu Zaifu was arousing much discussion and controversy with his writings on subjectivity (*zhutixing*) in
literature. His attempt is to make the case for an independent, autonomous, subjective individual on the three levels of author, character, and
reader.[14] Conceptualizing literature as a process of the writer's self-
realization (*ziwo shixian*), Liu also argues for self-determining, independent characters who are neither tools nor puppets, and finally for the subjectivity of the reading experience through which readers and critics may
discover meanings beyond what the writer intended. What the new post-
Mao literature has rediscovered, according to Liu Zaifu, is (the hu)man
(*ren*), but one very different from the earlier discovery by May Fourth
literature. During that period

> the affirmation of man was sought from "society," a demand that society
> change its history of eating people, that society affirm the value of man, in-
> cluding the value of little people. Their hope was the realization of a "human
> society." In literature of the new era, they are not looking toward society,
> looking toward others, but are looking toward the "self" (*ji*), toward one self
> (*ziwo*). . . .
>   What they are seeking is self-affirmation, self-liberation . . . self-realiza-
> tion.[15]

These ideas were understandably seen as posing a threat to "the fate of
Marxism in China, the fate of socialist literature in China,"[16] for to affirm an independent, autonomous subject à la Western humanism would

seem tantamount to resisting the party's definition and domination of the self.

But to achieve the "affirmation," "liberation," and "realization" for the subjective self in and through the practice of writing has turned out to be a complex and problematic matter. In certain works of "roots-searching" fiction there is a conspicuous absence of a conscious, coherent, and rational individual narrator or character as the center of meaning and purpose. What the narrative discloses instead is the apparent discontinuity between the self's past and present and the elusiveness of individual identity. The loss of the unified subject may be attributed to specific historical causes—namely, the disastrous disruptions of life and existence under the party's pernicious campaigns; in any case these narratives give rise to the question of whether political agency can be ascribed to such a precarious and unstable self as the site from which to resist authoritarian domination.

But even if it may be impossible to assert the humanist values of individual autonomy as advanced by Liu Zaifu, the textual representation of the subject in contemporary narratives can nevertheless demonstrate the potential power of literary practice to elude or undermine ideological control. This rise of the split and shifting subject in modern Chinese literature coincides with the influx of literary theories from the West. Just as May Fourth writers applied their own readings of nineteenth-century Western doctrines of realism and romanticism to mount assaults against the hold of Chinese tradition, these writers of the 1980's will expropriate or bend Western poststructuralist notions about subject and textuality to challenge party domination over literature. In the post-Mao era, aesthetic theories and narrative praxis will again, as they did sixty years earlier, provide the base for a political—or antipolitical, as some Chinese writers would have it—but similarly utopian agenda.

The issue of self-representation is heavily implicated in contemporaneous debates over the ontological status of literature in its relation to reality and language. If literature claims to be a matter of "expressing the self" (biaoxian ziwo), has it not then, as some have claimed, turned its back on its primary task of "reflecting reality" (fanying xianshi), the central doctrine of Marxist criticism? Apart from the question of whether the two concepts of literature are mutually exclusive, there is the assumption that self-expression is somehow "bourgeois" or "antisocialist." Moreover, is it not only in reflecting "reality" that literature can have a proper social effect (shehui xiaoguo) and fulfill its public mission?,

But perhaps the mission of literature is in itself double-edged and inherently self-contradictory. When literature first emerged from the shambles of the Maoist-dominated literary scene, there was initially much celebration of the "new realism" or the "return to realism"—Gao Xiaosheng's fiction was hailed as producing prime examples of that—for the requirement that "literature be in the service of politics" had, so it seemed, merely produced a "fake realism" in the past. But the question that soon followed was whether a "realistic literature" that severed itself from political service was actually possible. The realist project may well have been doomed from the start due to the writer/intellectual's long-standing role and self-image in the Chinese system.

According to this view, the tradition of intellectuals participating in the political establishment, either as scholar-officials in the imperial past or as party cadres under communism, meant that they have never been able to speak the truth in literature.[17] Innately weak and cowardly to begin with, intellectuals have been even more intimidated in recent decades by campaigns and persecutions, and even less capable of speaking up in an independent voice. Furthermore, what has hampered them has been precisely the persistent belief that literature must perform a practical and didactic function, the modern engaged author's "intervening in life" (*ganyu shenghuo*) being merely an up-to-date version of the age-old principle of "literature as vehicle of the Way" (*wen yi zai dao*). If writers have embraced realism, labored to simulate or represent reality in literature, it has mainly been because they have always considered themselves to be "sociologists, moralists, reformers, etc."[18] From the time of "its emergence in the mother's womb, the Chinese form of realism has carried the fetal mark of pragmatism," as Li Hangyu, a prominent "roots-searching" writer, put it.[19] The fact that realism has always carried a moral or political agenda, grounded in a "vision of the world and system of values"[20] means that it can never deny its own subordination to or complicity with prevailing ideology.

As Jing Wang puts it well in her incisive discussion of aesthetic modernity in post-Mao China, "the historical burden of 'modernist' artists and writers fell on their potential exposure of what was 'unreal' about socialist reality and on their discovery and radicalizing of the private space of the subject."[21] Rather than challenging head on socialist reality's lack of "reality," many post-Mao writers and critics have adopted the modernist stance that the only way literature could break free from the constraints of reflecting an officially sanctioned model of the world would

be to renounce the realist project altogether. Reconceptualized as an independent, self-contained process, literature would abdicate any claims
to referentiality. Instead of maintaining that it has some clear and direct
correspondence with the world "out there," it would turn to focus on
"doing its own thing" with the medium it has to work with—language.

From early on the argument against realism was also strongly reinforced by controversies over the referentiality of language in the new poetry. In fact the post-Mao "revolt of language" (*yuyan de fanpan*), as it
has been termed, had begun with the "Misty Poetry" (*Menglong shi*) that
first appeared in the pages of the unofficial journal *Jintian* (*Today*) in
December 1978;[22] it had then "struck the first blow against Maoist language."[23] Widely attacked for being unintelligible, incomprehensible, as
constituting a "misty" or "obscure" school of poetry, the poets themselves gladly welcomed the pejorative label. What it did was to call attention to their deliberate experimentation with form and imagery, to
their efforts of exploring the cutting edge between language and meaning, all in effect questioning the assumption that the function of language was to express clear and explicit (official) "truths." The writers of
"root-searching" fiction likewise possessed a very strong "language consciousness"; they did not, as the writer Wang Zengqi points out, see
"language only as a means for expression, but as the 'thing-in-itself,' the
content of the work."[24]

In his article "1985," Li Tuo has particularly emphasized the central
role of this fiction during that year of "sudden change" or "mutation"
(*tubian*), when Chinese literature went "modernist." "In 1985, due to the
rise of 'root-searching literature' . . . the history of 'worker, peasant, sol-
dier literature and art' (*gongnongbing wenyi*) finally reached its terminal
point." That literature led the way in signaling the end of the road for
the "brand new popular mass culture that had been created by Mao Zedong to fit in with the revolution he led."[25]

The break with the Maoist language system and the ideological code
embedded in it may be more sharply evident in the openly antirealist experimental or avant-garde fiction (*shiyan xiaoshuo* or *xianfeng xiaoshuo*)
of such writers as Ma Yuan, Yu Hua, and others, which began about the
same time but would increasingly come to occupy the center of attention
in the next two years or so. For "root-searching" fiction appropriates
rather than totally discards certain features of that "worker, peasant, sol-
dier" literature, including some of its themes, tropes, mise-en-scènes, as
well as its cast of characters, even as it subjects all to ironic and self-

conscious interrogation. Unlike avant-garde fiction, it may continue, although in varying degrees, to locate itself in some kind of identifiable temporal context with references to recent history, while at the same time its textual operations will disrupt or question that referential relationship. It both employs and subverts the political rhetoric and ideological codes that have long shaped and defined the subject matter of fiction on the countryside. In this respect it can be seen as an example of what Linda Hutcheon, in her discussion of the politics of postmodernism, has provocatively termed "historiographic metafiction," a paradoxical form in which "its historical and sociopolitical grounding sits uneasily alongside its self-reflexivity."[26]

"Root-searching" fiction reflects a wide range of ideological and aesthetic issues, but my discussion will be mainly limited to those aspects that are manifest in the intellectual/peasant encounter. The process of representing/constructing a peasantry outside the confines of a reformist or revolutionary ideology involved this fiction in many of the other questions under debate at the time. Who or what is that subjective self that is consciously rejecting the interpellation of ideology, even as it must confront the world of a peasant "other"? Can this subjective self be a center of knowledge and authenticity? How should the contextual world in which the encounter between self and "other" takes place be represented through language? What are the sources of narrative authority in speaking for either self or the other? Han Shaogong, Mo Yan, and Wang Anyi will each explore such issues through a variety of experimental practices in subjectivity, representation, and narrative.

HAN SHAOGONG AS EXEMPLARY "SEARCH

FOR ROOTS" WRITER?

In 1985, Han Shaogong produced several texts that have been seen as practically synonymous with the "root-searching" movement. These include what has been regarded as the movement's "manifesto," "Wenxue de 'gen'" ("The 'Roots' of Literature"), as well as several exemplary short stories. His experiences as an "educated youth" were typical of many of his generation. Born in 1953 in Changsha, Hunan, he was sent to the countryside upon graduation from middle school and spent nine years of rustification in Changle, Miluo county, Hunan. He was transferred to the local cultural center in 1974 and graduated from Hunan Teachers' College in 1982. Although he had published several stories between 1974 and 1983, it was not until 1985, when he had gone on a trip to Western Hunan, that he began the "root-searching" phase of his literary career."[27]

Two months after the "manifesto" of April 1985, Han Shaogong followed with "Ba Ba Ba," which was soon considered by many to be the "root-searching" story par excellence.[28] However, whether the manifesto can indeed serve as *the* explanatory program even of that very story is quite another matter.

The manifesto begins with a query about where the "many-splendored" culture of Chu had gone, a query raised since this writer from Changsha, Hunan, is, in Joseph Lau's words, "a bona fide native of the ancient state of Chu."[29] When Han Shaogong spent his stint in the countryside near the Miluo River not far from Qu Yuan's Temple, he had found traces in local speech that suggested connections with the *Li-sao* of Qu Yuan, though not much more. But as the essay proceeds, he is not so much concerned with those qualities of "mystery, romantic strangeness, freedom, lack of inhibition or indignation," that are, in his view, characteristic of Chu culture and once embodied in its poetic tradition, as with something that might be regarded as quite outside literature proper altogether.

Referring to Taine's *Philosophy of Art* (1865–1869), Han Shaogong goes on to discuss his search as one for the deeper levels of a nation's culture, the substratum, the "magma that lies under the earth's shell," the traditional culture as "coagulated" in the countryside, as seen in "slang, unofficial history, legends, jokes, folk songs, stories about gods and spirits, customs, forms of sexual love, etc.," that mostly do not form part of written tradition or fall within the confines of orthodox norms.[30] The countryside (*xiangtu*) is the locus for this magma, for the countryside is seen as the "past of the city."

While Han Shaogong may claim to be representing in his fiction a countryside with its customs and folkways that is distinctive of the regional culture of Chu, paradoxically the powerful impact of his celebrated *xungen* story "Ba Ba Ba" comes rather from its being read as a much broader, more generalized portrait of China as a whole. For its audience the story seems to have produced a symbol, comparable to Lu Xun's celebrated Ah Q, of China's overall backwardness and "primitive mental state."[31]

Such generalized readings are encouraged by the story's deliberate blurring of the boundaries of time and space, and Han Shaogong has acknowledged that his goal in the story was indeed to blend historical truths.[32] Cock's Head Village, where the story's events take place, is de-scribed as being deep in mountains perched high in the clouds; when walking out one is always surrounded by a sea of white clouds, as if floating on a tiny isolated island without end.[33] There are some historical references in the story that could place it at the end of the Qing, but oth-ers seem to place it after Communist liberation. When the villagers plan to file a complaint with the authorities, a dispute breaks out over whether it should be referred to by the old term "supplication" (*bingtie*, as to one's official superiors) or by the modern sounding "report" (*baogao*). At the end, as the villagers, devastated by famine and defeat in war, embark on a journey of migration "over the mountains" (*guoshan*), they sing the same song about their origins that begins the story, when, guided by a phoenix, their ancestors arrived from the shores of the East Sea. Time need not be specified for time here is circular; in this stagnant culture, history can only endlessly repeat itself.

The looking forward and looking backward in time is represented by members of two generations in one family. Shi Ren or Renbao is the only one in this insular, enclosed community who has occasional con-tacts with the world beyond—Qianjiaping, the village down below—and who carries with him some suggestions of possible change. When he re-turns from down below he will bring back some new plaything, "a glass bottle, a broken lantern, an elastic band that could stretch or contract, an old newspaper, a photograph of someone or other" (p. 13). His status is enhanced when he uses such new terms as "too conservative" to com-plain about the village, and by his frequent repetition of "It will begin soon," or "This is the beginning." The remarks certainly impress every-body, but what is going to begin, the beginning of what? No one under-stands what he is really talking about. And apparently neither does Ren-bao himself. The utter ineffectuality of this "personage of the new school" (*xinpai renwu*) is underscored by the fact that he is a bachelor getting on in years who tries to assuage his sexual frustration by poking around with animal parts, or by spying on bathing or peeing women. But then his voyeurism is frustrated by his poor eyesight.

At the opposite pole, forever looking backward toward the old ways, is his father, Zhong Man, the tailor, who likewise inspires a certain re-spect in the village, because he possesses the rudiments of literacy, having read a few "tattered thread-bound books with no beginning or end," and thus acquired some "apparently either true or fictitious" knowledge about the past. The villagers listen to him tell stories about historical figures as he laments the decline of the present age. Now that there is no Sleeping Dragon—Zhuge Liang, the sage minister of the Three Kingdoms period and Zhong Man's idol—manners and morals can only go from bad to worse, and he foresees that Cock's Head Village will soon come to an end (p. 18). And so it does.

With no food, repeatedly defeated in their armed feuds against their neighboring village, in the end the villagers must move on deeper into the mountains so that the young men and women among them will be able to survive, beget descendants, and continue to serve their ancestors. It is Zhong Man the tailor who follows what their ancestors supposedly, as recorded in the clan book, had done before and who mixes the powerful poison to administer to the old and weak in the village who must be left behind. He may have let his ancestors down but his consolation is that in this matter he has maintained the ancient traditions. There is an almost overwhelming poignancy in the final pages of the story, as this collective suicide is accepted with pathos and dignity by the old members of the community who have to feed the poison to their grandchildren and then drink it themselves.

While the father-and-son pair represent two opposing perspectives on time, both are characterized by the same noncomprehension and nonarticulation that pervades this story of timeless stagnation. There have been several perceptive analyses of "Ba Ba Ba" as an allegory and critique of traditional Chinese culture, and particularly of the character of Bingzai as an image of the Chinese national character.[34] What I would like to explore further are the questions raised by the story concerning the role of literacy and language in its attempt to represent the substratum of culture.

Far removed from the splendors of romance, mystery, and poetry that Han Shaogong saw in the *Chuci* tradition, "Ba Ba Ba" is dominated by the misshapen and grotesque figure of Bingzai, the ageless "little old man" in a permanent stage of undevelopment, an emblem of a community stuck in time. His most outstanding trait is his inability to speak, to say anything beyond the two phrases "Ba ba ba," uttered when he is in a good mood, and "F—mama" when otherwise. Apart from this absurdly minimized expression of the cosmic principle of the *yinyang* bipolarity, Bingzai is a creature without language and utterly lacking in subjectivity or self-awareness; in comparison, the idiot Benjy in Faulkner's *The Sound and the Fury,* at least had "some brains" and a "sexual consciousness."[35] The Bingzai in Han Shaogong's story becomes a mere cipher, a blank space onto which the villagers can play their crude jokes, take out their aggressions, or project their superstitious beliefs. At one moment he is a human sacrifice picked to appease the grain god, merely saved when a thunder clap suggests that the Heavens might be displeased with such a poor offering; at another he is venerated as an oracle, addressed as Master, Lord, Immortal Bing, whose meaningless gestures are taken as a guide to the villagers who are plotting war against the neighboring Cock's Tail Village, while they prostrate themselves before him. (Could this alternation between cruel victimization and exalted veneration be taken as a parody of the Communist Party's treatment of those at the lower strata, Mao Zedong's "poor and blank" masses both oppressed yet glorified?) But in his inadequate command of language—to put it mildly—Bingzai is not just an isolated freak; he is but an exaggerated example of what is true of his entire community.

The ignorant, superstitious, and irrational way in which this village community responds to events and makes fatal decisions—they offer human sacrifice to the grain god in times of drought, consult geomancers or observe the way the slaughtered ox falls to decide about going to war—is reflected in the peculiar way they speak. Their language is different from that of others, sprinkled with archaic words, confusing even in such fundamental matters as kinship terms. They are shown over and over again as seemingly unable to express themselves or communicate with others; they cannot manage to articulate their motivations for actions, explanations for decisions, or whatever it is they understand about their world. The songs they sing about their history have been pronounced by an official historian who once visited Qianjiaping as having no truth in them. Delong, the singer of ancient songs with his wonderful voice, left the community long ago, leaving behind his son Bingzai, the inarticulate moron.

The story of this linguistically deficient community is told by a seemingly self-effacing third-person narrator who constantly withholds interpretation, explanation, or commentary on the events he relates. While using vocabulary that obviously is beyond that used by the villagers, the narrator employs a matter-of-fact tone that for the most part simply appears to "go along" with the community's "naive" way of looking at things. At one point he refers to "our ancestors," as if he were one of its members (p. 8).

In one sense the narrator is "omniscient" in that he follows different characters around, although never beyond the community, but in another he is not, in that he does not express an external or higher overall commanding view of the story. Information is given as uncertifiable, events introduced by such phrases as "allegedly" (*jushuo*), "apparently" (*sihu*), "for some unknown reason" (*buzhi wei shenme*), etc. Events are often presented to be uncertain, and to remain so. Did Third Grandpa of Cock's Tail Village die of a bite from a huge centipede, and was one of his feet half-eaten away by rats? A bad omen if true, but then he was seen by someone later. So "Third Grandpa seemed there and not there, his very existence became a question" (p. 16).

At times the narration will present events from the point of view of Bingzai's uncomprehending consciousness, as when the village decides to slaughter an ox in order to predict its own fortune in the coming battle. The cheer that goes up in the crowd when the ox falls forward after its head is cut off frightens Bingzai and he begins to mutter. Then "he saw a thread of something red flowing from the under the tangle of the grown-ups' feet, like a slithering crimson snake. He squatted down to pinch it; it felt slimy. But when he got it onto his clothes, it looked real pretty" (p. 24). He covers his body and face with ox blood. His mother drags him home, gives him a good beating, and ties him to a chair. He takes a nap, and when he woke up "he heard the clang of gongs in the distance, then the sound of ox horns, and then all was quiet. Later on, he had no idea when, he heard the noisy din of footsteps, people yelling, the sound of metal clashing. Then he heard the sound of women wailing. . . . Something had happened outside" (p. 25). The "something" is a battle that has been fought and lost with much loss of life. It will turn out to be the climactic event that finally seals the community's fate, but it is not otherwise described.

While the narration does not often "descend" to the level of Bingzai's noncomprehension, the general absence of commentary or evalution, as well as other signs of an abdication of narrative authority, would seem to be a strategy to let the story and its participants "speak for themselves," even as they are shown to be incapable of "speaking." But such a narrative strategy reveals a rather paradoxical or dubious relationship between the cultivated, literate culture in which the writing inevitably participates and the subculture it seeks to represent. Why is this "lower" culture made out to be so mindless, inarticulate, and "dumb"? Is the implied author, speaking from his own superior position as a writer/intellectual exercising his privileged control of language all the more with his apparent self-effacing restraint? Or does this restraint signify his own status as an outsider, his lack of access to the conscious life of this community? How can one give voice to those who—apparently—hardly know how to speak? How should one represent in literature those who are seemingly beyond or beneath the conscious level of language? How can the hardly verbal substratum of Chinese culture—if that indeed is where its "roots" are to be found—be represented by those who are part of the self-conscious, self-perpetuating literary tradition above?

One could even go on to ask if the searchers for cultural roots know what it is that they are doing, or what they are looking for. Wang Zengqi refers to "root-searching" as "a vague and confusing notion." No one can really say what it really is. "But this may be a good thing. 'Root-searching' was basically a kind of hope, a quest, an impulse, without a unified norm or measure."[36] The gap between "root-searching" theory and narrative performance, the paradox of attempting to represent what might not be representable, as seen in "Ba Ba Ba," are indications of how undefined that hope or quest may well be.

These writers may have all along been rather unclear about what they meant by "culture" (*wenhua*) to begin with; the main point was that in some vague way, culture stood in opposition to politics.[37] What the new "cultural agenda" of such stories as "Ba Ba Ba" did first of all was to provide writers with a new area of literary exploration, a means to break away from dominant ideological molds in representing the "peasant others" by reconstructing them as forming the base of Chinese society and culture, however understood. Nothing could be further removed from the glorified images of the vanguard peasant masses with their boundless revolutionary potential that had filled the party-approved pages of socialist realism than the bleak portrayal of Bingzai and his ignorant and backward community. That he alone survives famine, war, and fatal poison at the end of the story strongly suggests that idiocy may be the permanent state of the culture he exemplifies.

THE CRISIS TO THE SELF: IDENTITY AND

MORAL RESPONSIBILITY

If peasant representation is no longer bound by Maoist ideology, the intellectual at the opposite pole, concomitantly released from a prescriptive discursive position, is driven to examine the self on its own now increasingly uncertain terms. In 1985, both Han Shaogong and Mo Yan wrote stories about the crises to the self that are brought on when the intellectual is forced to confront that self by revisiting the rural communities where he had lived for a time before.

Han Shaogong's "Guiqulai" ("Homecoming") draws more explicitly than "Ba Ba Ba" upon the literary tradition of Chu culture. Joseph Lau sees "Guiqulai" as a "*baihua* variant of Zhuangzi's famous Butterfly Dream parable," an example of Han Shaogong's "tacit claim of spiritual ancestry with the Chu philosophers and poets.[38] Jeffrey Kinkley has pointed out its echoes or allusions to Qu Yuan's "Summons of the Soul" and Tao Qian's poem "Return" as well as the Shangri-La in his "Peach Blossom Spring."[39] While such references point to a reaching back to the literary past of the Hunan region, the themes of exile, wandering, confused identity, and search for utopia in these particular examples happen also to resonate powerfully with Han Shaogong's story about the elusive quest for self.

"Guiqulai" has been variously translated as "The Homecoming," "Homecoming?," "Déjà Vu," the titles themselves reflecting different degrees of uncertainty in reading the "facts" of the story's events,[40] for one point of the story is precisely the difficulty of sorting out the relationship between external reality and the subjective consciousness of dream, memory, and perception.

The story centers around an "educated youth" who may or may not be Huang Zhixian, as he visits a mountain village where he may or may not have lived in exile ten years ago. When the narrative begins, the I-narrator finds himself negotiating a mountain path and encountering many scenic details which seem "both very familiar and very strange." He tells himself that he couldn't have been there before, that it was "absolutely impossible," but the villagers seem to recognize him as "Glasses Ma," a nickname that immediately sets him off as an intellectual. Their comments suggest that he had been a sent-down "educated youth" and won their respect and affection as a dedicated teacher.

After vainly protesting that he is Huang Zhixian, he half-willingly goes along with this conferred identity so as to, he tells himself, take advantage of their friendly hospitality. But other more ominous revelations about "his" past emerge. Apparently "he" had been jailed for killing the local bully, Shorty Yang, who everyone agrees deserved what he got, and had also misled a local girl into falling in love with him. She had subsequently turned into a bird who is always calling for him, "don't go [or do that] brother" (*xing bude ye gege*). Had "he" as Glasses Ma been guilty of murdering one person, and of seducing and possibly causing the death of another? The question of identity then is not only one of memory or cognition, but involves the even more indeterminate question of moral culpability.

The split in the self that is reflected in the shifting identities of the "I" is also dramatized in the frequent dialogues between two selves, the self-observation and self-questioning in the unfolding narrative process that alternately confirms and denies knowledge and responsibility about what he encounters.

He seems to be verging onto a moment of "truth" when in accordance with some local custom, he is made to take a bath. Looking at himself through the blue mist he "suddenly had a weird feeling, as if this body were unfamiliar, strange. There was no adornment here and no stranger, no one to cover up or put on an act for and no conditions for it, only my naked self, my own reality."[41] He sees a scar on his calf; had it been caused by the spiked shoe on the soccer field (in that case when he was a student) or here in the village by the bite of the murdered victim in his death struggle? Like every "educated youth" of his generation he carries scars from his past experiences; it is the specific cause that is uncertain here. Details of that horrible struggle on the narrow mountain path as Shorty Yang was being killed seem to come to his mind. He is afraid to look at his own hands. Was there a smell of blood on them? But if his memory might be on the verge of clearing up the mystery of his identity—if he is indeed the guilty Glasses Ma—he immediately feels compelled to deny it: "I struggled now to convince myself I had never come here before and never known any Shorty. Never, even in a dream, had I seen this circle upon circle of blue mist. Never" (p. 233).   In   spite   of this denial, he slips out to see the old house where "he" had lived before and carries on a conversation about the past with the dead Old Grand-dad, who uses the "voice of a crow to cough and the rustle of the leaves to speak with me." Then when he next encounters the younger sister of the betrayed woman who had become a bird, he seems to act as if he can no longer get away with being Huang Zhixian, an outsider from town passing through. He begins to acknowledge that he could be someone deeply implicated in what had happened there in the past.

Without taking proper leave he secretly flees the village and checks into an inn in town. He has a dream in which he is still walking and walking on that mountain road, the road always under his feet. Could he have been in this recurring dream when the story opens with him walking on that mountain road? But somehow there is a parrot with him in the inn, concrete evidence perhaps of an actual visit to the village but also of an unshakable link with the past. Questions of reality, dream, memory, identity become harder to sort out, but no matter where he goes, he has the same dream. When he wakes up he is stunned to be addressed over the phone as Huang Zhixian. "Was there a Huang Zhixian in the world, too? And was I that Huang Zhixian?" (p. 237) Even if he may have now returned to the world of Huang Zhixian, he "will never be able to get out of that gigantic I. Mama!"[42]

So the story concludes, the question of his identity unresolved. For if he cannot remember who (or which person) he once was, he cannot know who he is now. What the generation of "educated youth" experienced when they were "sent down" to the countryside will haunt them for the rest of their lives; it changed them into something other, whether literally or metaphorically, than what they had been, leaving them forever uncertain of who they are.[43] The notion of a fractured self, the lack of a coherent, continuous, autonomous subject, may coincide with the theories of postmodernism, but it can be seen no less as the product of a specific history: the destructive effects on selfhood from the countryside experience during the Cultural Revolution.

In Mo Yan's story "Baigou qiuqian jia" ("White Dog and the Swings"), published in the same year as "Homecoming," what creates a dilemma for the intellectual I-narrator when he returns to visit the countryside after a ten-year absence, is not a split identity but his advanced class status and the question of his moral obligations toward those left behind.[44]

Unlike the two other writers discussed in this chapter, Mo Yan spent his early life in the countryside and therefore may claim, as he puts it, to possess a "peasant consciousness."[45] He was born into a poor rural community in Shandong. As a member of an "upper-middle peasant" family he attended school until the fifth grade, when the Cultural Revolution broke out and he went back to attending cows, cutting grass, "happy, but somewhat discomforted every time I passed by school."[46] In search for a future (chulu) he joined the army in 1976. He began writing fiction in 1981 and five years later passed the entrance exam of the literature department in the Liberation Army's School of Arts. While Mo Yan often insists on his rural origins, many of his stories on the countryside are actually told through the perspective of an I-narrator who long ago left it for the city.[47] The "peasant consciousness," however understood, will be mediated by this narrator's self-reflective language. And the confrontation between intellectual and peasant will be all the more fraught with complex moral issues, precisely because the "I" now returns to his home village not as the peasant he once might have been but *as* an urbanized and alienated intellectual.

In "White Dog and the Swings" a college teacher revisits his home village and re-encounters Nuan, a high school friend—in some ways she could be considered a childhood sweetheart—only to discover the hardships and degradation of her existence and the enormous difference in status now between them. "Strongly reminiscent of Lu Xun's "homecoming" stories "The New-Year Sacrifice" and "My Old Home," as David Der-wei Wang has observed,[48] the critical encounter with the peasant turns into a moral crisis on the part of the I-narrator. In Lu Xun's stories, the intellectual's guilty conscience is the occasion for indulging in uneasy self-reflection or perhaps in speculation over possible hopes for improved relations in the younger generation, but at the narrative's close he is free after all to turn his back on the discovered "other" and return to resume his life in the city. The "I" in Mo Yan's "White Dog and the Swings" is not allowed to "get off" so easily. The story ends with his being confronted with a direct and urgent plea from his former friend, and he must make an on-the-spot choice, so to speak—right there in the midst of the trampled-down sorghum—as to whether he will engage in an immediate, physical act that might possibly alleviate the horror of her situation and thereby redeem himself.

One night over ten years ago, when both were in high school, he had dragged Nuan out to a swing, causing her to lose an eye when the rope broke and she fell into a clump of thorns. Horribly disfigured at age seventeen, the talented and once beautiful girl loses her chance, or so she thinks, to marry a flirtatious PLA officer. In her despair she also decides to discontinue her relationship with the narrator when he leaves for college. Instead she is reduced to marrying a coarse mute, gives birth to three deaf and dumb children, and is condemned to a life of hardship, poverty, and utter loneliness. Seizing the opportunity of the narrator's return visit, she contrives to meet with him in a sorghum field and pleads with him to "save" her by helping her to conceive a child, a child that can speak.

The story ends in midair as her pleading voice trails off; he is deeply moved, but we do not know his response. Apart from other dilemmas— he has a fiancée in the city—there is the physical disgust that she refers to and that he must overcome in acceding to her desperate request. From the very first moment when Nuan appears on the scene bent under the weight of the big load of sorghum leaves on her back, the narration takes pains to establish the disagreeable aspects of her physical appearance. The narrator is struck by the pungent smell of her sweat, observes her dirt-streaked face, the terrible looking bloodshot left eye. Then there is that sunken right eye socket marked with only a jagged line of eye lashes. Although later she puts in an artificial eye to make herself more acceptable to him, he can't bear to look at it: "It was lifeless, glowed dully like porcelain" (p. 282). All these graphic descriptions are there to emphasize the sad, brutal conditions of her life, reminders of how far she has fallen from what she once was or might have been.

The deaf-mute husband whom the I-narrator meets when he eats at their house is particularly grotesque and repulsive. He "exudes a bestial odor," rubs the "grey dirt looking like rat droppings" off his exposed chest, "laughs like a barking dog," is capable of uttering nothing but "argh, argh." There is a moment, fraught with sexual connotations, when the narrator observes the brutish husband grab his wife by the hair, pull her head back, and use two "cucumberlike" black fingers to force a piece of candy covered with his own sticky saliva into her small, delicate mouth.

Of all the writers discussed so far, Mo Yan is unique for the way he exploits sensory details to evoke the earthy body presence of his peasant characters. Zhao Shuli's peasants had been sanitized into revolutionary heroic models, but even Lu Xun's oppressed peasants, as depicted through the eyes of the narrator, have, in comparison with Mo Yan's, a distant and abstract quality to them. Not only are the peasant figures physically particularized in Mo Yan's fiction—their smell, dirt, body functions, described in graphic detail—he shows a marked predilection for those who are disfigured, deformed, physically maimed, mentally retarded, sexually impotent, and so on. While they are reactions against the haloed peasant images in so much party-directed fiction of the past, these damaged characters are also telling examples of as well as metaphors for the hardships and deprivations of peasant existence.

When the narrator in "White Dog and the Swings" enters his village and first sees the huge, swaying load of sorghum leaves approach from afar, his "heart senses its heavy weight":

> I knew all too well what it felt like to push your way in the summer through the dense, stifling sorghum fields to cut leaves. Needless to say your body is drenched in sweat and your chest feels too tight to breathe. But what feels

worst is the way the tiny hairs on the sorghum leaves scratch against your sweat-soaked skin. (p. 268)

His present status as an intellectual has freed him from having to bear such heavy burdens. As a college teacher, soon to be promoted to lecturer, he has become, as Nuan terms him, "upper class" (*gaoji*) while she is "lower class" (*diji*) (p. 276). His twenty-five yuan blue jeans, pretend as he may that they cost only three yuan and sixty cents, arouses the villagers' hostility; it is an embarrassing reminder of how utterly out of place he is there. Due to his higher station in life his uncle disapproves of his going to visit his old school friend. To the uncle it shows that even after all that studying, his nephew is rather "crazy": "You tell me what you're going out to see her for; they're either blind or dumb over there, won't people in the village laugh at you? Fish stay with fish, shrimp with shrimp; you shouldn't be stooping below your station!" (p. 278). He has to go, though, linked to her not just because of their old friendship but also because of the terrible burden of guilt he carries with him, and of which he is reminded by every feature of her harsh existence.

Particularly symptomatic of the sharp class division in the story is the fact that Nuan is now stuck with a family of mutes. What she begs for from the narrator is not a renewal of their past relationship, but for him to give her someone she can talk with, speak to. But even if he should find it impossible to refuse her request and gives in to have sex with her, the enormous gulf between them that has been created by the unequal access to language is not one that can be bridged.

Nuan's request may well be based on an understanding of genetics that is less than scientific. In any case it is doubtful whether the defining boundary—the nexus of speech and writing, privilege, power, authority—that bars the lower-class peasant from the world of the upper-class intellectual can be transcended by an act of copulation. Having gone to school herself, Nuan is not merely a passive victim submitting without protest to her inferior station in life, but she is unable to do more than make a desperate appeal to the more powerful male intellectual for a child with speech. (In this case inequality of class status is reinforced by gender difference.) The story leaves the two characters confronting each other in the sorghum field, its lack of closure emphasizing the persistent and unresolvable issue of the moral responsibility of the intellectual— ever aware of his privileged status—when forced to come face to face with that insurmountable (pardon the pun here) fact.

Problematic endings, as we have also seen in Han Shaogong's "Home-coming," are a common phenomenon in post-Mao fiction. Such acknowledgment of ambiguity or indeterminacy in itself represents a significant departure from the past, when party intervention or the application of some Maoist idea could provide an answer to every question and all stories concluded with all problems solved. In Mo Yan's novel *Honggaoliang* (Red Sorghum), ambiguity and indeterminacy are there not just in the ending but also on many levels within the text; they are everywhere written into the narrative process itself.

THE INTELLECTUAL WRITING SELF AS UNWORTHY DESCENDANT IN 'RED SORGHUM'

"White Dog and the Swings," like Han Shaogong's story "Homecoming," is set in the post–Cultural Revolution era. Mo Yan's *Red Sorghum*, which began appearing in 1986,[49] covers an extended history that begins in 1923 and perhaps goes to 1985. A giant of a novel, running to almost five hundred pages, complex, multifaceted, it has inspired much critical comment and acclaim since its appearance. It was the basis of one of the first films to win recognition abroad for its then novice director Zhang Yimou and Chinese contemporary cinema in general.[50]

An epic account of the exploits and tragedies of his ancestors by their "unworthy descendant," *Red Sorghum* is the exploration of the relationship between the writing/intellectual self and the peasant "other," transposed to a personal level, brought close to home, so to speak, by being located within the family. The representation of that relationship, now conceptualized as "filial," has also been raised to an unprecedented level of sophistication and complexity. My focus will primarily be on the work's narrative mode, most particularly its ironic interaction with established genre conventions, and its distinctive employment of the narrating "I," as means both for examining the novel's ambivalent attitude toward that relationship and how that ambivalence is interwoven into various self-reflexive operations within the narrative process.

The double-edged relation between the narrating self and those ancestors whose stories he is narrating is immediately evident in the novel's unusual dedication. It borrows from, but simultaneously subverts, both form and language from the traditional ritual of offerings made to the dead. While notifying readers of the purpose of his novel, Mo Yan's unique mixture of professed respect and ironic self-deprecation also alerts them to what will be the most characteristic of its narrative tone and mode:

> With this book I respectfully invoke the heroic, aggrieved souls wandering in the boundless bright-red sorghum fields of my hometown. As your unfilial son, I am prepared to carve out my heart, marinate it in soy sauce, have it minced and placed in three bowls, and lay it out as an offering in a field of sorghum. Partake of it in good health![51]

From its opening the novel casts itself as a partly ironic exercise of self-expiation by an unfilial, unworthy son/grandson (*bu xiao zisun*), who is also a self-styled effete and inferior urban intellectual. The hero-guerrilla-bandits who "killed and plundered, loyally served their country, enacted scene after scene of heroic, tragic, and stirring drama," are referred to by the I-narrator as "Granddad," "Grandma," or "Father."[52]

The narrator's ambivalent attitude, a combination of extreme love and extreme hate, toward his homeland, Gaomi Dongbeixiang, is announced right from the beginning. After growing up and working hard to study Marxism,[53] he finally realized that his homeland was easily "the most beautiful and the most ugly, the most elevated and the most vulgar, the most sacred and the most filthy, the most heroic and the most son-of-a-bitch, the hardest-drinking and hardest-loving place on earth" (p. 2) (p. 4). As portrayed in the novel his ancestors were glorious war heroes, larger than life in their passions, in their loyalty and heroism, in their capacity to live life to the fullest and to die with courage. But at the same time they were also lawless bandits who engaged in suicidal factional fights, robbed, looted, and betrayed those who loved them. Just as they mixed their urine and their blood into the sorghum wine they brewed and drank to give it its distinctive taste, their characters are a mixture or blend of the positive and the negative.

On the formal level, the novel is similarly a rich "brew" as it draws upon diverse ingredients from several narrative genres, incorporating them while simultaneously parodying them. Indeed *Red Sorghum* may be seen as a telling example of Bakhtin's heteroglossia, the hybridization characteristic of the novel that is "connected with a disintegration of stable verbal-ideological systems," the "decentering" that occurs when "a national culture loses its sealed-off and self-sufficient character."[54] While Bakhtin is characterizing the novel as a whole, his notion of the disintegration of verbal systems, which are also in themselves ideological, seems particularly applicable to the historical and "disintegrating" moment of the post-Mao era and the "hybrid" fiction it has produced. The "hybridization" of *Red Sorghum*, its challenge to the domination of any single unitary discourse, is carried out most notably in the way it sets itself in dialogic tension with multiple genre conventions.

While on the one hand the novel is a story about the War of Resistance against Japan (as Zhang Yimou's film interprets it), on the other, it has "'dismembered' or 'deconstructed' the conventional didactic stories on that theme,"[55] since guerrilla fighters are portrayed both as patriotic heroes and members of murderous outlaw gangs. The narrator claims that he is erecting a monument for his family in compiling this chronicle (*shubei lizhuan*), but its decidedly mixed picture of his ancestors both recalls and parodies (as did the novel's dedication) the conventions of hagiographic family history. Zhou Yingxiong has suggested that we approach *Red Sorghum* as a "*yanyi* historical novel,"[56] referring particularly to the moment when Five Troubles, a bandit gang member who has been "studying the *Sanguo* (*Romance of the Three Kingdoms*) and the *Shuihu* (*The Water Margin*) since childhood," decides to throw in his lot with Granddad Yu Zhan'ao. In his view Granddad is the only true leader who has the ability "to put the nation (*tianxia*) in order" (p. 387) (p. 283). It is not clear that Granddad actually entertained grandiose ambitions of being another Zhuge Liang, but in the conception of his character there are not a few allusions to the bandit-heroes of *The Water Margin*.

Zhu Ling has persuasively argued that the construction of masculinity in *Red Sorghum* is consistent with the sadistic misogyny and glorification of violence that pervades that sixteenth century novel.[57] At first glance Granddad Yu Zhan'ao may appear to exhibit one trait that marks him as a different kind of hero—his sexual energy, since in *The Water Margin* a test of the true hero, a "good guy" (*yingxiong haohan*) is precisely his ability to rise above sexual temptation. Yet *Red Sorghum*'s endorsement of sexuality is not without its misogynous bias.

The novel makes a conscious attempt to build up Grandma Dai Fenglian, the beauty with the smallest feet of any in the village, as a "hero of the resistance, a trailblazer for individual liberation, a model of woman's independence." She has the ability to take over and run the family's distillery business, she instigates and plans the ambush against the Japanese truck convoy, she has a possible affair with the foreman Uncle Arhat, and at one time leaves Granddad and runs off to Black Eye, a rival bandit leader. But in spite of the celebration of her resourcefulness and her open sexuality, she is still "owned" by Yu Zhan'ao who asserts the right to kill anyone who might have touched her, still constructed as an eroticized, desirable "field" on which the male can demonstrate his sexual prowess. The woman's body in *Red Sorghum,* in Lu Tonglin's words, is both perceived as a symbol of "natural force and primitive energy," an "idealized origin supposedly free of Communist influence," but also used "as a location on which brutal masculine power displays its force."[58] Grandma may be upheld as a "model of women's independence," but she belongs to Yu Zhan'ao, his overwhelming power over her beginning with the rape in the red sorghum field, the proof of his masculinity.

The assertion of "brutal masculine power" in post-Mao fiction can be understood as a form of protest against emasculation as a result of decades of political oppression. Women were proclaimed to be "equal" to men as they were emancipated by the Communist Party; emancipation thus erased women's difference, while denying subjectivity to all equally. In the process of rejecting their own "feminization" by the party and reasserting themselves as masculine subjects, male writers in the past two decades have fallen back on misogyny, returning women to their old status as inferior "others."[59] *Red Sorghum*'s apparent rebellion against traditional patriarchal discourse in fact continues it; it tries, but ultimately fails, through its glorification of masculinity and attempted representation of a "trailblazing liberated woman," to have it both ways.

There are other dialogic complexities in the novel's inheritance of *The Water Margin* "model." In his search for the anti-Confucian, "prefeudal" primordial human that may represent the "roots" of Chinese culture, Mo Yan attempts to represent the "primitive" man that lives beyond or "below" the established mainstream political and moral system, as did the bandit-heroes of that earlier novel. *Red Sorghum*'s graphic descriptions of battles, duels, and gunfights appear to celebrate such "uncivilized virtues" as bravado, physical prowess, and the savage thirst for vengeance, especially when's one personal honor is at stake. Yet the novel also departs significantly from the bandit-heroic tradition in stressing that unremitting bloodshed and escalating violence lead to internecine rivalries and self-destruction. *The Water Margin* had at one time been much touted by Marxist critics as a classic par excellence about peasant uprisings, but while *Red Sorghum* emphasizes the anti-establishment qualities of its bandit-heroes, it strongly highlights the brutality and destructive consequences of such "peasant" behavior as well.

While the novel's ambivalent representation of the narrator's peasant ancestors is carried out through these double-edged allusions to various prior texts and genre conventions that ambivalence is most tellingly reinforced within the narrative process by its shifting positioning of the I-narrator, the presumed "unfilial descendant" who is telling the story.

For the most part the narrative is presented as if by a super-omniscient third-person narrator whose knowledge of his characters is so detailed that it even extends to the grain-size piece of steel pellet firmly lodged between two of Grandma's back molars. But shortly after the novel begins, an I-narrator irreverently inserts himself into the text, while creating a sense of ambiguity as to his identity and role in the story. Was he in fact the bare-bottomed boy with the snowy white goat who once stood on the tombstone of his father's grave and peed furiously, then sang at the top of his voice the patriotic anti-Japanese song that will run like a refrain through the text? "Some have said that the boy with the goat was me. I don't know whether it was me or not" (p. 2)(p. 4).

This unworthy descendant/I-narrator then continues to appear as child or adult overtly and sporadically in the text with personal responses and commentary on the unfolding events. His continual referring to the characters through kinship terms undermines the illusion of the novel as the representation of an objective, self-contained world by calling attention to his own omnipresence behind the scenes; at the same time it underlines his distant yet intimate relation with those he is presenting. Such uncertainty of distance is a challenge to the reader, who is required to negotiate between the normal associations of an appellation like *nainai,* "granny" or "grandma," for example, and the novel's depiction of the vivid, beautiful young woman whose story begins with her wedding journey at sixteen and ends with her killing by the Japanese at age thirty.

The alternation or merging of first and third person, the shifting of the I-narrator between diegetic and extradiegetic narrative levels, the moving back and forth between layers of time, constantly open up multiple perspectives on all that happens. This lack of a stable one-point perspective from which a "reality" is perceived and portrayed, further undermines any illusion of the novel as a direct representation of objective events, but foregrounds it as one that oscillates and mediates between remembered history and imaginative reconstruction, as a narrative in continual process.

For what, the story asks, are the authoritative sources "out there" from which the novel can be derived? As one attempts to recuperate the past

history of one's ancestors, what is revealed to have been lost through
human atrophy or through the passage of time? The enormous gap between what the I-narrator may actually have witnessed in person and the
multitude of past events he is at present in the process of retelling, is
particularly highlighted in a poignant moment toward the end of the
first of the novel's five chapters. This chapter, entitled "Red Sorghum"
(*Honggaoliang*), had been constructed around an account of the heroic
ambush in 1939 of the Japanese truck convoy at the Jiaoping Highway
led by his grandfather, the "world-famous legendary hero Commander
Yu Zhan'ao," as he is introduced in the opening sentence. Interpolated
into the account of the ambush by means of flashbacks was also the story
of Yu Zhan'ao's kidnapping of Grandma as a young bride fifteen years
earlier in 1923, and their romantic lovemaking in the red sorghum field.
In 1958, almost twenty years later, the I-narrator as a two-year old was
present at a ceremony welcoming and hailing his grandfather as a returning hero who had "brought glory to the whole county." What the
child observed then was an old man, enfeebled by age and years of hard
labor in the wild mountains of Hokkaido, incapable of speech, awkwardly rising to his feet, his grayish white pupils rolling, mumbling
"wo—wo—gun—gun" in reply to the county magistrate's toast, while
the wine dribbled down his chin and chest (p. 91) (p. 78). As recalled
now, almost another thirty years later in the writing of the novel, what
that scene points to is not just the pathetic decline of the once virile hero
whose grand exploits have just been described, but the vast distance that
narrative must bridge in order to recuperate him as he once might have
been.

For the purpose of writing his novel and thus raising a monument
memorializing his family, the "I" had returned to his village for what he
thought would be a large-scale investigation. His single informant is a
ninety-two-year-old woman, one of the few survivors of the massacre of
their village that was carried out by Japanese soldiers in savage revenge
seven days after the ambush. Her version of events is given either in dog-
gerel storytelling rhyme (*banhua*) or in scattered, confused words "like
wind-blown leaves rolling on the ground." A pithy account of a few
events leading up to the ambush is contained in the county gazetteer. It
is from such meager sources that the richly detailed, highly dramatic, often moment-to-moment suspenseful action of the novel will be constructed.

The I-narrator presents himself within the text as witness, as reporter, as commentator, but also as one engaged in the search for his story. He is in search also for the appropriate genre of his story, which he variously refers to as tragedy (*beiju*), mythical story (*shenhua gushi*), family legend (*jiazu de chuanshuo*), and history (*lishi*). Its process of "hybridization," its use and deconstruction of generic tropes and conventions, preclude the narrative from settling into a well-defined genre. Most particularly and emphatically it represents a total rupture with the Marxist model and ideology of "realistic" literature as a direct reflection of history. As the narrative in *Red Sorghum* moves back and forth between different levels of "reality," many of its seemingly meticulously documented "historical facts" are transformed into legend. For this purpose it has also borrowed from Western literature.

Red Sorghum shows the influence of the magic-realism of Gabriel Marquez's *One Hundred Years of Solitude,* even to the extent of containing parallel passages.[60] That the fictional world of this novel and indeed of much of Mo Yan's other fiction is located within the boundaries of Gaomi Dongbeixiang (Northeast Gaomi Township) also invites comparisons with Faulkner's Yoknapatawpha County. While both writers share the theme of a culture or way of life in decline, the small corner of Shandong that is Mo Yan's home village is first of all reimagined and elevated into a mythical setting for grand epic events.

The functioning of the I-narrator as presumed "witness" is further complicated when he is not present "in person," so to speak, and utilizes a center of consciousness that functions like a stand-in for himself. This most often is Douguan, the father. The novel begins with the fourteen year old "Father" as he goes off with Granddad Yu Zhan'ao, who is leading the band of thirty to forty villagers armed with primitive agricultural implements and rusty rifles, all on their way to carry out the famous ambush. The fog is heavy and drizzly as they leave the village and make their way through the dense sorghum field. Clutching onto a corner of Commander Yu's jacket, "Father" listens for the sound of the river while trying to figure out the direction in which they are going. During the long trek through the sorghum, the boy/father feels his way uncertainly in an environment of shadowy figures and strange sounds, while assailed by the red smell of fresh blood, a color and smell that will increasingly pervade the novel. Speculations about future events, memories of the dimly understood past, both of what that young boy had witnessed and what he could not have known, are interwoven into detailed descriptions of a world in which it seems that only what is immediate

and sensory can be apprehended. Yet paradoxically, it is the very precise
representation of such sounds, sights, and smells that must rely the most
on the narrator's creative imagination.

Rather than an account of the overall action from a vantage point
above, the narration here follows the father Douguan through the thicket
of fog and sorghum, presenting events as filtered through his shadowy
semicomprehension of what is going on. This focus on Douguan's state
of mind, together with the constant movement from past to present to
future, the uncovering of layers of memory and consciousness, can be
seen as a mirroring of the I-narrator's own struggles to recuperate and
reimagine the experience in the novel.

"Father" and "I," "focalizer"[61] and narrator, two young descendants
from two different generations, are engaged in parallel efforts to come to
terms with the legacy of their forefathers and confront the world of heroism, cruelty, and despair that awaits them.[62] While this mutually mirroring relationship is most concretely demonstrated in the trek through
the sorghum, it prefigures a general pattern for much of the rest of the
novel, where events are very often presented as filtered through the experiences of the young father growing up. At one point in the text the narrating "I" addresses this Father: "My fantasies (*huanxiang*) were pursuing
yours, just as yours were pursuing what was in Granddad's mind" (p.
212) (p. 181). Yet at the same time the narrator is capable of seeing beyond what the Father saw: "Father did not know what romantic, tragi-
comic dramas my Grandma had enacted on this road. I know. Father
did not know that Grandma's splendid jade white body had once lain on
the black earth under the sorghum's shadow. But I know" (p. 5) (p. 6).
At such moments the I-narrator openly acknowledges his own textual
operations, as when he goes beyond the one who is "there" directly experiencing and contemplating the events: "Father was still young then, he
could not have thought in such fancy phrases (*huayan qiaoyu*), this is
what I thought" (p. 26) (p. 24). He thus calls attention to the production
and processes of literature itself, as he simultaneously constructs and deconstructs the writing of his "history."

The novel comes into being in these opening pages with Douguan's
participation in the ambush as a rite of passage, a test that initiates him
into adulthood. The Japanese kill his mother, but he is acknowledged by
his true father, Yu Zhan'ao, and through his fearlessness he is recognized
as a true son, one truly from the same stock.[63] Chapter one thus moves
back and forth between the sexual awakening and death of Grandma in

the sorghum field, the one resulting in Douguan's conception, the other his rite of passage. But what kind of adult world is he being initiated into? Since Yu Zhan'ao's ambush of the Japanese truck convoy includes among the enemy killed a major-general, it goes down in history and into legend as a great victory, but the human costs are immense. The entire band of peasant guerrillas that Commander Yu, father and son, started out with is lost; they are the only two survivors. Seven days later the Japanese massacre the village in revenge, leaving only a handful of mostly teenage children among the smoking ruins.

In one of the most surreal yet powerful chapters in the novel, "Gou dao," ("Dog Ways") as opposed to "rendao," the way of man, the line between what is human and what is bestial becomes increasingly blurred. With Yu Zhan'ao wounded, fourteen-year-old "Father" takes command and leads the few surviving village children in a desperate warfare against the five to seven hundred dogs that are running wild and gorging themselves fat on hundreds of human corpses. Human beings survive only by a kind of cannibalism once-removed; they feed on the dogs that feed on dead humans, and are transformed into what they eat and kill.[64] The village boys put on dog skins to trap their enemy; in time they assume an appearance thirty percent human and seventy percent canine (sanfen xiang ren, qifen xiang gou).

It is in part the dwelling on such scenes of human degradation that has led some Chinese critics to describe the novel as "deconstructing" through language the customary significations of such signifiers as the "anti-Japanese War" (kangri zhanzheng.)[65] But the dark and repulsive side of human actions is also frequently depicted as being so proximate to extraordinary feats of bravery and endurance, that they seem to be almost two sides of the same coin. It is in such interlocked dualities that some of the most memorable effects of the novel are achieved.

The novel abounds in images that show the metamorphosis from the gruesomely ugly into the beautiful. An example is the description of the corpses of mules putrefying among the shallow grasses in the river until their distended bellies split open under the sunlight, "their gorgeous innards overflowing like blooming flowers" (huali de changzi xiang huaduo yiyang yi chulai) (p. 44) (p. 39).

As this perhaps rather self-parodic sentence exemplifies in microcosm, Red Sorghum is ultimately a novel that celebrates the transforming power of language and narration. Many a horrifying and tragic episode in the novel is turned into legend through the act of telling. After the agonizing death of Uncle Arhat, the chief steward of the family's brewery business, through flaying—described in excruciating, and, unfortunately, unforgettable, detail—his body and skin and blood are washed away completely by a night of heavy rain; the disappearance is told and retold by the people, told from this generation to the next, until it becomes a beautiful mythical story (p. 42)(p. 37). The waylaying of Grandma's bridal procession at Toad Hollow (Hama keng) similarly becomes an important family legend (p. 52)(p. 46). These are *mise en abyme,* or embedded instances of the operations of the text as a whole, the transformation of the brutal facts of history and human experience through narrative process into transcendent tales of wonder.

Most particularly the novel does this in two important death scenes that frame the book. The prolonged description in chapter one of Grandma's dying, interwoven with flashbacks to the scene of lovemaking between her and Yu Zhan'ao in the sorghum fields, during which Father was conceived, ends in her apotheosis as she joins with the pigeons in their heavenward flight.[66] The novel concludes with the death of the narrator's Second Grandma (*Er nainai*), the servant girl who brings grief to her mistress (since there is a hellish as well as a heavenly side to love) when Granddad takes her as his concubine. Brutally raped by Japanese soldiers, she is possessed by an evil spirit before she dies.[67] The attempts at exorcism and the strange manner of her death become the matter of different legends circulating in the village.

This death occurs in the last chapter and is the final event narrated in *Red Sorghum*, although chronologically it takes place before the ambush that begins the novel. It is while paying his respects before the tomb of Second Grandma that the I-narrator, in the last pages of the text, directly confronts himself in relation to his family's past, a confrontation that also highlights the particular nature of his narrative enterprise. "Second Grandma's brief but colorful life added a striking page to the family's 'most heroic most son-of-a-bitch' history," and the "eerie, transcendent process of her dying awakened a mysterious emotion in the depths of the souls of the Gaomi Dongbei villagers." It is an emotion that germinates in the memory of the ancient villagers, then grows and develops to "become a powerful mental tool for grasping the world of the unknown" (p. 450)(pp. 356–357), a linking of memory and imagination that can be seen as an image of the germination of narrative itself.

The I-narrator has returned to his home village after a ten-year absence, infected by the hypocrisies of smart high society, and with a "body oozing from every pore the foul smell that comes from having been immersed in the stinking water of filthy urban life" (p. 450)(p. 356). As he stands before Second Grandma's tomb she leaps out, and holding a golden-hued mirror, commands the "grandson not borne by her" to look at himself. She urges him to cleanse his body and soul in the river and soak himself there for three days and three nights. While there may be more than a tinge of irony in the hyperbolic language of self-deprecation, the narrator goes on to suggest a parallel between the decline of the race or family stock and what has happened to the "red sorghum, red as a sea of blood," whose praises he had "celebrated and sung over and over." Lashed by the "floodtide of revolution," nothing is left now of that red sorghum; in its place is a "short-stalked, thick-stemmed, densely leaved hybrid plant, covered with white powder and having tassels as long as dogs' tails" (p. 452)(p. 358).

Many meanings cluster around the red sorghum, the central symbol in the novel. Existing in an intimate symbiotic relationship with humans, nourishing their spirit and their lives, the sorghum is also the blood-soaked field of their deaths, and continually nurtured by that blood. A symbol of the spirit of those ancestral figures the narrator is celebrating, red sorghum represents the nostalgia for all that is forever gone, whether it may ever have once existed or not. The novel closes in a chorus of voices, as the spirits of all his departed ancestors enjoin their "pitiful, weakly, suspicious, stubbornly biased, wine-besotted child" to sacrifice everything and search for the one stalk of pure red sorghum left, the symbol of Gaomi Dongbeixiang's traditional spirit, the family's glorious totem, as well as his talisman as he knocks about in a treacherous and perilous world (p. 453)(p. 359).

So ends the novel, the quest by an "unworthy descendant (*zisun*)" for the story of his ancestors. But then Mo Yan appends a brief postscript with further reflections about the ambiguous relation between truth and fiction, revelation and intimation, self and narrative. Speaking here now in the persona of implied author, he describes his anxiety over writing a long novel, and then the discovery that it was just a matter of putting in a little more time, adding a few more characters, and "fabricating a few more authentic lies (*zhenshi de huanghua*). One should treat long novels the way one treats certain species of dogs; better be bitten to death than be scared to death by them." Deeply ashamed of his failure to write a good novel, he has, in any case, he states, placed many hints (*fubi*) there, creating an opportunity for him to present (*biaoxian*) both the family and himself.[68] This is not to say that the I-narrator is himself, an identification that Mo Yan has denied repeatedly in other writings,[69] but rather that he has set up a continual interplay between writer, implied author, and the I-narrator(s).

For the search for roots, as Mo Yan openly states here, is concomitantly a search for the writing self. In a 1989 article, "My View of Peasant Consciousness" ("Wo de 'nongmin yishi' guan"),[70] Mo Yan comments explicitly on his treatment of the peasant in *Red Sorghum* and relates it to his conception of himself as a writer. His view of peasant consciousness is as he expressed in the opening of that novel; it is bifurcated (*yi fen wei er*) and absolutely dialectical (p. 42). While we are the product of peasants, "their most reliable sons," we are also "rebels," "the ones to dig their graves" (p. 40). He is uncertain how to think about peasant consciousness in relation to China's future. What is important for the writer, though, is not to save the souls of all the people, but to save his own soul. Therefore he continues to struggle in pain and perplexity, but should these once be resolved, he would no longer exist as a writer, for it is only in the process of painful struggle and contradictions that the writer can survive and have value (p. 42). Further perspectives are opened up on the novel in these comments by Mo Yan, in the persona now of the author commenting two years later on this text from another text, adding ever more levels of self-reflexivity to the writing of his novel.

In writing his long novel and thus confronting head on, so to speak, the dog that can bite or scare one to death, Mo Yan was confronting head on the ambivalences toward his "most heroic most son-of-a-bitch" peasant ancestors and his own contradictions as a writer. These ambivalences and contradictions are mirrored and carried out on the formal level in *Red Sorghum* through the self-questioning of its own narrative operations and the indeterminacies of the textual process. Wang Anyi will comment on the role and coming-into-being of literature in a very different way in her novel *Bao Village*.

WRITING ABOUT BAO VILLAGE: THE WRITER INSIDE AND OUTSIDE THE TEXT

While Mo Yan can claim to write as an "unworthy son" of peasant ancestors because he grew up in the countryside, Wang Anyi's rural experience was mainly as an "educated youth" sent down during the Cultural Revolution. Her mother is the noted author Ru Zhijuan, who became prominent in the late 1950's. Three years after Wang Anyi was born in 1954, her father was denounced as a rightist. Nevertheless she was raised in a relatively sheltered and privileged environment, "in a lane off Shanghai's wealthiest and most prosperous thoroughfare, Huaihai Road."[71] But at age fifteen, after graduating from junior high, her years of rustication began in a backward and impoverished area of northern Anhui. In 1972 she was assigned to a cultural troupe in Xuzhou and began publishing short stories four years later. She did not return to live in the urban milieu of Shanghai until 1978.

When Wang Anyi's novel *Bao Village* (*Xiaobaozhuang*) appeared in 1985,[72] a striking departure for a writer known more up till then for her fiction about young men and women wrestling with the issues of art, love, and sexuality, it was quickly greeted as a successful effort to climb aboard the "root-searching" bandwagon. Unlike the stories of Mo Yan or Han Shaogong discussed above, *Bao Village* does not revolve around a "personalized" intellectual or I-narrator who comes to the rural community to find the self confronting some sort of identity or moral crisis. There is, however, an intellectual, or rather, an aspiring writer within Wang Anyi's novel, the minor character Bao Renwen, whose all-consuming struggle is to make it as an author by attempting to record the lives of people in the village. Thus there are two writers involved in the narrative, both drawing upon the same material for their literary production, as it were: an implied author and a fictional author, one outside and one situated inside the text. Issues of ideology and representation become foregrounded in their parallel yet contrasting writing efforts, as events in Bao Village are presented in differing "versions" to the reader. Bao Renwen, the fictional author created by the implied author, writes by following official formulas, whereas *Bao Village,* the very narrative within which he is producing his writing, questions and challenges them.

In an article, "Wo weishenme xiezuo" ("Why I Write"),[73] published the same year as *Bao Village,* Wang Anyi describes how she once wrote party-line fiction herself. It was those days of "hardship and loneliness" in the countryside that drove her to become a writer. During an educational campaign in elementary school she had declared that her ideal goal in life was "to be a peasant," since the countryside seemed mysterious and wonderful then to the "little romantic." But once she arrived in northern Anhui, she knew that she could not be content with or resigned to (*bunenggou ganxin*) being a peasant. She turned to writing as a way out. One early piece was about an "educated youth" growing up in the countryside, and "going against my own true feelings, I sang its praises." Later when she came to write *Bao Village* she would write both against the idealized peasantry and the officially sanctioned way of representing it.

Wang Anyi breaks away from the party's conception of the peasantry and its ascribed role in revolutionary history first of all by placing the life and mores of her village within a broader mythical context that transcends historical time. This has encouraged many critics to read her depiction of a small, isolated peasant community in the backward and impoverished area of northern Anhui province as a representative and timeless image of the Chinese, where "history has coagulated, a people's fate has coagulated (*chengu*)"; it's a "totalistic reflection of a people, of a history."[74] Her own postface seems to suggest such a reading as well. There she refers to her own unsettling experience of visiting America in 1983 that led to the profound discovery that she was indeed Chinese and to the decision to "write on China" (*xie Zhongguo*) when she returned.[75] The peasantry in *Bao Village* would seem to be the age-old bedrock foundation on which that "China" is constructed.

The most famous and influential portrayal of the Chinese peasant, and by extension, the Chinese people, in literature, is, of course, *The Good Earth* by Pearl S. Buck, who "invented China" for generations of Americans.[76] Particularly noteworthy here is the fact that Suxian, where Wang Anyi settled (*chadui*) as an "educated youth," and Nanxuzhou, where Pearl Buck spent the first two and a half years of her married life and which "provided her with her subject, the Chinese characters who would populate *The Good Earth*,"[77] are located in the same area of northern Anhui.[78] Widely dissimilar as these two works of fiction might be, they are set in the same locale, and both have been read, respectively, by American readers in the 1930's and 1940's, and by Chinese readers in the 1980's, as portraits of China's enduring peasantry.

Han Shaogong's very different "Ba Ba Ba," as we have seen, has also been viewed as a microcosm of the Chinese countryside. The question is not which work of fiction gives us the "real" Chinese peasant, but rather what it is in each text that invites such generalizing readings. Whereas Han Shaogong's story revolves around melodramatic, catastrophic events such as famine, warfare, collective suicide, or mass migration, Wang Anyi's novel, apart from major floods at the beginning and toward the end, focuses rather on such experiences of everyday life as childbirth,

sexual maturation, marriage, old age, and, in the end, death, that are ordinary and ongoing.

Bao Village further creates the effect of timelessness with a distinctive
narrative method that moves back and forth among several different levels of time. It begins in an unspecified time long ago when after seven
days and seven nights of rain a flood covers the entire village. In time, "as
short as the blink of an eye or as long as a century, a tree emerges sepa-
rating heaven and earth" (p. 243)(p. v).[79] Next follows the legend of the
village's founder, a high official who settles in the lowest area under Bao
mountain after falling into disgrace because of his failure to control the
waters. Through transmissions and embellishments from generation to
generation, the villagers come to see themselves as descendants of the
Great Yu (founder of the prehistoric Xia dynasty). The first flood in the
novel foreshadows the one toward the end, for flooding goes back to
prehistoric times and continues periodically into the present; it is a recurring event that defines and encloses the community's existence.

While allusion to specific events apparently locates the novel in recent
history, those events are presented as happenings of far away:

> A thousand miles away in Beijing, the battle over control of the country was
> taking place.
>   A thousand miles away in Shanghai, things were set for the guns to go off.
> (p. 265)(p. 34)

These two lines, referring vaguely to the upheavals in the wake of Mao
Zedong's death and the fall of the "Gang of Four," compose the whole
of chapter ten, but meanwhile in the other chapters, everyday life in the
village more or less goes on.

Another dimension of time is introduced by the passages of "flower-
drum ballads" (*huaguxi*) that punctuate the novel. Through his singing,
Bao Bingyi, the old bachelor who feeds the cows and lives in the cow
pen, can conjure up "in one stanza heroes from the past five thousand
years." The five ballad sections are interspersed throughout the novel but
form their own sequence as indicated by the characters of one to ten then
back to one contained in each couplet; only finally in the epilogue is the
ballad "sung to its conclusion." Drawn randomly from history, myth,
and popular literature, the heroes and events in the ballad have no evident bearing upon what is going on in the narrative, but they serve as
fragmentary reminders of the enduring backdrop of Chinese culture

which has filtered down into the consciousness of the villagers and against which they are living out their lives.

Ballad singing and the novel's prose narration, progressing along unsynchronized paths toward a common terminal point, are yet another means by which different time levels in the novel are juxtaposed. Bao Bingyi is both a character within the novel, one who interacts with other characters, but also a character outside the novel's events, in that his singing provides a broader historical perspective that frames or transcends the *present* of what is happening. (He is a figure that recalls the folk artist in Zhao Shuli's "Rhymes of Li Youcai," but one major difference is that Li Youcai is totally caught up as actor and commentator in the unfolding political struggles of a precisely noted historical present.) All these strategies enhance the sense that the novel is not just about one particular village community at a particular given moment in history, but resonates with myth, legend, folk art, and tradition to portray through that village a comprehensive view of what has long existed in time.

The novel's unusual narrative structure, what has been termed its "simultaneous temporal mode" (*gongshitai*), has been much commented on as reinforcing the impression of generality.[80] Going against the convention of chronological linearity and causality in organizing events—a technique that likewise breaks through the restrictions of time—the narrative shifts back and forth in its forty chapters among several parallel plot lines: (1) the Bao Yanshan family and their youngest son Laozha (Dregs), a central character whose death and apotheosis will be the main business toward the end of the book; (2) and in the same family, the growing love between Little Jade (Xiaocui) the child-bride and her prospective brother-in-law, Culture (*Wenhuazi*); (3) the strange, suggestively Oedipal relationship between Shilai (Picked-Up) and the "aunt" who had found him by the road and was rearing him; (4) the marriage between Bao Bingde and his mad wife; (5) the literary aspirations of Bao Renwen, nicknamed the "Crazy Writer" (*Wenfengzi*) by the villagers. Interspersed with these is the ballad singing of Bao Bingyi. Wang Anyi uses a similar narrative technique in her novella "Daliuzhuang" ("Liu Village"), which is about a village, to judge by mutual references, not far from Bao Village, but the effect is very different. In that text the alternation in its seven chapters between the lives of several educated youth in Shanghai preparing to go down to settle in the countryside and those in the village which will be receiving them underlines above all the great gap that exists between two disparate worlds. Considerable suspense is created through this method as to what will happen when the twain finally meet, but the novella ends before the youths ever arrive. It concludes with a dialogue, in itself a comment on the ambiguity of the rural experience for "educated youth," about the ambiguous distance—geographical, but also psychological and cultural—between Shanghai and Daliuzhuang as "not close," "but not far either."[81]

Rather than emphasizing difference, the shifting among plot lines in *Bao Village* reinforces the sense of the villagers' common mode of existence. Not only does most of the community (Picked-Up, the outsider, is an exception) bear the surname Bao and belong to the same clan, its members also share the same world view and moral values. Above all the village is repeatedly said to be widely known for its virtue (*renyi*). To uphold *renyi* as the defining characteristic of the culture represented in the novel would seem, in contradistinction to other "root-searching" fiction, to take its peasants beyond the primal stage onto a level informed by the basic teachings of traditional Confucianism. But as it works out in practice, and particularly in its relationship with the "socialist morality" as propounded by the Communist Party, *renyi* is revealed to be a problematic principle that carries many self-contradictions.

The people in Bao Village take in orphans, look after the aged, help one another during the flood, and Bao Bingde, for example, refuses to go against *renyi* and divorce his insane wife. But in accepting the dire poverty, the deprivation of their lives, and the constant threat of recurrent disaster without complaint, these virtuous villagers are also shown to be conservative, passive, and fatalistic. They lack strong individualities and the entrepreneurial spirit, continuing to stake all on farming—"if you have food or grain (*liangshi*) you don't have to worry about anything"—even when post-Mao economic reforms permit them to engage in trade, for "trading means entrapping people" (p. 327)(p. 125). The age-old ethical culture they have inherited and continue to represent is stagnant, somnolent; it fosters an unquestioning submission to their place and lot in the world.

Other negative sides of this "virtuous" traditional culture are most clearly dramatized in the fates of several women. Little Jade, the beggar orphan girl, is indeed taken in, but actually as a child-bride, to be exploited first for her slave labor, and then later as producer of heirs for the family. Bao Bingde's wife goes mad after having five stillbirths, for which she had been beaten by her husband. When Second Aunt, an older widow with children, takes up with a wandering peddler, the grown-up Picked-Up, and has him move into her house, she is ostracized. Her former brother-in-law organizes a mob of clan members to give the two a severe beating. The traditional culture of *renyi* is patriarchal, male-centered; it oppresses women through its chastity code and the pressure to produce descendants.

But at the same time, there are women who are shown to be transgressors, who dare to challenge the expected rules of behavior. Most of the characters in the novel are represented as conformist members of a more or less uniform community, but these women are more strongly individualized, particularly in their sexual relationships.

After Second Aunt and Picked-Up are beaten by the clan members, he offers to leave, saying that he's done her wrong for having "ruined your family's good name (*baile ni jia de menfeng*). You should beat me!" (p. 299)(p. 85). But she boldly asks him to stay: "'If you don't mind my being old, don't mind my many children, don't mind my being so poor . . . then . . . don't go!' She said this and abruptly turned away" (p. 299)(p. 86). Moved to tears, he decides to remain. The township does later rule that it is legal for a widow to remarry and for the man to move into the woman's house, but as an outsider, "a calabash fallen into a basket of melons," and living with an older woman, Picked-Up continues to be an eyesore to the village, a target of ridicule.

An even more promising example of women protesting their fate and taking the initiative to change it is Little Jade, the child-bride destined for Construction (*Jianshezi*), the eldest son in Bao Yanshan's family. When at sixteen she gets wind that wedding plans are under way, Little Jade protests and weeps, holding onto a willow tree and refusing to let go until the family agrees to postpone the marriage for two years. It is the younger brother, Culture (*Wenhuazi*), that she loves, but he is apparently unaware of it. He has been helping with housework but she acts as if he is somehow an "enemy":

> Finally one day he intercepted her at the well:
> "What is it, Little Jade? What have I done to you?"
> "You haven't done anything to me."
> "Then what are you mad about?"
> "Mad, that you haven't done anything," she teased, picking up the carrying pole to leave.
> Culture held down the pole so she couldn't lift it.

"Can't you say clearly what you mean?"
"My words couldn't be more clear."
"Then why is it that I don't understand?"
"You've got no ears, you've got no heart."
"Why are you swearing at me?"
"I am swearing at you, you're heartless, gutless!"
(pp. 282–283) (p. 60)

As in many of these relationships, the underlying complexity of the woman's feelings is conveyed without explicit comment but subtly suggested through dialogue and gestures. Little Jade finally runs away from home and only after she is gone does Culture realize that she is in love with him. She occasionally steals back to meet him, and on the day the elder brother is married to someone else she returns home.

By assuming active roles in their relationships and refusing to be bound by patriarchal rules, women like Second Aunt and Little Jade reveal cracks in the uniform age-old *renyi* cultural structure, showing not only their own potential agency as a destabilizing force but also suggesting possibilities for change in the future. Wang Anyi's novel thus poses questions both for the Communist Party's vaunted project of liberating women and for its claims of overturning the old "feudal" order. For what the women achieve, they achieve on their own without party support or intervention. In fact *Bao Village*'s portrait of China's enduring peasant society for the most part marginalizes the Communist Party to a remote, almost irrelevant presence. What the novel highlights are the unchanging ways of the peasants' traditional way of life, the revolution notwithstanding, while *renyi*, in both its positive and negative aspects, remains the abiding principle that governs their relationships and their lives.

When the party finally enters the picture after the village is devastated by another catastrophic flood, it is mainly to appropriate the traditional idea of *renyi* to serve its own specific propagandist purposes of the moment. In its role as both political and moral mentor of the people, the Communist Party has launched the campaign of Five Efforts (to improve courtesy, civilization, order, hygiene, and morality) and Four Beauties (of mind, language, behavior, and environment) (*wujiang simei yundong*).[82] It so happens that March is to be "Courtesy month" and the local leadership is in need of a model to coordinate with the campaign. Dregs (*Laozha,*) a boy of nine, who from birth had been seen as the embodiment of *renyi* due to his selflessness and compassion for others, had drowned during the flood in a vain attempt to save an old neighbor. The novel's account of how the party authorities go all out to exalt the child posthumously—a child who had known nothing but hunger and poverty in his short life—into a "Youth Hero" (*shaonian yingxiong*) by constructing in his honor a monumental tomb on a raised platform with a tall and imposing plaque, including plans for a memorial hall, is bitterly ironic.

The fortunes of the community's one aspiring writer, Bao Renwen, will be deeply implicated in this project since literature must be called into service for the party to carry out its attempts to make Dregs into a model hero. It is the party's apotheosis of Dregs that makes it possible for Bao Renwen finally to be a published author. Through its account of the process by which Bao Renwen manages to realize his dream and attain this glorious status, the novel explores the relation between literature and ideology, and interrogates the relation of both to "reality" as the writer performs his assigned role.

Bao Renwen had studied for two years at the county middle school and learned about the Soviet writer Gorky, a great writer who never had a day of schooling. He also owns copies of *Chuangye shi* (The Builders) and *Linhai xueyuan* (Miles of Forests and Plains of Snow),[83] the authors of which had either come from the countryside or began as soldiers in the army and were barely literate; all these provide evidence that "anyone could become a writer, if only he were diligent enough" (p. 252)(p. 12). Bao Renwen works so hard day and night at writing that he is nicknamed "Crazy Writer" (*Wenfengzi*) by his fellow villagers.

Taking such typical examples of socialist realism or revolutionary romanticism as his models, Bao Renwen looks around in Bao Village for material from "life" to turn into literature. He pesters an old revolutionary for his memories of battles against the Kuomintang in the late 1940's so he can write a novel he has already entitled *Baoshan ernü yingxiong zhuan (A Tale of the Heroic Sons and Daughters of Bao Mountain)*. Their conversations lead nowhere, since the old revolutionary is unable to oblige by recalling any of his actual thoughts and motivations at the time of battle, and, in any case, is more concerned these days with filling the mouths of his family.

Bao Renwen makes other attempts. He writes a piece that is broadcast by the commune radio about Bao Bingde's refusal to divorce his crazy wife, with the title either of "Class Feelings Deep as the Sea" or "Class Feelings Deeper than the Sea." This piece has the effect of making him

locally known, but also of making it impossible for Bao Bingde to divorce his wife, even if he had wished to. For this Bao Bingde harbors
some resentment.

Another piece Bao Renwen sends to the radio station is about the relationship between Picked-Up and Second Aunt, a piece of much
"literary flavor," under the title "Sublime Love," in which the two are described as working hard by day and making plans to get rich (this is the
time of economic reform, when "to get rich is glorious") at night. Bao
Renwen reaches the pinnacle of his literary career thus far when the piece
is even broadcast at the district radio station. Now that they were famous, it did not seem proper for Picked-Up and Second Aunt to fight so
much between themselves, but since they couldn't really stop fighting,
they now closed the door tight and yelled at each other softly.

Party-sanctioned literature stops at the door short of entering into the
reality of people's lives; it must gloss over that to render them ideologically correct. In contrast to the novel *Bao Village* itself, Bao Bingwen's
literary efforts follow the Maoist prescriptions for literature. This is the
source of the discrepancies between the characters as the novel represents
them and what Bao Bingwen makes of them.

The big break for Bao Bingwen comes when Dregs loses his life; he
writes a piece of reportage literature (*baogao wenxue*) about the event and
finally sees himself in print. He had made a "determined effort," copying
his report many times over and sending it off to various periodicals,
newspapers, and youth magazines of the cultural centers of the province,
the region, the district. When the district leadership finds it needs a
model for "Courtesy Month," they take another look at his piece and see
its potential. A reporter from the local *Morning Star News* is assigned to
"cooperate" in the rewriting. In fact, Bao Renwen merely talks while the
reporter writes. At first, when "A Little Hero of Bao Mountain" appears
in the newspaper with his name following that of the reporter's, "his
heart beat so fast it seemed to be about to jump out of his throat" (p.
329) (p. 127), but then he discovers that "there was not a single line in the
article that had been written by him." Only after rereading it over several
times, and after much effort, does he recognize his own labor between
the lines. When the published article has been made over beyond recognition even by the author himself in order to serve a designated political
purpose, can it still be considered to be truly his own?

If the relation between writer and literary production is dubious when writing is controlled and managed by party cadres, what about the relation between literature and the "reality" it is supposedly writing about? This issue becomes all the more acute when the province decides to go on and make a big propaganda campaign out of Dregs. Cadres and reporters descend in jeeps onto the village to gather material on the little hero. In a parody of an interview they ask the bewildered family such incomprehensible questions as what heroes the nine-year-old Dregs had most admired, what were the influences on his life, etc. Another article appears in the provincial newspaper: "The New Style of Youth, Sacrificing the Self for Others: The Little Hero, Bao Renping" ("Youmiao xinfeng, ji sheji weiren xiaoyingxiong Bao Renping"); the provincial publishing house sends a writer to come to work with Bao Renwen on a book entitled "The Story of the Little Hero."

But when the county sends people to collect Dreg's personal belongings for display in the planned memorial hall they run into serious problems, since in accordance with village custom things of little ghosts must not remain in the house, and everything ever owned by him has been burned. At one point it is discovered that his signature survives on the mud wall of a privy. Can they be sure it is the handwriting of the little hero? "Absolutely" says a young friend. "The two of us were taking a shit together, and we each wrote our names for fun" (p. 338)(p. 140). Unfortunately the privy's mud wall begins to crumble as soon as people try to lift it, so they have to leave it where it is.

Behind the comedy of this episode the poignant question raised is what happens in the midst of all the flurry of literary productions to the actual subject himself. Where are the traces of the child Dregs who once lived, where the evidence, where the truth of his life? How much of him is there in the literature written about him, or has he vanished into all that hyperbole? When Culture, Dreg's older brother, reads Bao Renwen's article to his mother, surprisingly "her face was expressionless, as if she was hearing the story of someone else. All those stirring words seemed to have little effect on her. The Dregs in the article seemed very distant from them, a stranger" (p. 329)(p. 128). Perhaps it is the father's repeated lament that brings out what to him is the central fact of his son's brief existence. During Dregs' funeral and to each group of interviewing reporters, he says through his tears, "The child had a hard life, never once had a decent meal."

Peasants may be exalted by the Communist Party into model heroes when needed for specific purposes, but if they "never once had a decent meal," the fundamental reality of their lives, as the novel suggests, is simply passed over in officially sanctioned literature.

As an author situated within the text, Bao Renwen's experience in attempting to write stories about the characters and events in Bao Village form a parodic counterpoint to what the implied author outside the text is doing. His endeavors to produce literature that accords with official formulas thus function as a reverse mirror of the novel's own narrative process. *Bao Village* is a self-reflexive text that both contains and subverts an example of the kind of literature it is writing against.

As the novel approaches its end, there are signs of hope for the betterment of the peasants' lot. The county party secretary comes to visit and sees to it that the little hero's family is given materials for a new house. The older brother is placed in a rural factory. More food is available. In the epilogue, new brick houses with blue-tiled roofs are seen going up behind Dreg's monumental tomb. Yet the novel does not end conclusively with the confident sense of history progressing toward a brighter future.

Historiographic referentiality and the conventions of socialist realism are further undermined by the addition of a second epilogue at the end of the novel. Just as *Bao Village* had begun with two prefaces, the two epilogues each frame events within different time levels, leaving ambiguous the issue of whether peasant life and culture will continue on in its immemorial stagnant condition or are poised at a historical threshold of change and a possible new future. In the second epilogue Bao Bingyi continues his transhistorical ballad with references to Chinese legends of the remote past; the old revolutionary, Bao Yanrong, recalls battles he has been through, while an old wandering peddler who is passing through stares fixedly at Picked-Up, who is sitting in the doorway. The sound of his peddler's drum had been heard off and on throughout the novel, but he is never identified. Could he perhaps be Picked-Up's long-lost father? Picked-Up looks back, wondering if this is someone he might have known. The two sets of eyes meet in a state of mutual questioning while the music of the ballad singing continues, and *Bao Village* ends in a lack of closure, suspended in indefinite time.

IN MAKING THE ontology of the peasant an essential part of their "search for roots" projects, Mo Yan, Han Shaogong, and Wang Anyi have greatly broadened the range of images, notions, and perceptions about the peasant in modern fiction. Whether portrayed as repositories of traditional virtue or of mindless stagnation and backwardness, as passionate larger-than-life bandit-heroes or victims crushed and crippled by the hardship of their lives, their peasant characters are widely diverse and much more complexly constituted than those of the reform agendas of the May Fourth generation, as well as those of the Communist Party's class-specific revolutionary ideology. The self-reflexivity of their fiction has furthermore shifted attention from the peasant as object to the literary processes that had traditionally sought to objectify them.

Gao Xiaosheng's ironic appropriation of the party's rhetoric into his own narratives was both a rewriting of revolutionary history as well as an exploration of the relationship between language and reality. The "modernist" fiction of our three writers has carried the undermining of the realist project much further. Han Shaogong's skepticism about memory and identity, Mo Yan's uncertain quest for ancestral history and narrative stance, Wang Anyi's shifting perspectives on time, among their other experimental techniques, have resulted in fiction that revolves around tensions, ambivalence, and indeterminacies. Their moral and psychological self-investigations are transmuted into various forms of textual self-reflexivity; in the process of dismantling the ideological mold of the peasant, they have even more radically rebelled against conventional forms of writing.

These writers had all spent their youth or an important part of their formative period in the countryside, and in revisiting it in person or in their writings, they have constantly recalled that profoundly unsettling historical past. To different degrees they have each alluded to or employed the political rhetoric and ideological tropes that have long formed the staples of the Communist master narratives on the peasant, while simultaneously challenging them. And with their fiction, the modern tradition in which the peasant had for so long figured as prime literary object approaches its inconclusive end.

Epilogue; or, What Next?

The story that gave "scar literature" or "literature of the wound" its name, Lu Xinhua's "The Wound," had opened with the protagonist, Xiaohua, traveling by train to Shanghai. She returns to the city to discover that she has lost the mother she had denounced nine years ago and also any hope she might have had of resuming the life she had before she left. Whatever new uncertainties the city may now have to offer, that journey away from the countryside, undertaken en masse by rehabilitating "educated youth," represents a significant change of direction for modern Chinese literature. It marks a decisive turning away from the broad rural landscape, primarily of the northern Chinese hinterland, the vast site of class wars and utopian socialist construction projects that had loomed so large in literary representation for thirty-some years. In the new modernizing China of the post-Mao era, the urban experience with all its volatility and restlessness will be where the "action" is. As the city begins to dominate the literary imagination, "mass culture"—or culture for the "masses" (no longer denoting the revolutionary peasantry)—will take on a totally different meaning.

When the urbanized or re-urbanized intellectual youth happen to return for visits to the countryside, it is not for the purpose as before of merging with and learning from the life and work of the vanguard peasantry, but rather to affirm the individual self as one that is set apart, disoriented, and alienated when placed in an impoverished and stagnant rural world. In Lu Hsun's "My Old Home" the barrier between the I-narrator and his childhood friend Runtu had been their mutual recognition of the traditional hierarchy between gentry and peasant class, but in Mo Yan's "White Dog and the Swings" the main division between the I-narrator and his old friend Nuan arises from the fact that he has been privileged to move away to the city, whereas her deformity has denied her any opportunity to leave the countryside. She is doomed to remain, as she herself terms it, underclass (*diji*) because of where she is.

The revolution that Mao Zedong had conceived of as a matter of "surrounding the city by the countryside"—and overwhelming it—has been side-stepped for the goal of economic modernization in post-Mao China. Now it is the city that has moved to the forefront, leading the way in commerce, industry, entertainment, and cultural production and leaving the countryside behind.[1] "Root-searching" literature of the mid-1980's turned to the countryside in part as a reaction against the accelerating globalization of Chinese culture and society. But the countryside it seeks to represent is not concretely set up as a clear-cut alternative or oppositional space to the city. Han Shaogong's mountain village surrounded by a sea of white clouds, Mo Yan's legendary Northeast Gaomi County with its formerly blood-red sorghum fields, Wang Anyi's virtuous village community evoking several dimensions of time, are not in fact represented as actually, geographically "there"; they are rather nostalgic projections or imagined constructions that transcend the historical realities of time and place.

If the countryside and the peasantry that abides there are losing their centrality as tropes of literature in the post-Mao era, it is because concomitantly they are also losing their validity as totalistic unified constructs. While the peasant has indeed undergone various redefinitions in the narratives of our four literary "generations," underlying all has been an assumption that the peasantry, in widely different ways to be sure, represents some kind of massive ongoing, perennial constant in history, about which one can generalize and posit as "others" to the writing/intellectual self.

In Lu Xun's "My Old Home," the shift in representation from Runtu as a childhood friend to an adult member of the peasant class suggests that he is no longer perceived as an distinct individual in himself. The eleven- or twelve-year-old Runtu in the I-narrator's memory had been given to depicting in lively and colorful detail such wondrous things as

catching birds with propped-up threshing baskets and ways of going after elusive *zha* crunching on watermelons in the moonlight. But all that
the grown-up Runtu can do when he meets the I-narrator thirty years
later is to speak rather vaguely about poverty, bad harvests, and high
taxes. Once he is identified in the narrator's perception as a lower-class
peasant, Runtu is transformed from a freely talkative, vividly particularized childhood friend into an inert and barely articulate victim; he has
become but a generalized representative of all oppressed peasants.

Zhao Shuli's progressive peasants are conceptualized according to a
prescribed ideological mold for carrying out the Communist Party's
revolutionary agenda of class struggle, an agenda extended to a retrospective reading of Chinese history as characterized from the beginning
by recurrent peasant uprisings. Gao Xiaosheng's peasants, while deluded
and victimized by the party's rural policies, are shown to possess a steadfast core of honesty and goodness that places them above their rulers,
qualities that also made their victimization possible. Now their supposedly hidebound ways are making it difficult for them to adjust to a rapidly changing, kaleidoscopic world. Han Shaogong and Wang Anyi both
emphasize the cyclical nature of history and the permanent character of
the peasant, although their specific definition of that character is very
different. Mo Yan looks for the primal, precivilized nature of his peasants; they are the ancestors who can always rise from the grave to haunt
their descendants. For the generation of sent-down "educated youth"
who experienced rural life firsthand, the fact that the party's reinvention
of the peasant as vanguard revolutionaries turned out to be so far removed from reality seems to have reinforced even more an image of a
massive and timeless peasantry. But in one way or another, however perceived or conceived, the peasant, as some sort of totalized entity, has
seemed to have been there, has inescapably always been there.

At first glance post-Mao notions of an enduring, stagnant countryside
may seem to be a resuscitation of the peasant "invented" during the early
decades of this century as a reservoir of "backwardness," the obstacle to
agendas of reform and modernization. But to say that the construction of
the peasant since that time has merely followed a circular path, so that
things are back to where they started, is to oversimplify the matter and
ignore some real developments in modern history. The political and literary focus on peasants for over five decades since May Fourth has inevitably increased the awareness of their specific conditions, as is particularly evident in the post-Mao fiction of Gao Xiaosheng and the

"search for roots" writers, conditions that have found their way into literary representation.

There has indeed been a closer and more intensive interacting relationship with the peasant since the May Fourth period, a relationship that has been enormously complicated, thrown into disorder, one might say, by the events of political history. To many disillusioned intellectuals the turn taken in the relationship between intellectual and peasant under communism is in fact the crux of everything that has happened, or even of everything that has gone wrong, during the past fifty years of the Maoist revolution. To put their thinking in a nutshell, the peasant-based revolution in their view turned out more than anything else to be an anti-intellectual revolution, indeed an anti-intellectual*s* revolution. The age-old relationship between intellectual and peasant became primarily one of opposition and contention, leading not only to the failure of party policies—because without intellectual expertise it is assumed that nothing can be accomplished—but also to the persecution of many hundreds and thousands of intellectuals. That hostility toward intellectuals became only too apparent during the violent decade of the Cultural Revolution.

On the other hand, there are those who do not believe that the "blame" for that disastrous period should all be placed on peasants, or the revolution that was carried out in their name. Intellectuals themselves must bear no small responsibility for their own tragic fate. In the view of one outspoken critic, what happened during the Cultural Revolution was not just due to Communist Party policies but also to the traditional Confucian political philosophy that had always considered the "people" to be the foundation of everything (*minben*):

> Our having gone through the great restoration of feudalism in the guise of Marxism—the "Great Cultural Revolution"—can help us reflect on history. During the "Cultural Revolution," the highest powers were conferred on workers, peasants, and soldiers, the word "people" (*renmin*) was sacred like God. ..."The people are the masters of the nation," "To serve the people" ... all the slogans took on the coloring of *minben*.[2]

The explicit target of criticism here is not so much the "people" themselves, but the intellectuals who in submitting since antiquity to the "people as foundation" idea have in the process relinquished all independence and become willing slaves of the state system.

The statement quoted above may be seen first of all as an apparent reversal with multiple ironic twists of the traditional bifurcation between the scholar-gentry and the laboring people (*min*). It seems to dismiss from consideration the fact that even as traditional intellectuals had been co-opted into the imperial system and become its "slaves," they had formed part of the elite class that ruled over the laboring peasants who were down below. Furthermore, the power, authority, and legitimacy of the ruling elite was supposedly based on their fulfilling the obligation to nurture and look after the welfare of the ruled; it was in that sense that "people" were the foundation of the entire system. In turning the old hierarchical structure on its head, the Chinese Marxist revolution made it possible, particularly during the Cultural Revolution, for the "people" to exercise their power and authority over the once elite intellectuals. If intellectuals continue as slaves of the system, it is now with the "people" on top. Class positions have been reversed, but the "feudal" hierarchy remains.

Whether or not one assents to this view of the Chinese revolution as the "restoration of feudalism," what is notable and characteristic here is how history, whether past or present, is persistently conceived in terms of the mutual positioning of the two broad ongoing categories of intellectual versus peasant. But it is precisely this paradigm of the intellectual versus peasant (or "people") bifurcation, as inherited or even as significantly altered from the traditional past, and indeed the historical practice of generalizing with such age-old totalizing concepts, that may well be losing their relevance and validity in the rapidly changing economic situation in post-Mao China. First of all, the peasant, for so long essential and essentialized in Chinese politics and ideologies, is becoming a much more ambiguous category. Fragmentation, dispersal, and shifts in economic status have increasingly highlighted the multiplicity, the many internal differentiations in Chinese rural life and culture.

Looking back from the perspective of recent developments we can see that the peasantry as a monolithic mass was a questionable notion even when the Communist Party was developing its vision and strategy for a peasant-based revolution in the 1930's. The misery of the countryside was certainly there to be exploited, but there were vast regional variations in the degree of that misery. In some areas under Republican China, peasants were gradually becoming better off—at least up till 1937, the time of the Japanese invasion. In other words, it is less likely that the party could have succeeded in mobilizing the peasantry from the coastal areas of Jiangnan or Guangdong in its struggle for political power. Historical circumstances drove the party to the most impoverished and deprived countryside of China; from such a base it forged the ideology and techniques that would enable it successfully to expand its revolution.

The discrepancies in the situation of the peasantry from region to region have become even more pronounced in the last two decades. In parts of the prosperous southern Jiangsu countryside, for example, particularly the areas around Yixing, Wuxi, Jiangyin, etc., over ninety percent of the households in a village may be working in new factories while the few remaining households are subsidized to work the fields with imported Japanese machinery. It makes little sense to lump them together with those struggling with antiquated farming methods to wrest a subsistence living from the soil in remote areas of northern Shaanxi. As China's economy continues to develop and bring about further changes in the countryside, one can expect the situation of the peasants to manifest a greater range of forms, a broader and ever more dynamic spectrum of transformations, so that "peasant" as a general, unitary, fundamental category could well be on its way to passing out of history.[3]

WOMEN AND THE INTELLECTUAL/PEASANT
"OTHER" PARADIGM

While modernization may be accelerating the dismantling of the intellectual versus peasant paradigm, women have long been positioned to problematize it in diverse ways. In the relative power relations of that paradigm, it has always been control over language, speech, and literary authority on the part of the intellectuals that enables the representation of the "other." No less than peasants, women have been objectified and represented as "others," and from the beginning of modern Chinese literature women and peasant have often been seen as analogous. Both have been perceived first as oppressed victims of the old society and then appropriated as liberated subjects under the party. Several of the stories discussed above have featured peasants who are also women, and in these stories voice and language often become foregrounded issues, issues that will uncover underlying problems and inner contradictions in the narrators' ideological agendas.

Under the old imperial system women had no public role and were totally excluded from the matrix of knowledge, political power, and literary authority in which writing was situated. But they were often "heard," not in their own voices, but as literary vehicles through which the out-of-favor scholar-official could project his protest and lament.

Sima Qian on the indignity of his castration and Qu Yuan on the sorrow of his exile are early examples in the literary tradition of intellectuals who adopted a "feminized" stance vis-à-vis political domination. The "feminization" of the self was, to be sure, an acknowledgment of one's subordinate status, but it also provided a literary platform, a position from which to lament one's own fate and, significantly, to protest against or question the ruler's political power from a higher moral ground. Perhaps this borrowed paradoxical stance was possible because women were outside others to begin with, not directly implicated in the ideologies or power practices of the imperial system; while subservient, they could be utilized and their condition presented as some kind of external measure for evaluating the system.[4] The fact that women were supposed to be well acquainted with suffering supplied the tropes of emotional appeal for this literary convention.

During the May Fourth period women were "discovered," together with peasants, as serious subjects for literature. Both were seen as readily available evidence for making an all-out assault against traditional society. The case of victimization could be made doubly effective by having woman and peasant blend into one. To emphasize their overall powerlessness, both women and peasants have often been portrayed as passive, inarticulate, and even to some extent mindless. Whatever subjectivity or inner life they might have has seemed to be beyond the reach, or perhaps the interest, of the writer who has undertaken to lament or be indignant over their lot.

Lu Xun's story "The New-Year Sacrifice," like many others of the time, centers around a victim who is doubly oppressed because she is both a woman and a peasant. The failure of the self-styled "modern" intellectual to respond adequately to her plea for help may have contributed toward her death. While the story is about Xianglin's Wife, it is even more about the narrator's moral crisis. The split in narrative mode is characteristic; "her story" is told from the outside by a distant third-person narrator; "his story" is told by a reflective, introspective first-person narrator. Actually it is an initiative act of Xianglin's Wife, the challenging question she puts to the I-narrator, that sets the narrative in motion and exposes his inadequacies as an intellectual, his inability to come up with a pragmatic solution to her problem. What he can do is to go on to tell her story, but only by enclosing it within his own. Ultimately she is dependent on him for her story to be told.

Oppressed as she is, Xianglin's Wife does act to resist her fate in many ways. That she runs away from her husband's home to seek employment for herself and puts up that fierce fight at her forced second marriage shows that she is not totally without an independent will and mind of her own. To represent her mainly as passive, stupefied, if not "dumb," suggests that she is lacking in a reflective consciousness of her own, or at any rate in the capacity to articulate it effectively. The complex issues of who should speak, who can speak, and who should speak for whom, are dramatized in the narrative process, even as it emphasizes how the woman is additionally victimized because no one will listen to her.

The situation of Meng Xiangying in Zhao Shuli's story, written two years after Mao Zedong's "Talks at the Yan'an Forum on Literature and Art," shows some surface similarities—poverty, cruel mothers-in-law, bondage through marriage—to that of Xianglin's Wife's. But the outcome of their stories stands in diametrical contrast. Xianglin's Wife dies an ostracized beggar, while Meng Xiangying is glorified as a labor heroine, leading the villagers' fight against famine and working for the emancipation of women. The difference, of course, is the Communist Party. Meng Xiangying's empowerment is mainly accomplished through her acquisition of party language. As Meng Xiangying "stands up," she also speaks up—to communicate the standard revolutionary message. In the case of Xianglin's Wife, it is up to the writer, with his privileged access to the resources of language and mastery of the appropriate forms of discourse, to speak of and speak for the woman to reveal her condition. In the case of Meng Xiangying, it is the party who speaks for her and who puts words into her mouth; the woman dedicated to the goals of the collective is similarly denied a private self. Whatever individual voice either woman might have of her own is rendered immaterial.

Gao Xiaosheng's story about Liu Yu, who comes back to writing after twenty years of political banishment and thus causes the death of his peasant wife, is a harsh indictment of the self-centered and self-important writer. When his wife in effect is sacrificed from overwork so that he can finish writing his book, he speculates that she might well have had "something she wanted to say," a subjectivity also seeking expression. But while Liu Yu expresses his remorse for writing at the expense of the labor of the peasant, the story also stresses the woman's utter inability—in spite of their years of marriage—to comprehend what writing is all about.

One might say that in Mo Yan's "White Dog and the Swings" the old schoolmate friend of the I-narrator could once have qualified as an aspiring intellectual, since she had likewise once been the backbone of the middle school propaganda team. That her ability and opportunities to speak are forever constrained with her "descent" into peasant life is symbolized by her being bound up with a family of mutes.

In Wang Anyi's *Bao Village,* however, the representation of women is somewhat different. The young peasant girl Little Jade, in spite of her lively mental capacities, is not allowed to go to school as the boys are, but she is capable of protesting her fate and taking an active role to change it. She puts up an effective resistance to her arranged marriage, later runs away from home, and she is first to speak up to express her feelings to Culture (*Wenhuazi,* is there symbolism in the name?), the younger brother of her betrothed. The story suggests toward the end that she will probably be able to realize her desire to marry the man she wants, pointing to a positive outcome for this articulate and assertive woman. It is the women who are not afraid to speak up about their own needs and desires who have the potential to destabilize the enduring structure of village society.

Wang Anyi has been more widely known as a woman writer who portrays young women confronting issues of sexuality and identity in boldly innovative fiction. She is highly regarded as one of the younger writers in the post-Mao "second flowering" or "high tide" of women's writing in modern China, the first having occurred during the May Fourth period. The fifty-year hiatus between the two periods may be explained by a dominant Marxist ideology that did not allow room for what was considered gender-specific literature.[5] In fact, during that long period, women authors, with the exception of a few like Ru Zhijuan and Ding Ling (who got into trouble with the party for what she wrote), were conspicuous largely by their absence. Women writers did not go along to produce very much party-directed literature; perhaps that means they have less to apologize for.

A major theme during both of the "high tides" of women's writing has been the exploration of subjectivity and sexual difference in the symbolic area, and how they may relate to issues of power, language, and meaning. One common explanation these days for the post-Mao upsurge in writing by women is that women are especially "good at" writing about such subjects as love, sexuality, personal relationships, nuanced emotions, etc., subjects that had been taboo in literature sponsored by the party.[6] Whether or not one wants to consider women's literary production as essentially different from that of men, the fact is that women's writing does not fit easily into one side or the other of the intellectual-peasant dichotomy.

Throughout the developments in modern Chinese literature, women have been alternately or simultaneously situated on both sides of the equation: actively struggling to affirm and give voice to woman's subjectivity while also objectified and silenced as oppressed "others." Male writers may represent women mainly in terms of the latter. But during the May Fourth period, even as they similarly came to discover oppressed peasant women as literary subjects, women writers tended to represent them as more than the passive, silent, mindless victims the male writers claimed to be speaking *for*. In Ding Ling's "Shui" ("Flood") of 1931, for example, among the disembodied voices of peasants huddling in the night while the rising water threatens the dikes, it is the old grandmother's bitter recollections of her hard life that is heard above all. *Shengsi chang* (*Field of Life and Death*), Xiao Hong's 1934 novel about peasant life in northeast China, has Old Mother Wang as the primary reflective consciousness and articulate commentator on events. Women may be victims in these stories, but they are not denied a voice with which to speak about their suffering.

In the formulaic fiction that generally conforms to party prescriptions on literature, a woman writer like Ru Zhijuan, one the very few who continued to be productive in the 1950's and early 1960's, is more likely to make space for a woman's subjective feelings. In her characteristically titled story "Chunnuan shijie" ("In the Warm Springtime"), the devoted housewife and mother learns to overcome the barriers between herself and her more progressive husband by "catching up with him"—that is, by actively assuming a role in the local Production-Welfare Co-op. Predictable as the upbeat ending of this 1959 story may be, the female protagonist is portrayed as coming to her own "standing up" (*fanshen*) not so much simply through external circumstances brought about by the party, as might be the case in a story by Zhao Shuli, but through the stages of her own awakened subjective consciousness.[7]

Due to the duality of their perspective, women have been in a position to crisscross but also to contest the defining boundaries of the intellectual/writing self and peasant "other" dichotomy. In recent decades, far from limiting themselves to gender-specific literature, or what women are supposed to be "good at," women writers have been increasingly moving in from the margins to play a vanguard role in challenging the mutually implicated discourses of political ideology and literary authority.

In Can Xue's 1985 story "Shan shang de xiaowu" ("Hut on the Hill"),[8] the I-narrator, who is subjective and obsessive to the point of apparent paranoia,[9] describes the world as she perceives it, simultaneously projecting and denying meaning to all events. She (actually the gender of this narrator/central character remains ambiguous, but is unavoidably specified in English translation) is forever tidying her drawer, a private space the self struggles to hold on to or put in order, while her family, constantly metamorphosing into nasty animals and insects and all with their own obsessive actions, are forever encroaching upon and sabotaging her efforts. The hut on the hill, whose existence is stated in the story's opening sentence and thereafter constantly referred to, turns out to be an elusive and illusory object. That "there was no hut"—a negation of its beginning premise—is the outcome of the story's main plot or "action." Characters speak at or past each other, for in such a world there is no dialogue, no conversation; language itself seems to have lost both its referentiality and its function as communication. On another level, however, the nightmarish "unreality" of the story becomes "intelligible" and "reasonable" as a portrayal of the incongruities, the denial of normal relationships, the loss of identity and meaning brought about by recent Chinese history; through this complex interplay between language and historical "reality" the text enacts the interrogation of all explanatory paradigms and master narratives.

Wang Anyi's "Lao Kang huilai" ("Lao Kang Came Back"),[10] published in the same year as "Hut on the Hill" and also as her own *Bao Village*, may be seen as subversive in another way. Twenty years after being sent to Qinghai as a "rightist," Lao Kang is permitted to return to his brother's home in Shanghai. But just before embarking on the trip home he had apparently suffered a stroke and now is able to perform only the basic functions of existence with continuing care. Having lost the power of speech or understanding, he spends his waking hours tracing over and again with his finger the one character *mi* (rice). The I-narrator is an old school friend who visits him twice but is not recognized by him. A chance conversation the narrator has with Lao Kang's brother as they speculate in vain about what may have happened to him and try to puzzle out the meaning of his repetitive mimetic gesture brings the story to an end. As a young scholar, Lao Kang had harbored the ambition of writing a history of Chinese music and spoke often of China's being the first country to compile its history as well as his own determination to carry the tradition forward. But he never actually produced anything.

Whatever aspirations he might have once had were put to an end when he was sent away as a "rightist," and his intellectual endeavors are now limited to this minimal repetitive act whose meaning is impossible to fathom.

For the brother and the old schoolmate, helplessly confronting what Lao Kang has become, his past and the person himself have become an unknowable empty space. If what he compulsively traces "really is an ideogram" then it could stand for something truly "engraved onto his bones and heart" (*kegu mingxin*)," but they wonder whether they have the heart (*buren*) to look into it further; on the other hand, it could also be totally meaningless.

Lao Kang exemplifies the ineffectuality of Chinese intellectuals who are then reduced to nothing as a result of political persecution, and the story can be read as a commentary on the fate of modern Chinese intellectuals and their helpless response to it. In contemplating the historical experience of others or of themselves, intellectuals find it to be neither accessible nor within the capacity of language or memory to recuperate and describe. They can no longer perform their usual role of putting things into words or giving meaning to people and events. The text becomes a metafiction on writing and representation, or rather, on the impossibility of both.[11]

Both Can Xue and Wang Anyi create fictional worlds with events and characters that undermine official versions of history. But even as they break away from the dominating discourse, they go further to raise questions about the expected means for creating a counterdiscourse—language, representation, and literary authority—in their own narrative processes. With Wang Anyi's story showing literature to be in a state of impasse, our various textual journeys can be said to have arrived at their appropriate termination.

THE UNCERTAIN STATE OF THE
WRITER/INTELLECTUAL

These two stories by Can Xue and Wang Anyi were both published at the end of the period covered by this study. In retrospect they can be seen as anticipating the sense of "crisis and perplexity" (*weiji yu kunhuo*) that would within a few years dominate discussions of Chinese literature.[12] The almost euphoric self-congratulations in the mid-1980's about the new possibilities of literature as it broke with realism and went "modernist" with the emergence of "root-searching" fiction, soon gave way to much *soul*-searching as to where literature was going, if anywhere at all.

What seemed striking and disconcerting for scholars and critics was that the "root-searching" literary movement apparently was not succeeded by any identifiable trend. Literary history in modern China has customarily been periodized by its link to specific developments in political history: the May Fourth Literary Revolution with its reform agenda, War of Resistance Literature produced during the Sino-Japanese War, and Revolutionary Literature under the guidance of the Communist Party reflecting successive stages of social construction, from land reform to co-ops to communes. During the post-Mao period, the pace of change accelerated. Literature of the Wounded looked back on the scars of the Cultural Revolution, Literature of Reform portrayed problems of the Four Modernizations Program, and these were followed by Reflective Literature which reflected on historical events while considering the nature of literature itself. The "root-searching" generation of the mid-1980's attempted to encompass a broader view of history and culture; it was also marked by its diversity, wide range of narrative methods, and its self-conscious, self-exploratory processes. Nevertheless there was a common "cultural agenda" critics could point to. This turned out to be the last time that a group of more or less contemporaneous works could be linked under a single descriptive label with some sort of theme or agenda or explicit ideology. Now, in the absence of anything like these, how should one characterize or describe what has been happening in modern Chinese literature since?

Such has been the Chinese critics' dilemma. Even "modernism," as a response to the revolution's aftermath and with its antirealist and anti-ideological oppositional stance, could be perceived to have an ideology.[13] What followed has been critical debates over such terms as "postmodernism" or "pseudo-postmodernism," and then beginning in the 1990's, over such period labels as "post-new-era literature," even "postcriticism."[14] Whatever their precise meaning (and the point is that they were not found to have any) this uncertain groping among a multitude of faddish controversial terms signals an unprecedented state of affairs in Chinese history—the loss of a clearly defined role for literature, and together with it the self-image of the writer/intellectual as someone who in certain specified ways intensely matters.

Up to this point in history, one thing that has been remarkable is how aspects of the traditional roles and self-conceptions of intellectuals have continued throughout nearly a century of turmoil and revolution. What stands out immediately—because it is also the most painful to contemplate—is the persistent renewal of the writer/intellectual as martyr syndrome. Among the writers we have considered, Lu Xun suffered persecution from the Guomindang, forcing him to take refuge in the foreign settlements of Shanghai. One often hears intellectuals in China today, who have this fixed image of Lu Xun as a courageous fighter, speculate among themselves on what his fate and behavior—presumably as a literary martyr—would have been had he survived to live under Communist rule. Most ironically it is the tragic life and career of Zhao Shuli, created by the party itself as a model peasant writer, who finally exemplifies the impossibility of living and writing according to its prescriptions. Gao Xiaosheng was exiled to the countryside to do labor reform for over twenty years because he once wrote a manifesto for an aborted literary periodical, and his self-ironic story of the rehabilitated writer Liu Yu explicitly recalls Sima Qian's text on literary martyrdom. The writers of the "search for roots" generation, nine or ten years old at the beginning of the Cultural Revolution, got off relatively lightly. After spending part of their youth in the countryside or border areas, they have had enough life and time left to develop important careers. All of the above writers together represent only the tiniest tip of the iceberg. The path of modern Chinese literature is strewn with the dead bodies or broken lives of intellectual martyrs; what is truly extraordinary is why so many have made the fateful life and death decision to write.

Even more painful may be the realization that what has happened to China's modern intellectuals has also been to a large extent a result of events they had brought on themselves. As Ying-shih Yü has observed,

> The real tragedy in the history of Chinese revolutions is that it was always the radicalized Chinese intellectuals who imported and sowed the seeds of revolution while the harvest was, without exception, reaped by those anti-intellectual elements who knew best how to manipulate the revolution in order to seize its power. For the intellectuals, the seeds of revolution turned out to be seeds of their own destruction.[15]

That intellectuals have actively contributed to their own martyrdom is also inextricably tied to their double-edged position in relation to power in the state system. While no longer part of the establishment as scholar-officials were in the past, twentieth-century intellectuals have nevertheless, as state-employed professional writers, editors, research workers, or cultural bureaucrats, been incorporated into the system. In spite of contemporary accusations that they have been "cowards" and "slaves," Chinese intellectuals have not been totally or uniformly subservient to state power. Indeed not a few have struggled to live by a Marxist version of something akin to the old Confucian continuum that links self-fulfillment and moral idealism to social vocation and political service. As they "sowed the seeds of revolution," participating in what seemed at first to be a great experiment to build a utopian socialist society of justice and egalitarianism, they were perhaps even more fervently holding onto that old "sense of mission," of "worry or concern for the country and the people (*youguo youmin*)." But whatever the apparent similarities with the imperial past there might have been during the early days of the Communist Revolution, subsequent historical developments began to expose that ideal of personal fulfillment combined with public service to be an unattainable illusion.

Under the old imperial system there had been, of course, skeptics, cynics, and nonbelievers, and for long periods in Chinese history a Daoist-type withdrawal for large numbers of intellectuals seemed the only possible response. But most of the time the political establishment and its ideological underpinning maintained enough credibility to call forth the commitment of enough members of the intellectual elite to sustain the system and make it work. What may be new in the Chinese polity now is first, the unprecedented pervasiveness and totalitarian power of the dominating ideology for a brief thirty-some years and, second, once the hold was loosened, its subsequent rapid loss of credibility.

One of the most important symptoms of the current state of affairs is the tenuous condition of the official language. The Confucian notion of "the correctness or rectification of names and terms" (*zhengming*) emphasized the assumed unity between language, morality, and political authority. It is an assumption that has been carried to extremes by the Chinese Communists to the point of making language the key index to ideological correctness and public performance. But after investing so much of their power and authority to maintain the hegemony of the Maoist discourse, they are discovering that it could be rapidly undermined should historical developments begin to challenge its applicability or authenticity.

The malfunctioning of the political system, the failure of its leadership to maintain even a facade of morality, have all the more intensified the need to hold onto the official language. This obsession with the "right" language can only further expose its basic irrelevance, thus setting up a self-defeating circular process. Perry Link provides some examples, which would be amusing were they not so tragic, of the "language game" or "linguistic engineering" going on at the official level in contemporary China, where "the surface meanings of words should make sense at the level of pretense, whereas actual meanings lie deeper." At the same time everybody has to pretend that no pretending is going on.[16]

All these developments have led to the widespread alienation of the majority of intellectuals, those who had derived their identity and purpose as nodes within an enclosed network of moral responsibility and political power, an identity and purpose reinforced and manifest in their mastery of language. The disintegration of that network due to the external forces of a globalizing market economy has intensified the identity crisis for intellectuals as they become ever more aware of their increasing marginalization in the system and in the eyes of their audience. On the other hand, the acknowledgment of their own diminished relevance may well be the best "cure" for the intellectual-as-martyr syndrome that has endured for so long.

At the end of Wang Anyi's story "Lao Kang Came Back," a theater bell rings to indicate that a movie will soon begin. Thereupon the I-narrator and the brother break off their despairing discussion over the fate of Lao Kang, one of thousands of martyred intellectuals, to go to the movie. It is a telling sign of the new times. In China's expanding urbanized market economy, the flood of imported cultural products from the outside world—movies, television, videos, rock music, and many other forms of media and entertainment—is eclipsing the visibility of literature. And even within the realm of literature, popular fiction, stories about crime and detection, the martial arts, hoodlums, the supernatural, sex, and violence are pushing serious literature (*yansu wenxue*), the kind that supposedly carried moral and political messages and was linked to pragmatic agendas or social action, to the side.

One of the most prominent exemplars of what may be happening in contemporary Chinese culture is Wang Shuo, whose sale of nearly 100 million copies of more than twenty best-sellers since 1984 has made him one of the most popular Chinese writers of the twentieth century, if not of all Chinese history. Since he stopped writing fiction in 1991, turning full-time to television, film-writing, and directing, his audience has reached hundreds of millions more. What has been labeled his "hooligan or riffraff literature" (*pizi wenxue*) focuses on the urban scene through the dealings and relationships of grifters, shady dealers, "bad girls," pimps, etc. "They never think about the future, for they do not believe there is a future," says the blurb on his 1993 novel with its characteristic title *Get Your High and Die* (*Guoba yin jiu si*).

Whether such irreverence or nihilism should be taken as representative of the current state of Chinese culture, the "Wang Shuo phenomenon," even as it may be showing signs of being an ephemeral one, has communicated a powerful message in its open contempt for intellectuals. Unsurprisingly, this "scorner of intelligentsia culture," as the title of one article has it,[17] has been the subject of much study by that very same culture in scholarly conferences and critical studies. He has been discussed and made much of as a "postmodernist" but of course denies knowing what that is.[18] His avowed goal is to "thoroughly knock out the superior position of intellectuals in culture" (p. 7). They "derive their power from moral status," whereas he himself had "never written anything [he] thought was necessary for society."[19] He claims to be dedicated to making his own fortune; his "sense of mission" (*shiminggan*) is only for himself.

If Wang Shuo's frequent spitting at intellectuals is a pose, it nevertheless targets intellectuals most tellingly for their traditional self-conception as being crucially positioned within the moral and political order of society. Some critics have attributed the flourishing of "vulgar, superficial, consumer culture" to the loss of "such ultimate convictions and traditional spiritual props as ideals, beliefs, and morality (*daoyi*)",[20] but the truth is more likely the other way round. With the increasing fluidity of Chinese society—money being the great solvent—it is economic changes that have brought about the erosions in traditional beliefs and values, and with it questioning about the function of literature. In Zhao Zhenkai's story "In the Ruins," with which this study began, the question whether the condemned intellectual Wang Qi in the end found a reason to go on with his life may be unanswered. But even while contemplating the devastations of Chinese history and his own suicide, he was confident that his books, in spite of the criticisms they had been subject to, would be validated and survive him. Given the state of literature today, such belief in the transcendent value of literature may have to be built on very different and perhaps shifting foundations.

In recent years the recognized boundaries of modern Chinese literature have also greatly expanded to encompass literature produced in

Taiwan and Hong Kong and by the growing numbers of writers in dias-pora, particularly since 1989, who may be writing "about China" in Chi-nese but are publishing their works abroad. Such global developments will require the reconceptualization and rewriting of modern Chinese lit-erary history.

The diversity of the peasantry, the marginalization of the intellectual, the multiplicity of literary and cultural productions, have together brought to a final end the obsessive dualistic theme of the intellectual vis-à-vis the peasant in modern Chinese literature. Inherited and adapted from the traditional self-conception and role of the scholar-official (*shi*) toward the "people" (*min*), the fictional self-representation of the writer/ intellectual and construction of the peasant "other" in modern Chinese literature have undergone several "generational" changes against a shift-ing historical context. But now this dualistic relationship is fading into the past as Chinese literature undergoes the seismic transformations of the present and faces its highly uncertain future.

Reference Matter

Chronological List of Major
Texts Discussed

(Dates represent year of completion of work unless otherwise noted.)

LU XUN 魯迅 (1881–1936)

"Kuangren riji" 狂人日記 ("A Madman's Diary") 1918.4
"Yijian xiaoshi" 一件小事 ("A Small Incident") 1920.7
"Fengbo" 風波 ("A Passing Storm") 1920.8
"Guxiang" 故鄉 ("My Old Home") 1921.1
"Ah Q zhengzhuan" 阿Q正傳 ("The True Story of Ah Q") 1921.12
"Zixu" 自序 ("Preface" to *Nahan*) 吶喊 1922.12.3
"Zhufu" 祝福 ("The New-Year Sacrifice") 1924.2

ZHAO SHULI 趙樹理 (1906–1970)

"Xiao Erhei jiehun" 小二黑結婚 ("Blackie Gets Married") 1943.5
"Li Youcai banhua" 李有才板話 ("The Rhymes of Li Youcai") 1943.10
"Meng Xiangying fanshen" 孟祥英翻身 ("Meng Xianying Stands Up") 1944.11
Sanliwan 三里灣 (*Sanliwan Village*) Serialized in *Renmin wenxue* 人民文學
  1955.1–4

GAO XIAOSHENG 高曉聲 (1928–)

"Jixin dai" 繫心帶 ("Bond of Hearts") 1978.12
"Li Shunda zaowu" 李順大造屋 ("Li Shunda Builds a House") 1979.3
"'Loudouhu' zhu" '漏斗戶'主 ("The 'Funnel House-holder'") 1978.12.7–11

"Chen Huansheng shangcheng" 陳奐生上城 ("Chen Huansheng Goes to Town") 1980.1

"Cheng Huansheng zhuanye" 陳奐生轉業 ("Chen Huansheng Transferred") 1981.1

"Chen Huansheng baochan" 陳奐生包產 ("Chen Huansheng Under Production Contract") 1982

"Liu Yu xieshu" 劉宇寫書 ("Liu Yu Writes a Book") 1981.8

Qingtian zaishang 青天在上 (*The Blue Heavens Above*) 1987.10.8 (revised 1990.1–6)

"Chen Huansheng chuguo" 陳奐生出國 ("Chen Huansheng Goes Abroad") 1991.12

ZHAO ZHENKAI 趙振開 (SHI MO) 石默 (1949–)

"Zai feixu shang" 在廢墟上 ("In the Ruins") 1978

LU XINHUA 盧新華 (1954–)

"Shanghen" 傷痕 ("The Wound") Published in *Wenhuibao* 文匯報 1978.8.11

HAN SHAOGONG 韓少功 (1953–)

"Wenxue de 'gen'" 文學的'根' ("The 'Roots' of Literature") 1985.1

"Ba Ba Ba" 爸爸爸 ("Pa Pa Pa") 1985.1

"Guiqulai" 歸去來 ("The Homecoming") 1985.1

MO YAN 莫言 (1956–)

"Baigou qiuqianjia" 白狗鞦韆架 ("White Dog and the Swings") 1985.4

Hong gaoliang jiazu 紅高粱家族 (*Red Sorghum*) Chapter 1 published in *Renmin wenxue* 1986.3; the entire five chapters in 1987

WANG ANYI 王安憶 (1954–)

Xiaobaozhuang 小鮑莊 (*Bao Village*) 1984.12

"Lao Kang huilai" 老康回來 ("Lao Kang Came Back") Published in *Chouxiaoya* 醜小鴨 1985.10

CAN XUE 殘雪 (1953–)

"Shanshang de xiaowu" 山上的小屋 ("Hut on the Hill") Published in *Renmin wenxue* 1985.8

Notes

INTRODUCTION

1. This Zhao Zhenkai story was first published in *Jintian,* 1978, under the pen name Shi Mo. The writer is more widely known as the poet Bei Dao. English translation in Bonnie McDougall, *Waves,* pp. 1–8.

2. Bonnie S. McDougall, to whom we are indebted for her skillful translations of Zhao Zhenkai's poetry and fiction, sees Wang Qi as an "unusually wooden figure in Zhao Zhenkai's fiction" ("Zhao Zhenkai's Fiction," p. 119). In my view the story is remarkable for its emblematic intellectual-peasant encounter, not for its realistic portrayal of individual character.

3. This reading of the scene was confirmed by Zhao Zhenkai himself when he visited my class on modern Chinese literature at the University of Michigan on November 16, 1993. In response to a student's question as to what he'd had in mind when he wrote this scene, he said that he had forgotten, but "coming to this scene as a reader," he believed that the child's situation made the professor realize that the peasant was worse off than himself.

4. See, for example, Liu Xiaobo, "Wu fa huibi de fansi," p. 108.

5. Mao Zedong's "Talks at the Yan'an Forum on Literature and Art" (1942), refers constantly to the "great masses of workers, peasants, and soldiers." But since workers scarcely existed as a class, and the ranks of soldiers were made up of peasants, for all practical purposes, Mao was referring to the great masses of peasants.

6. The concept of "generation" has often been used by scholars, most notably Li Zehou and Vera Schwarcz, to analyze the shaping of the distinct fate, experiences, and collective identity of Chinese intellectuals by political events. See

their "Six Generations of Modern Chinese Intellectuals." Li Zehou had earlier offered a brief outline of his "six generations" in an 1979 article on the development of Lu Xun's thought, "Lüelun Lu Xun sixiang de fazhan," esp. p. 543. Li's generations are roughly fifteen years apart. I begin my "four generations" later and they do not correspond to his six. But I have found the concept useful for emphasizing the ways historical contexts influence—while also being incorporated into their distinctive narrative texts—the writers in this study.

CHAPTER I

1. For a discussion of these terms, see Benjamin Schwartz, "The Limits of 'Tradition Versus Modernity.'"

2. Pierre Bourdieu, *Language and Symbolic Power*, See especially sections "The Production and Reproduction of Legitimate Language," pp. 43–65; "On Symbolic Power," pp. 163–70.

3. See Edward Shils, "Intellectuals," esp. p. 413.

4. Jerome B. Grieder, *Intellectuals and the State in Modern China*, pp. 6, 30.

5. Tu Wei-ming, *Way, Learning, and Politics*, p. 19.

6. Ibid., p. 22.

7. Frederic Wakeman, "The Price of Autonomy," compares the situation and self-conceptions of intellectuals during the Tunglin struggles and the scholarly reformers of the 1890's.

8. Wm. Theodore de Bary, *Self and Society in Ming Thought*, p. 6.

9. See Pei-yi Wu, *The Confucian's Progress*, for a fascinating and pioneering study of the subject, including examples of spiritual autobiographies and "conversion narratives" which began to make their appearance in the fifteenth century.

10. Jerome B. Grieder, *Intellectuals and the State in Modern China*, p. 34.

11. Antonio Gramsci, "The Intellectuals," *Selections from the Prison Notebooks*, p. 8.

12. Merle Goldman, ed., with Timothy Cheek and Carol Lee Hamrin, *China's Intellectuals and the State*, p. 2.

13. It was highly instructive to hear the "Confucian" echoes as Ding Ling, for example, spoke to me, when I visited her in 1981, about her long relationship with the party that had condemned and expelled her as a "rightist" for twenty years. She maintained that her stance had never changed, that she had always remained loyal to the party. It was only that the party had deviated from its "proper path," but now in the post-Mao era—and presumably in its rehabilitation of her and many others—had returned to it.

14. David Johnson, "Communication, Class, and Consciousness in Late Imperial China," p. 56.

15. Writers who wrote for profit tended to be producers, editors, or anthologists of literature in the vernacular language. Feng Menglong is an outstanding

example of someone who straddled the two types of classical literature and vernacular literature. But most writers, like Feng, even the authors of the great novels, did not openly claim authorship for their vernacular works; it was not what would inscribe one's name in the literary tradition. "Significantly . . . there are no works in the vernacular, no matter how serious they are, that carry Feng's own name." Patrick Hanan, "Feng's Life and Ideas," in *The Chinese Vernacular Story,* p. 82.

16. During the Qing dynasty, an aspirant had about one chance in sixty of getting the lowest prefectural level *shengyuan* degree. By 1850 only *jinshi,* those who were successful at the national level, could be sure of getting official posts. Each of the two million students taking the prefectural examination in any given year had only one chance in six thousand of such an appointment. See Frederic Wakeman, Jr., *The Fall of Imperial China,* p. 22.

17. Although there were women in upper-class households who may have received a classical education, since they were barred from holding office and the possibility of any public role, the goals of their education were very different.

18. John King Fairbank, *The United States and China,* pp. 37–38.

19. As for example in Liu E's 1904–1907 novel *Lao Can youji,* ch. 14.

20. Cao Pi, "Dian lun lun wen," p. 45.

21. Questions about the Chinese intellectual's past and present relation to language and how it is affected by the relation between knowledge and government are raised by Rey Chow in her thoughtful reflections on the Tiananmen Massacre of June 1989. See her "Pedagogy, Trust, Chinese Intellectuals in the 1990's," pp. 191–207.

22. Wendy Larson, *Literary Authority and the Modern Chinese Writer,* p. 16.

23. "Taishigong zixu," p. 5207. For a discussion of the "assimilation of personal identity into tradition" in Sima Qian, see Stephen W. Durrant, "Self as the Intersection of Traditions," pp. 33–40.

24. "Bao Ren Shaoqing shu," p. 361. Trans. J. R. Hightower, in Cyril Birch, comp. and ed., *Anthology of Chinese Literature: From Early Times to the Fourteenth Century* (New York: Grove Press, 1965), pp. 95–102. Whether or not this letter was actually written by Sima Qian himself, it remains one of the most powerful and influential texts in defining the tradition of literary martyrdom. A somewhat shorter list with much identical wording is included in the postface to the *Shiji.* Sima Qian follows it immediately to describe his own writing of the history, again pointing to his self-perception as being in that tradition. See *Shiji huizhu kaozheng,* ch. 70, in 10: 5209.

25. Trans. Hightower, p. 101.

26. The often quoted notion that great poetry is possible only when one is in difficult circumstances, or frustrated in official life, *shi bi qiuong er hou gong,* is another example of this tradition of literary martyrdom. For a famous expression of the idea see Ouyang Xiu, "Mei Shengyu shiji xu," pp. 197–98.

27. "Qu Yuan Jia Sheng liezhuan," p. 3841.

28. David Hawkes uses this expressed relationship between the historian and the poet to argue that the biography is indeed by Sima Qian. See *Ch'u Tz'u*, p. 17. I have used Hawkes' translation for the quoted passages.

29. See Hawkes' discussion of these issues. Ibid., pp. 16–19.

30. Lu Xun quotes lines 94 to 97 of the *Lisao* as the epigraph for his short story collection *Panghuang*, published in 1926. One version of Zhao Zhenkai's story "In the Ruins" also has the head of the History Department quoting one of these same lines: *"Lu man man qi xiu yuan xi,"* (Long has been my road and far the journey). See Anne Wedell-Wedellsborg, "Chinese Modernism?" p. 109.

31. For example, see Rudolf Wagner's meticulous allegorical reading of historical dramas produced between 1958 and 1966, which are "historical screens" for debates or criticisms of contemporary political events and personalities, in *The Contemporary Chinese Historical Drama*. Bai Hua placed himself in this tradition in his 1979 screenplay *"Kulian"* ("Unrequited Love") by quoting Qu Yuan at the outset. He can be said subsequently to have suffered a "fate" similar to that of Qu Yuan, when his work became the target of a national campaign in 1981. See Richard Kraus, "Bai Hua." Ralph Crozier provides examples of the Qu Yuan legacy in the field of art in "Qu Yuan and the Artists."

32. This is not to say that the question of whether the Qu Yuan analogy is applicable to the relationship between intellectuals and the state has not in itself been a contentious matter. When Bai Hua was criticized for his filmscript of "Unrequited Love" in 1981, he admitted his error: "I equated the fate of intellectuals since the feudal society of Qu Yuan with the unjust treatment suffered as a result of Leftist mistakes committed by the Party in its policies. . . . This was naturally wrong of me. I should not have confused the nature of different societies and drawn similarities between the two." *Jiefangjun bao,* December 23, 1981. Quoted in David S. G. Goodman, "PRC Fiction and Its Political Context," p. 143.

33. Liu Zaifu, "Zhongguo zhishifenzi de mingyun yu zhongguo dangdai wenxue de mingyun."

34. Liu Zaifu, *Xingge zuhe lun*, p. 19.

35. Vera Schwarcz, *The Chinese Enlightenment*, p. 2. This was one of the "particularities" of the Chinese enlightenment, as compared with its European precedent.

36. See the foreword by John Israel to *China's Establishment Intellectuals* for an account of the Chinese intellectual's stages of transition from independent critic of the May Fourth period to increasingly dependent establishment intellectual.

37. Wang Youqin, "Zuojia de shiming gan," uses Qu Yuan and Lu Xun as two representative figures to compare the sense of mission in ancient and modern intellectuals.

38. *Mencius,* Book I, Part A, section 7. Trans. Lau, p. 58.

39. "Peasant" or "peasantry" is the term used in Auerbach's and Jameson's discussion of the La Bruyère passage In the following section I will discuss the implications of using "peasant" rather than "farmer" to refer to food producers.

40. The passage is quoted by Eric Auerbach, *Mimesis,* p. 366. Auerbach sees the "moralizing emphasis" as clearly of its century. For Fredric Jameson's discussion of the same passage see *The Prison-House of Language,* pp. 56–57.

41. "Tianjia yu" in *Mei Yaochen shixuan* (1980), pp. 44–45. I have benefited from consulting the translation of Jonathan Chaves in his *Mei Yao-ch'en and the Development of Early Sung Poetry,* pp. 164–65. This is the same poet who had been praised by Ouyang Xiu as an example of how great poetry is the product of suffering.

42. For other poetic uses of the Poetry Collector office see Qian Zhongshu, *Song shi xuan zhu,* p. 20.

43. Zhu Dongrun in *Mei Yaochen shixuan,* p. 13.

44. Michel Foucault, "The Subject and Power": "While the human subject is placed in relations of production and of signification, he is equally placed in power relations which are very complex," p. 209. See also Kaja Silverman, *The Subject of Semiotics* for a discussion of how the "strategies for understanding persons and places" are "really ways of signifying and controlling those persons and places. Those epistemological strategies also determine the position from which power is exercised, and therefore must be seen as exceeding the agent who occupies that position," p. 254.

45. Zhang Yiwu, "Zhongguo nongmin wenhua de xingsheng yu weiji," pp. 144–45.

46. For an illuminating study of translingual practice and cultural crossings in the early twentieth century, see Lydia H. Liu, *Translingual Practice.* Her useful Appendix D: "Return Graphic Loans: 'Kanji' Terms Derived from Classical Chinese" includes the example of *nongmin* in the early Chinese text.

47. Myron L. Cohen, "Cultural and Political Inventions in Modern China," p. 154.

48. An example of a story which contains the two apparently contradictory images of the peasant as oppressed victim and as revolutionary vanguard is Mao Dun's "Shuizaoxing" ("Algae"). See Yi-tsi Mei Feuerwerker, "The Dialectics of Struggle."

49. For an overall discussion of the issues in approaching the peasant as a "multidimensional being," see Philip C. C. Huang, *The Peasant Economy and Social Change in North China,* esp. pp. 3–9.

50. Eric R. Wolf, *Peasants,* pp. 3–4. Thirty years later, this book is still regarded as an important benchmark, a "comprehensive review and synthesis of the ethnography and theory of peasant society." It is subject to criticism now that anthropologists have come to consider "the kinds of others" in their own

history and the problem of "peasant essentialism." "Peasant," more or less a successor to "the primitive," has been a category that anthropology has "objectified ethnographically and assigned primordial ontologies." The attention has been shifting from "the presumed objects of peasant literature to the literature that objectifies them," to the problems of representation itself. See Michael Kearney, *Reconceptualizing the Peasantry,* esp. pp. 1–3, 59–60. His book is yet another example of how anthropology is turning more and more into an approximation of literary studies. "Peasant essentialism" is, of course, a core issue in my own book, which may be said to be above all a study of representation.

51. Ying-shih Yü, "The Radicalization of China in the Twentieth Century," p. 141.

52. For a discussion of the evolution of this term from *zhishi jieji* (intellectual class, 1905–1919) to *qimeng xuezhe* (enlightened scholars, 1919–1927) to *zhishifenzi* as the discursive product or "subject position" settled on by 1927, see Tani E. Barlow, "*Zhishifenzi* [Chinese Intellectuals] and Power," pp. 210–11.

53. Benjamin Schwartz, "The Intelligentsia in Communist China," p. 169. The term "intelligentsia," Russian in origin, was introduced into the Russian language in the 1860's, but had its origins in the "circles" of the 1830's and 1840's. With the name, the group then assumed a specific identity. Intelligentsia does not include all the well-educated class, but has connotations of "critical thought," opposition, alienation, moral passion. In that sense intelligentsia does not completely overlap with the Chinese term *zhishifenzi* but is comparable in the ways discussed by Schwartz.

54. For a study of this movement, primarily of its effect on intellectuals, see Chang-tai Hung, *Going to the People.*

55. For a discussion comparing the populism in the two countries, see Maurice Meisner, "Leninism and Maoism."

56. See ibid.

57. Many Western scholars have seen the notion of "class analysis" as having forced an inappropriate model onto Chinese society, particularly in the context of China's dense social continuum and high social mobility and the lack of "natural breakpoints" in the continuum. See, for example, Mark Elvin's "No Controlling Vision," p. 87. The article is a review of Jonathan D. Spence, *The Search for Modern China* (New York: W. W. Norton, 1990).

58. Tani E. Barlow, "*Zhishifenzi* [Chinese Intellectuals] and Power," p. 216.

59. This was a major political issue and effectively used as a source of narrative tension, for example, in Ding Ling's land-reform novel *Taiyang zhao zai Sangganhe shang (The Sun Shines on the Sanggan River),* published in 1948.

60. Mao Zedong, "Daliang xishou zhishifenzi." Trans. in *Selected Works of Mao Tse-tung,* pp. 301–3.

61. Merle Goldman, *China's Intellectuals,* p. 9.

62. Zhou Yang on the fortieth anniversary of the Yen'an Forum on Literature and Art, *Renmin ribao,* June 23, 1982.

63. Michel Foucault, "Truth and Power," p. 67. Bonnie S. McDougall makes a similar point about the "universal intellectual" in China, in "Writers and Performers: Their Works, and Their Audiences in the First Three Decades," p. 279.

64. For example, see Tatyana Tolstaya's review of *The Great Terror* by Robert Conquest, p. 6.

65. Chen Sihe, "Zhongguo xinwenxue fazhan zhong de chanhui yishi," p. 81. See Mau-sang Ng, *The Russian Hero in Modern Chinese Fiction,* pp. 63–64, for a discussion of the influence of repentant characters in Russian novels on Chinese writers.

CHAPTER 2

1. Hu Shi, "Wenxue gailiang chuyi."

2. Edward Gunn, *Rewriting Chinese,* p. 39.

3. Qu Qiubai, "Puluo dazhong wenyi de xianshi wenti," p. 310. May Fourth writers may have been advocates of democracy, but they have been charged with elitism in their attitude toward the popular literature (so-called Butterfly literature) that reached a wider public than they did themselves. They attacked this literature for the common people, which was also more traditional in style, for its lack of serious moral and political purpose. For a discussion of the contradictions in May Fourth discourses on literature see Feng Lipeng, "Democracy and Elitism."

4. For a discussion of the relationship between Mao's ideas on literature and the influence of Qu Qiubai see Paul G. Pickowicz, *Marxist Literary Thought in China,* esp. pp. 222–42.

5. Mao Zedong, "Zai Yan'an wenyi zuotanhui shang de jianghua," pp. 521–22. Translation is from *Selected Works of Mao Tse-tung,* 3, p. 72.

6. David E. Apter and Tony Saich, *Revolutionary Discourse in Mao's Republic,* pp. 294, 263.

7. Confucian *Analects,* bk. 13, ch. 3. Rey Chow, "Against the Lures of Diaspora," pp. 29–30, refers to the same passage in making the important observation about the continuity between the Confucian and the Chinese Communist attitude toward language. My point here is that Confucians did not quite push language to the same extent to *make* things real.

8. D. W. Fokkema and Elrud Kunne-Ibsch, *Theories of Literature in the Twentieth Century,* p. 111.

9. Michael Schoenhals, *Doing Things with Words in Chinese Politics,* pp. 31–53. I am grateful to Lydia Liu for calling my attention to this work.

10. See note to Zhao Shuli, "Huiyi lishi, renshi ziji," p. 1825. The excerpted text focusing on his relation with literature runs from p. 1825 to p. 1844.

11. Li Tuo, "The New Vitality of Modern Chinese," p. 74.

12. Li Tuo, Zhang Ling, Wang Bin, "'Yuyan' de fanpan,"p. 79.

13. *Sanguo yanyi* (*The Romance of the Three Kingdoms*), by Luo Guanzhong (ca. 1330–ca. 1400) is one notable example.

14. J. Hillis Miller, *Tropes, Parables, Performatives*, p. ix.

15. Roland Barthes, *S/Z*, p. 16.

16. Deconstruction has rejected the assumptions of New Criticism about coherence and unifying meanings, but it has to an even greater degree continued with the practice of close reading. See, for example, Barbara Johnson's discussion of deconstructive reading in *The Critical Difference*, esp. pp. 3–6.

17. Jacques Derrida, *Of Grammatology*, p. 158.

18. Stephen Greenblatt has made a similar point in discussing what is meant by cultural analysis. See "Culture," p. 227.

19. Linda Nochlin, *Realism*, p. 13.

20. The argument for the "alliance of socialism and realism" has been made with greater sophistication by Georg Lukács, but he ultimately resorts to openly ideological assertions. When he writes that "in no other aesthetic does the truthful depiction of reality have so central a place as in Marxism," he gives the following reason: "For the Marxist, the road to socialism is identical with the movement of history itself. . . . Thus, *any* accurate account of reality is . . . a blow in the cause of socialism." See "Critical Realism and Socialist Realism," in *Realism in Our Time*, pp. 93–135, esp. p. 101. But see also Terry Eagleton's criticism of Lukács as being committed to "the great humanist tradition of bourgeois realism," *Marxism and Literary Criticism*, p. 53. Marxist criticism and its insistence on realism is of course a direct inheritance from nineteenth-century "bourgeois realism," adding yet another level of ironic contradictions to this literary doctrine.

21. Zhuang Zhongqing, *Zhongguo xiandai wenxue yanjiu*, pp. 31–35.

22. James J. Y. Liu, *Chinese Theories of Literature*, p. 67.

23. Marston Anderson, *The Limits of Realism*, p. 37.

CHAPTER 3

1. Yang Yi, *Zhongguo xiandai xiaoshuoshi*, 1: 171.

2. The close, rather than dichotomous, relation between the two groups and their slogans is discussed by Leo Ou-fan Lee, "Literary Trends, I," pp. 474–75.

3. Kirk A. Denton, *Modern Chinese Literary Thought*, pp. 35–36. Denton follows with a persuasive argument on the "distorting influence" of "traditional cosmology and literary thought" on the reception of Western realism and romanticism, so that in the end both take on quite different meanings in the Chinese context. In Denton's view the "realist" and "romantic" theorists "shared fundamental assumptions about the origin and function of literature."

4. Marston Anderson, *The Limits of Realism*, p. 36.

5. Linda Nochlin, *Realism*, p. 23. Although this is a book on Western art, Nochlin's discussion of realism in relation to the social and political upheavals of nineteenth-century Europe contains (apart from the origins of my theatrical metaphor) many useful insights into its nature.

6. Leo Ou-fan Lee, *The Romantic Generation of Modern Chinese Writers.*

7. James J. Y. Liu, *Chinese Theories of Literature,* esp. pp. 69–70, 75. For a variety of modes of expression of the Chinese literary self, see the collection of essays in *Expressions of Self in Chinese Literature,* ed. Robert E. Hegel and Richard C. Hessney.

8. This traditional Chinese notion of literature anticipates in some intriguing ways Roland Barthes' conception of the text as a "tissue of quotations" when he pronounced the "death of the author." See "The Death of the Author," p. 146. The first thing that Barthes "deconstructs" is of course the idea of the "independent creative writer, the autonomous genius" which was the result of political, social, and economic changes brought about by the Industrial Revolution. See Raymond Williams, *Culture and Society,* pp. 30–32. The May Fourth Chinese writer was facing a somewhat similar predicament in having to fall back on the self.

9. Yu Dafu, *Zhongguo xinwenxue daxi, sanwen erji daoyan,* p. 2887. Yu Dafu's introduction is dated Apr. 1935.

10. Jaroslav Průšek, "Mao Tun and Yu Ta-fu (from *Three Sketches of Modern Chinese Literature*)" in *The Lyrical and the Epic,* p. 143.

11. For a fuller analysis of this story see my "Text, Intertext, and the Representation of the Writing Self in Lu Xun, Yu Dafu, and Wang Meng." The story can be found in *Yu Dafu daibiao zuo,* pp. 1–39. It has been translated by C. T. Hsia and Joseph S. M. Lau in their *Twentieth-Century Chinese Stories,* pp. 3–33.

12. The creative artist as suicidal genius has been a widespread image in the West since nineteenth-century Romanticism, and its influence is everywhere evident in Yu Dafu's story. My interest here is to see it also as exemplifying one particular effect when modern Chinese writers, in contrast to writers of the past, sought to cut themselves loose from their own literary tradition.

13. Leo Ou-fan Lee, "Literary Trends I," p. 473.

14. Raymond Williams discusses the alienation of the romantic artist due to the passing of the patronage system in England from the mid-eighteenth century on. See *Culture and Society, 1780–1950,* p. 32. Compare also Leo Ou-fan Lee's comment: "The May Fourth generation of writers (with few exceptions) often asserted their individual personalities and life-styles externally against an environment that they found confusing and alienating." See "The Solitary Traveler," esp. p. 294.

15. As Patrick Hanan has noted, "Each story of Lu Hsun's is a venture in technique, a fresh try at the perfect matching of subject and form." "The Technique of Lu Hsun's Fiction," p. 53.

16. Jaroslav Průšek, "The Changing Role of the Narrator in Chinese Novels at the Beginning of the Twentieth Century," in *The Lyrical and the Epic,* pp. 110–20; Milena Doleželová-Velingerová, *The Chinese Novel at the Turn of the Century.* A little-known example of first-person narration from 1906 is discussed in Yang Yi, *Zhongguo xiandai xiaoshuoshi,* p. 29.

17. Milena Doleželová-Velingerová, *The Chinese Novel at the Turn of the Century,* p. 71.

18. Chen Pingyuan discusses the author's incomplete efforts on this matter in *Zhongguo xiaoshuo xushi moshi de zhuanbian,* pp. 82–83.

19. Lu Xun, "Xie zai *Fen* houmian." The volume includes twenty-three essays written between 1907 and 1925; the postface is dated Nov. 11, 1926, published in 1927. Numbers in parentheses following quotations indicate page numbers in this text.

20. Leo Ou-fan Lee's important book on Lu Xun contains an extended discussion on the "transitional mentality" in "this interim figure living on the eve of the Chinese revolution." *Voices from the Iron House,* see esp. pp. 170ff.

21. See Kaja Silverman, *The Subject of Semiotics,* for a discussion of the subject that combines theories of psychoanalysis and semiotics, particularly the first chapter, "From Sign to Subject, A Short History," pp. 3–53. Wayne Booth's seminal term "implied author" for the "second self," the system of norms and beliefs that govern the text, is useful for differentiating it from the historical author, but nevertheless it is more useful to think of that "self" as a reconstruction of the reader rather than as a manifestation of the author. Wayne C. Booth, *The Rhetoric of Fiction,* pp. 71–77.

22. The "author" is allowed to survive his poststructuralist demise at least as a label that "permits one to group together a certain number of texts" in order to establish among them a "relationship of homogeneity, filiation . . . reciprocal explication or concomitant utilization." Michel Foucault, "What Is an Author?," p. 107. On that level at least, Lu Xun may be said to "exist," and most certainly as a "label" for grouping together a certain number of "his" texts for critical consideration.

23. Lu Xun, "Kuangren riji." Trans. Yang Xianyi and Gladys Yang, *The Complete Stories of Lu Xun,* pp. 1–12. I have consulted this translation but slightly revised it to emphasize the original meanings of the text. The story is discussed from a somewhat different point of view in my article "Text, Intertext, and the Representation of the Writing Self in Lu Xun, Yu Dafu, and Wang Meng."

24. Theodore Huters, "Lives in Profile," p. 276. My reading of the story can be seen as a "supplement" to Huters' perceptive analysis and is in agreement with it in many ways. However I am focusing more on the textual representation of the self.

25. David Der-wei Wang, *Fictional Realism in Twentieth-Century China,* p. 10.

26. In such parodic stylization, the "intentions of the representing discourse are at odds with the intentions of the represented discourse; they fight against them, they depict a real world of objects not by using the represented language as a productive point of view, but rather by using it as an exposé to destroy the represented language." M. M. Bakhtin, *The Dialogic Imagination,* p. 364.

27. Liu Zaifu and Lin Gang see the cannibalism, "eating people," as existing on three levels: (1) the harsh oppression and humiliation inflicted by those above on those below; (2) the eating of those weaker than themselves by those "being eaten"; and (3) the eating of the self, the suppression and extinguishing of one's self. See their "Chi ren yanxi de faxian" ("The Discovery of the Banquet of Cannibalism"), *Chuantong yu Zhongguo ren,* pp. 85–95.

28. See *Lu Hsun's Vision of Reality,* p. 270.

29. A distinction made by Emile Benveniste in "The Nature of Pronouns." The speaking subject, the individual who participates in discourse, whether speaker or writer, is the "referent," and the subject of speech, the discursive element with which the discoursing individual identifies, is the "referee." They are separated by the barrier between reality and signification. See the discussion of this issue in Kaja Silverman, *The Subject of Semiotics,* pp. 45–46.

30. Meng Yue, "Shijiao wenti yu 'wusi' xiaoshuo de xiandaihua," p. 83.

31. Leo Ou-fan Lee, *Voices from the Iron House,"* p. 53.

32. Lu Xun, "Zi xu," p. v. Yang and Yang, trans., *The Complete Stories of Lu Xun,* p. ix.

33. Leo Ou-fan Lee, *Voices from the Iron House,* p. 87.

34. Lu Xun, "Ah Q zhengzhuan." Trans. Yang and Yang, *The Complete Stories of Lu Xun,* pp. 66–113. William A. Lyell prefers "Ah Q—The Real Story" for his translation in *Diary of a Madman and Other Stories,* pp. 101–172. The irony, of course, is that the story is neither "true" nor "real."

35. Martin Weizong Huang, "The Inescapable Predicament." Huang's analysis contains many perceptive insights into the narrator's role. I have two minor questions, as to whether (1) the narrator in the introduction and the narrator of the story should necessarily be conflated as one and the same, or whether the introduction and the "story proper" might represent two different types of discourse (cf. "A Madman's Diary"); and (2) whether the narrator is more a rhetorical stance, a "speaker" of the text, than a character within the text interacting with Ah Q (cf. "The New-Year Sacrifice"). But perhaps the fact that these questions cannot be conclusively answered is due again to the ironic use of the narrator.

36. The phrase is from the *Zuozhuan,* twenty-fourth year of Duke Xiang's reign, recording the words of the Shu Sun, a *dafu* of Lu. The three means to immortality (*san bu xiu*) were virtue, military achievement, and writing.

37. Patrick Hanan, "The Technique of Lu Hsun's Fiction," p. 81.

38. Zhou Xiashou (Zhou Zuoren), "Ah Q," *Lu Xun xiaoshuo li de renwu,* pp. 64–65.

39. Lu Xun, "Da *Xi* zhoukan bianzhe xin," p. 117. See also "Ah Q zheng-zhuan de chengyin," p. 281. "When the story began appearing in *Beixin zhoukan* under the pen name Ba Ren, there were those who were in fear and trepidation because they suspected their own secret behavior was being attacked."

40. Lydia H. Liu, *Translingual Practice,* particularly the chapter on "Trans-lating National Character: Lu Xun and Arthur Smith," pp. 45–76.

41. Is the cult of "face," as unique to Chinese culture, another product of missionary discourse? See Lydia Liu, *Translingual Practice,* pp. 65–66.

42. Leo Ou-fan Lee, *Voices from the Iron House,* p. 77; Lin Yü-sheng, "The Morality of Mind and Immorality of Politics," p. 112.

43. For a succinct summary of the argument on the mode of existence of character, whether they are "people" or "words," see Shlomith Rimmon-Kenan, *Narrative Fiction,* pp. 31–34.

44. This is a question formulated by Beckett and discussed by Michel Fou-cault in "What Is an Author?," pp. 101–2. Foucault's point is that writing is a matter of creating a space into which the writing subject constantly disappears. In the story of Ah Q, the creation of a narrated subject who continually appears only to disappear can be seen as a parallel to what is happening to the narrating subject. Marston Anderson discusses this break in the narrative in Ah Q's final moments as a "personal plea" or "direct expression of indignation" that may have "originated in the critical consciousness of the narrator." See *The Limits of Realism,* p. 84.

45. Although a photo of the execution of a Russian spy in 1905 has come to light, suggesting that there could be a factual base for this slide event, the exact relationship between the two has not been fully established. In any case, whether real or fabricated, this incident or "image" remains an overriding metaphor in Lu Xun's work. Lydia Liu focuses on the "rhetoric of representation" in her analysis of this event. See her *Translingual Practice,* pp. 62–63.

46. See Lin Zhihao, ch. 3, "Wenhua geming de weiren—Lu Xun" ("Lu Xun—Great Man of Cultural Revolution"), in *Zhongguo xiandai wenxueshi,* 1: 41–113, esp. pp. 67–68.

47. Lin Fei, "Lun 'Ah Q zhengzhuan,'" p. 115.

48. Liu Shousong, *Zhongguo xin wenxueshi chugao,* 1: 46, quoting from Zhou Yang: "Fayang 'wusi' wenxue geming de zhandou chuantong" ("Carry forward the fighting tradition of the May Fourth literary revolution").

49. Lu Xun, "Yingyiben 'Duanpian xiaoshuo xuanji' zixu," p. 632.

50. See editors' notes to this preface in *Lu Xun quanji,* 7: 830.

51. Famous examples include No. 113 of the Mao text, "Shuo shu" ("Big Rat"). One commentator sees it as composed by a tenant farmer (*diannong*) protesting "against the cruel exploitation of the landlord." *Shijing jinzhu,* pp. 148–49. Trans. Burton Watson, *The Columbia Book of Chinese Poetry,* p. 32.

52. See for example, Waley's translation of the text: "God said to King

Wen, / 'I am moved by your bright power. / Your high renown has not made you put on proud airs, / Your greatness has not made you change former ways, / You do not try to be clever or knowing, / But follow God's precepts.'" Arthur Waley, *The Book of Songs,* p. 258. Also see *Shijing jinzhu,* p. 392, n. 60: "These two lines state that King Wen unawares and naturally followed the laws of God."

53. Lu Xun, "Fengbo." Trans. William A. Lyell, in *Diary of a Madman and Other Stories,* pp. 77–88. See Lin Fei, "Lu Xun de 'Fengbo' he 'Guxiang' duiyu nongcun ticai xiaoshuo de kaituo," for an analysis of the two stories and an account of other contemporaneous stories about the countryside.

54. Zhou Xiashou (Zhou Zuoren), *Lu Xun xiaoshuo li de renwu,* provides many examples. Two notable exceptions that employ an I-narrator to tell the story but without apparent autobiographical implications are "A Madman's Diary," discussed above, and "Regret for the Past," which is based on "Juansheng's notes."

55. Lu Xun, "Zixu," p. 1. Yang and Yang, trans., *The Complete Stories of Lu Xun,"* Preface to *Call to Arms,"* pp. v–x.

56. Patrick Hanan discusses the different uses of the narrator/persona in Lu Xun's stories and the effects of irony achieved through varying measures of authorial distance in "The Technique of Lu Hsun's Fiction," p. 93

57. Leo Ou-fan Lee, *Voices from the Iron House,* p. 63.

58. M. M. Bakhtin, *The Dialogic Imagination,* p. 250.

59. "Guxiang." Yang and Yang, trans., *The Complete Stories of Lu Xun,* pp. 55–65.

60. The collision between the two worlds, the imagined one of illusory memory and the present one of dismal reality, makes the story a "powerful metafiction concerning the representation of the individual imagination" when literature is committed to an ideology of realism. See Theodore Huters, "Ideologies of Realism in Modern China," p. 165.

61. "Zhufu." Yang and Yang, trans., *The Complete Stories of Lu Xun,* pp. 153–71.

62. Marston Anderson, *The Limits of Realism,* p. 88; also "The Morality of Form," p. 41. In an insightful essay, Rey Chow discusses this story as a paradigm also for First World representation of the "Third World," in her "'It's You, and Not Me': Domination and 'Othering' in Theorizing the 'Third World,'" pp. 152–61.

63. William A. Lyell, *Diary of a Madman and Other Stories.*

64. Lu Xun, *Panghuang tici,* p. 425.

65. David Hawkes, *Ch'u Tz'u,* p. 28. I have altered Hawkes' translation somewhat, especially of the second line: "I would go up and down to seek my heart's desire," since what Lu Xun was "seeking" is less specifically spelled out; but my version is less poetic.

66. Besides Rey Chow's article, see the two excellent essays by Yue Mingbao,

"Gendering the Origins of Modern Chinese Fiction," pp. 47–65; and Carolyn T. Brown, "Woman as Trope: Gender and Power in Lu Xun's 'Soap,'" pp. 55–70.

67. I am grateful to Yu-shih Chen for calling my attention to this point in her comments on a paper I presented on "Gender, Power, Language: Some Heard/Unheard Voices in Modern Chinese Fiction," at the forty-third Annual Meeting of the Association for Asian Studies, April 14, 1991.

68. Qian Xingcun, "Si qule de Ah Q shidai."

69. Leo Ou-fan Lee, *Voices from the Iron House,* see esp. ch. 7, pp. 133–50. One needs to keep in mind also the occasional and reactive nature of the later writings, many of which were commissioned by ideological journals and papers, delivered as speeches before a specific audience, or formed polemical essays against his critics and opponents. This has not discouraged Chinese critics from analyzing in endless studies the development of Lu Xun's thought (*sixiang*).

70. Lu Xun, "Geming shidai de wenxue," p. 16.

71. Lu Xun, "Duiyu Zuoyi Zuojia Lianmeng de yijian," p. 187.

72. Lu Xun, "Zhonguo wuchanjieji geming wenxue he qianqu de xue," pp. 221–22.

73. See Ding Jingtang and Qu Guangxi, eds., *Zuolian wulieshi yanjiu ziliao bienmu,* p. 2, for the names of thirteen others who were also executed at the same time. But, as the title indicates, the book gives hardly any information about them.

74. Lu Xun, "Shanghai wenyi zhi yipie," p. 186.

75. Mao Zedong, "Xin minzhu zhuyi lun," p. 187. Trans. *Selected Works of Mao Tse-tung,* 2: 372.

76. Lin Zhihao, *Zhongguo xiandai wenxueshi,* p. 50. The history was first written in 1960; this revision has already incorporated some of the more "liberated" views of the post-Mao period.

77. A typical view, for example, is expressed by Lin Zhihao on the story "Guxiang": "The primary reason why 'Guxiang' is famous at home and abroad, is not its portrayal of the first-person 'I,' but that it has created (*suzao*) in Runtu the typical image (*dianxing xingxiang*) of an average peasant." See "Tan 'Guxiang' de zhuti sixiang," p. 299.

78. Tang Tao, *Zhongguo xiandai wenxueshi,* p. 116.

79. Feng Guanglian, "'Nahan' 'Panghuang' laodong renmin xingxiang yanjiu zhong de pianxiang," p. 58.

80. Lu Xun, "Kong Yiji."

81. Lu Xun, "Zai jiulou shang." Lin Yü-sheng has persuasively analyzed the story in terms of Lu Xun's "implicit intellectual and moral commitment to some traditional Chinese values." See *The Crisis of Chinese Consciousness,* pp. 142–51.

82. Lu Xun, "Shangshi." For a perceptive analysis of the self-contradictions in this text see Lydia H. Liu, "Narratives of Modern Selfhood," esp. pp. 106–13. Ching-kiu Stephen Chan has analyzed this story as an example of how "the tex-

tual organization of the (male) intellectual 'self' in relation to the (female) emotional 'other' . . . is an objectifying process of the identity crisis." See "The Language of Despair," p. 17. There are interesting analogies between peasant and women when both are examined as "others" posited in relation to the self, but if the woman is "new," her objectification will have further ramifications, as Chan's article argues.

83. Lu Xun, "Yijian xiaoshi." Yang and Yang, trans., *The Complete Stories of Lu Xun,* pp. 36–38. William A. Lyell underlines the irony of the title by translating it as "An Unimportant Affair." See *Diary of a Madman and Other Stories,* pp. 67–69.

84. This story is particularly cited by Chen Sihe as an example of the "penitential consciousness" in modern Chinese literature in "Zhongguo xinwenxue fazhan zhong de chanhui yishi," p. 81. See Mau-sang Ng, *The Russian Hero in Modern Chinese Fiction,* pp. 63–64, for a discussion of the influence on Chinese writers of repentant characters in Russian novels.

85. Lu Xun, "Shanghai wenyi zhi yipie," p. 187.

86. Mao Dun has discussed his method of writing "Chuncan" as first investigating the conditions of the rural industry and the silk market before coming up with the plot and characters of the story; he began with a "sociological theme." See "Wo zenyang xie 'Chuncan.'"

87. Even if it may be a landscape that "exists only in Shen Congwen's imagination." See David Der-wei Wang, *Fictional Realism in Twentieth-Century China,* p. 274.

88. See Helen F. Siu's well conceived anthology *Furrows,* p. vii.

CHAPTER 4

1. Liu Zaifu, Lou Zhaoming, and Liu Shijie, "Lun Zhao Shuli," p. 317. The Zhao Shuli school of creative writing is referred to in this article as the "Shanxi School" or the "Huohua School," after the periodical in which their fiction was frequently published. These writers, who include (among others) Ma Feng, Xi Rong, and Shu Wei, are all from Shanxi province and under Zhao Shuli's influence focused on writing about peasant life in Shanxi. They began to be prominent in the 1950's, when they also became known as the *Shanyaodan pai* (potato school), because of the down-to-earth character of their writing.

2. [Chen] Huangmei, "Xu," p. 2.

3. This comment is still repeated in a 1981 biography: Huang Xiuji, *Zhao Shuli pingzhuan,* p. 276.

4. For example, Wu Yang, "Yipian waiqu shishi de xiaoshuo," p. 484. The article was originally published in 1959.

5. Cheng Fangwu, "Cong wenxue geming dao geming wenxue," p. 136. The article was originally published in *Chuangzao yuekan* 1:9 (Feb. 1, 1928). It has been translated by Michael Gotz in *Revolutionary Literature in China,* ed. John Berninghausen and Ted Huters, pp. 34–36.

6. Song Yang (Qu Qiubai), "Dazhong wenyi de wenti," pp. 395–96. The article was originally published in *Wenxue yuebao* 6: 10 (1932). It has been translated by Paul Pickowicz in *Revolutionary Literature in China,* ed. John Berninghausen and Ted Huters, pp. 47–51.

7. Ralph Thaxton, *China Turned Rightside Up.*

8. Ramon H. Myers, "The Agrarian System," p. 257.

9. For example, Chalmers A. Johnson, *Peasant Nationalism and Communist Power.*

10. Mao Zedong, speech at the Second Plenary Session of the Seventh Central Committee of the Chinese Communist Party, Xibaipo Village, Pingshan County, Hebei, Mar. 5–13, 1949. Quoted in Dong Dazhong, *Zhao Shuli pingzhuan,* p. 214.

11. Lucien Bianco, "Peasant Movements," pp. 326–27, 328.

12. David E. Apter and Tony Saich, *Revolutionary Discourse in Mao's Republic,* p. 130.

13. Mao Zedong, "Hunan nongmin yundong kaocha baogao," p. 208. Trans. *Selected Works of Mao Tse-tung,* 1: 23–24.

14. Roy Hofheinz, Jr., *The Broken Wave,* p. 35.

15. "Zai Yan'an wenyi zuotanhui shang de jianghua," p. 519. Trans. Bonnie S. McDougall, *Mao Zedong's "Talks at the Yan'an Conference on Literature and Art,"* p. 58.

16. Bonnie S. McDougall, "Writers and Performers, Their Works and Their Audiences in the First Three Decades," p. 269.

17. Ellen R. Judd, "Prelude to the 'Yan'an Talks,'" p. 380.

18. Interviews by David E. Apter and Tony Saich with surviving Yan'anites, including a significant number of students and intellectuals, contain many examples of how they were "swept up by the revolution." See their *Revolutionary Discourse in Mao's Republic.*

19. I have discussed this aspect of Ding Ling's experience in *Ding Ling's Fiction,* pp. 94–99. Ding Ling's exhilarating account of the work of the corps is contained in *Yi nian (One Year),* Chongqing, 1939.

20. For an in-depth and illuminating study of how *yangge* was transformed into a major vehicle of revolutionary consciousness in Yan'an, see David Holm, *Art and Ideology in Revolutionary China.* For parallels with traditional fiction and drama in post–Yan'an Forum literature, see Robert E. Hegel, "Making the Past Serve the Present in Fiction and Drama."

21. Zhao Shuli, "Huiyi lishi, renshi ziji," pp. 1839–40. These three traditions and their "class backgrounds" are discussed in several of his talks on literature as well.

22. Huang Xiuji, *Zhao Shuli pingzhuan,* p. 5.

23. Chief among these are Huang Xiuji, *Zhao Shuli pingzhuan,* 1981; Dong Dazhong, *Zhao Shuli pingzhuan,* 1990; Gao Jie, Liu Yunhao, Duan Chongxuan,

Gao Zhongwu, and Ren Wengui, *Zhao Shuli zhuan,* 1982; Han Yufeng, Yang Zong, Zhao Guangjian, and Gou Youfu, *Zhao Shuli de shengping yu chuangzuo,* 1981; and Dong Dazhong, *Zhao Shuli nianpu,* 1982. What is interesting in this collection of biographies is how the same themes are repeated. Dong Dazhong's 1990 biography is the most comprehensive and informative.

24. Huang Xiuji, *Zhao Shuli pingzhuan,* p. 10.

25. Ibid., p. 15.

26. Ibid., p. 5.

27. Dong Dazhong, "Zhao Shuli sanshi niandai de liangpian zawen," p. 29.

28. Zhao Shuli, "'Sanliwan' xiezuo qianhou," p. 29.

29. This point was made with much emphasis by Ma Feng in a talk at a panel on literature which I attended at Xiamen University in May 1981.

30. Dong Dazhong, *Zhao Shuli nianpu,* p. 55.

31. Gao Jie, Liu Yunhao, Duan Chongxuan, Gao Zhongwu, and Ren Wengui, *Zhao Shuli zhuan,* p. 66.

32. "Xiao Erhei jiehun." The story has been translated by Sidney Shapiro as "The Marriage of Young Blacky" in *Rhymes of Li Youcai and Other Stories,* pp. 86–109. I have tried to be more literal in my translations for the purpose of bringing out more clearly some features of Zhao Shuli's language. I also prefer Cyril Birch's rendition of the story's title, "Blackie Gets Married." See, "Literature Under Communism," p. 751.

33. Zhao Shuli, "Ye suan jingyan," p. 1397. Originally written in 1949.

34. Dong Junlun, "Zhao Shuli zenyang chuli 'Xiao Erhei jiehun' de cailiao." The article was originally published in 1949.

35. Dong Junlun, "Zhao Shuli zenyang chuli 'Xiao Erhei jiehun' de cailiao," p. 338.

36. Zhao Shuli, "Xiao Erhei jiehun," p. 1.

37. Zhao Shuli, "Ye suan jingyan," p. 1397.

38. Huang Xiuji, *Zhao Shuli yanjiu,* p. 100.

39. In the opening of the 1959 story "Lao Dinge" ("Old Quota"), the writer notes that some comrades have urged him to use fewer nicknames, and he agrees with them, but a nickname happens to be necessary for this story. *Zhao Shuli xiaoshuo xuan,* p. 413.

40. Guo Zheng, "Lun Zhao Shuli zuopin zhong zhuanbian renwu de yiyi," p. 64.

41. Zhao Shuli, "Meng Xiangying fanshen (xianshi gushi)." The story is translated by W. J. F. Jenner, *Modern Chinese Stories,* pp. 121–38. In the quoted passages I have made some revisions in trying for a more literal version.

42. Zhao Shuli, "'Meng Xiangying fanshen' xiaoxu," p. 3.

43. Zhao Shuli, "Buyao jiyu xie, buyao xie ziji bu shuxide—Zhao Shuli tan chuangzuo," p. 1929. These were notes based on a talk he gave on November 12, 1962, published in *Guangxi ribao,* Nov. 18, 1962.

44. Mencius and Mao Zedong may be said to have in common a belief in the inherent potential of human beings that is capable of development, hence the efficacy of models. In Mencius the potential is "moral" and equally shared by all human beings, whereas in Maoism the potential is "revolutionary" and limited to those of the right class background.

45. "Meng Xiangying fanshen," p. 70.

46. See Ann Anagnost's "Transformation of Gender in Modern China," for a succinct summary of the issues and scholarly positions on the matter.

47. In a 1961 story, "Shiganjia Pan Yongfu," this diffident attitude of the narrator toward the central character is emphasized even more. Written as a counterexample to the "extravagant, boastful style of work" (*fukuafeng*) Zhao Shuli regarded as prevalent at the time, the story is about a poor peasant who has risen to be chairman of the district workers' union. In the introduction the narrator states that the story was based on several interviews with Pan, and, praising Pan's high moral character, adds, "I would like to learn from him," p. 439.

48. Zhao Shuli, "Li Youcai banhua," p. 20. The story has been translated by Sidney Shapiro, *Rhymes of Li Youcai and Other Stories,* pp. 1–66. I have consulted this translation but tried to be more literal in my quotations.

49. Li Youcai is "rather like the interlocutor (*fumo*) in plays of the old *chuanqi* tradition of aristocratic drama or like the narrator of a Ming-Qing novel," as Robert Hegel has commented. See "Making the Past Serve the Present in Fiction and Drama," p. 207. But Zhao Shuli's innovation lies not only in providing "this traditionally anonymous narrator/interlocutor with a personality"; he also makes him into a narrated character who is a poor peasant, a member of a specific class, victimized and then liberated like the others.

50. C. T. Hsia, *A History of Modern Chinese Fiction,* p. 483.

51. Zhao Shuli's works in this genre include "Weisha yao zu pinmintuan" ("Why We Must Form Poor People Groups"), 1948; "'Chun' zai nongcun de bianhua" ("The Changes in 'Spring' in the Countryside"), 1958; "Guzi hao" ("The Millet Is Good"), 1960. All texts are in *Zhao Shuli quyi wenxuan,* pp. 126–34.

52. Edward Gunn, *Rewriting Chinese,* p. 134. I am indebted to Gunn's insights into how stylistic features can reflect broader issues, but am attempting to carry his argument somewhat further in the question of power and discourse.

53. Edward Gunn, *Rewriting Chinese,* p. 137.

54. Zhao Shuli, "Dengji," p. 162.

55. Zhao Shuli, "Lingquandong."

56. "Shi Bulan ganche" is also a different case. As the introductory remarks give it, the story is based on a poem by Tian Jian. Although the story alternates verse and prose and much of the text is given over to Shi Bulan speaking in first person when he tells his audience at the inn about what had happened to him in the past, there is no sharing of the burden of narrative and commentary with the author as in "The Rhymes of Li Youcai."

57. Chen Huangmei, "Xiang Zhao Shuli fangxiang maijin," p. 199.

58. Zhou Yang, "Lun Zhao Shuli de chuangzuo," p. 184.

59. Wu Yang, "Yipian waiqu xianshi de xiaoshuo," p. 483. The article was originally published in *Wenyibao,* 1959.

60. Quoted in Dong Dazhong, *Zhao Shuli nianpu,* p. 143.

61. A quotation from the blurb of Zhao Shuli, *Sanliwan,* the novel's sixth printing, in 1956.

62. Ba Ren, "'Sanliwan' duhou gan—wei *Zhongsu youhao bao* er zuo," p. 444. Article reprinted from a 1957 volume by Ba Ren.

63. C. T. Hsia, *A History of Modern Chinese Fiction,* p. 493.

64. Zhao Shuli, *Sanliwan,* p. 91.

65. The readiness with which present and future can be confused is borne out by personal experience. One of the privileges I enjoyed when visiting the PRC as part of an American scholarly delegation in 1973 was to be taken to visit various *dianxing* (model or typical?) communes or production brigades. During the briefings we would be given, at times with the aid of paintings or of models, accounts of how far the area had come, its present situation, and plans for the future. The glorious developments of the future were at times discussed as if they were already in place, but it was only with persistent questioning that this became clear.

66. Maynard Solomon, ed., *Marxism and Art,* p. 67.

67. Zhao Shuli, "'Sanliwan' xiezuo qianhou," p. 29.

68. Dong Dazhong, *Zhao Shuli pingzhuan,* p. 248.

69. Zhao Shuli, "Ye suan jingyan," p. 5.

70. Zhao Shuli, "'Sanliwan' xiezuo qianhou," p. 30. The article was originally published in 1955.

71. Instead of giving a detailed history of the ups and downs of Zhao Shuli's writing career, when he was in and out of political favor, I will mention only some highlights to indicate the overall pattern.

72. Zhao Shuli, "Dangqian chuangzuo zhong de jige wenti," p. 183. The talk was first published in *Huohua* 6 (1959). He discusses again his stories as "problem stories" on p. 186.

73. Zhao Shuli, "Gongshe yinggai ruhe lingdao nongye shengchan zhi wojian." The original article is lost; only a brief excerpt is included in his selected writings. See *Zhao Shuli wenji.* This article and other unpublished works by Zhao Shuli on agricultural problems are discussed in Wang Zhongqing and Li Wenru, "Ji Zhao Shuli de zuihou wunian." In the view of the authors, the persecution of Zhao Shuli during the Cultural Revolution was due less to his literary works than to his political views as a "capitalist roader," p. 153.

74. For accounts on this Dalian meeting see Huang Xiuji, *Zhao Shuli pingzhuan,* pp. 235–38.

75. Dong Dazhong, *Zhao Shuli pingzhuan,* p. 311.

76. Zhao Shuli, "Huiyi lishi, renshi ziji," p. 1841.

77. Wang Zhongqing and Li Wenru, "Ji Zhao Shuli de zuihou wunian," p. 153.

78. Zhao Shuli, "Huiyi lishi, renshi ziji," pp. 1831, 1834. According to the editors of Zhao Shuli's works, this piece was written as part of his self-criticism during the Cultural Revolution, probably in 1966, when the pressure was not as great as it would become later, and therefore probably closer to the author's own ideas than the other seven examples of self-criticism they had seen. Unfortunately, even this selection is not included in its entirety.

79. Dong Dazhong, *Zhao Shuli nianpu,* p. 177.

80. Xian Yin, "Rang laolao shaoshao dou neng kan—ji Zhao Shuli zai yici 'pindaohui' shang," p. 66. The author notes that this was as reported by those giving an account of the meeting, and therefore "relatively reliable."

81. For a discussion of this issue, see Dai Guangzhong, "Guanyu 'Zhao Shuli fangxiang' de zai renshi," esp. p. 15.

82. See Zhao Shuli, "Huiyi lishi, renshi ziji," p. 1833.

83. "Tao bu zhu de shou" (1960) and "Shiganjia Pan Yongfu" (1961) are both in *Zhao Shuli xiaoshuo xuan.* The first story has been translated by Nathan K. Mao and Winston L. Y. Yang in Hsu Kai-yu, ed., *Literature of the People's Republic of China,* pp. 494–502.

84. For more detailed accounts of the campaign see Wang Zhongqing and Li Wenru, "Ji Zhao Shuli de zuihou wunian"; and Han Yufeng, Yang Zong, Zhao Guangjian, and Gou Youfu, *Zhao Shuli de shengping yu chuangzuo,* pp. 57–62. The *wanyan shu* was particularly attacked for "singing the same tune" as Peng Dehuai's criticisms of the party at the 1959 meeting at Lushan.

85. Huang Xiuji, *Zhao Shuli pingzhuan,* p. 266.

86. Dong Dazhong, *Zhao Shuli nianpu,* p. 190. The article was written by Chen Yonggui.

87. Both poems, written to the tune of "Busuanzi" ("Song of Divination"), can be found in Wu-chi Liu and Irving Yucheng Lo, eds., *K'uei Yeh Chi,* pp. 170, 233. Translations are included in the editors' *Sunflower Splendor,* Lu Yu's poem, trans. James J. Y. Liu, p. 385; Mao Zedong's poem, trans. Eugene Eoyang, p. 519. The two poems are also translated and discussed in Hua-ling Nieh Engle and Paul Engle, *Poems of Mao Tse-tung,* pp. 122–24.

88. An excellent point made in the comments of the anonymous reviewer of my manuscript.

CHAPTER 5

1. These comments are taken from an interview I had with the writer in July 1984. See Yi-tsi Mei Feuerwerker, "An Interview with Gao Xiaosheng, p. 119.

2. Fan Boqun, "Gao Xiaosheng lun," p. 39.

3. Ji Hongzhen, "Tongyi lishi zhuti de liangge shidai yuezhang," p. 49. It was

Gao Xiaosheng himself who without comment called my attention to this article.

4. For example, see Fan Boqun, "Chen Huansheng lun," especially the point-by-point comparison between the two characters, pp. 14–17.

5. Many articles have compared the techniques (*bifa*) of Gao Xiaosheng and Lu Xun. See, for example, Yan Gang, "Lun Chen Huansheng," and Shi Hanren, "Gao Xiaosheng he 'Lu Xun feng.'"

6. Bonnie S. McDougall, *Mao Zedong's "Talks at the Yan'an Conference on Literature and Art*," p. 81.

7. Yan Gang, "Lun Chen Huansheng," p. 29.

8. Yu Bin, "Dui xianshizhuyi shenhua de tansuo," p. 85.

9. Michael Duke, "Chinese Literature in the Post-Mao Era," p. 3.

10. See, for example, Qiu Lan, "Dui yige 'jishou timu' de sikao."

11. See "Zhongguo dangdai wenxue xuehui 1981 nian Lushan nianhui taolun zongshu" for a range of views on the issue.

12. Published in 1953. Li Zhun himself has admitted that his works from those years are dead.

13. For an example of a tortuous argument to salvage such works, see Tian Jingbao, "Ruhe dui nongye hezuohua ticai xiaoshuo chuangzuo zai pingjia."

14. Zhao Junxian, *Zhongguo dangdai xiaoshuo shigao*," p. 55.

15. Among these, "Jieyue" (1954) has been translated as "The Broken Betrothal," the title story in an anthology of Gao Xiaosheng stories, pp. 7–24. Particularly notable is his story "Buxing" for its critical portrayal of a high-level cadre, published in 1957.

16. Gao Xiaosheng, Fang Zhi, et al., "Yijian he xiwang." For a translation and discussion of the documents relating to the only "programmatic statement on literature formulated in the spirit of the Hundred Flowers," see Rudolph G. Wagner, "Documents Concerning *Tanqiuzhe.*"

17. In *Yuhua* 10 (1957), pp. 13–15. Trans. Wagner, "Documents Concerning *Tanqiuzhe*," pp. 139–45.

18. Yi-tsi Mei Feuerwerker, "An Interview with Gao Xiaosheng."

19. Gao Xiaosheng, "Tantan youguan Chen Huansheng de jipian xiaoshuo," p. 24.

20. Gao Xiaosheng, "Jixindai," pp. 1–10.

21. See, for example, Ye Zhicheng, "The String that Will Never Break."

22. See his preface to *Gao Xiaosheng xiaoshuo xuan*, p. i.

23. Gao Xiaosheng, "Tantan youguan Chen Huansheng de jipian xiaoshuo," p. 24.

24. Gao Xiaosheng, "Li Shunda zaowu." The story has been translated by Madelyn Ross in *The Broken Betrothal*, pp. 25–57; and by Ellen Klempner in *The New Realism: Writings from China after the Cultural Revolution*, ed. Lee Yee (New York: Hippocrene Books, 1983), 31–55.

25. Leo Ou-fan Lee, "The Politics of Technique." Written while Gao Xiao-

sheng was still near the beginning of his postrehabilitation literary career, Lee's article provides a perceptive analysis of the story's style, particularly on how "ironic readings of the text . . . whether or not intended by the author, are made possible by the author's consummate technique." In view of Gao Xiaosheng's later works, I would go further than the article in attributing "intentionality" to Gao's irony. Michael Duke, in *Blooming and Contending,* also writing about the early works of Gao Xiaosheng, sees a falling off in the quality of his works after this story.

26. Gao Xiaosheng, "'Li Shunda zaowu' shimo," p. 70.

27. Leo Ou-fan Lee, "The Politics of Technique," p. 175.

28. Gao Xiaosheng, "'Li Shunda zaowu' shimo," p. 71.

29. Gao Xiaosheng, "Li Shunda zaowu," p. 13.

30. This type of "double-voiced discourse" is discussed by Mikhail Bakhtin in *Problems of Dostoevsky's Poetics,* pp. 193–94.

31. Mao Zedong's version can be found in *Mao zhuxi yulu,* pp. 172–73.

32. Leo Ou-fan Lee, "The Politics of Technique," p. 175.

33. In a talk given at the University of Michigan, Mar. 17, 1988, Gao Xiaosheng commented that the song of the strange was a widespread folk form, the words of which might be altered as it circulated. He retained some of the lines and made up others. He also incorporated and altered proverbs. The song "enabled Li Shunda to express imagistically his views of the 'ten years of turmoil.'" The talk has been published as "Wo de xiaoshuo tong minjian wenxue de guanxi"; see p. 95.

34. Gao Xiaosheng, "Tantan youguan Chen Huansheng de jipian xiaoshuo," p. 29. In 1981 he wrote the story "Shuwai chunqiu," in which the Chen Huansheng featured is not the same Chen Huansheng of the series, but the "original," "historical" Chen Huansheng on which the character is supposedly modeled. This enables Gao Xiaosheng to indulge in a further playful scramble of fiction and reality.

35. All seven stories are collected in Gao Xiaosheng, *Chen Huansheng shangcheng chuguo ji,* with the name Chen Huansheng omitted from each title.

36. Yu Bin, "Dui xianshizhuyi shenhua de tansuo," p. 84.

37. Gao Xiaosheng, "'Loudouhu' zhu."

38. Gao Xiaosheng, "Tantan youguan Chen Huansheng de jipian xiaoshuo," p. 25.

39. Yan Gang, "Lun Chen Huansheng—shenme shi Chen Huansheng xingge?" p. 31.

40. Gao Xiaosheng, "Tantan youguan Chen Huansheng de jipian xiaoshuo," p. 25.

41. Ibid., p. 24.

42. Ibid., p. 26.

43. Gao Xiaosheng, "(Chen Huansheng) shangcheng," p. 26.

44. Ibid., p. 15. An English version translated by Yu Fanqin as "Chen Huansheng's Adventure in Town" is included in *The Broken Betrothal,* pp. 71–81. It makes little attempt to preserve the lively storyteller style of the narration, reading almost like a bland, prosaic paraphrase of the original.

45. A term used by Shlomith Rimmon-Kenan in her useful discussion of what other critics have called "angle of vision," "point of view," or "perspective" in narrative. See her *Narrative Fiction,* p. 74.

46. Gao Xiaosheng, "(Chen Huansheng) zhuanye," p. 28. The story has been translated by Kuang Wendong and is included in *The Broken Betrothal,* pp. 82–119.

47. Gao Xiaosheng, "(Chen Huansheng) baochan."

48. Zhao Junxian, *Zhongguo dangdai xiaoshuo shigao—renwu xingxiang xilie lun,* p. 86.

49. Ibid., p. 229.

50. Fan Boqun, "Chen Huansheng lun," p. 11.

51. Zhang Zhong et al., *Dangdai Zhongguo wenxue gaiguan,* p. 506.

52. Gao Xiaosheng, "Zhanshu."

53. Gao Xiaosheng, "Zhongtian dahu."

54. Gao Xiaosheng, "Chuguo."

55. Gao Xiaosheng's visit to America from February to July 1988 was sponsored by the Visiting Scholar Exchange Program of the former Committee on Scholarly Communication with the People's Republic of China. He was in residence at the University of Michigan from Feb. 5 to the end of March, then visited and lectured at various college campuses on the East and West coasts. Many of the experiences and characters in "Chen Huansheng Goes Abroad" will be "recognized" by those involved in arranging his activities and working with him while in this country. Some of my own actions and remarks have found their way into the story, attributed to a minor character which I will leave unnamed here.

56. Gao Xiaosheng, "Xiwang nuli wei nongmin xiezuo," p. 12.

57. Gao Xiaosheng, "Shenghuo, mudi, he jiqiao," p. 16.

58. Gao Xiaosheng, "Kaituo yanjie," p. 65.

59. Gao Xiaosheng, "'Li Shunda zaowu' shimo," p. 74.

60. Gao Xiaosheng, "Tantan wenxue chuangzuo," p. 72.

61. Gao Xiaosheng, "'Li Shunda zaowu' shimo," p. 76.

62. Gao Xiaosheng, "Da haoren Jiang Kunda," pp. 81–82.

63. Gao Xiaosheng appeared to acknowledge this interpretation in our interview. See Feuerwerker, "An Interview with Gao Xiaosheng," p. 120.

64. Wu Liang, "Bingfei nanjie zhi mi—ping Gao Xiaosheng wanjin de xiaoshuo," p. 75.

65. Gao Xiaosheng, "Kaituo yanjie," p. 193.

66. Gao Xiaosheng, "Diejiao yinyuan."

67. Gao Xiaosheng, "Hutu."

68. Gao Xiaosheng, *Qingtian zaishang*. The title may be an allusion to the traditional nickname for a just magistrate, for example, Bao Qingtian. Thus it can be seen as a protest against the injustice that causes the tragic fate of the characters in the novel.

69. Gao Xiaosheng told me about the deeply personal meaning of the novel for him when he showed me the galley proofs in March 1988. It is about the wife he lost, and "60 percent" of the novel is based on fact. Most particularly he wanted me to know that it is her picture that graces the title page of the book. These points are reiterated in a letter to Dai Fang dated Apr. 5, 1991.

70. To some extent this split is analogous to what Scholes and Kellogg have discussed as the difference between "illustrative" and "representational" characterization. "Illustrative characters are concepts in anthropoid shape or fragments of the human psyche masquerading as human beings." Robert Scholes and Robert Kellogg, *The Nature of Narrative*, p. 88.

71. Gao Xiaosheng, "Liu Yu xieshu."

72. Feuerwerker, "An Interview with Gao Xiaosheng," p. 128. The story is drawn from personal experience, and he did not have the "peasant" specifically in mind when he wrote the story; these were "implications that only came out in the writing process."

73. Gao Xiaosheng, "Liu Yu Writes a Book." Worried about what will happen to his wife after his death, Liu Yu "often thought of Xiang-lin's wife after her son had been eaten by a wolf," p. 128.

74. Sima Qian, "Bao Ren Shaoqing shu," p. 212. I discuss the letter in chapter 1.

75. Zhuangzi, "Tian zi fang," in which Confucius is quoted as saying, "*ai mo da yu xin si, er ren si yi ci zhi*": "There is no grief greater than the death of the mind—beside it, the death of the body is a minor matter." Burton Watson, trans., *The Complete Works of Chuang Tzu*, p. 223.

76. For example, see Zhou Jianming, "Gao Xiaosheng—Lu Xun youmo fengge de chengchuanren": "In this work that moves one to tears (*cuiren leixia*), Gao Xiaosheng has instilled much of his own experience and ideas. The pail of well water (like an ice box) and the methane gas lamp (like a stove) are drawn from his own life. Many of the philosophical ideas and feelings towards suffering, towards life, towards death, towards the new life during the new era, all come from his heart," pp. 273–74.

77. For example, see Wang Xiaoming, "Zai fukan Chenjiacun zhiqian."

78. See Feuerwerker, "An Interview with Gao Xiaosheng," pp. 125–27.

CHAPTER 6

1. There are of course many other writers who have written in new ways on the intellectual/peasant encounter during this period as well. One notable exam-

ple is Zhang Xianliang, whose fiction adds the dimension of gender and sexuality to that encounter, since the "peasant other" is a woman who has the capacity to make the emasculated intellectual, a former prisoner from a labor camp, "into a man again." His best known works on this theme include "Lühuashu" (1984) in *Zhang Xianliang xuanji* (Tianjin: Baihua wenyi chubanshe, 1986), pp. 161–338 (trans. Gladys Yang as *Mimosa* [Beijing: Panda Books, 1985], pp. 13–181); and *Nanren de yiban shi nüren* (1985) in *Zhang Xianliang xuanji*, 399–618 (Martha Avery, trans., *Half a Man Is Woman* [New York: Ballantine Books, 1991; first published in 1988]). However he was not generally perceived as having been part of the "search for roots" movement.

2. Song Yaoliang, *Shinian wenxue zhuchao*, p. 246.

3. See, for example, Li Jie, "Lun Zhongguo dangdai xinchao xiaoshuo," p. 116. Li Jiefei dates the beginning of "new wave fiction" from 1984, to include the publication of fiction by Ah Cheng, Ma Yuan et al. See "Xinshiqi xiaoshuo de liangge jieduan ji qi bijiao," p. 80.

4. Tang Xiaobing makes the important observation that both "realism" and "modernism," "like many other loaded catchwords, are less meaningful as terms describing a certain aesthetic style or cultural logic than as rigid epithets for political alignment and power distribution" ("The Function of New Theory," p. 280). There was much debate from the mid-1980's about whether "modernism" or "postmodernism," or even "pseudopostmodernism" would be the more applicable to the new developments in the literary scene. Whether "postmodernism," as appropriated from the West in China's "rush to theory," is the most fitting label for the literary practice of these three "search for roots" writers is not the issue. The point that critics are trying to emphasize is their radical violations of continuities with the past.

5. See Jing Wang, *High Culture Fever*, esp. pp. 208–17, for an insightful discussion of the "tradition versus modernity" issue regarding *xungen* fiction in contemporary Chinese criticism.

6. Li Jie makes the point in "Lun Zhongguo dangdai xinchao xiaoshuo." See also Shao Jian and Fan Bo, " 'Xungen' lun."

7. Chen Xiaoming, "Lishi zhuanxing yu houxiandai zhuyi de xingqi," p. 198.

8. Zheng Wanlong: "Wo de gen"; Li Hangyu: "Li yi li women de gen."

9. For a report on this meeting see Li Qingxi: "Xungen: huidao shiwu benshen."

10. See, for example, Shao Jian and Fan Bo: " 'Xungen' lun," pp. 27, 28.

11. David Der-wei Wang, "Imaginary Nostalgia: Shen Congwen, Song Zelai, Mo Yan, and Li Yongping." Wang's discussion focuses on his four writers as producers of native soil literature, whose subject matter, for obvious reasons, can be found to overlap with that of "search for roots" practitioners. I am particularly indebted to his many insights into the three Mo Yan texts which I also discuss, although with a different emphasis.

12. Lu Xinhua, "Shanghen," p. 257. The story has been translated several times, including a translation by Kenneth J. DeWoskin, "The Wounded," in Robert F. Dernberger et al., eds., *The Chinese: Adapting the Past, Facing the Future*, 2d ed. (Ann Arbor: University of Michigan, 1991), pp. 631–44. The quotation is from p. 632.

13. Kam Louie, "Educated Youth Literature," p. 94.

14. Liu Zaifu, "Lun wenxue de zhutixing."

15. Liu Zaifu, *Xingge zuhe lun*, pp. 28, 29.

16. Chen Yong, "Wenyi xue fangfalun wenti."

17. Li Zhaozhong, "Xuanzhuan de wentan," p. 26.

18. Ibid., p. 25

19. Li Hangyu, "Li yi li women de 'gen,'" p. 78.

20. Quoting Gerard Genette on seventeenth-century French literature, Jonathan Culler discusses *vraisemblance*—one of the levels on which texts are naturalized into the reader's world—as "what we should today call an 'ideology': a body of maxims and prejudices which constitute both a vision of the world and a system of values." See *Structuralist Poetics*, p. 144.

21. Jing Wang, *High Culture Fever*, p. 143. Her comprehensive mapping of the cultural territory of China in the 1980's is also highly illuminating regarding how "roots-searching" fiction intersects with contemporary issues of cultural politics, aesthetic modernity, and the literary elite's self-image.

22. *Jintian* began "publishing"—first in the form of big character posters and later in mimeograph or typescript form—in December 1978 during the "Beijing Democracy Wall Movement." Until it was banned after nine issues by the government in September 1980, the journal was a major outlet for new or underground writings. It has been revived and published outside China since 1990 and now serves as a major outlet for writers and scholars in exile.

23. Li Tuo, "The New Vitality of Modern Chinese," p. 75.

24. Wang Zengqi, "Xu," p. 5.

25. Li Tuo, "1985," pp. 66, 64.

26. Linda Hutcheon, *The Politics of Postmodernism*, p. 15.

27. Joseph S. M. Lau discusses Han Shaogong's transformation from "a reluctant disseminator of certified Party truths to that of anguished rootseeker" as an example of the writer's "self-transcendence." See "Visitations of the Past in Han Shaogong's Post-1985 Fiction," p. 21.

28. See, for example, Shao Jian and Fan Bo, "'Xungen' lun," p. 25: "Without reading it ["Ba ba ba"] one cannot speak about *xungen*, without understanding it, one cannot really discuss *xungen.*"

29. Joseph S. M. Lau, "Visitations of the Past in Han Shaogong's Post-1985 Fiction," p. 27.

30. Han Shaogong, "Wenxue de 'gen,'" pp. 2, 4.

31. For example, see Fang Keqiang, "Ah Q he Bingzai," p. 9.

32. Lin Weiping, "Wenxue he renge," pp. 73–74.

33. Han Shaogong, "Ba Ba Ba," p. 5. I have consulted the translation by Martha Cheung in *Homecoming? And Other Stories* (Hong Kong: Chinese University of Hong Kong [Renditions], 1992), pp. 35–90.

34. In addition to the articles by Joseph Lau and Fang Keqiang mentioned above, these would include Jeffrey Kinkley, "Shen Congwen's Legacy in Chinese Literature of the 1980's," pp. 100–103; and Liu Zaifu, "Lun Bingzai."

35. Li Qingxi, "Xungen: huidao shiwu benshen," p. 21.

36. Wang Zengqi, "Xu," p. 1.

37. Wang Xiaoming, "Bu xiangxin de he bu yuanyi xiangxin de," p. 24.

38. Joseph S. M. Lau, "Visitations of the Past in Han Shaogong's Post-1985 Fiction," p. 27.

39. Jeffrey Kinkley, "Shen Congwen's Legacy in Chinese Literature of the 1980's," p. 99.

40. "The Homecoming," in *Spring Bamboo: A Collection of Contemporary Chinese Short Stories*, comp. and trans. Jeanne Tai (New York: Random House, 1989), pp. 21–40; "Homecoming?" in *Homecoming? and Other Stories,* trans. Martha Cheung (Hong Kong: Chinese University of Hong Kong [Renditions], 1992), pp. 1–20; "Déjà Vu," in *Furrows,* pp. 223–37.

41. Han Shaogong, "Guiqulai," pp. 34–35. My quotations are taken from the story as translated by Margaret Decker, p. 232.

42. Perhaps there is an echo here of the ending of Gogol's "Diary of a Madman," a story about one man's descent into insanity and confused identity. This is of course the same story that had played an influential role in Lu Xun's "Diary of a Madman."

43. Five years later, in an article that refers to many descriptive details of the story, Han Shaogong gives an explanation about why the countryside experience was so "unforgettable." The hardship, the extreme deprivation, and the suffering keep coming back to fill the memory, "for only in the soil of suffering will one have the rich harvest of memories." Han Shaogong, "Jiyi de jiazhi," p. 58.

44. Mo Yan, "Baigou qiuqian jia." Quotations are my translations from this text. I have consulted Michael Duke's translation in Michael Duke, ed., *Worlds of Modern Chinese Fiction* (Armonk, N.Y.: M. E. Sharpe, 1991), pp. 45–62.

45. Mo Yan, "Wo de 'nongmin yishi' guan," p. 39.

46. "Mo Yan xiaozhuan," p. 174. This brief biography of a mere fourteen lines is typical of the writer's unconventional, nonchalant, self-deprecating way of writing about his own life, but as usual with some picturesque details thrown in.

47. To Ji Hongzhen, the parallel between these I-narrators and Mo Yan's own background show them to be "artistic projections of the writer's personality." See "Shenhua shijie de renleixue kongjian," p. 68.

48. David Der-wei Wang, "Imaginary Nostalgia," pp. 125–26.

49. The first chapter, "Red Sorghum," was published in *Renmin wenxue* 3 (1986).

50. *Red Sorghum* was Zhang Yimou's first directorial effort. Made in 1988, it was awarded the Golden Bear at the Berlin Film Festival. Based primarily on chapters one and two of the novel, it has primarily been seen as a patriotic film about Chinese guerrilla resistance in 1939 to the brutal Japanese invasion.

51. Mo Yan, *Honggaoliang jiazu*. Page numbers in first parentheses refer to this edition. Page numbers in the second parentheses refer to Howard Gold-blatt's translation of the novel: *Red Sorghum: A Novel of China*. Quoted passages are from this translation with occasional minor revisions. Although the full title of the novel in Chinese is *Honggaoliang jiazu* (*Red Sorghum Family*), as distinguished from the title of its first chapter, "Honggaoliang," I will follow the translator and refer to the novel as *Honggaoliang* or *Red Sorghum* in my text.

52. At one point in the novel the I-narrator departs from this practice and explains why he refers to his grandfather by his name of Yu Zhan'ao in describing certain events. See p. 113.

53. This phrase on studying Marxism is omitted from the Taiwan edition of the novel, an inexplicable omission, since the reference to Marxism is hardly a positive one, but almost a parody.

54. M. M. Bakhtin, *The Dialogic Imagination*, pp. 370, 371.

55. Li Tuo, Zhang Ling, and Wang Bin, "'Yuyan' de fanpan," p. 77.

56. Zhou Yingxiong, "Honggaoliang jiazu yanyi," p. 518.

57. Zhu Ling, "A Brave New World?" pp. 131–32.

58. Lu Tonglin, "'Red Sorghum': Limits of Transgression," in *Misogyny, Cultural Nihilism, and Oppositional Politics*, pp. 51–74, esp. pp. 58, 69.

59. These are important points that Lu Tonglin makes in her book, ibid. See esp. pp. 4–8.

60. For a discussion of the influence of Gabriel Marquez's novel on modern Chinese literature see Meng Fanhua, "Mohuan xianshi zhuyi zai Zhongguo." The anthology includes the first two chapters of Mo Yan's novel. Page seven of Meng's article gives an example of parallel passages from Gabriel Marquez and Mo Yan.

61. I am using Shlomith Rimmon-Kenan's term from her *Narrative Fiction*. See chapter 6, "Text: Focalization," pp. 71–85.

62. For a Freudian analysis of this blurring of "Father" and "I" in the narrative process see Li Jiefei and Zhang Ling, "Jingshen fenxixue yu 'Honggaoliang' de xushi jiegou."

63. The ordeal that initiates one to adulthood is an important theme in the novel. At age fifteen, the mother is lowered into a dry well—in both sexual imagery and action (or lack of it), a contrast to "Father's" initiation—by her parents as the Japanese soldiers approach the village. The three days of her ordeal, described in excruciating detail, bring about the onset of her menstruation.

64. In his talk "Wo de 'nongmin yishi' guan," Mo Yan makes the point that "what war does is call forth our beastly nature and obliterate human nature," p. 40.

65. Li Tuo, Zhang Ling, and Wang Bin, "'Yuyan' de fanpan," esp. p. 77.

66. There are echoes here of the description of the death and levitation of Remedios the Beauty in Gabriel Garcia Marquez's *One Hundred Years of Solitude,* p. 222ff.

67. See Zhu Ling's perceptive analysis of this character as the embodiment of excessive female sexuality, and her fate as an expression of male fear of it. "A Brave New World?" pp. 129–31.

68. The connection between the "search for roots" and the "search for the self" has been much commented on. See, for example, Li Qingxi, "Xungen: huidao shiwu benshen," esp. pp. 16–17.

69. For example in the note appended to the end of "Honghuang" and in "Maoshi huicui." There are many other Mo Yan stories that are also located in Gaomi township and contain characters referred to as Granddad, Father, and Mother. In some cases they appear to be telling about "what happened" to characters from *Red Sorghum* as they refer to events about "themselves" there. These stories, mixed in with other stories in collections, fill in gaps of time and information of the novel: Father as a people's militia supplying food to the front in 1948 (this explains his limp) or Granddad when he was in Hokkaido. How these fit or do not fit into events referred to or hinted at in *Red Sorghum* may not be possible to determine until we have the "whole story"—that is, all that Mo Yan intends to tell about the I's ancestors. On the other hand this intertextual play also means that *Red Sorghum* is "unfinished," the boundaries between it and other writings of the author remain in a state of flux.

70. Mo Yan, "Wo de 'nongmin yishi' guan," pp. 40, 42.

71. Wang Anyi, "Biographical Note—My Wall," p. 233.

72. I will refer to this work as a novel to avoid the more cumbersome term novella, even though it is just under one hundred pages long. It was completed in December 1984 and published in *Zhongguo zuojia 2 (1985).* Its title has been translated as *Bao Town,* but it is more a village community. *Bao Town,* trans. Martha Avery.

73. Wang Anyi, "Wo weishenme xiezuo," p. 102.

74. Chen Sihe, "Shuangchong dieying, shenceng xiangzheng," p. 17; Li Jie, "Shi linmo, yeshi kaituo—'Ni biewu xuanze' he 'Xiaobaozhuang' zhi wojian," p. 24.

75. Wang Anyi, "Houji," p. 453.

76. Peter Conn, *Pearl S. Buck,* p. xiv.

77. Ibid., p. 68.

78. In her preface to the volume *Xiaobaozhuang,* Bing Xin claims that Sai Zhenzhu (Pearl Buck) had informed her that Suxian was the background of *Dadi (The Good Earth).* Bing Xin, "Xu," p. 2.

79. The second page number in parentheses refers to Martha Avery's translation of the novel, but I have at times revised it into language that is closer to the original.

80. For example, Li Guotao, "'Xiaobaozhuang' de wenti ji qita"; Cheng Depei, "Yizhong gongshitai de xushu: cong 'Xiaobaozhuang' kan Wang Anyi chuangzuo zhuti shang de zhuanbian."

81. There is one novella, "Yunhe bianshang," by Wang Anyi of the experiences of an "educated youth" in a production brigade on the banks of the Grand Canal in which some of the same names, if not characters, of Daliu-zhuang appear. The focus there is not the encounter between intellectual and peasant but rather on the aspirations and struggles of the protagonist to become an artist, and her relations with a local teacher.

82. The actual campaign took place in 1982–83.

83. The first part of *Chuangye shi* by Liu Qing (1916–1978) was published in 1959. Persecuted during the Cultural Revolution, he was not able to publish sections of part two until it was over, and he died in 1978 without having completed the work. The novel's main subject matter is the socialist revolution in the countryside. *Linhai xueyuan* by Qu Bo (b. 1923) was published in 1957. It is about the early days of the civil war between the CCP and the Nationalist troops in Manchuria. Both these novels, as well as those by Gorky, are examples of socialist realism, the kind of literature *Xiaobaozhuang* is writing against.

EPILOGUE

1. Even though China's rapid economic development has been largely fueled by the great strides in rural industry, it is mainly in those rural areas that are adjacent to large cities.

2. Liu Xiaobo, *Yu Li Zehou duihua*, p. 73. This is one outspoken critic who has been silenced, as he is now serving a three-year prison term.

3. Some Western anthropologists are now engaged in the process of "reconceptualizing the peasantry." In considering recent developments and drawing examples mostly from Mexico, Michael Kearney believes that "the category *peasant*, whatever validity it may once have had, has been outdistanced by contemporary history . . . Peasants are mostly gone and global conditions do not favor the perpetuation of those who remain." See *Reconceptualizing the Peasantry*, pp. 1, 3. As Daniel Kelliher puts it, under Deng Xiaoping the Chinese Communist Party's "theory-bound observations" about the peasantry were "rigid and formulaic" and "ossified." See his "Chinese Communist Political Theory and the Rediscovery of the Peasantry," pp. 409–10. This underlines all the more the diminishing relevance of all "essentialist" theories about the peasant.

4. In his discussion of Sima Qian's theory that "great literature is the result of great suffering," in the light of the castration (a symbol of his feminization/marginalization) that he suffered for offending the emperor, Martin Huang

advances the provocative idea that "we can almost conclude that all great literature has to be feminine in one way or another." See his *Literati and Self-Re/Presentation,* p. 80. While such "femininity" may not have been explicitly acknowledged as the precondition for great literature, what I want to emphasize here is that because of its marginality, it was conventionally adopted as a stance to represent a moral authority higher even than the ruler's power.

5. Wendy Larson discusses the "creation of a literary ideology that makes no allowances for a gender-specific literature" as Chinese writing makes the transition into the 1930's in "The End of 'Funü wenxue.'"

6. For the complexities of the issues raised see Lydia H. Liu, "Invention and Intervention."

7. Chen Shunxin compares the different treatments of the theme of women "standing up" in Ru Zhijuan and Zhao Shuli in her *Zhongguo dangdai wenxue de xushi yu xingbie.* See pp. 66–69.

8. Can Xue, "Shan shang de xiaowu" was first published in *Renmin wenxue,* Aug. 1985. Translations include "Hut on the Mountain" in Ronald R. Janessen and Jian Zhang, trans., *Dialogues in Paradise* (Evanston, Ill.: Northwestern University Press, 1989), pp. 46–53; "The Hut on the Hill," trans. Michael S. Duke, in Duke, ed., *World of Modern Chinese Fiction* (Armonk, N.Y.: M. E. Sharpe, 1991), pp. 41–44.

9. Lu Tonglin takes on those male critics who attribute Can Xue's originality to her madness or paranoia. In a textual analysis of three stories other than "Hut on the Hill" and drawing upon Luce Irigaray's theories on female subjectivity and the "fluidity of language," she makes the argument for Can Xue's lucidity. See the chapter "Can Xue: What Is So Paranoid in Her Writings?" in her *Misogyny, Cultural Nihilism, and Oppositional Politics,* pp. 75–103.

10. Wang Anyi, "Lao Kang huilai," was first published in *Chou Xiaoya* in Oct. 1985. The story has been translated by Jeanne Tai in *Spring Bamboo: A Collection of Contemporary Chinese Short Stories* (New York: Random House, 1989), pp. 41–55.

11. In his discussion of "univocality" or "authoritarian narration" as a central feature of modern Chinese literature," Theodore Huters sees the story as posing questions because the main character is "too weak to qualify as a worthy vessel for the omniscient voice." For the purposes of this study I am reading it as posing questions about the possibilities of writing in general, given the historical pressures on all intellectuals. See Huters, "Lives in Profile," pp. 270 and 282.

12. Cheng Ma et al., "Wenxue duihua."

13. This is one of the important points made by Tang Xiaobing in "Residual Modernism."

14. For example, see Li Qingxi, "Baiwu liaolai de 'houpiping.'"

15. Ying-shih Yü, "The Radicalization of China in the Twentieth Century," p. 146.

16. Perry Link, *Evening Chats in Beijing*, p. 179.

17. Mu Gong, "Wang Shuo—zhishifenzi wenhua de bishizhe," p. 152.

18. Liu Xiaobo, "Wang Shuo," p. 1. The interview was first published in *Lianhebao*, May 30, 31, 1982.

19. Yu Wong, "Wang's World," p. 46.

20. Wang Lijun, "Guanyu 'houxinshiqi wenxue' de taolun."

Works Cited

Anagnost, Ann. "Transformation of Gender in Modern China." In Sandra Morgen, ed., *Gender and Anthropology: Critical Reviews for Research and Teaching*. American Anthropological Association, 1989, 313–29.

Anderson, Marston. *The Limits of Realism: Chinese Fiction in the Revolutionary Period*. Berkeley: University of California Press, 1990.

————. "The Morality of Form: Lu Xun and the Modern Chinese Short Story." In Leo Ou-fan Lee, ed., *Lu Xun and His Legacy*. Berkeley: University of California Press, 1985, 32–53.

Apter, David E., and Tony Saich. *Revolutionary Discourse in Mao's Republic*. Cambridge, Mass.: Harvard University Press, 1994.

Auerbach, Eric. *Mimesis: The Representation of Reality in the Western World*. Trans. Willard R. Trask. Princeton: Princeton University Press, 1953.

Avery, Martha, trans. *Bao Town*. New York: Viking, 1989.

Ba Ren 巴人. "'Sanliwan' duhou gan—wei *Zhongsu youhao bao* er zuo" 「三里灣」讀後感—爲『中蘇友好報』而作 ("Reflections After Reading 'Sanliwan'—Written for the *Sino-Soviet Friendship Journal*"). *In Zhao Shuli zhuanji* 趙樹理專集(*Works of Zhao Shuli*). Fuzhou: Fujian renmin chubanshe, 1981, 442–48.

Bakhtin, Mikhail M. *The Dialogic Imagination*. Ed. Michael Holquist; trans. Caryl Emerson and Michael Holquist. Austin: University of Texas Press, 1981.

————. *Problems of Dostoevsky's Poetics*. Ed. and trans. Caryl Emerson. Minneapolis: University of Minnesota Press, 1984.

Barlow, Tani E., ed. *Gender Politics in Modern China: Writing and Feminism.* Durham: Duke University Press, 1993.

———. "*Zhishifenzi* [Chinese Intellectuals] and Power." *Dialectical Anthropology* 16 (1991): 209–32.

Barthes, Roland. "The Death of the Author." In *Image—Music—Text.* Trans. Stephen Heath. New York: Hill and Wang, 1977, 142–48.

———. *S/Z: An Essay.* Trans. Richard Miller. New York: Hill and Wang, 1974.

Benveniste, Emile. "Subjectivity in Language." In *Problems of General Linguistics.* Trans. Mary Elizabeth Meek. Carol Gables, Fla.: University of Miami Press, 1971, 223–30.

Berninghausen, John, and Ted Huters, eds. *Revolutionary Literature in China: An Anthology.* White Plains, N.Y.: M. E. Sharpe, 1976.

Bianco, Lucien. "Peasant Movements." In John K. Fairbank and Albert Feuerwerker, eds., *The Cambridge History of China,* vol. 13: *Republican China 1912–1949,* pt. 2. Cambridge: Cambridge University Press, 1986, 270–328.

Bing Xin 冰心. "Xu" 序 ("Preface"). In *Xiaobaozhuang* 小鮑莊 (*Bao Village*). Shanghai: Shanghai wenyi chubanshe, 1986, 1–4.

Birch, Cyril. "Literature Under Communism." In Roderick MacFarquhar and John K. Fairbank, eds., *The Cambridge History of China,* vol. 15: *The People's Republic,* pt. 2, "Revolutions Within the Chinese Revolution 1966–1982." Cambridge: Cambridge University Press, 1991, 743–812.

Booth, Wayne. *The Rhetoric of Fiction.* Chicago: University of Chicago Press, 1967.

Bourdieu, Pierre. *Language and Symbolic Power.* Ed. John B. Thompson; trans. Ginor Raymond and Matthew Adamson. Cambridge: Mass: Harvard University Press, 1991.

Brown, Carolyn. "The Paradigm of the Iron House: Shouting and Silence in Lu Xun's Short Stories." *Chinese Literature: Essays, Articles, Reviews* 6 nos. 1–2 (July 1984): 101–19.

———. "Women as Trope: Gender and Power in Lu Xun's 'Soap.'" *Modern Chinese Literature* 4 (Spring/Fall 1988): 55–70.

Can Xue 殘雪. "Shan shang de xiaowu" 山上的小屋 ("Hut on the Hill"). In Cheng Depei 程德培 and Wu Liang 吳亮, eds., *Tansuo xiaoshuoji* 探索小說集 (*Anthology of Exploratory Fiction*). Shanghai: Shanghai wenyi chubanshe, 1986, 543–48.

Cao Pi 曹丕. "Dian lun lun wen" 典論論文 ("On Literature"). In Yan Henfu 顏亨福 and Zhou Caizhu 周才珠, eds., *Guwen jinghua yijie* 古文精華譯解 (*Essence of Ancient Prose,* annotated). Guiyang: Guizhou renmin chubanshe, 1987.

Chan, Ching-kiu Stephen. "The Language of Despair: Ideological Representations of the 'New Woman' by May Fourth Writers." In Barlow, *Gender Politics in Modern China,* 13–32.

Chaves, Jonathan. *Mei Yao-ch'en and the Development of Early Sung Poetry*. New York: Columbia University Press, 1976.

Chen Huangmei 陳荒煤. "Xiang Zhao Shuli fangxiang maijin" 向趙樹理方向邁進 ("Strive forward in the direction of Zhao Shuli"). In *Zhao Shuli zhuanji*, 198–202. (First published in *Renmin ribao*, 1947.8.10.)

[Chen] Huangmei 荒煤. "Xu" 序 ("Preface"). In Yang Zhijie 楊志杰, *Zhao Shuli xiaoshuo renwu lun* 趙樹理小說人物論 (*The Characters in Zhao Shuli's Fiction*). Taiyuan: Shanxi renmin chubashe, 1983, 1–6.

Chen Jihui 陳繼會. "Nongcun ticai xiaoshuo de lishi yu xianshi—ershi shiji Zhongguo nongcun ticai xiaoshuo zonglun zhi yi" 農村題材小說的歷史與現實－二十世紀中國農村題材小說綜論之一 ("History and Reality in Fiction on Countryside Themes—One Discussion of Twentieth-Century Chinese Fiction on Countryside Yhemes"). *Xiaoshuo pinglun*, 1987.6: 55–60.

———. "Xin wenxueshi shang nongcun ticai de liangwei kaituozhe—lüelun Zhao Shuli yu Lu Xun" 新文學史上農村題材的兩位開拓者－略論趙樹理與魯迅 ("Two Pioneers in the History of the New Literature on Themes on the Countryside—On Zhao Shuli and Lu Xun"). *Zhao Shuli xueshu taolunhui jinianji* 12 (1982).

Chen Pingyuan 陳平原. *Zhongguo xiaoshuo xushi moshi de zhuanbian* 中國小說敘事模式的轉變 (*The Changes in Narrative Modes in Chinese Fiction*). Shanghai: Shanghai renmin chubanshe, 1988.

Chen Shunxin 陳順馨. *Zhongguo dangdai wenxue de xushi yu xingbie* 中國當代文學的敘事與性別 (*Narrative and Gender in Chinese Contemporary Literature*). Beijing: Beijing daxue chubanshe, 1995.

Chen Sihe 陳思和. "Shuangchong dieying, shenceng xiangzheng—du 'Xiaobaozhuang' li de shenhua moshi" 雙重迭影, 深層象征－讀「小鮑莊」裏的神話模式 ("Doubled Reflections, Deep Layered Symbolism—On the Mythical Mode in *Xiaobaozhuang*"). *Dangdai zuojia pinglun*, 1986.1: 16–18.

———. "Zhongguo xinwenxue fazhan zhong de chanhui yishi" 中國新文學發展中的懺悔意識 ("The Penitential Consciousness in the Development of the New Chinese Literature"). *Shanghai wenxue*, 1986.2: 76–85.

Chen Xiaoming 陳曉明. "Lishi zhuanxing yu houxiandai zhuyi de xingqi" 歷史轉型與後現代主義的興起 ("The Transformation of History and the Rise of Postmodernism). *Huacheng* 2 (1993) 24–35.

Chen Yong 陳涌. "Wenyixue fangfalun wenti" 文藝學方法論問題 ("The Methodology of Literature and Art"). *Hongqi* 8 (1986): 21–32.

Cheng Depei 程德培. "Yizhong gongshitai de xushu: cong 'Xiaobaozhuang' kan Wang Anyi chuangzuo zhuti shang de zhuanbian" 一種共時態的敘述：從「小鮑莊」看王安憶創作主體上的轉變 ("A Type of Contemporaneous Narrative: The Transformation of the Creative Subject by Wang Anyi in *Xiaobaozhuang*"). *Wenhuibao*, 1985.6.3.

Cheng Fangwu 成仿吾. "Cong wenxue geming dao geming wenxue" 從文學革

命到革命文學 ("From Literary Revolution to Revolutionary Literature"). In Modern Literature Study Section, Literature Research Institute, Chinese Academy of Social Sciences, ed., *"Geming wenxue" lunzheng ziliao xuanbian* 「革命文學」論爭資料選編 (*Selections from Materials on the Debates over "Revolutionary Literature"*). Beijing: Renmin wenxue chubanshe, 1981, 1: 130–37.

Cheng Ma 程麻, Chen Xiaoming 陳曉明, Li Jiefei 李潔非, Jin Dacheng 靳大成, and Chen Yangu 陳燕谷. "Wenxue duihua: weiji yu kunhuo" 文學對話: 危機與困惑 ("Dialogue on Literature: Crisis and Perplexity"). *Dangdai zuojia pinglun,* 1989.3: 4–12.

Chow, Rey. "Against the Lures of Diaspora: Minority Discourse, Chinese Women, and Intellectual Hegemony." In Tonglin Lu, ed., *Gender and Sexuality in Twentieth-Century Chinese Literature and Society*. Albany: State University of New York Press, 1993, 23–45.

———. "'It's You, and Not Me': Domination and 'Othering' in Theorizing the 'Third World.'" In Elizabeth Weed, ed., *Coming to Terms*. New York: Routledge, 1989, 152–61.

———. "Pedagogy, Trust, Chinese Intellectuals in the 1990s—Fragments of a Post-Catastrophic Discourse." *Dialectical Anthropology* 16 (1991): 191–207.

Cohen, Myron L. "Cultural and Political Inventions in Modern China: The Case of the Chinese 'Peasant.'" *Daedalus,* Spring 1993, pp. 151–70.

Conn. Peter. *Pearl S. Buck: A Cultural Biography*. Cambridge: Cambridge University Press, 1996.

Crozier, Ralph. "Qu Yuan and the Artists: Ancient Symbols and Modern Politics in the Post-Mao Era." *Australian Journal of Chinese Affairs* no. 24 (July 1990): 25–50.

Culler, Jonathan. *Structuralist Poetics: Structuralism, Linguistics, and the Study of Literature*. Ithaca: Cornell University Press, 1975.

Dai Guangzhong 戴光中. "Guanyu 'Zhao Shuli fangxiang' de zai renshi" 關於「趙樹理方向」的再認識 ("Reappraisal of 'The Direction of Zhao Shuli'"). *Shanghai wenlun,* 1988.4: 13–17, 62.

de Bary, Wm. Theodore, and the Conference on Ming Thought. *Self and Society in Ming Thought*. New York: Columbia University Press, 1970.

Denton, Kirk A., ed. *Modern Chinese Literary Thought: Writings on Literature, 1893–1945*. Stanford: Stanford University Press, 1996.

Derrida, Jacques. *Of Grammatology*. Trans. Gayatri Chakravorty Spivak. Baltimore, Md.: John Hopkins Press, 1976.

Ding Ling 丁玲. "Shui" 水 ("Flood"). In *Ding Ling duanpian xiaoshuo xuan* (*Selected Short Stories of Ding Ling*), vol II. Beijing: Renmin wenxue chubanshe, 1981, 297–332.

Ding Jingtang 丁景唐 and Qu Guangxi 瞿光熙, eds. *Zuolian wulieshi yanjiu ziliao bienmu* 左聯五烈士研究資料編目 (*Bibliography of Research Materials on the Five Martyrs of the League of Left-wing Writers*), enl. ed. Shanghai: Shanghai wenyi chubanshe, 1981.

Doleželová-Velingerová, Milena. *The Chinese Novel at the Turn of the Century.* Toronto: University of Toronto Press, 1980.

Dong Dazhong 董大中. *Zhao Shuli nianpu* 趙樹理年譜 (*Chronicle of Zhao Shuli's Life*). Taiyuan: Shanxi renmin chubanshe, 1982.

―――. *Zhao Shuli pingzhuan* 趙樹理評傳 (*Critical Biography of Zhao Shuli*). Tiantsin: Baihua wenyi chubanshe, 1990).

―――. "Zhao Shuli sanshi niandai de liangpian zawen" 趙樹理三十年代的兩篇雜文 ("Two Essays by Zhao Shuli in the 1930s"). *Shanxi wenxue,* 1982.3: 69.

―――. "Zhao Shuli zai huabei Xinhua ribao she de liangnian" 趙樹理在華北新華日報社的兩年 ("Zhao Shuli's Two Years with the *Xinhua Daily* in North China"). *Xinwenxue shiliao (Historical Materials of the New Literature),* 1983.3: 143–52.

Dong Jian 董健. "Lun Gao Xiaosheng xiaoshuo de sixiang he yishu" 論高曉聲小說的思想和藝術 ("On the Ideas and Art of Gao Xiaosheng's Fiction") *Wenxue pinglun congkan* no. 10 (1981.8): 68–89.

Dong Junlun 董均倫. "Zhao Shuli zenyang chuli 'Xiao Erhei jiehun' de cailiao" 趙樹理怎樣處理「小二黑結婚」的材料 ("Zhao Shuli's Treatment of the Material for 'Xiao Erhei's Marriage'"). In *Zhao Shuli zhuanji,* 335–38 (originally published in 1949).

Duke, Michael. *Blooming and Contending: Chinese Literature in the Post-Mao Era.* Bloomington: Indiana University Press, 1985.

―――. "Chinese Literature in the Post-Mao Era: The Return of 'Critical Realism.'" In Michael Duke, ed., *Contemporary Chinese Literature: An Anthology of Post-Mao Fiction and Poetry.* Armonk, N.Y.: M. E. Sharpe, 1984, 3–6.

―――. "Reinventing China: Cultural Exploration in Contemporary Chinese Fiction." *Issues and Studies* 25, no. 8 (Aug. 1989): 29–53.

Durrant, Stephen W. "Self as the Intersection of Traditions: The Autobiographical Writings of Ssu-ma Ch'ien." *Journal of the American Oriental Society* 106, no. 1 (1986): 33–40.

Eagleton, Terry. *Marxism and Literary Criticism.* Berkeley: University of California Press, 1976.

Elvin, Mark. "No Controlling Vision." *National Interest* no. 21 (Fall 1990): 86–90.

Engle, Hua-ling Nieh, and Paul Engle, trans. *Poems of Mao Tse-tung.* New York: Delta, 1972.

Fairbank, John King. *The United States and China.* 4th ed. Cambridge, Mass.: Harvard University Press, 1979.

Fan Boqun 范伯群. "Chen Huansheng lun" 陳奐生論 ("On Chen Huansheng"). *Dangdai zuojia pinglun,* 1984. 1: 9–17.

———. "Gao Xiaosheng lun" 高曉聲論 ("On Gao Xiaosheng"). *Wenyibao,* 1982.7: 39–45.

Fang Keqiang 方克強. "Ah Q he Bingzai: yuanshi xintai de chongsu" 阿Q和丙崽:原始心態的重塑 ("Ah Q and Bingzai—Primitive Mental State Reportrayed"). *Wenyi lilun yanjiu,* 1986.5: 9–17 .

Feng Guanglian 馮光廉. "'Nahan' 'Panghuang' laodong renmin xingxiang yanjiu zhong de pianxiang" 「吶喊」,「彷徨」勞動人民形象研究中的偏向 ("Biases in the Studies of the Images of the Laboring People in *Nahan* and *Panghuang*"). *Shandong shida xuebao,* 1986.5: 58–63, 72.

Feng Lipeng. "Democracy and Elitism: The May Fourth Ideal of Literature." *Modern China* 22, no. 2 (Apr. 1996): 170–96.

Feuerwerker, Yi-tsi Mei. "The Dialectics of Struggle: Ideology and Realism in Mao Dun's 'Algae.'" In Theodore Huters, ed., *Reading the Modern Chinese Short Story.* Armonk, N.Y.: M. E. Sharpe, 1990, 51–73.

———. *Ding Ling's Fiction: Ideology and Narrative in Modern Chinese Literature.* Cambridge, Mass.: Harvard University Press, 1982.

———. "An Interview with Gao Xiaosheng." *Modern Chinese Literature* 3, nos. 1 and 2 (Spring/Fall 1987): 113–35.

———. "Text, Intertext, and the Representation of the Writing Self in Lu Xun, Yu Dafu, and Wang Meng." In Ellen Widmer and David Der-wei Wang, eds., *From May Fourth to June Fourth: Fiction and Film in Twentieth-Century China.* Cambridge, Mass.: Harvard University Press, 1993, 167–93.

Fokkema, D. W., and Elrud Kunne-Ibsch. *Theories of Literature in the Twentieth Century.* New York: St. Martin's Press, 1977.

Foucault, Michel. "The Subject and Power." In Hubert Dreyfus and Paul Rabinow, *Michel Foucault: Beyond Structuralism and Hermeneutics.* Chicago: Chicago University Press, 1983, 208–26.

———. "Truth and Power." In Paul Rabinow, ed., *The Foucault Reader.* New York: Pantheon Books, 1984, 51–75.

———. "What Is an Author?" In *The Foucault Reader,* 101–20.

Gao Jie 高捷, Liu Yunhao 劉蕓灝, Duan Chongxuan 端崇軒, Gao Zhongwu 郜忠武, and Ren Wengui 任文貴. *Zhao Shuli zhuan* 趙樹理傳 (*Biography of Zhao Shuli*). Taiyuan: Shanxi renmin chubanshe, 1982.

Gao Xiaosheng. *The Broken Betrothal.* Beijing: Panda Books, 1987.

———. 高曉聲. "Bu xing" 不幸 ("Misfortune"). *Yuhua,* 1957.6: 16–18.

———. "(Chen Huansheng) baochan" (陳奐生) 包產 ("Chen Huansheng Under Production Contract"). In *Chen Huansheng shangcheng chuguo ji,* 61–80.

———. "(Chen Huansheng) shangcheng" (陳奐生) 上城 ("Chen Huansheng Goes to Town"). In *Chen Huansheng shangcheng chuguo ji,* 15–27.

———. *Chen Huansheng shangcheng chuguo ji* 陳奐生上城出國記 (*Chen Huansheng Goes to Town, Travels Abroad*). Shanghai: Shanghai wenyi chubanshe, 1991.

———. "(Chen Huansheng) zhuanye" (陳奐生) 轉業 ("Chen Huansheng Transferred"). In *Chen Huansheng shangcheng chuguo ji*, 28–60.

———. "Chuguo" 出國 ("Going Abroad"). In *Chen Huansheng shangcheng chuguo ji*, 133–222.

———. "Da haoren Jiang Kunda" 大好人江坤大 ("The Very Virtuous Fellow Jiang Kunda"). In *Gao Xiaosheng 1981 nian xiaoshuo ji* 高曉聲1981年小說集 (*Gao Xiaosheng 1981 story collection*). Beijing: Renmin wenxue chubanshe, 1982, 51–82.

———. "Diejiao yinyuan" 跌跤姻緣 ("Falling into a Marriage"). In *Gao Xiaosheng 1984 nian xiaoshuo ji* 高曉聲1984 年小說集 (*Gao Xiaosheng 1984 Story Collection*). Beijing: Zhongguo wenlian chuban gongsi, 1986, 1–43.

———. *Gao Xiaosheng xiaoshuo xuan* 高曉聲小說選 (*Selected Stories of Gao Xiaosheng*). Beijing: Renmin wenxue chubanshe, 1983.

———. "Hutu" 糊塗 ("Muddled"). *Huacheng*, 1983.4: 4–21, 60.

———. "Jixindai" 繫心帶 ("Bond of Hearts"). In *Gao Xiaosheng xiaoshuo xuan*, 1–10.

———. "Kaituo yanjie" 開拓眼界 ("To Broaden Our Outlook"). *Xiaoshuo lin*, 1983.7: 65–66.

———. "Li Shunda zaowu" 李順大造屋 ("Li Shunda Builds a House"). In *Gao Xiaosheng xiaoshuo xuan*, 11–32.

———. "'Li Shunda zaowu' shimo" 「李順大造屋」始末 ("The story of 'Li Shunda Builds a House'"). In Mu Zhongxiu 牟鐘秀, ed., *Huojiang duanpian xiaoshuo chuangzuo tan: 1978–1980* 獲獎短篇小說創作談: 1978–1980 (*Discussions of Prize-winning Stories*). Beijing: Wenhua yishu chubanshe, 1982, 68–77.

———. "Liu Yu xieshu" 劉宇寫書 ("Liu Yu Writes a Book"). In *Gao Xiaosheng 1981 nian xiaoshuo ji*, 121–38.

———. "'Loudouhu' zhu" 「漏斗戶」主 ("The 'Funnel-Householder'"). In *Gao Xiaosheng xiaoshuo xuan*, 100–113.

———. *Qingtian zaishang* 青天在上 (*The Blue Heavens Above*). Shanghai: Shanghai wenyi chubanshe, 1991.

———. "Shenghuo, mudi, he jiqiao" 生活,目的,和技巧 ("Life, Purpose, and Technique"). *Xinghuo*, 1980.10: 15–19.

———. "Shuwai chunqiu" 書外春秋 ("Historical Annals Outside Books"). In *Gao Xiaosheng 1982 xiaoshuo ji* 高曉聲1982 小說集 (*Gao Xiaosheng 1982 Story Collection*). Chengdu: Sichuan renmin chubanshe, 1983, 30–40.

———. "Tantan wenxue chuangzuo" 談談文學創作 ("Comments on Writing Literature"). *Changjiang wenyi*, 1980.10: 69–76.

———. "Tantan youguan Chen Huansheng de jipian xiaoshuo" 談談有關陳奐生的幾篇小說 ("Some Remarks on the Stories Concerning Chen Huansheng"). *Wenyi lilun yanjiu*, 1982.3: 24–30.

———. "Wo de xiaoshuo tong minjian wenxue de guanxi" 我的小說同民間

文學的關係 ("The Relationship Between My Fiction and Folk Literature"). *Suzhou daxue xuebao (zhexue shehui kexue ban)*, 1981.1: 95–101.

———. "Xiwang nuli wei nongmin xiezuo" 希望努力爲農民寫作 ("Hoping to Work Hard to Write for Peasants"). *Wenyibao*, 1980.5: 12–14.

———. "Zhanshu" 戰術 ("Tactics"). In *Chen Huansheng shangcheng chuguo ji*, 81–106.

———. "Zhongtian dahu" 種田大戶 ("The Rich Farming Household"). In *Chen Huansheng shangcheng chuguo ji*, 107–32.

Gao Xiaosheng 高曉聲, Fang Zhi 方之, Ye Zhicheng 葉至誠, et al., "Yijian he xiwang" 意見和希望 ("Opinions and Hopes") *Yuhua*, 1957.6: 7–9.

Garcia Marquez, Gabriel. *One Hundred Years of Solitude*. Trans. Gregory Rabassa. New York: Avon Books, 1970.

Goldblatt, Howard, trans. *Red Sorghum: A Novel of China*. New York: Viking Penguin, 1993.

Goldman, Merle. *China's Intellectuals: Advise and Dissent*. Cambridge, Mass.: Harvard University Press, 1981.

Goldman, Merle, ed., with Timothy Cheek and Carol Lee Hamrin. *China's Intellectuals and the State: In Search of a New Relationship*. Cambridge, Mass.: Harvard University Press, 1987.

Goodman, David S. G. "PRC Fiction and Its Political Context, 1978–82: To Write the Word of 'Man' Across the Sky." In Helmut Martin, ed., *Cologne Workshop 1984 on Contemporary Chinese Literature*. Deutsche Welle, Kohn, 1986, 127–48.

Gramsci, Antonio. *Selections from the Prison Notebooks of Antonio Gramsci*. Ed. and trans. Quintin Hoare and Geoffrey Novell Smith. New York: International Publishers, 1971.

Greenblatt, Stephen. "Culture." In Frank Lentricchia and Thomas McLauglinn, eds., *Critical Terms for Literary Study*. Chicago: University of Chicago Press, 1980, 225–32.

Grieder, Jerome. *Intellectuals and the State in Modern China: A Narrative History*. New York: Free Press, 1981.

Gunn, Edward. *Rewriting Chinese: Style and Innovation in Twentieth-Century Chinese Prose*. Stanford: Stanford University Press, 1991.

Guo Zheng 郭政. "Lun Zhao Shuli zuopin zhong zhuanbian renwu de yiyi" 論趙樹理作品中轉變人物的意義 ("The Meaning of Characters that Change in Zhao Shuli's Works"). *Shanxi wenxue*, 1982.3: 63–66.

Hamrin, Carol Lee, and Timothy Cheek. *China's Establishment Intellectuals*. Armonk, N.Y.: M. E. Sharpe, 1986.

Han Shaogong 韓少功. "Ba Ba Ba" 爸爸爸 ("Pa Pa Pa"). In *Tansuo xiaoshuo ji*, 1–43.

———. "Guiqulai." 歸去來 ("Homecoming"). *Shanghai wenxue*, 1985.6: 30–37.

———. *Homecoming? and Other Stories*. Trans. and intro., Martha Cheung. Hong Kong: Chinese University of Hong Kong, 1992.

———. "Jiyi de jiazhi" 記憶的價值 ("The Value of Remembering"). *Wenxue ziyou tan*, 1990.3: 57–58.

———. "Wenxue de chuantong" 文學的傳統 ("The Tradition of Literature"). In *Shengzhan yu youxi* 聖戰與游戲 (*Sacred War and Playing Games*). Hong Kong: Oxford University Press, 1994, 63–70.

———. "Wenxue de 'gen'" 文學的「根」 ("The 'Roots' of Literature"). *Zuojia* 1985.4: 2–5.

Han Yufeng 韓玉峰, Yang Zong 楊宗, Zhao Guangjian 趙廣建, and Gou Youfu 笱有富. *Zhao Shuli de shengping yu chuangzuo* 趙樹理的生平與創作 (*The Life and Works of Zhao Shuli*). Taiyuan: Shanxi renmin chubanshe, 1981.

Hanan, Patrick. *The Chinese Vernacular Story*. Cambridge, Mass.: Harvard University Press, 1981.

———. "The Technique of Lu Hsun's Fiction." *Harvard Journal of Asiatic Studies* 34 (1974): 53–96.

Hawkes, David. *Ch'u Tz'u: The Songs of the South: An Ancient Chinese Anthology*. London: Oxford University Press, 1959.

Hegel, Robert E. "Making the Past Serve the Present in Fiction and Drama: From the Yan'an Forum to the Cultural Revolution." In Bonnie S. McDougall, ed., *Popular Chinese Literature and Performing Arts in the People's Republic of China, 1949–1979*. Berkeley: University of California Press, 1984, 197–223.

Hegel, Robert E., and Richard C. Hessney, eds. *Expressions of Self in Chinese Literature*. New York: Columbia University Press, 1985.

Hightower, James Robert. *The Poetry of T'ao Ch'ien*. Oxford: Clarendon Press, 1970.

Hofheinz, Roy. Jr. *The Broken Wave: The Chinese Communist Peasant Movement, 1922–1928*. Cambridge, Mass.: Harvard University Press, 1977.

Holm, David. *Art and Ideology in Revolutionary China*. New York: Oxford University Press, 1991.

Hsia, C. T. *A History of Modern Chinese Fiction*. 2nd. ed. New Haven: Yale University Press, 1971.

———, ed., with Joseph S. M. Lau. *Twentieth-Century Chinese Stories*. New York: Columbia University Press, 1971.

Hsu Kai-yu, ed. *Literature of the People's Republic of China*. Bloomington: Indiana University Press, 1980.

Hu Shi 胡適. "Wenxue gailiang chuyi" 文學改良芻議 ("Tentative Proposals for a Reform of Literature"). In *Zhongguo xiandai wenxueshi cankao ziliao* 中國現代文學史參考資料 (*Reference Materials for Modern Chinese Literary History*), vol. 1, no. 1. Beijing: Gaodeng jiaoyu chubanshe, 1959, 44–50.

Huang, Martin Weizong. "The Inescapable Predicament: The Narrator and His

Discourse in 'The True Story of Ah Q.'" *Modern China* 16, no. 4 (Oct. 1990): 430–49.

———. *Literati and Self Re/Presentation: Autobiographical Sensibility in the Eighteenth-Century Chinese Novel.* Stanford: Stanford University Press, 1995.

Huang, Philip C. C. *The Peasant Economy and Social Change in North China.* Stanford: Stanford University Press, 1985.

Huang Xiuji 黃修己. *Zhao Shuli pingzhuan* 趙樹理評傳 (*Critical Biography of Zhao Shuli*). Xuzhou: Jiangsu renmin chubanshe, 1981.

———. *Zhao Shuli yanjiu* 趙樹理研究 (*Study of Zhao Shuli*). Taiyuan: Shanxi renmin chubanshe, 1985.

Hung, Chang-tai. *Going to the People: Chinese Intellectuals and Folk Literature, 1918–1937.* Cambridge, Mass.: Council on East Asian Studies, Harvard University, 1985.

Hutcheon, Linda. *The Politics of Postmodernism.* London: Routledge, 1989.

Huters, Theodore. "Ideologies of Realism in Modern China: The Hard Imperatives of Imported Theory." In Liu Kang and Xiaobing Tang, eds., *Politics, Ideology, and Literary Discourse in Modern China: Theoretical Interventions and Cultural Critique.* Durham, N.C.: Duke University Press, 1993, 147–73.

———. "Lives in Profile: On the Authorial Voice in Modern and Contemporary Chinese Literature." In Widmer and Wang, *From May Fourth to June Fourth,* 269–94.

Israel, John. "Foreword." In Hamrin and Cheek, *China's Establishment Intellectuals,* ix–xix.

Jameson, Frederic. *The Prison-House of Language: A Critical Account of Structuralism and Russian Formalism.* Princeton: Princeton University Press, 1972.

Jenner, W. J. F., ed. *Modern Chinese Stories.* London: Oxford University Press, 1970.

Ji Hongzhen 季紅眞. "Shenhua shijie de renleixue kongjian—shi Mo Yan xiaoshuo de yuyi cengci" 神話世界的人類學空間—釋莫言小說的語義層次 ("Anthropological Space of a Mythical World—Elucidating the Semantic Levels of Mo Yan's Fiction"). *Beijing wenxue,* 1988.3: 59, 67–74.

——— "Tongyi lishi zhuti de liangge shidai yuezhang—Zhao Shuli yu Gao Xiaosheng chuangzuo tezheng de bijiao" 同一歷史主題的兩個時代樂章—趙樹理與高曉聲創作特徵的比較 ("Two Period Movements of the Same Historical Theme—A Comparison Between the Literary Characteristics of Zhao Shuli and Gao Xiaosheng"). In Ji Hongzhen, *Wenming yu yumei de chongtu* 文明與愚昧的衝突 (*The Conflict Between Civilization and Ignorance*). Hangzhou: Zhejiang wenyi chubanshe, 1986, 47–66.

Johnson, Barbara. *The Critical Difference: Essays in the Contemporary Rhetoric of Reading.* Baltimore, Md.: Johns Hopkins University Press, 1980.

Johnson, Chalmers. *Peasant Nationalism and Communist Power: The Emergence of Revolutionary China: 1937–1945.* Stanford: Stanford University Press, 1982.

Johnson, David. "Communication, Class, and Consciousness in Late Imperial China." In David Johnson, Andrew J. Nathan, Evelyn S. Rawski, eds., *Popular Culture in Late Imperial China*. Berkeley: University of California Press, 1985, 34–72.

Judd, Ellen R. "Cultural Articulation in the Chinese Countryside, 1937–1947." *Modern China* 16, no. 3 (July 1990): 269–308.

———. "Prelude to the 'Yan'an Talks': Problems in Transforming a Literary Intelligentsia." *Modern China* 11, no. 3 (July 1985): 269–304.

Kearney, Michael. *Reconceptualizing the Peasantry: Anthropology in Global Perspective*. Boulder, Colo.: Westview Press, 1996.

Kelliher, Daniel. "Chinese Communist Political Theory and the Rediscovery of the Peasantry." *Modern China* 20, no. 4 (October 1994): 387-415.

Kinkley, Jeffrey. "Shen Congwen's Legacy in Chinese Literature of the 1980s." In Widmer and Wang, *From May Fourth to June Fourth*, 71–106.

Krauss. Richard. "Bai Hua: The Political Authority of a Writer." In Hamrin and Cheek, *China's Establishment Intellectuals*, 185–211.

Larson, Wendy. "The End of 'Funü wenxue': Women's Literature from 1925–1935." In Barlow, *Gender Politics in Modern China*, 58–73.

———. *Literary Authority and the Modern Chinese Writer: Ambivalence and Autobiography*. Durham, N.C.: Duke University Press, 1991.

Lau, Joseph S. M. "Visitations of the Past in Han Shaogong's Post-1985 Fiction." In Widmer and Wang, *From May Fourth to June Fourth*, 1–42.

Lee, Leo Ou-fan. "Literary Trends I: The Quest for Modernity, 1895–1927." In John K. Fairbank, ed., *The Cambridge History of China*, vol. 12, *Republican China, 1912–1949*, pt. I. Cambridge: Cambridge University Press, 1983, 451–504.

———. "Literary Trends: The Road to Revolution, 1927–1949." In Fairbank, *The Cambridge History of China*, vol. 12, *Republican China, 1912–1949*, pt. II, 421–91.

———. "The Politics of Technique: Perspectives of Literary Dissidence in Contemporary Chinese Fiction." In Jeffrey Kinkley, ed., *After Mao: Chinese Literature and Society, 1978–1981*. Cambridge, Mass.: Council on East Asian Studies, Harvard University, 1985, 159–90.

———. *The Romantic Generation of Modern Chinese Writers*. Cambridge, Mass.: Harvard University Press, 1973.

———. "The Solitary Traveler: Images of the Self in Modern Chinese Literature." In Hegel and Hessney, *Expressions of Self in Chinese Literature*, 282–307.

———. "Tradition and Modernity in the Writings of Lu Xun." In Leo Ou-fan Lee, ed., *Lu Xun and His Legacy*. Berkeley: University of California Press, 1985, 3–31.

———. *Voices from the Iron House: A Study of Lu Xun*. Bloomington: Indiana University Press, 1987.

Lewis, John Wilson, ed. *Peasant Rebellion and Communist Revolution in Asia.* Stanford: Stanford University Press, 1974.

Li Guotao 李國濤. "'Xiaobaozhuang' de wenti ji qita" 「小鮑莊」的文體及其它 ("The Form of 'Xiaobaozhuang' and Other Matters"). *Dangdai zuojia pinglun,* 1986.5: 95–101.

Li Hangyu 李杭育. "Li yi li women de 'gen'" 理一理我們的「根」 ("Attending to Our 'Roots'"). *Zuojia,* 1985.9: 75–79.

Li Jie 李劼. "Lun Zhongguo dangdai xinchao xiaoshuo" 論當代中國新潮小說 ("On the New Wave Fiction of Contemporary China"). *Zhongshan,* 1988.5: 116–38.

———. "Shi linmo, yeshi kaituo—'Ni biewu xuanze' he 'Xiaobaozhuang' zhi wojian" 是臨摹,也是開拓一「你別無選擇」和「小鮑莊」之我見 ("It's Imitation, It's Also Innovation—My Views on 'You Have No Other Choice' and *Bao Village*). *Dangdai zuojia pinglun,* 1986.1: 8, 19–24.

Li Jiefei 李潔非. "Xinshiqi xiaoshuo de liangge jieduan ji qi bijiao" 新時期小說的兩個階段及其比較 ("Comparison Between the Two Stages of New Era Fiction"). *Wenxue pinglun,* 1989.3: 73–86.

Lie Jiefei 李潔非 and Zhang Ling 張陵. "Jingshen fenxixue yu 'Honggaoliang' de xushi jiegou" 精神分析學與「紅高梁」的敘事結構 ("Psychoanalysis and the Narrative Structure of *Red Sorghum*"). *Beijing wenxue,* 1987.1: 75–80.

Li Qingxi 李慶西. "Baiwu liaolai de 'houpiping'—ye tan 'hou xinshiqi wenxue'" 百無聊賴的「後批評」一也談「後新時期文學」 ("A Bored 'Post-Criticism'—On 'Post New-Era Literature'"). *Wenyi lilun,* 1993.2: 129–30.

———. "Xungen: huidao shiwu benshen" 尋根: 回到事物本身 ("Search for Roots: Back to the Essence of Things") *Wenxue pinglun,* 1988.4: 14–23.

Li Tuo 李陀. "1985." *Jiantian* 今天 (*Today*) 3–4 (1991): 59–73.

———. "The New Vitality of Modern Chinese." In Wendy Larson and Anne Wedell-Wedellsborg, eds., *Inside Out: Modernism and Postmodernism in Chinese Literary Culture.* Aarhus, Denmark: Aarhus University Press, 1993, 65–77.

———. "Xu" 序 ("Preface"). In Mo Yan, *Touming de hongluobo* 透明的紅蘿卜 (*The Crystal Carrot*). Beijing: Zuojia chubanshe, 1986, 1–10.

Li Tuo 李陀, Zhang Ling 張陵, and Wang Bin 王斌. "'Yuyan' de fanpan—jin liangnian xiaoshuo xianxiang" 「語言」的反叛一近兩年小說現象 ("The Revolt of 'Language'—The Phenomenon in Fiction of the Last Two Years"). *Wenyi yanjiu,* 1989.2: 75–80.

Li Zehou 李澤厚. "Lüelun Lu Xun sixiang de fazhan" 略論魯迅思想的發展 ("On the Development of Lu Xun's Thought"). In Li Zongying 李宗英 and Zhang Mengyang 張夢陽, eds., *Liushinian lai Lu Xun yanjiu lunwen xuan* 六十年來魯迅研究論文選 (*Selected Essays on the Study of Lu Xun of the Past Sixty Years*). Beijing: Zhongguo shehui kexue chubanshe, 1982, vol. 2, 513–45.

Li Zehou and Vera Schwarcz. "Six Generations of Modern Chinese Intellectuals." *Chinese Studies in History* 17, no. 2 (Winter 1983–84): 42–56.

Li Zhaozhong 李兆忠. "Xuanzhuan de wentan—'xianshi zhuyi yu xianfeng pai wenxue' yantao hui jiyao" 旋轉的文壇—「現實主義與先鋒派文學」研討會紀要 ("The Turning Literary Scene—Summary of Conference on 'Realism and Avant-garde Literature'"). *Wenxue pinglun*, 1989.1: 23–30.

Lin Fei 林非. "Lu Xun de 'Fengbo' he 'Guxiang' duiyu nongcun ticai xiaoshuo de kaituo—'Zhongguo xiandai xiaoshuoshi shang de pianduan'" 魯迅的「風波」和「故鄉」對于農村題材小說的開拓—「中國現代小說史中的魯迅」片段 ("The Opening Up of Fiction on the Countryside by Lu Xun's 'A Passing Storm' and 'My Old Home'—Aspects of *Lu Xun in the History of Modern Chinese Literature*"). *Shehui kexue jikan*, 1986.5: 75–83.

———. "Lun 'Ah Q zhengzhuan'" 論「阿Q正傳」 ("On 'The True Story of Ah Q'"). In Lin Fei, *Lu Xun xiaoshuo lungao* 魯迅小說論稿 (*On Lu Xun's Fiction*). Tianjin: Tianjin renmin chubanshe, 1979, 111–30.

Lin Weiping 林偉平. "Wenxue he renge—fang zuojia Han Shaogong" 文學和人格—訪作家韓少功 ("Literature and Character: Interview with the Writer Han Shaogong"). *Shanghai wenxue* 1986.11: 68–76.

Lin Yü-sheng. *The Crisis of Chinese Consciousness: Radical Antitraditionalism in the May Fourth Era*. Madison: University of Wisconsin Press, 1979.

———. "The Morality of Mind and Immorality of Politics: Reflections on Lu Xun, the Intellectual." In Leo Ou-fan Lee, *Lu Xun and His Legacy*, 107–28.

Lin Zhihao 林志浩. "Tan 'Guxiang' de zhuti sixiang—yu An Yongxing tongzhi shangque" 談「故鄉」的主題思想—與安永興同志商榷 ("On the Main Theme of 'Guxiang'—A Discussion with Comrade An Yongxing"). *Zhongguo xiandai wenxue yanjiu congkan*, 1982.4: 298–302.

———, ed. *Zhongguo xiandai wenxueshi* 中國現代文學史 (*History of Modern Chinese Literature*). Beijing: Zhongguo renmin daxue chubanshe, 1979.

Link, Perry. *Evening Chats in Beijing: Probing China's Predicament*. New York: W. W. Norton, 1992.

Liu E 劉鶚. *Lao Can youji* 老殘游記 (*The Travels of Lao Can*). Jinan: Qilu shushe, 1981.

Liu, James J. Y. *Chinese Theories of Literature*. Chicago: University of Chicago Press, 1975.

Liu Kang and Xiaobing Tang, eds. *Politics, Ideology, and Literary Discourse in Modern China: Theoretical Interventions and Cultural Critique*. Durham, N.C.: Duke University Press, 1993.

Liu, Lydia H. "Invention and Intervention: The Female Tradition in Modern Chinese Literature." In Barlow, ed., *Gender Politics in Modern China*, 33–57.

———. "Narratives of Modern Selfhood: First-person Fiction in May Fourth Literature." In Kang and Tang, eds., *Politics, Ideology, and Literary Discourse in Modern China*, 102–23.

————. *Translingual Practice: Literature, National Culture, and Translated Modernity, China, 1900–1937*. Stanford: Stanford University Press, 1995.

Liu Shousong 劉綬松. *Zhongguo xin wenxueshi chugao* 中國新文學史初稿 (*Draft History of New Chinese Literature*). 2 vols. Beijing: Renmin wenxue chubanshe, 1979.

Liu Wu-chi and Irving Yucheng Lo, eds. *K'uei Yeh Chi* 葵曄集 (*Chinese Text of Sunflower Splendor*). Bloomington: Indiana University Press, 1976.

————. *Sunflower Splendor: Three Thousand Years of Chinese Poetry*. New York: Anchor Press/Doubleday, 1975.

Liu Xiaobo 劉曉波. "Wang Shuo: Zhongguo zuiyou shangyexing yu tongsuxing de zuojia—Liu Xiaobo dui Wang Shuo de fangtan lu" 王朔:中國最有商業性與通俗性的作家—劉曉波對王朔的訪談錄 ("Wang Shuo—China's Most Commercialized and Popular Writer—Liu Xiaobo Interviews Wang Shuo"). Preface to Wang Shuo, *Bianjibu de gushi* 編輯部的故事 (*Story of the Editorial Department*). Taipei: Fengyun shidai gongsi, 1993, 1–13.

————. "Wu fa huibi de fansi—you jibu zhishifenzi ticai de xiaoshuo suo xiangdau de" 無法回避的反思—由幾部知識分子題材的小說所想到的 ("An Unavoidable Reflection—Thoughts on Several Stories on the Theme of Intellectuals") *Zhongguo*, 1986.4: 103–11.

————. *Yu Li Zehou duihua* 與李澤厚對話 (*Dialogue with Li Zehou*). Shanghai: Shanghai renmin chubanshe, 1988.

Liu Zaifu 劉再復. "Lun Bingzai" 論丙崽 ("On Bingzai"). *Guangming ribao*, Nov. 4, 1988.

————. "Lun wenxue de zhutixing" 論文學的主體性 ("On Subjectivity in Literature"). *Wenxue pinglun*, 1985.6: 11–26; 1986.1: 3–19.

————. *Xingge zuhe lun* 性格組合論 (*On the Composite [Literary] Personality*). Shanghai: Shanghai wenyi chubanshe, 1986.

————. "Zhongguo zhishifenzi de mingyun yu zhongguo dangdai wenxue de mingyun—zai Bali dui Zhongguo liuxuesheng de jiangyan" 中國知識分子的命運與中國當代文學的命運—在巴黎對中國留學生的講演 ("The Fate of Chinese Intellectuals and the Fate of Contemporary Chinese Literature—Lecture to Overseas Chinese Students in Paris"). *Wenxue siji* 1 (Autumn, 1988): 256–64.

Liu Zaifu 劉再復 and Lin Gang 林岡. *Chuantong yu Zhongguo ren* 傳統與中國人 (*Tradition and the Chinese*). Hong Kong: Joint Publishing Co., 1988.

Liu Zaifu 劉再復, Lou Zhaoming 樓肇明, and Liu Shijie 劉士杰. "Lun Zhao Shuli chuangzuo liupai de shengchen" 論趙樹理創作流派的升沉 ("On the Rise and Fall of the Zhao Shuli School of Creative Writing"). In *Zhao Shuli zhuanji* 趙樹理專集 (*Works on Zhao Shuli*). Fuzhou: Fujian renmin chubanshe, 1981, 303–25.

Louie, Kam. "Educated Youth Literature: Self-Discovery in the Chinese Villages." In Louie, *Between Fact and Fiction: Essays on Post-Mao Chinese Literature and Society.* Victoria, Australia: Wild Peony, 1989, 91–102.

Lu Tonglin, ed. *Gender and Sexuality in Twentieth-Century Chinese Literature and Society.* Albany: State University of New York Press, 1993.

————. *Misogyny, Cultural Nihilism, and Oppositional Politics: Contemporary Chinese Experimental Fiction.* Stanford: Stanford University Press, 1995.

Lu Xinhua 盧新華. "Shanghen" 傷痕 ("The Wound"). In *Xinglai ba, didi* 醒來吧, 弟弟 (*Awake, My Brother*). Guangdong renmin chubanshe, 1979, 257–71.

Lu Xun 魯迅. "Ah Q zhengzhuan" 阿Q正傳 ("The True Story of Ah Q"). In *Nahan,* 68–114.

————. "Ah Q zhengzhuan de chengyin" 阿Q正傳的成因 ("The Origins of 'The True Story of Ah Q'"). In *Lu Xun quanji,* vol. 3, 279–86.

————. *The Complete Stories of Lu Xun.* Trans. Yang Xianyi and Gladys Yang. Bloomington: Indiana University Press, 1981.

————. "Da *Xi* zhoukan bianzhe xin" 答「戲」周刊編者信 ("Reply to a Letter from the Editor of *Drama Weekly*). *Qiejieting zanwen* 且介亭雜文 (*Essays*). Beijing: Renmin wenxue chubanshe, 1973, 115–20.

————. "Duiyu Zuoyi Zuojia Lianmeng de yijian—sanyue erri zai Zuoyi Zuojia Lianmeng chengli dahui jiang" 對于左翼作家聯盟的意見—三月二日在左翼作家聯盟成立大會講 ("Views on the League of Left-wing Writers—Lecture at the Inaugural Meeting of the League of Left-wing Writers, Mar. 2"). In *Lu Xun quanji,* vol. 4, 182–87.

————. "Fengbo" 風波 ("A Passing Storm"). In *Nahan,* 48–56.

————. "Geming shidai de wenxue—siyue bari zai Huangpu Junguan Xuexiao jiang" 革命時代的文學—四月八日在黃埔軍官學校講 ("Literature in a Time of Revolution—Lecture at Huangpu Military Officers' School, Apr. 8"). In *Eryi ji* 而已集 (*And That's That*). Beijing: Renmin wenxue chubanshe, 1973, 10–17.

————. "Guxiang" 故鄉 ("My Old Home"). In *Nahan,* 57–66.

————. "Kong Yiji" 孔乙己 ("Kong Yiji"). In *Nahan,* 14–19.

————. "Kuangren riji" 狂人日記 ("A Madman's Diary"). In *Nahan,* 1–13.

————. *Nahan* 吶喊 (*Call to Arms*). Beijing: Renmin wenxue chubanshe, 1979.

————. *Panghuang* 彷徨 (*Wandering*). Beijing: Renmin wenxue chubanshe, 1979.

————. "*Panghuang* tici" 彷徨題詞 ("Foreword to *Panghuang*"). In *Lu Xun quanji,* vol. 2, 425.

————. "Shanghai wenyi zhi yipie—bayue shierri zai Shehui Kexue Yanjiuhui jiang" 上海文藝之一瞥—八月十二日在社會科學研究會講 ("A Glance at Shanghai Literature—Lecture at the Social Science Research Association, Aug. 12"). In *Lu Xun zawen xuan* 魯迅雜文選 (*Selected Essays by Lu Xun*). Shanghai: Shanghai renmin chubanshe, 1973, 1: 178–96.

————. "Shangshi" 傷逝 ("Regret for the Past"). In *Panghuang,* 106–27.

———. "Xie zai *Fen* houmian" 寫在「墳」後面 ("Postface to *The Grave*"). In *Lu Xun zawen xuan*, vol. 1, 71–78.

———. "Yijian xiaoshi" 一件小事 ("A Small Incident"). In *Nahan*, 38–40.

———. "Yingyiben 'Duanpian xiaoshuo xuanji' zixu" 英譯本「短篇小說選集」自序 ("Preface to English Translation of 'Selected Short Stories'") (1933). In *Lu Xun quanji*, vol. 7, 632–33, 830.

———. "Zai jiulou shang" 在酒樓上 ("In the Tavern"). In *Panghuang*, 20–30.

———. "Zhongguo wuchanjieji geming wenxue he qianqu de xue" 中國無產階級革命文學和前驅的血 ("The Revolutionary Literature of the Chinese Proletariat and the Blood of the Pioneers"). In *Lu Xun quanji*, 4: 221–22.

———. "Zhufu" 祝福 ("The New-Year Sacrifice"). In *Panghuang*, 1–19.

———. "Zixu" 自序 ("Preface"). In *Nahan*, i–iv.

Lu Xun quanji 魯迅全集 (*Complete Works of Lu Xun*). Beijing: Renmin chubanshe, 1958.

Lukács, Georg. *Realism in Our Time: Literature and the Class Struggle*. New York: Harper and Row, 1972.

Lyell, William A. Jr. *Diary of a Madman and Other Stories*. Honolulu: University of Hawaii Press, 1990.

———. *Lu Hsun's Vision of Reality*. Berkeley: University of California Press, 1976.

McDougall, Bonnie S. *Mao Zedong's "Talks at the Yan'an Conference on Literature and Art": A Translation of the 1943 Text with Commentary*. Ann Arbor: Michigan Papers in Chinese Studies, 1980.

———. "Writers and Performers, Their Works, and Their Audiences in the First Three Decades." In McDougall, ed., *Popular Chinese Literature and Performing Arts in the People's Republic of China, 1949–1979*, 260–304.

———. "Zhao Zhenkai's Fiction: A Study in Cultural Alienation." *Modern Chinese Literature* 1, no. 1 (1984): 103–30.

———, ed. *Popular Chinese Literature and Performing Arts in the People's Republic of China, 1949–1979*. Berkeley: University of California Press, 1984.

———, ed. *Waves: Stories by Bei Dao*. Trans. Bonnie S. McDougall and Susette Ternent Cooke. New York: New Directions, 1990.

Mao Dun 茅盾. "Wo zenyang xie 'Chuncan'" 我怎樣寫「春蠶」 ("How I Wrote 'Spring Silkworms'"). In *Zhongguo xiandai zuojia tan chuangzuo jingyan* 中國現代作家談創作經驗 (*Modern Chinese Writers Speak About Their Writing Experience*). Jinan: Shandong renmin chubanshe, 1980, 1: 97–101.

Mao Tsetung. *Selected Works of Mao Tse-tung*. 5 vols. Peking: Foreign Languages Press, 1966–1977.

Mao Zedong 毛澤東. "Daliang xishou zhishifenzi" 大量吸收知識分子 ("Recruit Large Numbers of Intellectuals"). In Takeuchi Minoru 竹內實, comp., *Mo Taku-to shu* 毛澤東集 (*Collected Works of Mao Zedong*). Tokyo: Hokubosha, 1983, vol. 7, 87–89. Trans. in *Selected Works of Mao Tse-tung* 2: 301–3.

———. "Hunan nongmin yundong kaocha baogao" 湖南農民運動考查報告 ("Report on an Investigation of the Peasant Movement in Hunan"). In *Mo Taku-to shu*, vol. 1, 207–50. Trans. in *Selected Works of Mao Tse-tung* 1: 23–59.

———. *Mao Zhuxi yulu* 毛主席語錄 (*Sayings of Chairman Mao*). Beijing: Zhongguo renmin jiefangjun zongzhengzhibu bianyin, 1968.

———. "Xin minzhu zhuyi lun" 新民主主義論 ("On New Democracy"). In *Mo Taku-to shu*, vol. 7, 143–202. Trans. in *Selected Works of Mao Tse-tung*, vol. 2, 339–84.

———. "Zai Yan'an wenyi zuotanhui shang de jianghua" 在延安文藝座談會上的講話 ("Talks at the Yan'an Forum on Literature and Art"). In *Wenxue yundong shiliao xuan* 文學運動史料選 (*Selected Historical Materials of Literary Movements*). Shanghai: Shanghai jiaoyu chubanshe, 1979, vol. 4, 518–46. Trans. in *Selected Works of Mao Tse-tung*, vol. 3, 69–98.

Mei Yaochen shixuan 梅堯臣詩選 (*Selected Poems of Mei Yaochen*). Ed. Zhu Dongrun 朱東潤. Beijing: Renmin wenxue chubanshe, 1980.

Meisner, Maurice. "Leninism and Maoism: Some Populist Perspectives in Marxism-Leninism in China." *China Quarterly* 45 (Jan.–Mar. 1971): 2–36.

———. *Li Ta-chao and the Origins of Chinese Marxism*. Cambridge: Harvard University Press, 1967.

Mencius. Trans. with an introduction by D. C. Lau. New York: Penguin Books, 1984.

Meng Fanhua 孟繁華. "Mohuan xianshi zhuyi zai Zhongguo" 魔幻現實主義在中國 ("Magic Realism in China"). In *Mohuan xianshi zhuyi xiaoshuo* 魔幻現實主義小說 (*Fiction of Magic Realism*). Changchun: Changchun shidai wenyi chubanshe, 1988.11: 1–11.

Meng Yue 孟悅. "Shijiao wenti yu 'wusi' xiaoshuo de xiandaihua" 視角問題與「五四」小說的現代化 ("Point of View and the Modernizing of 'May Fourth' Fiction"). *Wenxue pinglun*, 1986.3: 60–74.

Miller, J. Hillis. *Tropes, Parables, Performatives: Essays on Twentieth-Century Literature*. Durham: Duke University Press, 1991.

Mo Yan 莫言. "Baigou qiuqian jia" 白狗鞦韆架 ("White Dog and the Swings"). In Li Tuo, *Touming de hongluobo*, 265–90.

———. *Honggaoliang jiazu* 紅高粱家族 (*Red Sorghum Family*). Beijing: Jiefangjun wenyi chubanshe, 1987.

———. "Honghuang" 紅蝗 ("Red Locust"). *Shouhuo*, 1987.3: 4–59.

———. "Maoshi huicui" 貓事薈萃 ("Exquisite Matters Having to Do with Cats"). *Shanghai wenxue*, 1987.11: 11–21.

———. "Mo Yan xiaozhuan" 莫言小傳 ("Brief Biography of Mo Yan"). *Zhongshan*, 1988.1: 174.

———. "Wo de 'nongmin yishi' guan" 我的「農民意識」觀 ("My View of 'Peasant Consciousness'"). *Wenxue pinglun jia*, 1989.2: 39–42.

Mu Gong 木弓. "Wang Shuo—zhishifenzi wenhua de bishizhe" 王朔—知識分子文化的鄙視者 ("Wang Shuo—Scorner of Intelligentsia Culture"). *Zhongshan*, 1991.1: 152.

Myers, Ramon H. "The Agrarian System." *The Cambridge History of China*, vol. 13, *Republican China 1912–1949*, pt. II, 230–69.

Ng, Mau-sang. *The Russian Hero in Modern Chinese Fiction*. Hong Kong: Chinese University Press, 1988.

Nochlin, Linda. *Realism*. Baltimore, Md.: Penguin, 1973.

Ouyang Xiu 歐陽修. "Mei Shengyu shiji xu" 梅聖俞詩集序 ("Preface to Mei Shengyu's Collected Poems"). In Liu Pansui 劉盼遂 and Guo Yuheng 郭預恒, eds., *Zhongguo lidai sanwen xuan* 中國歷代散文選 (*Selected Chinese Essays*). Beijing: Beijing chubanshe, 1982, 2: 197–99.

Owen, Stephen. "The Self's Perfect Mirror: Poetry as Autobiography." In Shuenfu Lin and Stephen Owen, eds., *The Vitality of the Lyric Voice:* Shih *Poetry from the Late Han to the T'ang*. Princeton: Princeton University Press, 1986, 71–102.

Pickowicz, Paul G. *Marxist Literary Thought in China: The Influence of Ch'u Ch'iu-pai*. Berkeley: University of California Press, 1981.

Průšek, Jaroslav. *The Lyrical and the Epic: Studies of Modern Chinese Literature*. Ed. Leo Ou-fan Lee. Bloomington: Indiana University Press, 1980.

Qian Xingcun 錢杏村. "Si qule de Ah Q shidai" 死去了的阿Q 時代 ("The Period of Ah Q Is Dead") (1928.3). In *"Geming wenxue" lunzheng ziliao xuanbian* 1: 180–94.

Qian Zhongshu 錢鐘書. *Song shi xuan zhu* 宋詩選注 (*Annotated Selection of Song Poetry*). Beijing: Renmin wenxue chubanshe, 1958.

Qiu Lan 邱嵐. "Dui yige 'jishou timu' de sikao—ping 'dui jianguo yilai nongcun ticai xiaoshuo de zai renshi'" 對一個「棘手題目」的思考—評「對建國以來農村題材小說的再認識」("Thoughts on a 'Thorny Topic'—A Critique of 'A Reappraisal of Fiction on the Countryside Since the Founding of the People's Republic'"). *Wenxue pinglun*, 1984.5: 33–40.

Qu Qiubai 瞿秋白. "Puluo dazhong wenyi de xianshi wenti" 普洛大眾文藝的現實問題 ("Practical Problems of Proletarian Art and Literature"). In *Zhongguo xiandai wenxueshi cankao ziliao*, vol. 1, no. 1. Beijing: Gaodeng jiaoyu chubanshe, 1959, , vol. 1, no. 1, 305–23.

Rimmon-Kenan, Shlomith. *Narrative Fiction: Contemporary Poetics*. London: Methuen, 1983.

Ru Zhijuan 茹志鵑. "Chunnuan shijie" 春暖時節 ("In the Warm Springtime"). In her *Baihehua* 百合花 (*Wild Lilies*). Beijing: Renmin wenxue chubanshe, 1984, 127–42.

Schoenhals, Michael. *Doing Things with Words in Chinese Politics: Five Studies*. Berkeley: Institute of East Asian Studies, University of California, ca. 1992.

Scholes, Robert, and Robert Kellogg. *The Nature of Narrative*. New York: Oxford University Press, 1966.

Schwarcz, Vera. *The Chinese Enlightenment: Intellectuals and the Legacy of the May Fourth Movement of 1919*. Berkeley: University of California Press, 1986.

Schwartz, Benjamin. "The Intelligentsia in Communist China: A Tentative Comparison." In Richard Pipes, ed., *The Russian Intelligentsia*. New York: Columbia University Press, 1961, 164–81.

———. "The Limits of 'Tradition Versus Modernity' as Categories of Explanation: The Case of the Chinese Intellectuals." *Daedalus*, Spring 1972, pp. 71–88.

Shao Jian 邵建 and Fan Bo 樊波. "'Xungen' lun" 「尋根」論 ("On 'Root-searching'"). *Piping jia* 2, no. 6 (1986.11): 21–30.

Shapiro, Sidney, trans. *Rhymes of Li Youcai and Other Stories*. Beijing: Foreign Languages Press, 1980.

Shi Hanren 時漢人. "Gao Xiaosheng he 'Lu Xun feng'" 高曉聲和「魯迅風」 ("Gao Xiaosheng and the 'Lu Xun Style'"). *Wenxue pinglun*, 1984, 4: 7–46.

Shih Mo 石默. (See Zhao Zhenkai 趙振開).

Shijing jinzhu 詩經近注 (*Recent Annotations to the* Shijing), by Gao Heng 高衡. Shanghai: Shanghai guji chubanshe, 1987.

Shils, Edward. "Intellectuals." In David Sills, ed., *International Encyclopedia* of *the Social Sciences*, vol. 7. New York: Macmillan, 1968, 399–414.

Silverman, Kaja. *The Subject of Semiotics*. Oxford: Oxford University Press, 1983.

Sima Qian 司馬遷. "Bao Ren An shu" 報任安書 ("Letter to Ren An"). In *Zhongguo lidai sanwen xuan*, 357–69. Trans. J. R. Hightower. In Cyril Birch, comp. and ed., *Anthology of Chinese Literature: From Early Times to the Fourteenth Century*. New York: Grove Press, 1965, 95–102.

———. *Shiji huizhu kaozheng* 史記會注考證 (*Shiji: Assembled Commentaries and Annotations*). Beijing: Wenxue guji kanxingshe, 1955.

———. "Qu Yuan Jia Sheng liezhuan" 屈原賈生列傳 ("Biographies of Qu Yuan and Jia Yi"). In *Shiji huizhu kaozheng*, 8: 3837–73.

———. "Taishigong zixu" 太史公自序 ("The Historian's Preface"). In *Shiji huizhu kaozheng*, 10: 5181–5246.

Siu, Helen F., ed. *Furrows: Peasants, Intellectuals, and the State: Stories and Histories from Modern China*. Stanford: Stanford University Press, 1990.

Solomon, Maynard, ed. *Marxism and Art: Essays Classic and Contemporary*. New York: Vintage Books, 1974.

Song Yang 宋陽 (Qu Qiubai 瞿秋白). "Dazhong wenyi de wenti" 大衆文藝的問題 ("The Question of Popular Literature and Art"). In *Wenxue yundong shiliao xuan*, 2: 391–99.

Song Yaoliang 宋耀良. *Shinian wenxue zhuchao* 十年文學主潮 (*Main Currents in Ten Years of Literature*). Shanghai: Shanghai wenyi chubanshe, 1988.

Tang Tao 唐弢. *Zhongguo xiandai wenxueshi* 中國現代文學史 (*History of Modern Chinese Literature*). Beijing: Renmin wenxue chubanshe, 1979.

Tang Xiaobing. "The Function of New Theory: What Does It Mean to Talk

About Postmodernism in China?" In Kang and Tang, *Politics, Ideology, and Literary Discourse in Modern China: Theoretical Interventions and Cultural Critique*, 278–99.

———. "Residual Modernism: Narratives of the Self in Contemporary Chinese Fiction." *Modern Chinese Literature* 7 (1993): 7–31.

Thaxton, Ralph. *China Turned Rightside Up: Revolutionary Legitimacy in the Peasant World*. New Haven: Yale University Press, 1983.

Tian Jingbao 田敬寶. "Ruhe dui nongye hezuohua ticai xiaoshuo chuangzuo zai pingjia" 如何對農業合作化題材小說創作再評價 ("How to Reevaluate Literary Works on the Theme of Forming Agricultural Cooperatives"). *Xueshu yanjiu congkan,* 1983.4: 125–29.

Tolstaya, Tatyana. "In Cannibalistic Times." Review of *The Great Terror: A Reassessment* by Robert Conquest. *New York Review of Books,* Apr. 11, 1991, pp. 3–6.

Tu Wei-ming. *Way, Learning, and Politics: Essays on the Confucian Intellectual*. Albany: State University of New York Press, 1993.

Wagner, Rudolf G. *The Contemporary Chinese Historical Drama: Four Studies*. Berkeley: University of California Press, 1990.

———. "Documents Concerning *Tanqiuzhe* [*The Explorer*], An Independent Literary Journal Planned During the Hundred Flowers Period." *Modern Chinese Literature* 3, nos. 1 and 2 (Spring/Fall 1987): 137–46.

Wakeman, Jr., Frederic. *The Fall of Imperial China*. New York: Free Press, 1975.

———. "The Price of Autonomy: Intellectuals in Ming and Ch'ing Politics." *Daedalus,* Spring 1972, pp. 35–70.

Waley, Arthur. *The Book of Songs*. London: George Allen and Unwin, 1954.

Wang Anyi 王安憶. "Biographical Note—My Wall." In *Lapse of Time*. San Francisco: China Books, 1988, 233–35.

———. "Daliuzhuang" 大劉莊 ("Liu Village"). In *Xiaobaozhuang*. Shanghai: Shanghai wenyi chubanshe, 1986, 131–242.

———. "Houji" 後記 ("Postface"). In *Xiaobaozhuang.* 451–53.

———. "Lao Kang huilai" 老康回來 ("Lao Kang Came Back"). In Wang Anyi, *Haishang fanhua meng* 海上繁華夢 (*Dreams of Prosperity*). Guangzhou: Huacheng chubanshe, 1989, 226–35.

———. "Wo weishenme xiezuo" 我爲什麼寫作 ("Why I Write"). *Nüzuojia,* 1985.2: 102–3.

———. *Xiaobaozhuang* 小鮑莊 (*Bao Village*). In *Xiaobaozhuang,* 243–339.

———. "Yunhe bianshang" 運河邊上 ("On the Banks of the Grand Canal"). In *Wang Anyi zhongduanpian xiaoshuoji* 王安憶中短篇小說集 (*Selected Novellas and Short Stories by Wang Anyi*). Beijing: Zhongguo qingnian chubanshe, 1983, 118–211.

Wang, David Der-wei. *Fictional Realism in Twentieth-Century China: Mao Dun, Lao She, Shen Congwen*. New York: Columbia University Press, 1992.

———. "Imaginary Nostalgia: Shen Congwen, Song Zelai, Mo Yan, and Li Yongping." In Widmer and Wang, *From May Fourth to June Fourth*, 107–32.

Wang Jing. *High Culture Fever: Politics, Aesthetics, and Ideology in Deng's China.* Berkeley: University of California Press, 1996.

Wang Lijun 王力軍. "Guanyu 'houxinshiqi wenxue' de taolun" 關於「後新時期文學」的討論 ("Discussions on 'Post New-Era Literature'"). *Renmin ribao,* Mar. 18, 1993.

Wang Shuo 王朔. *Guo ba yin jiu si* 過把癮就死 (*Get Your High and Die*). Hong Kong: Qinshiyuan chubanshe, 1993.

Wang Xiaoming 王曉明. "Bu xiangxin de he bu yuanyi xiangxin de—guanyu sanwei 'xungen' pai zuojia de chuangzuo" 不相信的和不願意相信的—關於三位「尋根」派作家的創作 ("What One Doesn't Believe and Doesn't Want to Believe—On the Writings of Three Writers of the "Root-Searching" School"). *Wenxue pinglin,* 1988.4: 24–35.

———. "Zai fukan Chenjiacun zhiqian—Lun Gao Xiaosheng jinnianlai de xiaoshuo chuangzuo" 在俯瞰陳家村之前—論高曉聲近年來的小說創作 ("Before Overlooking Chen Family Village—on Gao Xiaosheng's Recent Fiction"). *Wenxue pinglun,* 1986.4: 57–64.

Wang Youqin 王友琴. "Zuojia de shiming gan: Cong Qu Yuan dao Lu Xun" 作家的使命感: 從屈原到魯迅 ("The Writer's Sense of Mission: From Qu Yuan to Lu Xun"). *Xinhua wenzhai,* 1986.4: 148–53.

Wang Zengqi 汪曾祺. "Xu" 序 ("Preface"). In Li Tuo 李陀, ed., 中國尋根小說選 *Zhongguo xungen xiaoshuo xuan* (*Selected Chinese Root-searching Stories*). Hong Kong: Joint Publishing Co., 1993, 1–5.

Wang Zhongqing 王中青and Li Wenru 李文儒. "Ji Zhao Shuli de zuihou wunian" 記趙樹理的最後五年 ("The Last Five Years of Zhao Shuli"). *Xinwenxue shiliao,* 1983.3: 153–69.

Watson, Burton. *The Columbia Book of Chinese Poetry, from Early Times to the Thirteenth Century.* New York: Columbia University Press, 1984.

———, trans. *The Complete Works of Chuang Tzu.* New York: Columbia University Press, 1968.

Wedell-Wedellsborg, Anne. "Chinese Modernism?" In *Cologne Workshop 1984 on Contemporary Chinese Literature*, 96–126.

Williams, Raymond. *Culture and Society, 1780–1950.* New York: Harper and Row, 1958.

Wolf, Eric R. *Peasants.* Englewood Cliffs, N.J.: Prentice-Hall, 1966.

Wu Liang 吳亮. "Bingfei nanjie zhi mi—ping Gao Xiaosheng wanjin de xiaoshuo" 并非難解之迷—評高曉聲晚近的小說 ("Puzzles Not Difficult to Decipher—On Gao Xiaosheng's Recent Fiction"). *Yuhua,* 1983.11: 75–80.

Wu Pei-yi. *The Confucian's Progress: Autobiographical Writings in Traditional China.* Princeton: Princeton University Press, 1990.

Wu Yang 武養. "Yipian waiqu xianshi de xiaoshuo—'Duanlian duanlian' duhou gan" 一篇歪曲現實的小說—「鍛煉鍛煉」讀後感 ("A Story that Distorts Reality—Thoughts After Reading 'Making Tough'"). In *Zhao Shuli zhuanji*, 482–85.

Xian Yin 峴垠. "'Rang laolao shaoshao dou neng kan'—ji Zhao Shuli zai yici 'pindaohui' shang" 「讓老老少少都能看」—記趙樹理在一次「拼刀會」上 ("'So Old and Young Can All Read It'"—Notes on Zhao Shuli at a 'Bayonet Struggle Meeting'"). *Shanxi wenxue*, 1982.3: 66.

Xiao Hong 蕭紅. *Shengsichang* 生死場 (*Field of Life and Death*). Harbin: Heilongjiang renmin chunbanshe, 1980.

Yan Gang 閻綱. "Lun Chen Huansheng—shenme shi Chen Huansheng xingge?" 論陳奐生—什麼是陳奐生性格 ("On Chen Huansheng—What Is the Chen Huansheng Character?" *Beijing shifan xueyuan xuebao*, 1982.4: 28–38.

Yang Yi 楊義. *Zhongguo xiandai xiaoshuoshi* 中國現代小說史 (*History of Modern Chinese Fiction*). Beijing: Renmin chubanshe, 1986.

Ye Zhicheng 葉至誠. "The String That Will Never Break—Introducing the Writer Gao Xiaosheng." In Gao Xiaosheng, *The Broken Betrothal*, 212–18.

———. "'Tanqiuzhe'de hua" 「探求者」的話 ("Comments on 'The Explorer'"). *Yuhua*, 1979.5: 11–12.

Yu Bin 余斌. "Dui xianshizhuyi shenhua de tansuo" 對現實主義深化的探索 ("An Exploration of the Deepening of Realism"). *Wenxue pinglun*, 1982.4: 83–91.

Yu Dafu 郁大夫. *Yu Dafu daibiao zuo* 郁大夫代表作(*Representative Works of Yu Dafu*). Ed. Liu Jiaming 劉家鳴. Zhengzhou: Huanghe wenyi chubanshe, 1989.

———. *Zhongguo xinwenxue daxi, sanwen erji, daoyan* 中國新文學大系, 散文二集導言 (*Introduction to New Chinese Literature Series: Essays, vol. 2*). Hong Kong: Xianggang wenxue yanjiushe, 1963.

Yu Wong. "Wang's World." *Far Eastern Economic Review*, Aug. 8. 1996, pp. 46–48.

Yü Ying-shih. "The Radicalization of China in the Twentieth Century." *Daedalus*, Spring 1993, pp. 125–50.

Yue Ming-Bao. "Gendering the Origins of Modern Chinese Fiction." In Lu, ed., *Gender and Sexuality in Twentieth-Century Chinese Literature and Society*, 47–65.

Zhang Yiwu 張頤武. "Zhongguo nongmin wenhua de xingsheng yu weiji—dui ershi shiji wenxue yige cemian de sikao" 中國農民文化的興盛與危機—對二十世紀文學一個側面的思考 ("The Ascendance and Crisis of Chinese Peasant Culture—Reflections on One Aspect of Twentieth-century Literature"). *Xinhua wenzhai*, 1986.1: 144–48.

Zhang Zhong 張鐘, Hong Zicheng 洪子誠, She Shusen 佘樹森, Zhao Zumo 趙祖謨, and Wang Jingshou 汪景壽. *Dangdai Zhongguo wenxue gaiguan* 當代中國文學概觀 (*Survey of Contemporary Chinese Literature*). Beijing: Beijing daxue chubanshe, 1986.

Zhao Junxian 趙俊賢. *Zhongguo dangdai xiaoshuo shigao—renwu xingxiang xilie lun* 中國當代小說史稿－人物形象系列論 (*Draft History of Contemporary Chinese Fiction—Discussion of Character Series*). Beijing: Renmin wenxue chubanshe, 1989.

Zhao Shuli 趙樹理. "Buyao jiyu xie, buyao xie ziji bu shuxide—Zhao Shuli tan chuangzuo" 不要急于寫,不要寫自己不熟悉的－趙樹理談創作 ("Do Not Be in a Rush to Write, Do Not Write on What You Are Not Familiar with—Zhao Shuli on Creative Writing). In *Zhao Shuli wenji*, 4: 1928–31.

———. "Dangqian chuangzuo zhong de jige wenti" 當前創作中的幾個問題 ("Some Problems in Current Writing"). In *Zhao Shuli lun chuangzuo*, 182–93.

———. "Dengji" 登記 ("Registration"). In *Zhao Shuli xiaoshuo xuan*, 135–62.

———. "Gongshe yinggai ruhe lingdao nongye shengchan zhi wojian" 公社應該如何領導農業生產之我見 ("My Views on How the Commune Should Lead Agricultural Production"). Excerpt in *Zhao Shuli wenji*, 4: 1663–69.

———. "Huiyi lishi, renshi ziji" 回憶歷史,認識自己 ("Recalling History, Knowing Oneself"). In *Zhao Shuli wenji*, 4: 1825–44.

———. "Lao Ding'e" 老定額 ("Old Quota"). In *Zhao Shuli xiaoshuo xuan*, 413–26.

———. "Li Youcai banhua" 李有才板話 ("The Rhymes of Li Youcai"). In *Zhao Shuli xiaoshuo xuan*, 17–60.

———. "Lingquandong" 靈泉洞 ("Lingquan Cave"), Part I. In *Zhao Shuli quyi wenxuan*, 163–283.

———. "Meng Xiangying fanshen (xianshi gushi)" 孟祥英翻身(現實故事) ("Xiangying Stands Up: A True Story"). In *Zhao Shuli xiaoshuo xuan*, 67–81.

———. "'Meng Xiangying fanshen' xiaoxu" 「孟祥英翻身」小序 ("Short Preface to 'Meng Xiangying fanshen'"). In *Zhao Shuli lun chuangzuo*, 3.

———. *Sanliwan* 三里灣 (*Sanliwan Village*). Beijing: Tongsu duwu chubanshe, 1956.

———. "'Sanliwan' xiezuo qianhou" 「三里灣」寫作前後 ("About Writing 'Sanliwan'"). In *Zhao Shuli lun chuangzuo*, 19–30.

———. "Shi Bulan ganche" 石不爛趕車 ("Shi Bulan, Cart Driver"). In *Zhao Shuli quyi xuan*, 82–117.

———. "Shiganjia Pan Yongfu" 實干家潘永福 ("The Honest to Goodness Worker Pan Yongfu"). In *Zhao Shuli xiaoshuo xuan*, 438–63.

———. "Tao bu zhu de shou" 套不住的手 ("The Unglovable Hands"). In *Zhao Shuli xiaoshuo xuan*, 427-37.

———. "Xiao Erhei jiehun" 小二黑結婚 ("Blackie Gets Married"). In *Zhao Shuli xiaoshuo xuan*, 1–16.

———. "Ye suan jingyan" 也算經驗 ("Call It Experience"). In *Zhao Shuli wenji*, 4: 1397–99.

Zhao Shuli lun chuangzuo 趙樹理論創作 (*Zhao Shuli on Writing*). Shanghai: Shanghai wenyi chubanshe, 1985.

Zhao Shuli quyi wenxuan 趙樹理曲藝文選 (*Selected Folk Art Writings of Zhao Shuli*). Beijing: Zhongguo quyi chubanshe, 1983.

Zhao Shuli wenji 趙樹理文集(*Collected Works of Zhao Shuli*). vol. 4, *Lunshu, zagan, shuxin* 論述,雜感,書信 (*Essays, Random Thoughts, Letters*). Beijing: Gongren chubanshe, 1980.

Zhao Shuli xiaoshuo xuan 趙樹理小說選 (*Selected Fiction of Zhao Shuli*). Taiyuan: Shanxi renmin chubanshe, 1980.

Zhao Zhenkai 趙振開 (Shi Mo 石默). "Zai feixushang" 在廢墟上 ("In the Ruins"). Written in 1978 and first published in *Jintian* 今天 (*Today*) 1 (Dec. 23, 1978): 3–10. It was reprinted in *Lasahe* 拉薩河 2 (Apr. 1985) under the name Zhao Zhenkai. References are to the text reprinted in *Zhongbao yuekan* 中報月刊 (*Zhongbao Monthly,* Hong Kong), 1980.5 (June 1980): 97–100.

Zheng Wanlong 鄭萬隆. "Wo de gen" 我的根 ("My Roots"). *Shanghai wenxue,* 1985.5: 44–46.

"Zhongguo dangdai wenxue xuehui 1981 nian Lushan nianhui taolun zongshu" 中國當代文學學會1981年盧山年會討論綜述 ("Summary of Discussions at the 1981 Annual Lushan Meeting of the Society of Contemporary Chinese Literature"). *Wenxue pinglun,* 1981.5: 108–11.

Zhou Jianming 周鑒銘. "Gao Xiaosheng—Lu Xun youmo fengge de chengchuanren" 高曉聲－魯迅幽默風格的承傳人 ("Gao Xiaosheng—The Successor to Lu Xun's Humorous Style"). In his *Xinshiqi wenxue* 新時期文學 (*Literature of the New Era*). Kunming: Yunnan jiaoyu chubanshe, 1986, 251–75.

Zhou Xiashou 周遐壽 (Zuoren 作人). *Lu Xun xiaoshuo li de renwu* 魯迅小說裏的人物 (*The Characters in Lu Xun's Fiction*). Shanghai: Shanghai chuban gongsi, 1954.

Zhou Yang 周揚. "Lun Zhao Shuli de chuangzuo" 論趙樹理的創作 ("On the Writings of Zhao Shuli"). In *Zhao Shuli zhuanji,* 179–91 (First published in *Jiefang ribao* 解放日報, 1946.8.26).

Zhou Yingxiong 周英雄. "Honggaoliang jiazu yanyi" 紅高粱家族演義 ("Red Sorghum Family Saga"). Appendix to Mo Yan *Honggaoliang jiazu*. Taipei: Hongfan shudian, 1989, 499–520.

Zhu Ling. "A Brave New World? On the Construction of 'Masculinity' and 'Femininity' in *The Red Sorghum Family*." In Lu, ed., *Gender and Sexuality in Twentieth-Century Chinese Literature and Society,* 121–34.

Zhuang Zhongqing 莊鐘慶. *Zhongguo xiandai wenxue yanjiu: fangfalun yu shijian* 中國現代文學研究: 方法論與實踐 (*The Study of Modern Chinese Literature: Theories of Methodology and Practice*). Fuzhou: Fujian jiaoyu chubanshe, 1995.

Index

Library of Congress Cataloging-in-Publication Data

Feuerwerker, Yi-tsi Mei
    Ideology, power, text : self-representation and the peasant
"other" in modern Chinese literature / Yi-tsi Mei Feuerwerker.
        p.   cm.
    Includes bibliographical references and index.
    ISBN 0-8047-3319-8 (alk. paper).
    1. Chinese fiction—20th century—History and criticism.
2. Peasants in literature.   I. Title.
PL2419.P39F48   1998
895.1'350935263—dc21

                                                    97-49582
                                                    CIP

This book is printed on acid-free, recycled paper.

Original printing 1998
Last figure below indicates year of this printing:
07   06   05   04   03   02   01   00   99   98